CONTRIBUTORS

BARBARA COEYMAN HULTS, the author of a travel guide-book to Italy, has studied Italian civilization in Rome and has contributed articles to *Art & Antiques, Italy Italy,* and other magazines and newspapers. She has also written *Balloon,* a newsletter for travel fanatics, as well as a series of walking-tour tapes on several Italian cities. She travels in Italy five months a year and is the editorial consultant for this guide-book.

DWIGHT V. GAST, a longtime resident of Italy, has written about the country for numerous newspapers, magazines, and guidebooks.

JOANNE HAHN has lived and studied in Italy and returns there regularly. A contributor to several magazines, she is coauthor of a travel guidebook to Italy.

THE BERLITZ
TRAVELLERS GUIDES

THE BERLITZ TRAVELLERS GUIDE TO SOUTHERN ITALY

AND ROME

1992

ALAN TUCKER

General Editor

BERLITZ PUBLISHING COMPANY, INC.
New York, New York

BERLITZ PUBLISHING COMPANY LTD.
Oxford, England

THE BERLITZ TRAVELLERS GUIDE
TO SOUTHERN ITALY 1992

Berlitz Trademark Reg U.S. Patent and Trademark Office
and other countries—Marca Registrada

Published by Berlitz Publishing Company, Inc.
257 Park Avenue South, New York, New York 10010, U.S.A.

Distributed in the United States by
the Macmillan Publishing Group

Distributed elsewhere by Berlitz Publishing Company Ltd.
London Road, Wheatley, Oxford OX9 1YR, England

Originally published as part of the Penguin Travel Guide to Italy
by Viking Penguin, a division of Penguin USA Inc.

ISBN 2-8315-1767-2
ISSN 1057-4662

Designed by Beth Tondreau Design
Cover design by Dan Miller Design
Cover photograph by © Angelo Tondini/Focus Team
Maps by Nina Wallace
Illustrations by Bill Russell
Fact-checked in Italy by Iris Jones
Edited by Katherine Ness

Printed in the United States of America
1   3   5   7   9   10   8   6   4   2

THIS GUIDEBOOK

The Berlitz Travellers Guides are designed for experienced travellers in search of exceptional information that will enhance the enjoyment of the trips they take.

Where, for example, are the interesting, out-of-the-way, fun, charming, or romantic places to stay? The hotels described by our expert writers are some of the special places, in all price ranges except for the very lowest—not just the run-of-the-mill, heavily marketed places in advertised airline and travel-wholesaler packages.

We indicate the approximate price level of each accommodation in our description of it (no indication means it is moderate in local, relative terms), and at the end of every chapter we supply more detailed hotel rates as well as contact information so that you can get precise, up-to-the-minute rates and make reservations.

The Berlitz Travellers Guide to Southern Italy 1992 highlights the more rewarding parts of Rome and the South so that you can quickly and efficiently home in on a good itinerary.

Of course, this guidebook does far more than just help you choose a hotel and plan your trip. *The Berlitz Travellers Guide to Southern Italy 1992* is designed for use *in* southern Italy. Our writers, each of whom is an experienced travel journalist who either lives in or regularly tours the region he or she covers, tell you what you really need to know, what you can't find out so easily on your own. They identify and describe the truly out-of-the-ordinary restaurants, shops, activities, and sights, and tell you the best way to "do" your destination.

Our writers are highly selective. They bring out the significance of the places they *do* cover, capturing the personality and the underlying cultural and historical resonances of a city or region—making clear its special appeal.

The Berlitz Travellers Guide to Southern Italy is full of

reliable and timely information, revised and updated each year. We would like to know if you think we've left out some very special place. Although we make every effort to provide the most current information available about every destination described in this book, it is possible too that changes have occurred before you arrive. If you do have an experience that is contrary to what you were led to expect by our description, we would like to hear from you about it.

A guidebook is no substitute for common sense when you are travelling. Always pack the clothing, footwear, and other items appropriate for the destination, and make the necessary accommodation for such variables as altitude, weather, and local rules and customs. Of course, once on the scene you should avoid situations that are in your own judgment potentially hazardous, even if they have to do with something mentioned in a guidebook. Half the fun of travelling is exploring, but explore with care.

ALAN TUCKER
General Editor
Berlitz Travellers Guides

Root Publishing Company
330 West 58th Street
Suite 5-D
New York, New York 10019

CONTENTS

THE
BERLITZ
TRAVELLERS
GUIDE
TO
SOUTHERN
ITALY
1992

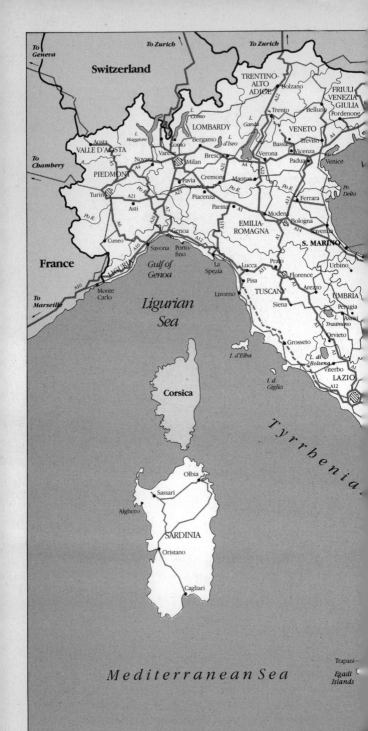

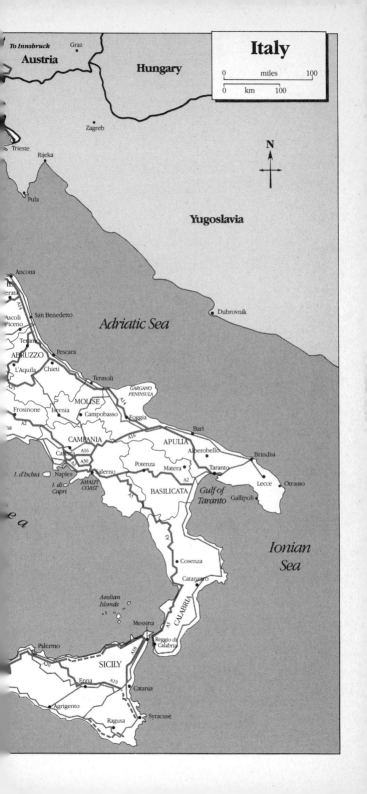

OVERVIEW

By Barbara Coeyman Hults

Barbara Coeyman Hults has lived, studied, and worked in Rome. Formerly the editor of Balloon, *a travel newsletter, she is the author of a travel guidebook on Italy and has written a series of walking-tour tapes on several Italian cities.*

There are three southern Italys.

One of them stretches luxuriously along the rocky coast from Sorrento to Amalfi, rushes up the cliffs to lofty Ravello, and jumps across the sea to the still-seductive Capri. This South is seen in other places: in Sicily's Taormina and along Puglia's eastern coast near Monopoli. This is the South of the sun worshiper, the sleek sailboat, the rich and famous, the boutique shopper. It's well groomed, glamorous, familiar.

The second is the South of antiquity: Roman Pompeii and Herculaneum; the ancient Greek cities of Agrigento, Siracusa, and Metapontum; and earlier shrines to Demeter and Diana. The more recent Baroque South—Sicily's Noto and Apulia's Lecce—would be included here as well.

The third South is in some ways more familiar because it has been transported to the Americas, Britain, and Australia in immigrant groups—the South of pizza and saint's day festivals, of Neapolitan exuberance and Sicilian restraint. It's also the South of Carlo Levi's novel, *Christ Stopped at Eboli.* For many who live in this South, life has changed little since that postwar book. Parts of the Abruzzi, Campania, Apulia, Calabria, and Sicily belong to this Other South, both in memory and in reality.

For travellers, this Other South offers fewer comforts in hotels and transportation and far less street-cleaning. In return it allows the possibility of discovering a new world, one rarely explored by foreign (or Italian) tourists.

We've included the region called Lazio or Latium, which is often overshadowed by its unequaled and unruly capital, Rome, because it can be visited en route to the Mezzogiorno—the Midday, as the South is known.

Sardinia belongs more to itself than to North or South, with a history unlike that of any other region. Its Emerald Coast shelters yachts and year-round tans, and its stone structures, the *nuraghi,* stand as they did in prehistoric Italy.

Probably the best way to see all aspects of the South is to choose comfortable bases in the first, the sleek South, from which to explore the others, mixing the familiar and the rare, the extravagant and the austere, the boutique and the souk.

Italy, we all know, is shaped like a delicate boot, with Sicily just off the toe. France, Switzerland, and Austria provide the northern political boundaries. The Alps turn into the Apennines, which follow the western part of the peninsula down its length. The eastern flatland ends in the marshy lagoons of Venice to the north, and beaches run down both coasts— with the best following Sardinia's island shoreline. Lakes dot the north above Milan, and the far northwest coast ends at the French border in an arc of Ligurian coast called the Italian Riviera.

Along their southwest boundaries, the north-central plains of Emilia-Romagna give over abruptly to the mountains of Tuscany, with Florence near its center. Umbria, between Tuscany and Rome's region of Lazio, follows ancient hills and valleys, and the provinces of Abruzzo and Molise, together familiarly called the Abruzzi, stretch from east of Rome to the Adriatic, rising at the center point to the Gran Sasso range, home to the highest peak of the Apennines. In the center of Lazio, on the west coast near the Tyrrhenian Sea, is Rome, the Eternal City, to which all roads have led for two thousand years—and where our journey begins.

Campania, south of Lazio, follows the beautiful rocky coast of Amalfi on the west side of Italy down to the toe of the boot, to Calabria's territory of mountains and lovely sea views. Eastward, the boot's instep is Basilicata, often neglected by travellers, partly because tourist facilities in its mountains and coastal villages are few. Its vineyards and olive groves, however, are beloved by those who take the time to know them. The high heel and spur of the boot are Apulia, the most industrially developed of the southern regions. Dramatic mountains cover its mystical northern

Gargano peninsula; in the south, the stunning rocky eastern coast continues around the tip to the lovely white-sand beaches and gentle harbors along the inner heel south of Taranto.

The island off the toe, Sicily, has a mountainous center yielding to plains, encircled with small cove beaches along the coast. The other major island, Sardinia, west of the mainland, is ruggedly mountainous at the center, while its coasts are rimmed with white-sand beaches that are admired around the world.

Italy's geographical variety is only part of its interest, however. Add to that the different historical destinies of its regions and you have the beginning of the myriad permutations in the country. Italy's history is exceedingly complicated, for rare is the conqueror who did not see something of value here, whether in natural resources or in enticing plunder.

"Ancient Italy" traditionally begins about 20,000 B.C., although areas throughout the peninsula and Sicily were inhabited long before then. Among many central Italian tribes, the Etruscans—whose origins have not been determined—emerged victorious.

Greek and Phoenician traders were then establishing trading ports in southern Italy, and soon they set up colonies as well. Tradition says that Rome was founded in 753 B.C. by Romulus and Remus, and this date, or at least that century, seems accurate, according to recent excavations.

The city's power grew, especially after kingship was abolished and Rome became a republic. Finally in 27 B.C., under Augustus, Rome became a full-fledged empire that ultimately stretched as far west as England, through North Africa, and east to Syria. Invasions of barbarians from the north began about the time of Marcus Aurelius, and by then the empire was on the wane. When Constantine (whose Edict of Milan ended the persecution of the Christians) moved the capital to Constantinople, the handwriting on the wall was etched in stone.

During the Middle Ages the Germanic Ostrogoths ruled from Ravenna while the papacy grew in influence, laying the groundwork for the Papal States that would follow. This was largely the work of Pope Gregory the Great (590–604), whose strength of purpose helped the papacy emerge as a major power from the muddle of the Middle Ages. In the year 800 the pope crowned Charlemagne Holy Roman Emperor, after which papal power increased as its troubles multiplied. After Frederick Barbarossa was crowned emperor in 1155 war broke out between his supporters, the Ghibellines, and the pope's backers, the Guelphs. During this period the Normans established a successful kingdom in Sicily.

Renaissance princes and dukes struggled in the city-states that had evolved, but foreign domination soon grew and lasted for centuries as France, Austria, and Spain held the reins. The Spanish Hapsburgs were a dominating force in Italy in post-Renaissance years, until the War of Spanish Succession (1701–1713) ended with Austria in control. Napoléon briefly annexed large portions of Italy, breaking the Austrian hold and moving Italy forward as a modern state. After the Congress of Vienna in 1815 the years were filled with riots, protests, and finally revolution as Mazzini, the great political thinker, joined forces with the man of action, Garibaldi, and with the brilliant Cavour, who would forge the new republic to Verdi's accompaniment.

In 1860 the revolution began, and by 1870 Italy was an independent republic with a king. After the wars of the 20th century the king's popularity diminished, and the last king, Umberto II, died in Portugal in exile.

Italy, once Europe's whiz kid, with an economy bulging with Made in Italy labels, recently has been seeing hard times. The prestigious label sells at an ever-increasing price, for residents as well as tourists. Public debt and labor costs have made Italy one of the most expensive countries in the world. Entering the Monetary System means that the old method of coping with debt—devaluing the lira—will no longer be possible. National elections in 1992 will mean a new coalition government, this time without the Communist Party, once Europe's largest. The new centrist Democratic Left Party, however, presents a serious challenge to the Christian Democrats, who have long held sway. The CD has sought to privatize part of the unwieldy public sector, tampering with the hallowed patronage system that has long supplied the public sector with workers and non-workers.

Other surprises from current data include a low birth rate (the lowest in Europe) and a growing population over age 70, the result, many think, of the very healthy diet and active life Italians enjoy. TV and fast food have not overtaken their vitality—a permanent condition, one hopes.

Northern and southern Italy are in many ways different countries. The South is Mediterranean; the North is European. The forces that fueled today's northern industries were largely French and Austrian, while in the South a history of exploitation and neglect, characteristics of Spanish viceroy rule, has contributed to the growth of the Mafia, which today discourages industry from expanding southward (with the exception of Apulia, whose prosperity is evident). A still-operative patronage system and public passivity are today's legacy, although demonstrations against organized crime have become frequent occurrences. The Renaissance, with its growth of the middle class, was by and large a northern phenomenon; even today, entrepreneurial exuberance in the South is possible only in certain areas, mainly where tourism is the industry.

At the time of Italy's unification in 1870, the North, many believe, took measures to encourage northern industry while keeping the South a source of cheap agricultural labor. The pattern has outlasted agriculture, which has shrunk in importance.

Organized crime—the Mafia in Sicily, the 'Ndrangheta in Calabria, and the Camorra in Campania—is today recognized as a serious problem not just in the South but also in Italy as a whole. The war against organized crime is now being waged as never before. By 1993, according to plans, Italy's economic system will be merged to a great degree with that of the rest of the European Community. Centuries of a "second" economy make public disclosure of resources unlikely, and the current economic state is chaotic.

Yet to everyone's amazement, including the Italians', the country goes on—the pasta is *al dente* and the sun shines in the piazza. Despite the fiscal disarray, Italy belongs to the group of industrialized nations. What does the future hold? *Che sarà, sarà.*

The Traveller's Southern Italy

Rome, the seductive, infuriating colossus, smugly aware that everyone will go there sooner or later, makes few adjustments to visitors. The traffic is ghastly, its unmufflered noise and gassy fumes at horror-show proportions. But should you then avoid Rome? Of course not. (Just be careful crossing the street when you get there.) Here you participate in Roman life; you do as the Romans do and you find it exhilarating. Rome provides visitors with layer upon layer of history—turning a corner may call up a new age altogether. You'll find the ghosts of Roman emperors and Renaissance popes, lavish Baroque churches, prisons and palaces, piazzas unchanged from the Middle Ages, arbors to dine under, and the Tiber winding calmly past it all. Each age makes its presence known in Rome, bizarrely juxtaposed as in a Fellini circus. An unexpected bonus in recent years is the unveiling of the many handsomely restored monuments, the magnificent statue of Marcus Aurelius among them.

Lazio, the region surrounding Rome, is a place where Etruscan tombs, ancient Roman apartment houses, and Renaissance castles are silhouetted against the sea and the sky, and where shepherds still lead their flocks along the airport road. (The urban sprawl around Rome is best sped past—unless you're a Roman who finds the modern comforts in these often unattractive areas more livable than the dark and unheated palazzi so romantic to the tourist.)

The **Abruzzi**, a land of wolves and witches and the highest mountains of the Apennines, is an eagle's nest a few hours east of Rome, and almost unknown to North Americans. Frederick II found this region to his liking and enriched its cooking with his Eastern flair—red-hot pepper is used with Moroccan abandon. The pear-shaped *scamorza* cheese of Abruzzo is cooked on a skewer, and almond sweets are a regional favorite.

The Abruzzi towns of L'Aquila and Sulmona are reached on roads that glide through a world of lush valleys, rushing streams, and Medieval towns perched on terraced hills. The ski trails here are superb, and a national park protects chamois, fox, and bear.

Southeast of Lazio, **Campania**, balm to body and soul, is known mainly for its splendid, rocky Amalfi coast and Capri's isle, for the ancient cities of Pompeii, Herculaneum, and Paestum, and, of course, for **Naples**. Neapolitan cooking comes as a wonderful surprise to those who think southern Italy is a poor cousin gastronomically.

In **Calabria**, down the Tyrrhenian coast from Campania, stark towns overlook mountain peaks and the sea, with its dramatic beaches and marinas. Cosenza's Medieval quarter encloses a bright cultural life of music, literature, and a brand-new university. A trip from town to town in this rural, mountainous region is an introduction to yet another Italy, fast disappearing as tape decks and television bring the remotest areas in contact with the world beyond.

Apulia, on the opposite side of the boot from Campania, is a newcomer to travellers' itineraries, although it became better known in 1991 when its ports were trying to cope with thousands of Albanian refugees who sailed across the Adriatic seeking, and sometimes demanding, asylum from their oppressive regime. Yet the region's prime attractions remain undisturbed: white beaches; whimsical *trulli,* conical stone dwellings that have enlivened the landscape for millennia on southern hills amid almond blossoms in spring; the easy sophistication of the southwestern coast; the new hostelries created from old farmhouses that were once fortified for enemy onslaughts; and Lecce's Baroque elaborations. Consider also the windswept cliffs of the Gargano peninsula, mystical with its saints, dramatic with its views of caves and crashing surf.

Between Apulia and Calabria lies **Basilicata**, to which we have devoted little time because its accommodations are so few. But it has its rewards: mountains and streams, white beaches, and especially the city of Matera, which seems like a camouflaged, almost abandoned village molded into the mountains. Metapontum, on the coast, is filled with the excavated ruins of a once-thriving Greek colony.

Sicily, the mystery that has finally opened to the world, reveals the brilliance of Arab-Norman cathedrals, the glory of Greek temples, elegant, restrained Baroque palaces, and the incomparably beautiful resort of Taormina, high on a terraced hill that looks out to beaches and sea and up to Mount Etna. Sicily's sophisticated cooking—more Arab in origin toward the island's west, more Greek to the east—takes advantage of the endless varieties of fish that fill the tropically blue seas around the island, and its desserts would please the sweetest teeth in Araby.

Sardinia is known for splendid white coves of beaches, but its dramatically varied interior is at once mountainous, carved with deep gorges, hollowed with grottoes, and flat with lagoons. Around the island are scattered some 7,000 *nuraghi,* ancient hollow stone structures as mystical as Stonehenge, some in the form of Medieval cities.

In smaller southern cities, and often in larger ones, travellers find themselves the object of rapt attention. Southern Italians, who find people fascinating, *stare.* Where you are from, what you are doing there, what you think of where you are, and whether you know a cousin in Rochester are vitally important questions. Life is more communal, more piazza-oriented, in the South—although using piazzas for parking lots, and the spread of TV antennas, seem likely to draw people indoors into the alienation of which the rest of the industrialized world complains. But for the moment, people-watching wins over any TV rating.

The late Sicilian writer Leonardo Sciascia described a man on a train looking at a woman. After an hour he was wondering what to name the baby, having progressed gradually in his thoughts from the first word through courtship and marriage.

This may be the Other South's most important gift to the traveller: the feeling of vitality that comes from living in the moment, observed and observing.

USEFUL FACTS

When to Go

Spring and fall (especially May, June, and October) are the ideal months—for climate, for flowers, and for lighter tourism and better prices. Summer is a cavalcade of tourists and winter is often drizzly. That said, both summer and winter have much to offer as well. Summer has the obvious advantages of beaches and water sports, and the unexpected discovery of cities—Rome in particular—when all the cars have gone. Anna Magnani said she felt the old Rome only in August, when she could walk through the medievally dark streets that surround the Pantheon and hear the echo of her own footsteps. Trattorias are unrushed then, and life is slow. The downside of summer is the same as the upside: Everyone *has* left the cities (in their cars), leaving many restaurants and shops closed, and those that remain open are filled with non-Italian faces for the most part. Museums, however, have recently realized that summer days are among their best attended, and they often stay open through August.

However, summer can mean blistering heat, and you may find your touring is limited to the length of the hotel pool.

Winter, too, has advantages, especially cultural: the opera, the theater, concert halls, and uncrowded museums. Because there are fewer tourists, there are fewer lines to wait in, restaurants are on their best behavior (in summer they sometimes think no one will know the difference if they take short cuts with the sauce), and the weather is often lovely—although showers and fog are common even in Sicily.

Entry Documents

Just a passport is necessary for travellers to Italy, or an identity card for citizens of the EC. Motorists need a driver's license and a civil-liability insurance policy if they rent a car (usually provided when the car is picked up; see "Renting a Car and Driving," below).

Arrival at Major Gateways by Air

Alitalia offers direct daily flights from New York to Rome and frequent flights from Los Angeles, Chicago, Boston, and Miami—with the added advantage of $100 fares to (and from) any Italian city. TWA flies from New York and Boston nonstop to Rome, and American Airlines has begun a direct service from Chicago to Rome. Delta has taken over Pan Am's routes from New York to Rome. Toronto and Montreal are linked to Rome several times a week by Alitalia, Air Canada, and Canadian Airlines.

From London, Alitalia and some British carriers provide service to Rome and Naples. Qantas and Alitalia fly from Sydney and Melbourne to Rome. Most flights from North America arrive in Italy during the morning, usually about 8:00 or 9:00. A good travel agent will work out the most convenient routing, by plane or train.

Rome's principal airport, at Fiumicino, has undergone a transformation so glamorous that Clinique cosmetics has opened a boutique there, for a flying re-do. (Only a cosmetic surgeon in the wings is lacking.)

Added to this glamor is a shiny new train, ready to whiz you to the Eternal City. (The clumsy old airport bus to Stazione Termini has of course been banished. No style.)

Sounds celestial? Not quite.

Unfortunately you can't get from the airport luggage carousel to the train if you need a luggage cart, as many international, and certainly intercontinental, passengers do. An escalator between airport and train prohibits carts.

Next, there are the two new station stops in Rome: The first incoming stop, Trastevere, is convenient only for those with room reservations at the Vatican; the second, Stazione Ostienze, was apparently chosen for those who wish to see Keats's grave immediately upon arrival. There is public transportation at these stops, but you must know which city bus to take, where it stops, and where to buy bus tickets before getting on. The Piramide Metro stop is within walking distance of Ostiense, for those without luggage. Taxis may be waiting at the station if it isn't raining.

Bureaucratic irascibility worthy of Tiberius is behind this state of transit—or is it the taxi union? In any case, at present the only way to enter the Eternal City with luggage is by taxi: about 60,000 lire ($50).

Before leaving on the trip, investigate with your travel agent the cost of fly-drive programs, which are often less expensive (don't ask for the smallest car unless you're under four feet tall), and also about special promotional offers and independent packages, such as TWA's, Alitalia's Italiatours, and those that CIT (the Italian government's official tour operator) offer, which include a choice of hotels without the disadvantages of group travel.

Many charter-flight organizations at present use regularly scheduled airlines, and reserved seats can be arranged in advance. You'll probably be the one in the center if the plane is crowded, however, because the higher-paying passengers will of course get the more desirable aisle or window seats. The Sunday editions of major city newspapers, such as the *Los Angeles Times, New York Times,* or *Toronto Sun* run ads regularly for special fares. In London, *Time Out* and the *Times* run similar ads.

One further suggestion: Book your stay in Rome through a tour that offers independent hotel packages that include airport transfers. Central Holidays (Tel: 800-526-6045) and Italiatour are among such packagers. Ask your travel agent.

Specialized travel agencies, such as Italy for Less (Tel: 800-794-8259 or 212-599-0577; Fax: 212-599-3288), will find the most economical fares. Summer and holiday fares are usually not discounted by the airlines. Other discounters are Access International (Tel: 212-465-0707) and TFI Tours International in New York (Tel: 212-736-1140), and Council Charter in New York (Tel: 212-254-2525) and Los Angeles (Tel: 213-208-3551). In Rome, call Skyreps for discounted European and worldwide fares: via Calabria 17, Tel: (06) 488-4208.

Travelling Around by Train

Italy's rail service is excellent, and improving. The Rome–Naples express flashes from point to point in 2 hours. The glamorous new first-class-only ETR 450 travels between Rome, Naples, and Bari. Rome to Naples takes 1 hour 40 minutes; Rome to Bari, 4½ hours. Reservations are required. A regular Rome–Palermo express requires 13 hours; sleepers are available.

Before leaving on the trip, check with your travel agent for the numerous train passes available, each with different advantages. For example, the Kilometric Ticket costs about $238 first class and $140 second class. Valid for two months, it permits 20 trips or a total of 1,875 miles. As many as five people, even unrelated, may travel together on it. If you are travelling elsewhere in Europe, the Eurailpass is also available. Apart from these passes, which should be purchased before departure if possible (some *must* be bought in North

America), youth, senior, and family passes are also sold at special rates.

Almost every city you will want to visit, large or small, has train service. For those that don't, bus connections are generally available though probably less frequent. If you are travelling any distance, ask about the InterCity trains, which are nonstop, at least between important cities on a given route. They run from Sicily to Venice or Genoa. Always reserve a seat if possible, especially on InterCity trains. They are heavily used by Italians as well as foreigners, midweek and midday as well as peak seasons. Even when it's not required, do it to avoid having to sit on your luggage in the aisle. It's worth the extra charge (no charge if you buy the special passes discussed above). Sleeping cars are available on long-distance trains and require supplements and reservations.

For information, ask your travel agent.

However you go, you can still expect experiences like D. H. Lawrence's, 70 years ago:

Sicilian railways are all single line. Hence, the *coincidenza*. A *coincidenza* is where two trains meet in a loop. You sit in a world of rain and waiting until some silly engine with four trucks puffs alongside. Ecco la coincidenza! Then after a brief conversazione between the two trains, *diretto* and *merce,* express and goods, the tin horn sounds and away we go, happily, towards the next coincidence. Clerks away ahead joyfully chalk up our hours of lateness on the announcement slate. All adds to the adventurous flavour of the journey, dear heart. We come to a station where we find the other diretto, the express from the other direction, awaiting our coincidental arrival. The two trains run alongside one another, like two dogs meeting in the street and snuffing one another. Every official rushes to greet every other official, as if they were all David and Jonathan meeting after a crisis. They rush into each other's arms and exchange cigarettes. And the trains can't bear to part. And the station can't bear to part with us. The officials tease themselves and us with the word *pronto,* meaning *ready!* Pronto! And again Pronto! And shrill whistles. Anywhere else a train would go off its tormented head. But no! Here only that angel's trump of an official little

horn will do the business. And get them to blow that
horn if you can. They can't bear to part.

Sea and Sardinia

Travelling Around by Air

Italy's domestic airlines are often attractively priced for weekend packages under the Nastro Verde (Green Ribbon) plan:
You must leave and return on specific days and hours, which
are different for each city but generally cover the weekend
period. These can be purchased only in Italy, however, at any
travel agent or Alitalia office. (All domestic airlines are
owned by Alitalia.)

Airports in the South are located in Naples, Reggio Calabria, Catania, Palermo, Pantelleria, Trapani, Bari, Brindisi,
Alghero, and Cagliari. These are serviced by Alitalia's domestic fleet, connecting with northern cities.

If you are making plans for railroad or air travel, make
sure no strike (*sciopero*) is planned for your day of departure. Strikes are announced in the newspaper, and your
hotel *portiere* should be able to forewarn you if you explain
your plans.

Travelling Around by Bus

Bus travel can best be arranged through travel agents. CIT,
American Express, Italiatours, Central Holiday, and TWA offer good programs, catering to independent travellers as
well as groups.

Each region has bus companies that vary from very comfortable, and frequently faster than local trains, to the
sardine-can variety. From Rome to L'Aquila (in the Abruzzi),
for example, bus travel is faster, as it sometimes is from
Palermo to Taormina. Travel agents and tourist offices in
Italy are your best sources of information.

Long-distance buses connect Rome with Naples, Palermo,
and smaller cities; travel agents book these intercity buses.

By Boat

The islands of Sicily and Sardinia and smaller islands along
the coasts are connected to the mainland by car ferry and
sometimes by hydrofoil, especially in summer. The Tirrenia
line is the largest of the long-distance lines (Naples–
Palermo, Rome/Civitavecchia–Cagliari, etc.), and can be
contacted in North America through Extra Value Travel,
Fountain Building, 683 South Collier Boulevard, Marco
Island, Florida 33937 (Tel: 813-394-3384; Fax: 813-394-
4848), or through a travel agent. Always reserve and go

first-class on the overnight runs. (In summer the deck may be hidden under backpacks, and an important soccer match will sell out the boat in a flash at any time during the season.)

Smaller islands, such as Capri and the Aeolians, are booked at the departure cities, as discussed in the "Getting Around" sections of the regions in which they are located.

The yacht *Argonaut* cruises the Italian shoreline under the scholarly auspices of the Smithsonian Institution. Ports of call include Venice, Ravenna, Urbino (Ancona), Bari, Syracuse and Palermo, Reggio di Calabria, Pompeii and Paestum, Tarquinia, Viterbo (Civitavecchia), Genoa, and Lake Maggiore. For information, Tel: (202) 357-4700.

By Taxi

Metered yellow cabs (the only ones you want) usually line up at cab stands, to be picked up there or telephoned. In most cities they don't pick up en route. If you call a taxi, the meter starts when and where the driver does. If you can't find a cab, go into a hotel or bar and ask whether they will call one for you. It's worth a tip.

Renting a Car and Driving

Although you'll want a car in the countryside to follow your inclinations to sea resorts and Greek temples, driving in any of the major cities is far more pain than pleasure. Congestion, speedway-style driving (Rome), hard-to-find parking, and auto theft in some cities are a few of the reasons you will be happier parking at the hotel or a good lot and walking or taking taxis or public transport.

All you will need is a valid license from your own country. Major rental car companies in Italy are Maiellano, Hertz, Avis, Budget, National (called Europcar in Europe), and Dollar Rent a Car (affiliated with InterRent). As mentioned above, the smallest compact is too small, so opt for at least the next larger. You may request an automatic (usually more than double the standard price, as is air-conditioning), but learn a bit about shifting gears just in case. Car rentals are subject to an 18 percent tax, higher for luxury cars.

If you rent a car, you can now obtain the 15 percent discount on gas long enjoyed by private automobiles. Gas coupons can be bought at car-rental desks at the Rome and Milan airports, and at entry points along the border. They are also sold by the Italian government tourist offices in Europe, and at offices of the Automobile Club of Italy.

In southern Italy, pick up your rental car in a smaller

town, such as Salerno, rather than in Naples. Rental cars leaving the Naples area have been a frequent target for robbery.

Insurance for all vehicles is compulsory in Italy. A Green Card (*Carta Verde*) or Frontier Insurance, valid for 15, 30, or 45 days, should be issued to cover your car at the Italian border or by the rental company. Access America provides a health and theft policy that includes collision damage. Many automobile and health insurance policies cover the same emergencies.

Telephoning

The international telephone country code for Italy is 39. When telephoning from outside Italy, omit the zero from the local area codes.

Plastic is the answer if you'll be using the telephone frequently, for calls within the country or abroad. For overseas calls, use your telephone card number. You can now reach an American operator to call collect or to use your telephone credit card: For AT&T dial 172-1011, for MCI 172-1022, and for Sprint 172-1877. You need a coin (200 lire) to activate the number. For other international operator assistance, dial 170 for non-European countries and 15 for Europe and Mediterranean countries. To dial directly (hotels charge a huge tax for this): dial 00-1 for the United States and Canada, 44 for the U.K., 61 for Australia, and 64 for New Zealand, and then the number.

To call within Italy, a SIP (Italian telephone company) card (*scheda*) is a great help, as Italian coins are heavy and phone calls require a lot of them. Buy SIP cards in denominations of 5,000 or 10,000 lire at SIP offices, airports, railroad stations, newspaper stands, or tobacconists. (Buy them when you are in a major urban area; smaller towns, especially in the South, are unlikely to have them.) The card is inserted in the phone box, and its remaining value is shown on a screen. An alternative is to use the telephone with a meter (*telefono a scatto*), which each town has in a bar (café) if you ask around; you pay the proprietor when you're through.

Regular calls within the same city cost 200 lire; tokens (*gettone*) are required less frequently, but it helps to keep a few with you.

The Post

Mail service in Italy is terrible. Use the telephone or fax whenever feasible. Urgent letters should be sent by DHL, Federal Express, or another guaranteed service. When in

Rome, try to do most of your mailing from the Vatican, which has its own—excellent—mail service.

Local Time

Italy is six hours ahead of Eastern Standard Time, one hour ahead of Greenwich Mean Time, and nine hours behind Sydney. During the changeover to and from daylight saving time there are a few days when Italy is an extra hour ahead or behind, so double-check relevant hours near that period.

Electric Current

Italian current is 220 volts, 50 cycles; a converter/adapter is necessary for North American appliances. Most hardware stores, electronics outlets, and computer dealers in this country have them.

Currency

The monetary unit is the Italian *lira,* plural *lire,* written Ł. Notes are issued in denominations of 1,000; 2,000; 5,000; 10,000; 20,000; 50,000; and 100,000 lire. Coins are 10 (rare); 20 (rare); 50; 100; 200; and 500 lire. The lira is valued at about 1,250 to the U.S. dollar, 1,123 to the Canadian dollar, 600 to the British pound, and 1,276 to the Australian dollar. The exchange rate is subject to daily variation; check with banks and daily newspapers for the current rates. On arrival at Rome's Fiumicino airport, you can change money just after clearing passport control, before claiming your luggage.

Travellers checks are changed in banks at (usually) better rates than elsewhere. The American Express office in Rome cashes personal checks for members carrying their cards. Few hotels will accept a personal check, and some do not accept credit cards.

Many banks throughout Italy give Visa and MasterCard cardholders cash advances. MasterCard advances are made in banks with Eurocard ("EC") stickers on the door. (Eurocard is equivalent to MasterCard for other purposes as well.) Try to obtain such an advance in larger cities, as not all small towns are prepared for this service and you may have to travel to ten banks, waving your card, to find out whether any do. (An advance is an *anticipo.*)

Business Hours

Learning Italian business hours would require a university course. They vary from region to region, with the North adhering in general to more European hours and the South keeping the siesta tradition of closing for most of the afternoon and reopening in the evening; "normal" business hours in the South would be from 9:00 A.M. to 1:00 P.M. and 4:00 P.M. to 8:00 P.M. Many shops are closed Monday mornings. Banks are open usually from 8:30 A.M. to 1:30 P.M. and sometimes from 3:00 or 3:30 P.M. to 4:00 or 4:30 P.M., but individual differences require that you double-check. Exchanges (*cambio*) keep store hours. Local post offices are open from 8:00 A.M. to 2:00 P.M., and the central office is usually open late in the evening in large cities. Barbers open from 8:00 A.M. to 1:00 P.M. and 4:00 P.M. to 8:00 P.M. and are closed Sunday afternoons and Mondays. Women's hairdressers are open 8:00 A.M. to 8:00 P.M., but most close all day Sundays and Mondays.

Museum and Church Hours. State museums are open mornings all week but close on Mondays. Double-check the specific museum you want to visit before setting out. Churches that are open to the public at specific hours are usually open mornings only, although some open afternoons as well. The dress code for churches is: no bare shoulders or bare legs, for men or women. Many churches require a 100 or 200 lire coin in the light box to illuminate certain dark chapels or paintings. Keep a supply, preferably in a tube such as those used for camera film; Italian coins are large and heavy.

Holidays

Offices and shops in Italy are closed on the following dates: January 1 (New Year's Day); January 6 (Epiphany); Easter Monday; April 25 (Liberation Day); May 1 (Labor Day); August 15 (Assumption of the Virgin); November 1 (All Saints Day); December 8 (Day of Immaculate Conception); December 25 (Christmas Day); December 26 (Saint Stephen).

Banks, offices, and shops may also be closed for local feast days, such as June 29 in Rome (Saints Peter and Paul), July 15 in Palermo (Santa Rosalia), September 19 in Naples (San Gennaro), October 30 in Cagliari (Saint Saturnino), and December 6 in Bari (Saint Nicholas). While you might not be able to do any banking that day, these holidays are often colorful and festive, and the celebrations are worth seeking out (see "The Local Festa," below).

Note: Beware of *ponte* (bridge) weekends—the three-day weekends that include a holiday, when banking and other services will be closed. Remember that on Labor Day, May 1, absolutely *everything* in Rome and many other cities closes. This means the bus and subway lines as well, and taxis are far from plentiful. Few restaurants are open, but hotel restaurants and a few others will keep you from starving.

When banks are closed, you can change money in an emergency at the airport or railroad station or, with a higher service charge, at your hotel.

The Local Festa

Each region has its own feast days to honor favorite saints. Parades and local food specialties are the rule, and each celebration is individualized by ancient traditions. Here are but a few:

January 6: Epiphany, or La Befana (the good witch who brings toys to children). Piazza Navona in Rome turns into a Christmas fair, and Romans visit the *Bambino* (Baby Jesus) displayed in elaborate *presepi* (mangers) in dozens of churches and in St. Peter's Square.

Celebrations occur throughout Italy.

February 3: Catania, Sicily, honors its patron saint, Agatha, with processions and pastries.

Holy Week and Easter (Pasqua): Easter is naturally celebrated with pomp at the Vatican and elsewhere in Italy, where flowers, music, and spring specialties, lamb and asparagus among them, greet the day. The day after Easter (*Pasquetta*) is also a holiday.

Good Friday is solemnized with special fervor in the South, with processions bearing the Cross in most cities and towns. In Sicily the city of Trapani is famous for its procession of the Mysteries—large figures that are paraded through the town. Sweets include sculpted lambs in marzipan. On Easter Sunday in the nearby town of Prizzi, the triumph of Good over Evil is enacted with devils escorting Death, who will be vanquished by the risen Christ and the Madonna. The favored pastry is *cannateddi,* braided dough surrounding a colored egg.

In Calabria, Catanzaro relives the Good Friday scene of Christ's flagellation with a procession of flagellants, whipping themselves as they accompany the Cross to Calvary.

May 8: In Puglia, Monte Sant'Angelo celebrates Saint Michael's appearance there (also on September 29).

May 7–8: In Bari, Christmas's Saint Nicholas is the patron; his statue is taken out in the harbor for a ride, while on shore the Barese have a seaside party.

Last Sunday in May: The Cavalcata Sarda takes place in Sassari, Sardinia. In one of Italy's most beautiful celebrations, lavish folk costumes from all Sardinia are paraded, accompanied by amazing displays of horsemanship.

May 31: Cavalcade of the Turks. In Potenza, Basilicata, galleons are paraded through the streets with costumed figures representing the downfall of the Turks.

July 3: In Matera, Basilicata, the Black Madonna is carried by cart through the town, and the cart is demolished by a sometimes frenzied crowd.

July 11: In Palermo, Sicily, their patron, Santa Rosalia, is fêted with fireworks and feasting.

August 15: The Feast of the Assumption, a national holiday, is especially festive in Reggio di Calabria—puppets and sweets.

August 16: In San Rocco, there is a Medieval-style religious procession of the lacerated *spinati,* who have pierced their flesh with thorns; votive offerings are sold along the streets.

September 1: Neapolitans celebrate the Feast of Piedigrotta, honoring the sanctuary with music, parades, and fireworks.

September 19: Naples' San Gennaro liquifies his blood in the Cathedral, a sign of good fortune.

October 30: In Cagliari, Sardinia, the Feast of Saint Saturnino is celebrated with parades.

October 31: The Day of the Dead, or *I Morti.* Graves are visited and decorated with flowers throughout Italy. Artistic marzipan creations, from a delicate *pietà* to a cavalier to an octopus, are on sale at a fair in Palermo and at local bakeries.

Safety

A great many problems are easily solved by purchasing or making a money belt or a small undercover silk or cotton pouch. Carry a credit card and enough cash for the day. Small towns are far safer (from thieves) than cities; thievery is a major problem in Rome, Naples, and Palermo at present. Be sure your homeowner's or renter's policy covers your valuables when travelling. Many do.

If you *must* transport valuables, do so in a plain plastic shopping bag, or one from Upim or Standa, Italy's five-and-dimes. Cameras are easily cut off if you wear them around your neck. Pickpockets thrive in buses (the No. 64, which goes to and from the Vatican, is notorious) and other crowded areas. Gypsy children (with parental supervision) are among the most obvious; don't read any cardboard signs they put in front of you or your wallet will disappear. They normally work the railroad station areas, among others. Vespa thieves, boys or girls, grab shoulder bags. The final word: Don't leave your valuables unguarded, even in St. Peter's.

The Emergency phone number throughout Italy is 113. The Police number is 112.

Receipts
All restaurants are required by Italian tax law to issue a *ricevuta fiscale,* a computerized cash-register receipt that you must carry with you upon leaving. You can be fined if you don't have it.

Day Hotels
Many services are offered by day hotels (*alberghi diurnali*), which are generally located near the main railroad stations. They are handy for day-trippers, providing baths, showers, barbers, hairdressers, shoeshines, dry cleaning, telephone, baggage checking, writing rooms, and private rooms for brief rest periods (overnight stays are not permitted). Railroad stations are usually not in the safest areas of town, and you must be aware of your neighbors when in the vicinity. Information desks in railroad stations or airports can tell you where day hotels are located. Usually signs indicating "diurnali" are clearly posted.

Hotels
Hotels are awarded stars by the government on the basis of amenities. If you don't need a television (in Italian) or a swimming pool, a deluxe hotel may not be required. (Deluxe hotels charge 17 percent IVA tax; others charge 9 percent.)

The *pensione,* in name, is no more. They are categorized as hotels now. Some "hotels," therefore, will be located on a separate floor of a building.

Motels
If you don't require traditional charm, Italian motels are excellent, and some have very good restaurants. AGIP and ACI are the organizations that operate motels, which are found on the main highways. (See the Tourist Office information booklet, below, for a listing.)

Youth Hostels
For a listing, see the Tourist Office information booklet, below, or contact the Associazione Italiana Alberghi

per la Gioventù, via Cavour 44, 00184 Rome; Tel: (06) 46-23-42; Fax: (06) 47-41-26.

Country Living

A delightful way to see Italy is through the Agriturist organization, which arranges for stays in country houses that range from beautifully groomed villas and ancient castles to rough-and-ready farms. At present some Agriturist offices are not set up for English-speaking people, but if you can communicate in Italian, do write or call. The main office in Rome is located at corso Vittorio Emanuele 101, 00186 Rome; Tel: (06) 651-23-42. There are many individual provincial offices also. Their addresses can be obtained from the Italian Tourist Office (see the booklet listed below) or the main Agriturist office.

Campgrounds and Mountain Cabins

More than 1,700 official campgrounds are in operation in Italy, varying from the simple to the well equipped, some with cottages. Write or call the Tourist Office (see below) for a current directory.

Longer Visits

If you are staying in one city for a week or longer, your best bet may be a *residence*, a hotel apartment that enables you to have your own living room and kitchen, usually for less than the price of a hotel room for that period. Many hotels have suites that are rented on a weekly or monthly basis as well. Contact the Italian State Tourist Office or local tourist authorities for a list of residences.

Apartments and houses can be rented in Italy through offices called Immobiliari, listed in the Yellow Pages. In Rome the newsletter *Wanted in Rome,* available at many hotels, at the Lion Bookstore (via Condotti 181), and at major newsstands, runs classified ads for those seeking and offering rentals in the city and throughout the country.

Many U.S. and British agencies handle villa and apartment rentals. The Italian Tourist Office lists a number of these (see below). This can be a great lira saver and a nice way to feel part of a community.

Cooking Classes

The ever-growing interest in Italian *cucina* has spawned a number of excellent cooking schools. These classes offer a long-lasting souvenir of your trip.

Jo Bettoja's Lo Scaldavivande in Rome: informal sessions

in a palazzo near the Fontana di Trevi, with participation and luncheons. Everyday home cooking is stressed. Jo Bettoja is the author of *Italian Cooking in the Grand Tradition* and *Southern Italian Cooking*. In the U.S., contact E & M Associates, 211 East 43rd Street, New York, NY 10017; Tel: (212) 599-8280.

Giuliano Bugialli's Cooking in Florence. Bugialli's professional kitchen in Florence is the usual site of classes, although he also organizes trips to other regions. His books include *The Fine Art of Italian Cooking* and *Foods of Italy*. Contact him at P.O. Box 1650, Canal Street Station, New York, NY 10013; Tel: (212) 966-5325; Fax: (212) 226-0601.

Country Cooking with Diana Folonari. Week-long courses in food and wine, conducted in a private home in Positano. Contact E & M Associates, 211 East 43rd Street, New York, NY 10017; Tel: (800) 223-9832 or (212) 599-8280.

Mario lo Menzo. Countess Franca and Count Giuseppe Tasca offer the opportunity to stay at Regaleali, their family estate and vineyard in Sicily (producing one of the island's finest wines), and learn the artistry of Mario lo Menzo, considered the last *monzù*—a term given to French master chefs during the 19th century. A rare and expensive week. Contact Ann Yonkers, 3802 Jocelyn Street NW, Washington DC, 20015; Tel: (202) 362-8228; or Anna Tasca Lanza, viale Principessa Giovanna 9, 90139 Palermo; Tel: (091) 45-07-27; Fax: (0921) 54-27-83.

Tourist Offices

Don't leave home without the booklet "General Information for Travelers in Italy," published annually by the Italian State Tourist Office. Major offices are located at:

630 Fifth Avenue, New York, NY 10111; Tel: (212) 245-4822; Fax: (212) 586-9249.

500 North Michigan Avenue, Chicago, IL 60611; Tel: (312) 644-0990; Fax: (312) 644-3019.

360 Post Street, San Francisco, CA 94108; Tel: (415) 392-6206; Fax: (415) 392-6852.

1 Place Ville Marie, Suite 1914, Montreal, Quebec H3B 3M9, Canada; Tel: (514) 866-7667; Fax: (514) 392-1429.

1 Princes Street, London WIR 8AY, England; Tel: (0441) 408-1254; Fax: (0441) 493-6695.

BIBLIOGRAPHY

Sir Harold Acton, *The Bourbons of Naples*. A witty evocation of an extraordinary time.

Corrado Alvaro, *Revolt in Aspromonte*. One of the few books available in English by this prolific writer; discusses problems in the Italian south during the mid-20th century.

Burton Anderson, *Vino: The Wines and Winemakers of Italy*. Even though it was published in 1980, it is still the best book on its subject—and with interesting asides on food, too—covering all 20 regions of the country.

Vernon Bartlett, *Introduction to Italy*. An amusing and unusually comprehensive overview of the country's history from ancient times to the present day.

Luigi Barzini, *The Italians*. Dr. Barzini explains his countrymen to the West, with wit and knowledge based on deep affection.

James Beck, *Italian Renaissance Painting*. A comprehensive and readable survey of one of the most important aspects of Western civilization.

Bernard Berenson, *The Passionate Sightseer*. Illustrated diaries of this essential art historian.

———, *Italian Pictures of the Renaissance*. One of the essential guides to Renaissance art.

Edward Bulwer-Lytton, *The Last Days of Pompeii*. A graphic yet historically respectable version of those days.

Jacob Burckhardt, *Civilization of the Renaissance in Italy*. Remains a classic work on that period, though it represents a somewhat old-fashioned type of history.

———, *At the Court of the Borgia*. The days of Pope Alexander VI (father of Cesare and Lucrezia).

Charles Burney, *Music, Men, and Manners in France and Italy 1770*. Burney's account of his travels is one of the classics of the history of music.

John Horne Burns, *The Gallery*. The Galleria Umberto in Naples as a metaphor for wartime Italy, with bartenders, prostitutes, gays, and WACs considered with a compassionate eye.

Baldassare Castiglione, *The Book of the Courtier*. An eyewitness account of one of the smaller ducal courts of the

Renaissance and a penetrating excursion into Renaissance thought.

BENVENUTO CELLINI, *The Life of Benvenuto Cellini*. One of the most fascinating autobiographies; Renaissance truth is as interesting as Renaissance fiction.

ELEANOR CLARK, *Rome and a Villa*. A novelist's portrait of the capital.

F. MARION CRAWFORD, *The Rulers of the South*. A two-volume history of southern Italy and Sicily.

VINCENT CRONIN, *The Golden Honeycomb*. A tour of Sicily that uncovers ancient myths and present pleasures.

DANTE ALIGHIERI, *Divine Comedy*. Heaven, Purgatory, and Hell, peopled with the author's candidates for each.

CHARLES DICKENS, *Pictures from Italy*. Evocative portraits of scenes encountered.

DANILO DOLCI, *Sicilian Lives*. Sicily experienced through individual life stories.

NORMAN DOUGLAS, *Old Calabria*. Historical and personal accounts of life in the south; many still hit home three-quarters of a century after publication.

————, *Siren Land*. The ancient siren myth is related as it touches the Campanian coast.

————, *South Wind*. Once a cult book, it offers readers an escape to Capri, disguised as Nepenthe.

UMBERTO ECO, *The Name of the Rose*. An intriguing novel set in the time of the Avignon papacy.

M. I. FINLEY, DENIS MACK SMITH, and CHRISTOPHER DUGGAN, *A History of Sicily*. A brilliant three-volume history compacted into one volume.

EDWARD GIBBON, *The Decline and Fall of the Roman Empire* (1776–1788). It is not commonly known that this classic work—hard to find in an unabridged edition—ends with the 15th century, not the 5th, and so has much discussion of the Visigoths, Byzantines, Arabs, Carolingians, Lombards, and other peoples who figure in the transition from Augustus to the early Renaissance. Gibbon—still—should be read by anyone interested in Italy.

JOHANN WOLFGANG VON GOETHE, *Italian Journey*. One of the most important Italian journals of its time.

ROBERT GRAVES, *I, Claudius.* An imagined autobiography by the classical poet and translator.

PETER GUNN, *A Concise History of Italy.* True to its title.

AUGUSTUS HARE, *Augustus Hare in Italy.* A compilation of the author's travel writings in turn-of-the-century Italy.

BARBARA GRIZZUTI HARRISON, *The Islands of Italy.* A lavishly illustrated tour through Sicily, Sardinia, and the Aeolian islands with a lively and opinionated guide.

———, *Italian Days.* Her personal journey through the country of her ancestors rewards us with an affectionate but razor-sharp view of everything from history and politics to food and local lore.

HOWARD HIBBARD, *Bernini* and *Michelangelo.* Biographies of the artists by one of the most respected art historians.

PAUL HOFMANN, *O Vatican! A Slightly Wicked View of the Holy See.* An insider's appreciation.

———, *Rome: The Sweet Tempestuous Life.* Sketches of all aspects of life in the Eternal City.

HOMER, *The Iliad.* Read the Sicilian and southern coast sections, especially regarding the Cyclops, the Sirens, and other myths.

HENRY JAMES, *Italian Hours.* His love affair with Italy. "At last—for the first time—I live!" he wrote.

WERNER KERNER, *The Etruscans.* A scholarly look, with illustrations.

GIUSEPPE TOMASI DI LAMPEDUSA, *The Leopard.* The sensuous and evocative story of a Sicilian prince facing the next generation of rulers: "We were the leopards... those who take our place will be little jackals."

D. H. LAWRENCE, *Sea and Sardinia, Etruscan Places,* and *Twilight in Italy.* All travel journals written with the Lawrencian passion.

CARLO LEVI, *Christ Stopped at Eboli.* Life in southern Italy during the Second World War.

GEORGINA MASSON, *The Companion Guide to Rome.* One of the best guides to Rome, divided by neighborhoods.

———, *Frederick II of Hohenstaufen.* A fine biography worth searching for.

————, *Italian Villas and Palaces.* A picture book full of good information.

MICHEL DE MONTAIGNE, *Travel Journal.* The 16th-century essayist's Renaissance insights into church, state, tepid baths, and tough crayfish.

CHARLES DE SECONDAT, BARON DE MONTESQUIEU, *Considerations on the Grandeur and Decadence of the Romans* (1734). Published 42 years before Gibbon's *Decline and Fall,* Montesquieu's commentary focuses on the ancient Roman republican virtues and the institutions behind them—and of course on how and why they weakened, with the well-known result.

ALBERTO MORAVIA, *The Woman of Rome.* A novel of a prostitute under Fascism.

H. V. MORTON, *A Traveler in Italy; A Traveler in Southern Italy;* and *A Traveler in Rome.* All three are filled with the lore and musings of the beloved tale-teller.

WILLIAM MURRAY, *The Last Italian: Portrait of a People.* An updated version of Barzini's *The Italians,* written by a resident foreigner.

JOHN JULIUS NORWICH, *The Italians: History, Art and the Genius of a People.* A comprehensive cultural history.

————, *The Normans in the South* and *The Kingdom in the Sun.* Delightfully written accounts of Norman Italy.

GEORGE PILLEMENT, *Unknown Italy.* Up-to-date and off the beaten track, with a focus on architecture.

PINDAR, *The Odes.* Those on Sicily's Olympic heroes are especially interesting.

PLINY THE YOUNGER, *Letters.* Those that deal with his uncle's death at Vesuvius are riveting.

WAVERLEY ROOT, *The Food of Italy.* Anecdotes and a pleasurable introduction to the country's food and wine.

STEVEN RUNCIMAN, *The Sicilian Vespers.* The revolt as it relates to European history, written with immediacy and clarity.

LEONARDO SCIASCIA, *The Day of the Owl.* A mafiosi mystery with insight. Sciascia (pronounced approximately sha-sha), who died recently, is the best known of Sicily's writers.

MARY TAYLOR SIMETI, *On Persephone's Island*. A Sicilian book of the seasons, the journal of a critical and compassionate American resident.

———, *Pomp and Sustenance*. The definitive book on Sicilian cooking (a disguise for a textured work on Sicilian history), beautifully illustrated with rare engravings.

KATE SIMON, *Italy: The Places In Between* and *Rome: Places and Pleasures*. Both are full of insightful observations.

D. MACK SMITH, *Cavour and Garibaldi 1860*. The definitive English-language study of the Risorgimento.

WILLIAM JAY SMITH and DANA GIOIA, EDS., *Poems From Italy*. Almost 800 years of Italian poetry in parallel text form.

LAURENCE STERNE, *A Sentimental Journey Through France and Italy*. Musings on the Continent by the 18th century's top wit.

SUETONIUS, *The Twelve Caesars*. He told what he knew and didn't know with great candor.

RACHEL ANNAND TAYLOR, *Invitation to Renaissance Italy* (1930). A vivid and highly entertaining account of the Renaissance and its major players and themes, forcing us to reconsider some strongly held notions of these fluid times.

GIORGIO VASARI, *The Lives of the Artists*. The life and times of the Renaissance masters; gives a sense of how they were judged by their peers.

HORACE WALPOLE, *The Castle of Otranto*. This forerunner of the Gothic novel gives an amusing idea of how exotic Apulia was viewed in the late 18th century.

JOHN WHITE, *Art and Architecture in Italy: 1250–1400*. A thorough study of the period that immediately preceded the Renaissance.

RUDOLPH WITTKOWER, *Art and Architecture in Italy, 1600–1750*. The noted Baroque historian's scholarly examination of the period.

A. G. WOODHEAD, *The Greeks in the West*. A concise, highly readable introduction to Greek expansion in Magna Graecia.

If the book you want is out of print or hard to find, stop when in Rome at **Books on Italy**, via Giubbonari 30, 00186 Rome, near campo dei Fiori. Call first for an appointment

(Tel: 06-654-5285), or write to Louise McDermott at that address for her mail-order catalog.

In the U.S., an excellent source is the Traveller's Bookstore, 75 Rockefeller Plaza, New York, NY 10019; Tel: (212) 664-0995. Ask for their catalog of travel books and related literature. Or for another good source, The Complete Traveller, 199 Madison Avenue, New York, NY 10016; Tel: (212) 679-4339; their catalog costs $1.

VIDEOGRAPHY
Some of Italy's artworks are films, many of which are now available on videotape, dubbed or with subtitles.

Of the early classics, *Bicycle Thief* (De Sica, 1949) and *Umberto D* (De Sica, 1952) are among the most shattering, painful, and powerful films ever made, great works of art and of human compassion. Another fine wartime film, *Open City* (Rossellini, 1946), gives neorealistic views of postwar Rome. A later (1971) De Sica film, *The Garden of the Finzi Continis,* photographs in exquisite color the elegant prewar world of a Jewish family as an unthinkable future descends.

Other directors who have brilliantly dominated the scene are:

Luchino Visconti (*Rocco and His Brothers*),

Federico Fellini (*Nights of Cabiria, La Strada, 8½, La Dolce Vita, Amarcord, Juliet of the Spirits*),

Michelangelo Antonioni (*Red Desert, L'Avventura*),

Paolo and Vittorio Taviani (*Night of the Shooting Stars, Padre Padrone*),

Giuseppe Tornature, the young Sicilian director whose *Cinema Paradiso* won an Oscar as Best Foreign Film, and

Lina Wertmuller (*Seven Beauties, Swept Away,* and, in an unusual collaboration with Franco Zefferelli, *Brother Sun and Sister Moon,* a life of Saint Francis, well played against a lyrical Umbrian landscape).

ROME

By Dwight V. Gast and Barbara Coeyman Hults

Dwight V. Gast is a former editor of Italy Italy *magazine and correspondent for the Associated Press in Rome. He has written about the city for numerous publications and is also the author of our chapters on Apulia and Calabria. Barbara Coeyman Hults is the editorial consultant for this guidebook.*

Ever whirling in watery arcs of fountains, citizens chattering and gesturing wildly, traffic like metallic legions marching into combat—Rome rushes at you. It can be overwhelming, overblown, exaggerated. The city is as colossal as the Colosseum, as pompous as the Baroque popes, as melodramatic as a street vendor. But just when you've had enough and given up on it, suddenly something unexpected happens. You see the Tiber sparkling sapphire in the night light, a waiter brings you a fresh taste from the oven as a gift, you're charmed by a cat admiring a column once reserved for the Caesars, and you decide to reconcile.

Federico Fellini once praised the city's expansive aspect: "Rome allows you all sorts of speculation, vertically. Rome is [also] a horizontal city, made of water and earth, spread out, and is therefore the ideal platform for flights of fancy. Intellectuals, artists, who always live in a state of friction between two different dimensions—reality and fantasy—here find an appropriate and liberating stimulus for their mental activity, with the comfort of an umbilical cord that keeps them solidly attached to the concrete. Because Rome is a mother—the ideal mother because she's indifferent. She's a mother who has too many children and who, not being able to take care of any one of them, doesn't ask anything of you, doesn't expect anything of you. She welcomes you when you come, lets you go when you leave."

33

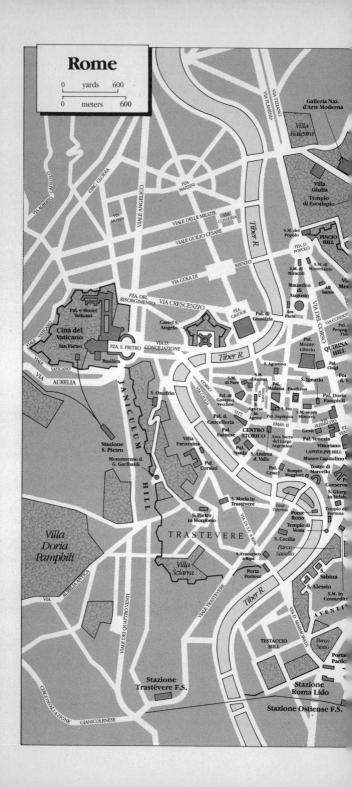

Rome

| 0 | yards | 600 |
| 0 | meters | 600 |

VIA TIZIANO

VIA FLAMINIA

Galleria Naz.
d'Arte Moderna

Villa
Balestra

VIA VETERBO

CIRC. CLODIA

VIALE ANGELICO

PZA.
MAZZINI

Villa
Giulia

VIA
MORIN

VIALE DELLE MILIZIE

VIA
COSSERIA

Tempio
di Esculapio

Tiber R.

VIALE GUILIO CESARE

S.M. del
Popolo

PINCIO
HILL

VIA COLA DI

RIENZO

PZA. D.
POPOLO

S.M. di
Montesanto

Via
Me

PZA. DEL
RISORGIMENTO

VIA CRESCENZIO

S.M. di
Miracoli

All
Saints

VIA DEL CORSO

VIA CONDOT

Mausoleo
di
Augusto

Pal. e Musei
Vaticani

Città del
Vaticano

San Pietro

PZA.
CAVOUR

Pal. di
Giustizia

Ara
Pacis

Pal.
Propag.
Fide

VIA VATICANO

Castel S.
Angelo

VIA D.
CONCILIAZIONE

Pal.
Monte-
citorio

QUIRINA
HILL

PZA. S. PIETRO

Tiber R.

Pal.
Chigi

Basilica

S. Agostino

For
d.

VIALE VATICANO

S.M.
d'Anima

S. Ignazio

VIA
AURELIA

S. Onofrio

CORSO

VIA DELLA

S.M.
di Pace

Pantheon

Pal. Doria
Pamphili

Pal.
Madama

VICOLA

Pal. di
Governo
Vecchia

Agnese
in Agone

S. Ivo

S.M. sopra
Minerva

Gesù

PZA
VEN

Pal. d.
Cancelleria

VITT.

Pal. Sapienza

EMAN. II

CENTRO
STORICO

Pal. Venezia

Vittoriano

Villa
Farnesina

Pal.
Farnese

Area Sacra
del Largo
Argentina

CAPITOLINE HILL

JANICULUM HILL

Stazione
S. Pietro

Pal.
Spada

S. Andrea
d. Valle

Museo Capitolino

Pa
Conserva

Monumento d.
G. Garibaldi

Pal.
Corsini

Pal.
Cenci

Teatro di
Marcello

S. Giorg
in Velab

Tempio
Maggiore

Tempio di
Fortuna

S. Maria in
Trastévere

Isola
Tiberina

Ponte
Rotto

Tempio di
Vesta

S. Pietro
in Montorio

S. Cecilia

Villa
Doria
Pamphili

TRASTEVERE

VIA B. S.F. ARIA

Parco
Savello

S
Sabina

S. Alessio

Villa
Sciarra

S. Francesco
a Ripa

Porta
Portese

S.M. in
Cosmedin

VIA AURELIA ANTICA

VIA

AVENTI

VIA D. MARMORATA

Tiber R.

VIALE DEI QUATTRO VENTI

VIALE TRASTEVERE

TESTACCIO
HILL

Parco
Sesto

Porta
Paolo

Stazione
Trastévere F.S.

CIRCONVALLAZIONE

GIANICOLENSE

Stazione
Roma Lido

Stazione Ostiense F.S.

Though quoted when he made his film *Roma* in the early 1970s, Fellini's words have an ageless quality about them—as befits the Eternal City. They recall the flights of fancy that created the legend about the foundation of Rome by Romulus and Remus, nursed by the she-wolf, the original mother of Rome.

That the contemporary reflects the ancient is the glory of Rome, a relationship immediately apparent on arrival. If your point of entry is the airport at Fiumicino, on your way to the city you'll pass the expanse of the E.U.R. suburb, begun under Mussolini for the Esposizione Universale di Roma, a world's fair that never took place. The use of Classical elements in its buildings portends the Postmodern movement in contemporary architecture, and Classical Rome itself is the reason most people visit E.U.R.—its Museo della Civiltà Romana houses a famous model of ancient Rome (currently closed). If instead you arrive at the train station, Stazione di Termini, you'll be confronted by another piece of modern architecture—the station itself. Immediately outside, however, are the remains of an ancient wall, and across the piazza stand the ruins of the Terme di Diocleziano (the Baths of Diocletian).

Between the deep red of the ancient brick and the stark white of modern marble and concrete are the mellower tones, now fixed by law, that dominate Rome and might have come out of a fruit basket in a Caravaggio painting. Peach, apricot, pomegranate, and honey hues decorate its palazzos and villas, the colors made even more striking in combination with the stately Renaissance style imported from Florence, or the exuberant Baroque born in Rome and favored by the popes. Rome's present look is a blend of all such styles, with a touch (but just a touch) of order added when the government of a newly united Italy lined the Tiber with travertine embankments when the city became its capital.

Rome's principal attractions are highlighted in the narrative below, but don't expect—or even attempt—to see everything the first time around. The jumble of the centuries is simply too confusing, even to longtime residents, who are used to the distractions of the unexpected church closures, the signs announcing *chiuso per restauro* (closed for restoration) and *chiuso per mancanza di personale* (closed for lack of personnel), the scaffolding and green gauze shrouding the monuments, the delightful tangent of discovering a hidden courtyard, witnessing a dramatic bit of street theater (though it's just the Romans going about their daily business), or lingering a little at table over a meal enlivened with good wine and better conversation.

Begin your visit on a leisurely note and let Rome's charms wash over you slowly. One way is by taking the free English-language tours on aspects of Rome from the ancient to the contemporary given regularly by the Dutch sisters of Foyer Unitas (via Santa Maria dell'Anima 30, Tel: 654-16-18). Include a Sunday or public holiday in your plans in order to see the city free of the traffic that normally engulfs its streets and monuments despite legislation attempting to restrict it. If it's a nice day (and it usually is, for the South begins in Rome, as evidenced by the palm trees and the slower pace), rent a bicycle, or sit in one of the cafés or restaurants in piazza Navona and watch the drama unfold in front of you against the piazza's Baroque backdrop. As a visitor, you'll be as much a part of the street scene as the "real" Romans, whose heroine Anna Magnani personified their fierce vitality on film. For despite nostalgic laments among many residents that the real Romans have been overrun by other Italians drawn to the capital to take patronage jobs, they are still here in force. A visit to campo dei Fiori or Trastevere will verify that.

And the city, which together with the Vatican is capital of church and state, is just as intensely bureaucratic and chaotic as any Fellini fantasy. But don't let it overwhelm you. Above all, take your time. Toss a coin into the Trevi Fountain to ensure you'll be back, for that oft-quoted expression about Rome, *non basta una vita* (one life is not enough), is true.

MAJOR INTEREST

The Roman Forum
The Palatine Hill
The Colosseum
The Pantheon
Piazza Navona's Baroque splendor
Walking through the Centro Storico (Old Rome, the historic center) for its large and small architectural pleasures
Piazza del Popolo's churches and cafés
The Spanish Steps
Shopping in the via Condotti area
The especially Roman areas of campo dei Fiori and Trastevere
Rome's restaurants, cafés, and bars
The museums at Villa Borghese, Palazzo Barberini, the Capitoline Hill, the ancient Roman Terme di Diocleziano, the Vatican (including the Sistine Chapel), and elsewhere
St. Peter's basilica and piazza

The visitor is constantly confronted with visual reminders of more than two thousand years of history: from the outline left by the Circus Maximus, built in the second century B.C., to the Stadio Olimpico, refurbished last year for the World Cup soccer finals. The Sabine and Etruscan kings ruled for more than two centuries (traces of the fortifications known as the Mura Serviane—traditionally attributed to the Etruscan king Servius Tullius, who ruled from 578 to 534 B.C.— may still be seen near the Mercato di Traiano [Trajan's Market]), until the Republic was founded around 500 B.C. The defeat of Carthage in 146 B.C. coincided with the conquest of Greek colonies in southern Italy, thus beginning the Greek influence on monumental Roman architecture, which expanded greatly during the Empire (27 B.C.–A.D. 395). It was during this era that most of what we see of ancient Rome was built, as well as when the engineering feats of the Aurelian Wall in the city (270–282) and the roads and aqueducts throughout the Empire were constructed.

Despite a series of sacks of Rome (by the Goths in 410, the Vandals in 455, the Saracens in 845, the Normans in 1084, and the German troops of Charles V in 1527), the papacy steadily established itself in the city, raising religious monuments and palazzi. The popes' effective political power began under Gregory I (590–604), but the development of the Holy Roman Empire—established when Leo III, in Rome, crowned Charlemagne emperor in 800—led to a series of conflicts between popes and emperors and eventually to the transfer of the papacy to Avignon (1309–1378). Rome's political and cultural importance was greatly diminished during this period.

With the end of the pope-antipope schism, and beginning with Martin V in 1417, Rome entered the Renaissance, and the popes began to commission great works from such artists as Michelangelo and Raphael. Sixtus V (1585–1590) began the first serious planning and development in the city in centuries, with straight roads, and under Urban VIII (1623–1644) and Innocent X (1644–1655) the Baroque we so associate with Rome today reached its zenith. During the relatively quiet political period that followed, such 18th-century works as the Spanish Steps and the Fontana di Trevi were built. Napoléon's troops occupied the city in 1798, and the French taste for Neoclassicism, typified by the works of Antonio Canova, Napoléon's favorite sculptor, also invaded the city's arts.

Following the defeat of Napoléon in 1814, the Italian

revolution (Risorgimento) began, and Rome became the capital of the united Kingdom of Italy in 1870. The over-blown monument to King Vittorio Emanuele, completed in 1911, set the stage for Mussolini's march on Rome in 1922, and the Fascist government he established imposed its order on the city by cutting such broad avenues as via dei Fori Imperiali and via della Conciliazione.

The liberation of Rome by the Allies in 1943–1944 brought about the Italian Republic we know today, and except for such scattered modern buildings as the New Audience Hall and a few hotels, the most important contribution to postwar building in Rome seems to be the Grande Raccordo Anulare (the 44-mile-long highway that rings the city)—an impressive feat of engineering, given Roman bureaucracy, almost in the tradition of the ancient Romans.

The discussion of the city that follows begins at the beginning, with *ancient Rome*. It continues chronologically with the monuments of the *Pantheon* and *piazza Navona* (formerly Diocletian's stadium), in the area where the mixture of ancient, Baroque, and Renaissance is most apparent: the *Centro Storico*. You'll then go south of the Centro Storico and see how the real Romans of today live, in the lively neighborhoods of *campo dei Fiori* and—across the Tiber—*Trastevere*. Then we return to ancient history in the *Capitoline* and *Aventine* hills back across the river west of the Roman Forum.

After a breather in Rome's largest park, *Villa Borghese,* you can trace the presence of foreigners in Rome (among them Napoléon's sister Pauline, who lived in the Villa Borghese); then, from the *piazza del Popolo,* take in that high point of the Grand Tour, the *Spanish Steps,* and from there go on to the haunt of the Hollywood stars in the 1950s and 1960s, the *via Veneto*. That area becomes a springboard to the city's Christian past, in the general neighborhood of the *Quirinal* and *Esquiline* hills, beginning with the Palazzo Barberini, built for Pope Urban VIII, and then heading generally south (into the area east of the Roman Forum) and back in time to Michelangelo's conversion of a portion of the Terme di Diocleziano into a church, to early Christian churches, and to two of Rome's major basilicas, Santa Maria Maggiore and San Giovanni in Laterano. Finally, you'll traverse the Tiber once again to the separate state surrounded by the city of Rome—*the Vatican*.

ANCIENT ROME

Traces of old Rome—an arch, a column, a fragment of sculpture, or even the colossal marble foot that gave via di Piè di Marmo its name—are strewn around the modern city. The ancient city itself, however, inhabits its very own zone. Behind the Vittorio Emanuele monument radiate the forums and the Palatine Hill, the Colosseum, the Circus Maximus, and the Terme di Caracalla. It is a world of venerable ruins intersected by avenues of rushing Roman traffic.

Before entering, pick up a copy of the red loose-leaf book titled *Rome: Past and Present,* with plastic overleafs that show the Forum now and then; it is essential to re-creating the whole from the assembly of stray columns and fragments you'll see before you. (Buy the book in a store as opposed to a stand near the monuments, where it will be double the price.)

The Palatine Hill evokes the Rome of Classical fantasy, umbrella pines shading fragments of ancient palaces. It's reached from the Roman Forum, whose main entrance is around to the left of the Vittoriano, as Romans call the modern-day monument, and is the best place to get an overview of the otherwise complicated Forum. When you reach the Forum grounds from the main entrance on via dei Fori Imperiali, you will see the Palatine ahead of you, rising above the ruins, an irregular mass of pine, oleander, and cypress interspersed with yawning arches. These arches are the ruins of the grand palaces that lined the hill (which gave us the very word "palace"): residences of Augustus, Nero, Caracalla, Tiberius, and Domitian. To reach the belvedere of the Palatine, from where you'll have a grand overview of the Forum, walk left through the Forum to its far side and then follow the path up the hill. Turn right and take the steps up to the terrace.

The Roman Forum

Few monuments so clearly represent the history and life of an entire civilization as does the great complex usually called the Roman Forum (Foro Romano). There are many forums, and the Roman is only a small part of the entire archaeological site, but for clarity the Roman Forum is considered to be that section entered from via dei Fori Imperiali through the admission gate.

Built in the valley between the Capitoline and Palatine hills, the Roman Forum reached the peak of its importance under

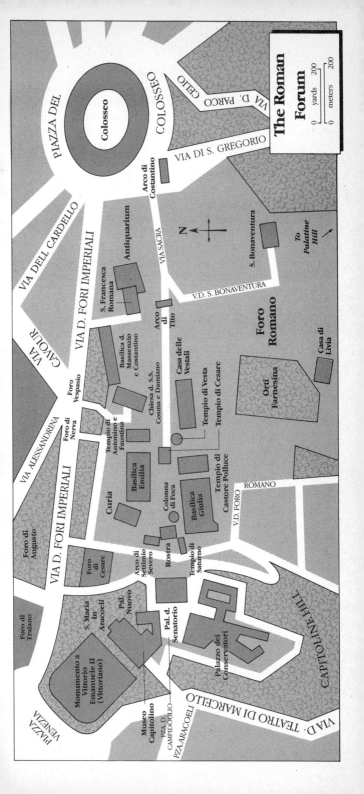

The Roman Forum

```
0       yards      200
0      meters      200
```

PIAZZA DEL COLOSSEO

Colosseo

CELIO

VIA D. PARCO

VIA D. PARCO CELIO

VIA DI S. GREGORIO

Arco di Costantino

VIA DELL CARDELLO

VIA D. FORI IMPERIALI

VIA SACRA

S. Bonaventura

N

To Palatine Hill

V.D. S. BONAVENTURA

VIA CAVOUR

Antiquarium

S. Francesca Romana

Basilica d. Massenzio e Costantino

Arco di Tito

Foro Romano

Casa di Livia

Foro Vespasio

Chiesa d. S.S. Cosma e Damiano

Casa delle Vestali

Tempio di Vesta

Tempio di Cesare

Orti Farnesina

Foro di Nerva

Tempio di Antonino e Faustina

VIA ALESSANDRINA

Curia

Basilica Emilia

Tempio di Castore Polluce

ROMANO

Colonna di Foca

Basilica Giulia

V.D. FORO

VIA D. FORI IMPERIALI

Foro di Augusto

Arco di Settimio Severo

Rostra

Tempio di Saturno

Foro di Cesare

CAPITOLINE HILL

Foro di Traiano

S. Maria in Aracoeli

Pal. Nuovo

Pal. d. Senatorio

Monumento a Vittorio Emanuele II (Vittoriano)

Palazzo dei Conservatori

PIAZZA VENEZIA

Museo Capitolino

PZA D. CAMPIDOGLIO

PZA ARACOELI

VIA D. TEATRO DI MARCELLO

Julius and Augustus Caesar. Both these emperors—and later ones—enlarged the area with their own forums, but it was here at the original Roman Forum that the framework of Western civilization was forged. Much of our own government system derives from this forum, and even the names here are standard in Western thought: "capitol" from the Capitoline Hill next to the Forum; the word "forum" itself; "rostrum" from the Rostra, where Mark Antony gave Caesar's obituary; "money" from the mint at the Tempio di Giunone Moneta on the Capitoline.

The original Forum predates most of the buildings you'll see, which were built during the time of Augustus, the beginning of the Roman Empire. At the right, just past the entry ramp, stand the ruins of the **Basilica Emilia**. It was built in 179 B.C. and was later nearly destroyed by fire and the Vandals. The original basilicas had no religious purpose but were commercial buildings with halls for conducting business. The building style was primarily functional, allowing light and air to circulate inside. The shape was rectangular and monumental, with two aisles and frequently a row of clerestory windows on top—the form adopted by many early Christian churches.

At the Emilia there were shops occupied by money changers—still an important profession for the tourist in Rome. When you walk up closer, in the nave you can see round green stains in the marble pavement, caused by copper coins dropped when the Goths set Rome ablaze in 410.

In front of the Basilica Emilia is the original Forum as devised by Tarquin, the Etruscan king of Rome, in the eighth century B.C. He and other kings brought the tribes that inhabited these marshy hills together to accomplish a communal project—draining the malarial marsh of the Forum area. This done, the stage was set for the first forum—really an early piazza. The **Tempio di Vesta** on the east side was there at that time, as was the original Curia—next to the basilica—which was the meeting place of the senate. The black stone called *lapis niger* is in a sacred enclosure dedicated to Romulus, as legend would have it.

The look of the place at that time was of modest buildings made of tufa with a stucco coat and terra-cotta decorations. Since wars laid claim to much of Rome's vitality for centuries, little was done to beautify the Forum until Augustus, who then boasted that he'd found a city of brick and transformed it into a city of marble.

City life was concentrated in the Forum, and all roads led

there. Political candidates addressed the crowds from the once grand **Rostra**, now just a stone platform behind the Column of Phocas. The Rostra was named for the prows (*rostra*) of ships captured as war booty and lined up here as war trophies. A later trophy would be Cicero's head and hands (43 B.C.), when he got on the bad side of Mark Antony. It was also at this spot that Caesar was cremated and Mark Antony delivered the funeral oration. Elections were held nearby, and victorious generals paraded along the **Via Sacra** (the oldest street in Rome, currently being excavated by an international team of archaeologists) to the Capitoline Hill, where the **Tempio di Giove** (Temple of Jupiter) stood.

Plautus, in his comedy *Curculio,* described the crowds: "In case you want to meet a perjurer, go to the Comitium; for a liar and a braggart, try the temple of Venus Cloacina; for wealthy married spendthrifts, the Basilica. There will be harlots, well-ripened ones . . . while at the fish market are the members of the eating clubs." But Roman society of that time—well before the wild days of Tiberius—was relatively reserved in dress and manners. Women were forbidden to wear jewelry or expensive clothes, partly because of the war efforts. Later, when Carthage was subdued in the Punic wars and Gaul was pacified—both events that filled the treasury—Rome changed, and its first capitalist class was born, for whom wealth was not in land but in money. After that, temples and basilicas sprang up in all the forums, including the adjacent Foro di Cesari and the Foro di Traiano—Trajan's Forum—across the present-day via dei Fori Imperiali (built by Mussolini and covering further riches known at this moment only to the gods).

Beyond the basilica stands the **Curia**, a brick building begun by Sulla in 80 B.C. that replaced the original Curia thought to have been built by King Tullius. Before the days of the Empire senators had considerable power. Judgments were sometimes helped along by augurs, who revealed the workings of fate by reading patterns in flights of birds or in the feeding movements of chickens. The Curia was a consecrated building, with an altar and statue to a pagan god of victory. Christians hundreds of years later objected to the statue, and Saint Ambrose, archbishop of Milan, finally had it removed by appealing to reason: "Where was Jupiter [when the Gauls attacked]?" he asked. "Was he speaking to the goose?"

In A.D. 203 the **Arco di Settimio Severo** (he was in charge of Britannia) was erected in honor of him and his two sons, and on top of the arch was placed a sculpture of all three in a chariot. One of his sons, however, was Caracalla, who murdered his brother, Geta, to ensure that he himself would become emperor—and erased Geta's name from this and other monuments throughout Rome, though the original inscription can still be made out under the obliterated fourth line across the top of the arch. Romans often used columns decoratively rather than structurally, which can be seen in the freestanding examples of the arch's portico.

To the side and slightly behind the Arch of Septimius Severus is the **Tempio di Saturno**, whose eight columns can still be seen. Dedicated to the god Saturn, it was the site of the Saturnalia, celebrated in December of each year, a time of wild public festivities and gift giving, with the quality and amount of the gifts no less carefully observed than they are today.

In front of the Rostra is the **Colonna di Foca**, dedicated to the tyrannical Eastern emperor who gave the Pantheon to Pope Boniface IV in 608. Next to the Temple of Saturn is the **Basilica Giulia**, named for Julius Caesar, who was murdered (not in the Forum but in Pompey's Theater near campo dei Fiori) before its completion. Some of the stones in the pavement were used as ancient gaming boards, traces of which can still be seen.

The most beautiful fragment in the Forum is from the **Tempio di Castore Polluce**: the three elegant columns east of the basilica, often photographed as a symbol of Classical grace. The temple was created during the fifth century B.C. after Roman troops saw the divine twins Castor and Pollux (the Dioscuri) fighting at their side in battle far from Rome. Then the heavenly twins appeared at this site, proclaiming the Roman victory.

The round **Tempio di Vesta** nearby, where the goddess's flame was kept burning by the Vestal virgins, is a favorite site, and was modeled on the circular hut used by the area's earliest known inhabitants. The Vestal virgins, women of noble birth pledged for 30 years to this cult, were charged with never letting the flame die. If it went out, they were severely thrashed; if they lost their virginity, they were buried alive after being driven in a covered hearse through the streets and forced to descend to their own tomb on a ladder. Because they enjoyed great privileges in Rome, it is sometimes assumed that Vestal virginity was a sought-after honor, but Suetonius tells of noble families doing everything to keep their daughters' names from getting on the list when a virgin died.

The house of the Vestal virgins was like a luxurious

convent, a self-contained unit surrounding a central garden court with pools and statues of the virgins. The name Claudia has been erased below the figure of one who converted to Christianity, an eternal reminder of her ignominy.

The **Tempio di Antonino e Faustina** (at the right of the entrance to the Forum area) is named for the emperor and his wife who adopted Marcus Aurelius and ruled after Hadrian in A.D. 138. Impressively set atop a long staircase, Etruscan style, it has nicely carved columns and a fragment of a statue on the porch. Alongside it is the **Church of Santi Cosma e Damiano**, once part of the Vespasian Forum. If the Forum-side entrance is open, you can see a delightful Neapolitan *presepio* (an exuberant, expansive Nativity scene). The church also merits a visit to see its sixth-century mosaics, among the earliest in Rome. Christ as the Lamb Enthroned is on the triumphal arch.

The name of the large **Basilica di Massenzio e Costantino** makes it sound as if the building were a collaborative effort, but it wasn't. It was begun under Maxentius, but after Constantine defeated him at the battle of the Milvian bridge in 312 it was given his name as well. Its original form is easy to imagine, and part of the coffered ceiling can still be seen. In the Museo Capitolino are some disembodied fragments of the 40-foot statue of the emperor Constantine that once stood inside the basilica. Encountering the enormous head and hand is an unforgettable Roman experience.

Three massive cross vaults of the nave rose 114 feet above the floor, their lateral thrust strengthened by concrete piers 14 feet in diameter. A Barberini pope appropriated the bronze tiles for St. Peter's, giving rise to the saying, "What the barbarians didn't take, the Barberini did." One of its gigantic marble columns ended up in front of Santa Maria Maggiore on via Cavour. This sort of papal modularism makes it seem probable that everything is really still here in Rome, if only massive rearranging could be done. But of course the jumble of the centuries is part of Rome's charm.

The **Arco di Tito** at the end of the expanse of the Forum was built in A.D. 81 to celebrate the sack of Jerusalem by the emperor; the friezes show the spoils being transported back to Rome in A.D. 70.

Next to the church (Santa Francesca Romana) between the basilica of Maxentius and Constantine and the Arch of Titus is the **Antiquarium**, a museum that has some interesting objects excavated from the Palatine and models of the huts in sarcophagus form. (A complete model of ancient

Rome is on display at the Museo della Civiltà Romana in the
suburban district of E.U.R.—but it is often closed; Tel: 592-
61-35. E.U.R. is accessible by Metro.)

The Palatine Hill

But now look at the Palatine Hill behind you.

> Come and see
> The cypress, hear the owl, and plod your way
> O'er the steps of broken thrones and temples.
> Ye whose agonies are evils of a day
> A world is at our feet as fragile as our clay.

This atmosphere of antiquity that enchanted Byron when
he wrote *Childe Harold* is readily evoked on the Palatine.
Here you can wander amid the umbrella pines of Rome that
must have inspired Respighi, and for the moment the world
is perfect in classical beauty. The Farnese spread gardens
along the hill, fragrant with roses and orange blossoms in
the spring. Down the steps are the excavations of Livia's
house, with its delicately painted walls, and beyond that the
unearthed huts of Romulus and Remus's time. To the southeast are remains of emperors' villas, including that of Augustus, which looks out over the Circus Maximus, on the other
side of the hill from the Forum.

The Circus Maximus

Although an oblong field, with wild flowers here and there,
is all that's left of the Circo Massimo's great chariot track, it is
enjoyable to walk where four chariots raced together for
seven laps around the two and a half miles. Originally, as
many as 385,000 spectators sat here amid marble columns—
nothing Rome did was less than colossal. Caligula loved the
chariots, and during his reign the number of races doubled
to 24 per day. In the stands, touts and wine-sellers worked
the crowds. The last race was held in A.D. 549.

The Arch of Constantine

On a nice day you'll notice lots of people on the Palatine
buried in books (or in one another's arms) under the trees,
and you may want to follow suit. Otherwise walk back down
the hill past the Arch of Titus and out on the via Sacra to via
San Gregorio and the Arch of Constantine (Arco di
Costantino), the largest and best preserved of the ancient

arches. It was erected to the emperor after his successful encounter with Maxentius. That battle is famous partly because of the vision that Constantine had before it began: He saw a flaming cross formed in the sky and heard the words, "*In hoc signo vinces*" ("In this sign thou shalt conquer").

The arch's unusual collection of reliefs was partly assembled from various other Roman monuments. On the inside of the central archway are reliefs from the frieze of a monument that commemorated Trajan's Dacian victories, but Constantine's head has been substituted for Trajan's. The frontality of the figures, a Byzantine convention, here foreshadows Constantine's transfer of the imperial capital from Rome to Byzantium (rebuilt as Constantinople) in 330, and the end of the glory days.

Beyond the arch looms the great oval mass that is the Colosseum, which may be contemplated alfresco at the **Hostaria Il Gladiatore** on the piazza in front of the Colosseum entrance.

The Colosseum

It was its colossal size that gave the Colosseum its name, but it was its games of bizarre cruelty that made this the most famous building in Rome. The Empire had many coliseums, and some exist today in better condition than Rome's, but this will always be *the* Colosseum. During the years when Christians were literally thrown to the lions, along with other "criminals," Claudius used to arrive at dawn to see the spectacle.

The building was begun in A.D. 72, during the reign of the emperor Vespasian, on the site where Nero had excavated a lake for the gardens of his Golden House (now in ruins across the street and rarely open). Outside stood a colossal 96-foot statue of Nero. Vespasian's spectacles of persecution were so sadistic that even Romans turned from them in disgust.

The niches that now seem to be open arches on the sides of the Colosseum were actually created to house Greek sculpture—including athletic motifs from Greece's unbloody games. The Greek athletic contests were introduced to the Romans but were apparently too tame in an age when combat to the death was the daily diet. Roman architects used niches not only for statuary but to glorify the massiveness of the walls by emphasizing their depth—something Greek architects with their airy colonnades would never have dreamt of.

The Colosseum was built of blocks of travertine excavated

from quarries near Tivoli and brought to Rome along a road created just for that purpose. It was apparently modeled after the Teatro di Marcello (see below), built during Julius Caesar's time. It rises in three levels, each decorated with columns, from the plain Doric at the bottom to Ionic and Corinthian; the fourth level held the cables that supported the huge awnings that could be billowed out across the spectators to protect them from rain or excessive sun. Scents were also sprayed on the crowd to keep the smell of blood away from their delicate nostrils.

At the first row of seats we can still see the names of important boxholders. In the second circle sat the plebians, with women and then slaves at the back. Galleries constructed between the seats and the outer walls provided a place to mill during intermissions. The Roman use of the crossed vault made such galleries possible.

Almost 50,000 could be seated with enviable efficiency. There were 80 entrances (four for the select boxholders), and each had a number that corresponded with the game-goer's ticket. Leaving was also facilitated by the vomitoria that "disgorged" the crowds down numerous ramps. Every detail was ingeniously worked out by the architects, who were sensitive to public comfort even as they watched gladiators and animals die agonizing deaths.

The games, too, were organized carefully. Gladiators were recruited from the ranks of those condemned to death and war prisoners—both groups with little to lose but the possibility of a dazzling future. They were housed nearby in the recently excavated *ludus magnus*. The floor could be flooded to create *naumachiae* (sea battles), and sometimes the gladiators fought in the water. (Not every program was just filled with gladiatorial strife, of course. There were circus acts with panthers pulling chariots and elephants that wrote Latin inscriptions with their trunks.)

During gladiatorial combat, participants sauntered around the arena, nonchalant, with their valets bearing their arms. They wore purple embroidered with gold, and when they came to the emperor's box they saluted by raising their right arm and saying, "*Ave Imperator, morituri te salutant*" ("Hail, Emperor. We who are about to die salute you"). The crowd screamed and cheered at each blow: *Verbera!* (Strike!) and *Ingula!* (Kill!). To ensure that a fallen warrior was dead, he was struck on the head with a mallet. A gladiator unable to continue could lie on his back and raise his left arm in appeal. Then the crowd could wave their handkerchiefs and show their raised thumbs to the emperor, who might take their advice and raise his, granting life. Or they might consider him cowardly and turn thumbs down. The emperor's down-turned thumb could not be contested.

Winners were given gold and the adoration of young girls. Cicero thought it a good way to learn contempt for pain and death, and Pliny the Younger thought the trials fostered courage. (Cicero and Pliny, however, did not have to fight.) What was fostered among the spectators was something basic to the Empire: Rome was about conquering.

Of all the forms created by Roman architects, the amphitheater, a huge bowl structure such as the Colosseum, has, in today's sports stadiums, been the most imitated. Maybe that's because it dovetails so neatly with our own modern sensibilities—both in its utilitarianism as well as in its striving for and achievement of grandiose and overwhelming effects.

The Baths of Caracalla

For more of ancient Rome, take a bus or taxi to the Terme di Caracalla south of the Colosseum. They were luxurious even for imperial Rome, their massive space shining with multicolored marble, the pools filled by jets of water spouting from marble lions' mouths, the nymphaeum of gardens and pools and statues, gyms, theaters, and libraries. Everyone—rich and poor—went to the baths to socialize and gossip. Caracalla began this project in 212, and his successors added to the glamorous surroundings. The ruins today, the evocative site of Rome's summer opera season, provide important insights into the social organization of ancient Rome.

Trajan's Column and
the Imperial Forums

Successive emperors laid out their own forums, and most are found across the via dei Fori Imperiali, Mussolini's idea of a triumphal highway, which split the forums into two parts.

Foro di Cesare (Caesar's Forum) is mostly on the Roman Forum side of the avenue. On the far side, close to the Vittoriano, is the **Colonna Traiana** (Trajan's Column), a depiction of the emperor's battle (triumphant, of course) long classified as one of the wonders of the world. Its spiral frieze rises 100 feet, and it would, if marble could be unrolled, extend some 215 yards. This masterpiece of intricate composition contains 2,500 figures and was once more easily seen by a spiral staircase. Now binoculars would be handy.

Although you can see the column and much of the several forums by walking along the sidewalk, go inside the **Foro di Traiano** (Trajan's Forum; entrance at via Quattro Novembre 94), because then you can see the **Mercato Traiano** as well; besides, there may be an exhibition going on, as there often is. Trajan's Market has the intimate fascination of ordinary places. It was a mall of 250 small shops on three levels where oil and wines, perfumes and shoes could be bought, and much of the original structure is well preserved. Beyond the Foro Traiano is the **Foro di Augusto** and then the **Foro di Nerva**—where two fine Corinthian capitals have been restored above a relief of Minerva; the friezes tell the story of Minerva's jealousy of Arachne when she heard the peasant girl could spin more beautiful garments. She slit the web Arachne had created, and Arachne hanged herself in shame. Repentant Minerva changed her into a spider, restoring her skill in spinning.

Returning to the Mercato Traiano to leave, you'll see the **Torre delle Milizie** rising above it, part of what was the fortress of Gregory IX (pope from 1227 to 1241). The hilly streets that radiate from here and around nearby piazza del Grillo (off via di Sant'Eufemia) are so Medieval in aspect they could be part of an Umbrian town, especially on Sunday when traffic is slow. The glimpses they afford of the forums through windows and arches and from parapets dramatize the ancient by contrasting the eras. From piazza del Grillo you can enter the **Casa dei Cavalieri di Rodi**, ancient seat of the crusading Order of St. John of Jerusalem. Go inside if it is open for the excellent view of ancient Rome from the loggia.

THE CENTRO STORICO

The Centro Storico, Rome's historic center, is the name traditionally given to the part of the city that occupies the bend of the Tiber across from the Vatican, where the Pantheon, piazza Navona, and a world of Renaissance palaces and piazzas, Baroque drama, and spacious courtyards unfold—sometimes gradually but often abruptly, seducing the senses.

Begin at the Palazzo Venezia, on the right corner of the via del Corso facing the Vittoriano, where the traffic is so frenetic that only nuns and mothers with small children (the only pedestrians for whom Roman drivers apply the brakes) dare cross. A traffic light eases some of the trauma, and once across you can weave a splendid path for yourself through streets that hold surprises even for those who tread their cobblestones daily. Most palaces along the way were created for noble families that numbered cardinals and one or even more popes among their members.

Peek into courtyards and look up at building decorations and tiny shrines. The traffic in this area is dreadful, and you might consider walking through it on a Sunday. Shops will be closed then, but almost everything else on this walk will be open, including the churches, though you will have to stop just before or just after mass to find them open to nonworshipers. If you can rent a bicycle to sail the virtually car-free streets, so much the better. Another good time is Saturday morning, when the **Galleria Colonna** (Palazzo Colonna, in piazza Santi Apostoli), with its outstanding collection—noted for its 17th-century landscapes—is open to the public.

Palazzo Venezia's crenellated, fortresslike mass was once the home of the Venetian Pope Paul II, but now it's better known for its balcony, at the center of the façade, from which Il Duce told Rome the Empire would rise again. Inside you sometimes can see his war room (Mappamondo). The museum in the palazzo has a good Medieval collection and hosts frequent shows and exhibitions. In 1564 the pope gave the palazzo to Rome as the Venetian Embassy, but now it belongs to the Italian Republic.

Tucked almost out of sight behind the palace is one of Rome's Byzantine jewels, the **Basilica of San Marco**. On its porch the popes once blessed the crowds as they do now from St. Peter's, but this small church usually escapes notice in a city where everything is grandiose.

The interior glows with mosaics and a coffered ceiling of blue and gold, with the heraldic crest and the crossed keys that always signify a pope. In the apse is a ninth-century mosaic of Pope Gregory IV offering Christ this church.

Across via del Plebiscito is the **Palazzo Doria Pamphili**, still partly inhabited by the noble Doria family, whose anti-Fascist resistance during World War II is remembered by Italians. The Genoese admiral Andrea Doria is a prominent ancestor. Cross via del Plebiscito and follow the little street behind the palace around to its inner courtyard and the museum, which is well worth seeing not only for the paintings but also for the apartment tour, a rare opportunity to see the interior of a Roman palace. (You must wait for a

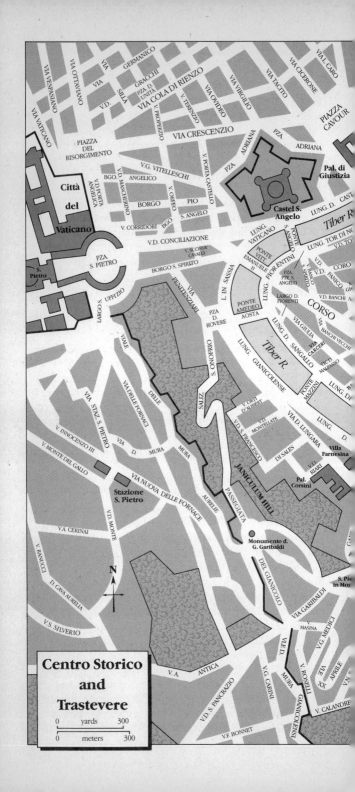

Centro Storico
and
Trastevere

| 0 | yards | 300 |
| 0 | meters | 300 |

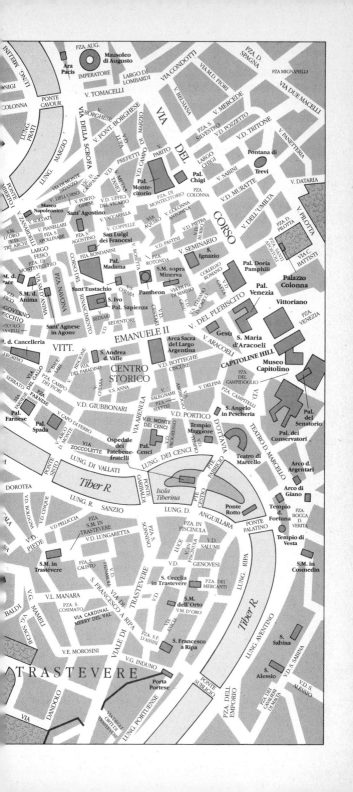

small group to be assembled, but you can see the paintings in the meantime.) The paintings have numbers only, so you may want to buy a catalog.

Among the highlights of the collection are *Salome* by Titian, and Caravaggio's *Penitent Magdalen* and *Rest on the Flight to Egypt* (the angel is superb but the gallery lighting isn't—it takes angling to see the painting without glare). Farther along is Parmigianino's *Adoration of the Shepherds;* then the bizarre *Olimpia Maidalchini,* whose less-than-sweet face, in a bust by Algardi, is found at the corner. The brother-in-law she bedeviled is around the corner: Innocent X, as seen in one of the greatest portraits ever painted, by Velásquez, and also in a portrait by one who knew him better, Gianlorenzo Bernini. We owe much of the neighborhood to Innocent's forcefulness—that is, until Olimpia cheated him out of all worldly goods, taking his last coin when he was on his deathbed, according to some reports. Notice also, in Room IV, the lunettes by the Carracci family and the *Flight into Egypt* by Annibale Carracci.

When you leave, follow the street in front, via di Piè di Marmo, past the large marble foot planted nonchalantly at the side of the street. A clothing designer known to *il tutto Roma* has a small shop in the piazza in back of the famous foot. **Teresa Trushnach** creates dresses, slacks, and blouses in sensuously beautiful fabrics and colors. Some ready-made clothes are also on display at her shop (via Santo Stefano 27, Tel: 67-97-450. Take your Italian dictionary.

If fabric shopping is on your itinerary, turn left at via del Gesù to **Bises** at number 93, the 17th-century palace that has sold fine yard goods to Roman matrons for many years. The frescoed ceilings serve as a remembrance of times past.

At the Gesù intersection, you'll see **piazza della Minerva** rearing its lovely obelisk, placed atop Bernini's small ele-phant. The elephant seems quite undisturbed by the size of the obelisk on his back; his trunk curls out cheerfully, like a horizontal bazaar snake. The obelisk was found near here and presumably came from the Temple of Isis that stood close by this spot. In fact, the marble foot may be the only remaining part of the figure of Isis.

The **Church of Santa Maria sopra Minerva** has a plain façade that hides its considerable riches. It's one of the few ancient Gothic churches in Rome, and it stands on the site of a temple to Minerva (as the name indicates), Isis, and Serapis—Egyptian religions having been brought to Rome when the Empire spread to Egypt. The first Christian church on the site was built during the eighth century, and much of the existing one dates from the 13th century—the work of Dominican brothers Fra Sisto and Fra Ristoro. As you advance along the impressive but dark aisle on the right, the first large chapel is the Aldobrandini crypt, where the parents of Clement VIII were laid to rest with a memorial by Giacomo Della Porta and Girolamo Rainaldi. At the transept is the delightful Carafa chapel, merrily frescoed with the life of Saint Thomas Aquinas by Filippino Lippi between 1488 and 1492.

To the right of the high altar is the Capranica chapel, with a *Virgin and Child* attributed to Fra Angelico. Beneath the altar is the crypt of Saint Catherine of Siena, the main patron saint of Italy and a Doctor of the Church. She lived near here and was instrumental in persuading the popes to return from their "Babylonian captivity" in Avignon. At the left is the tomb of the mystical Fra Angelico. Beyond is *Christ with the Cross* (1514–1521) by Michelangelo, apparently finished by another when the master found a flaw in the marble. Cardinal Bembo is buried at the altar (plaque in floor), as are Popes Leo X and Clement VII, in tombs sculpted by Sangallo the Younger. Works of art are clearly not lacking in this church; an inexpensive booklet is for sale here, detailing each of them, or take a look at the diagram near the entrance. Behind the altar you can see a small museum and rooms once occupied by Saint Catherine.

A fine dining option is found in nearby piazza Rondanini, where **Le Volte** has tables on the piazza; unfortunately, it's often used as a car park by government officials and their friends from the nearby ministries. (A special permit is needed to park in the Centro Storico.) At night, however, the bureaucrats vanish and youth emerges, to linger, stylishly dressed, in the piazza sipping a drink that **Le Cornacchie** provided, or to wander down, drink in hand, to **Hemingway**, in piazza delle Coppelle.

The Pantheon

As you walk toward the right, the mass of the Pantheon seems to sit in wait for you, as it has for millions of admirers over the centuries. Its massiveness is what seizes you first, followed by the grace of its columns and the piazza (piazza della Rotonda) that opens in front. The obelisk-topped fountain of wonderfully absurd faces spraying water, the young people sitting at the base, the open windows—always someone leaning out—make this one of the loveliest piazzas in Rome for people-watching while paying respects to the

Pantheon, the best preserved of all Rome's ancient buildings. Have a drink or coffee at one of the cafés and savor the day.

Across the top of the Pantheon's façade you'll see the name Agrippa in the inscription, signifying the son-in-law of Augustus who built the original Pantheon (27 B.C.), which later burned down. The existing structure is the work of the always-building Hadrian, and was begun in 118. In 609 it was consecrated as a Christian church, having originally been a temple to all the gods.

The outside gives little hint of what's to come—there is nothing like it in the world. The circular opening, way on top—with clouds passing some days, or even raindrops or an occasional snowflake—comes as a shock. The immensity of the round space so high above and the coffered ceiling around it are awe-inspiring. The tomb of Raphael, especially, and of the Italian kings Vittorio Emanuele II and Umberto I are impressive, of course, but it is the space that hushes chattering visitors when they come through the door. In fact, it was the first building ever conceived as an interior space, aided by the use of concrete and cross vaults that allowed Roman architecture to soar.

Walk around the Pantheon to the left as you leave, until you see the stag's head and antlers of the **Church of Sant'Eustachio**, the saint being the nobleman who converted to Christianity when hunting. His bow and arrow were aimed at a stag when suddenly Christ's face appeared in the antlers, according to the legend. Have coffee or cappuccino at the **Caffè Sant'Eustachio**, long considered by many the best in Rome, although the other coffee bar on the piazza allows you to move your table in sight of the swirling tower of Sant'Ivo, Borromini's masterpiece (see below).

Continue to the right into via della Scrofa for two streets to the **Church of San Luigi dei Francesi** (Saint Louis). You'll want to run inside to see the Caravaggio paintings, but stop outside for a moment to see a bit of drollery. At the bottom right of the façade is a salamander that bears the head of François I of France. The salamander was his insignia, but in his version did not bear his face.

Inside, the Caravaggio canvases are in the last chapel on the left. *The Vocation of Saint Matthew* glows with unreal light that hits each figure in a different way, some to follow Christ, some to remain in shadow. *Saint Matthew's Martyrdom* is one of the most dramatic of his works in terms of lighting effects. (The plumed figure at the top left is thought to be the artist himself.) *Saint Matthew and the Angel* was painted in 1602 and shows Matthew writing what the angel dictated.

Turn left from the church of San Luigi for two blocks, then left again to the **Church of Sant'Agostino** for Caravaggio's *Madonna di Loreto*. This painting was not at all what was expected, because he used the poor and humble as her supplicants instead of the usual rich patrons. The model for the Madonna was a local woman who had rejected a lawyer who sought her hand. The lawyer called Caravaggio a "cursed ex-communicant" for painting her; the artist, in turn, wounded him with a sword and had to escape to Genoa until things cooled down. Raphael painted the *Prophet Isaiah* in fresco here after he had seen the Sistine ceiling; the high altar is the work of Bernini.

From San Luigi it's a short walk south on via della Scrofa to Sant'Ivo. Turn right into corso del Rinascimento and walk past the well-guarded Palazzo Madama, named for Madama Margaret of Austria, illegitimate daughter of Charles V, who married a Medici and then a Farnese. The palace is now the Palazzo del Senato, named for the government body whose traditions go back to the Curia of the Forum.

While on the corso del Rinascimento stop at number 72, **Ai Monasteri**, where honey from sweetpea-frequenting bees and anchorite elixirs for curing colds made by Carmelites, Benedictines, and Trappists throughout Italy are sold.

Just beyond, at number 101, is the Palazzo della Sapienza, whose Renaissance façade is the work of Giacomo Della Porta. Inside now are the Vatican archives, but the reason to enter is to see Borromini's newly restored tower and **Church of Sant'Ivo** and the courtyard there that Borromini also designed. The Barberini bees that have been worked into the design indicate that a Barberini pope, Urban VIII, was the instigator. The courtyard is elegantly planned to lead the viewer to the campanile's upward movement. The church, constructed from 1642 to 1660, is an intricate play of convex and concave shapes inside, with a hint of the Rococo. Borromini's search for geometric perfection as a spiritual state comes close to fulfillment here.

Piazza Navona

Just across the street, behind a row of palaces, is piazza Navona. The façades that grace the piazza make the owners of these buildings among Rome's most envied residents. The piazza is beautiful in all lights and moods: in early morning when the street-sweepers swoosh through, and by the golden light of sunset when shadows make casual encounters seem dramatic. On Sundays it is still the village piazza, with the entire family here to watch the youngest balance his first two-wheeler while papa hovers above him. Artists set out their paintings, Africans sell belts, pigeons swoop, and rendezvous are agreed on with the eyes.

Festivity has always characterized piazza Navona. In ancient Rome it often took the form of *naumachiae,* when the piazza was flooded to create a sea for real ships to play war in—but it was not play, and deaths were part of the "excitement." During that era the piazza was the stadium of Domitian, which accounts for its elongated shape. Athletic contests (*agone*) were frequent, and gave the name to the church facing the center, Sant'Agnese in Agone.

Pope Innocent X, wanting a symbol of his family to be indelibly imprinted on Rome, as well as to beautify the city, called in Bernini to create a monument, stipulating that an obelisk be fetched from the Circus Maximus to be part of the design. Bernini's fountain shows four rivers and their continents, each represented by a person. The head of the figure representing the Nile was covered to indicate that the source was then unknown, but Romans said it was because Bernini's statue couldn't bear to look at his rival Borromini's dreadful façade on the church of Sant'Agnese. The Danube's outstretched arm, meant to connect the fountain visually with the façade, was said to be raised to ward off the church's imminent collapse. The Plate and the Ganges complete the quartet. Bernini himself, it's thought, finished the horse, rock, lion, and palm while working here in situ. His poetic use of realistic objects in an exuberant style has made the Fontana dei Fiumi (Fountain of the Rivers) symbolic of Rome itself.

The other two fountains in the piazza were finished by Bernini and his studio: Fontana del Moro con Tritone (the Moor) and Fontana del Nettuno (Neptune); the latter was largely rebuilt during the 19th century.

Inside the **Church of Sant'Agnese** is a bas-relief of Saint Agnes by Algardi, showing the miracle in which she was stripped naked in preparation for martyrdom, only to be covered immediately by her long, luxuriant hair, which suddenly grew to conceal her body from her persecutors.

Piazza Navona is the place to eat a delicious chocolate ice cream called *tartufo* at **Tre Scalini**—so what if it's crowded with tourists; the *tartufo* and Bernini together are not to be scorned. **Mastrostefano**, the terrace restaurant on the piazza, is another good place to sit and observe the piazza life, and the food can be surprisingly good for such a heavily visited location. Prints are found at **Nardecchia**, a 30-year-old institution at number 25. The finest of cameos and corals are to be found past Tre Scalini at **Giovanni Api**.

The streets off the western side of the piazza are popular with the young and trend-conscious. Wine bars and shops have sprung up, enlivening the area at night. Walk down to the north end of piazza Navona (on your right when facing Sant'Agnese), turn left to the church of Santa Maria dell'Anima, designed by Giuliano da Sangallo, past the charming vine-covered Hotel Raphael—protected by *carabinieri* because of its government guests—to the lovely **Church of Santa Maria della Pace**. Be there just after 10:30 mass on Sunday morning to see the Raphael frescoes of the sibyls. If it's closed, the façade and the polygonal piazza are delightful anyway. But if the church is open, you also can see its cloisters, Bramante's earliest Roman creation.

So popular it's often overflowing, the **Pace Bar** on nearby via Santa Maria dell'Anima is an old-fashioned, pleasant place to have an expensive drink.

One block north of Santa Maria della Pace is the merry **via dei Coronari**, an antiques-sellers' street that holds regular antiques fairs, when it is carpeted as if for royalty and festooned with flowers, banners, and candles. Paralleling the street to the north is the Medieval via dei Tre Archi, and all around for strolling are delightful streets near the bank of the Tiber.

Along the river at piazza di Ponte Umberto I is the **Museo Napoleonico**, with Bonaparte family portraits and the chaise on which Pauline reclined for her famous statue (now in the Museo Borghese; see below).

From here you can follow the via dell'Orso, the street of the bear, as it makes its romantic meanderings. The **Hostaria dell'Orso** is as atmospheric a place as Rome has to offer—a Medieval hostelry where you can stop for a drink at the beautiful bar on the ground floor or dine upstairs (though the food does not match the decor in quality). At night the lights from the river make the window views softly romantic.

For lunch stop at **L'Orso '80**, number 333, where freshly baked bread, an exceptional antipasto table, and grilled meats attract a stylish clientele. If unusual theater and movie posters and books for the devotee of the performing arts interest you, go to **Il Leuto** at via di Monte Brianzo 86; they have a foreign mail-order business as well.

Continuing back to the via del Corso, you may want to get

an ice cream at Rome's venerable *gelato* institution, **Giolitti**. If so, make a detour when you reach via degli Uffici del Vicario. The *semi-freddo* (partly frozen) varieties and fresh fruit flavors are sought after; for pastry-lovers, the *bigne a zabaglione* (a cream puff bursting with Marsala-laced cream) is one of their rich favorites. Farther along the same street, the **Gelateria delle Palme** is a relative upstart favored by younger *gelato* aficionados.

Via degli Uffici del Vicario leads to piazza di Montecitorio, where, in the **Palazzo Montecitorio**, the lower house of parliament meets—thus the heavy security and milling journalists when congress is in session. The palace itself was completed by Fontana in 1634, as requested by the ubiquitous Pope Innocent X Pamphili. The back of the palace has one of the few Art Nouveau touches in Rome—the stairway and portal designed by Basile, the Sicilian master of Liberty style, as Art Nouveau is called in Italy.

The obelisk at the center of the piazza was brought to Rome by Augustus, according to Pliny in his *Natural History;* it is one of the 13 that remain out of the nearly 50 that once graced the cityscape.

At the far end of the piazza a short street leads to **piazza Colonna**, dominated by the **Palazzo Chigi**, where the cabinet offices of the government are located. The Chigi Palace was designed by Giacomo Della Porta in 1562 for the Aldobrandini family, but the famous Chigi family of banking interests bought it. During the 18th and 19th centuries this piazza was sufficiently off the beaten track for coffee to be roasted here in the open air; the scent was then considered disagreeable. The column for which the piazza is named commemorates the campaigns of Marcus Aurelius and his victory over the Germanic tribes. The emperor's statue at the top was replaced by one of Saint Paul in 1588.

For a grand finale to your walk, cross the via del Corso to the right of the arcaded Galleria and continue straight ahead until the rush of water tumbling over boulders tells you that the **Fontana di Trevi** is near. This Baroque version of a nymphaeum, bursting with gods and steeds, was just another fountain until Hollywood, with *Three Coins in the Fountain,* and Fellini, who splashed Anita Ekberg in it in *La Dolce Vita,* made it part of the standard itinerary. Just restored to an almost too-pristine whiteness, it's most magical at night when fewer tourist cameras are clicking. Tradition dictates that you toss a coin into it from over your shoulder to ensure a return to Rome.

THE REAL ROMANS: CAMPO DEI FIORI TO TRASTEVERE

The Counter-Reformation, when the Roman Catholic church was attempting to draw back the parishioners who had strayed northward, was a time when popes commissioned artists, notably Bernini and Borromini, to seduce the viewer into the church's mysterious excitement. Façades waved convex and concave, statues gestured, putti cavorted over ceilings and dangled chubby legs from balustrade perches. What realism didn't accomplish, trompe l'oeil did.

No art form better expressed Italy's own vitality, and especially the famed exuberance of the people from Rome southward. To see Baroque at its most opulent, start at the church of Sant'Ignazio (Saint Ignatius, founder of the Jesuit movement) and continue to the Gesù, where he is buried. The contrast between today's Jesuits—sometimes condemned by the Vatican for their leftist policies—and the priests who accumulated the Gesù's gold and precious stones is as dramatic as the art itself.

The **Church of Sant'Ignazio** is near the Palazzo Doria, on a piazza best appreciated on a car-free Sunday. Sit on the church steps and you will discover yourself on a stage, the center of attention for the palaces that curve around the piazza, palaces whose waving convex and concave lines caused critics to call them "the bureaux"; the name spilled over into the tiny adjoining street, via del Burrò.

The church's visual impact starts with its façade, designed by the Jesuit Father Orazio Grassi, Algardi, and others, and financed by Cardinal Ludovisi, whose collection of antiquities is exhibited at the Museo Nazionale. Inside, a blaze of marble, stucco, and rich altar decorations set the tone. Algardi created several large statues for this church, but the pièce de résistance is the nave's vault, entirely frescoed by the Jesuit Andrea Pozzo, and showing Saint Ignatius's ascent into Paradise. Stand at the marble disc on the floor for the trompe l'oeil effect. (Baroque churches relied on viewer participation.)

The simple trattoria **Cave di Sant'Ignazio**, with an outdoor terrace on the piazza, is still a favorite with Romans at night, when the setting is even more scenic.

Several blocks south of the church is the via del Plebiscito. Turn right into it and soon you will see the **Church of the Gesù**, whose opulence makes Sant'Ignazio seem stark. The façade was designed by della Porta in collaboration with the Jesuit Father Valeriani. The church is the prototype for Counter-Reformation churches, with room for the congregation to hear the priest's address comfortably, and wide aisles for seating. The church design was by Vignola, for Cardinal Alessandro Farnese, and the idea was to lead the spectator into contact with the mystical by artistic means.

Father Pozzo again created a great ceiling in the chapel. The master of the quadrature painters, who treated entire ceilings as canvases, he organized the groups of heavenly participants by dark and light areas. Bernini's influence is seen here in the rays of light at the center, to which your eyes gravitate. There also appears the monogram IHS, signifying the Name of Jesus, a subject for contemplation in Ignatian meditation. But not everyone saw it as mystical: The grand duke of Tuscany said it meant *"Iesuiti Habent Satis"*—"the Jesuits have enough."

Another story attached to the church is that of the devil and the wind. The two were out walking in Rome when they came upon this church. "Wait for me," said the devil, entering the Gesù. Since he never came out, the wind is still waiting, which explains why that corner is one of the windiest in Rome.

Continue along corso Vittorio Emanuele II to the **Area Sacra del Largo Argentina**, where some of Rome's oldest buildings, temples from the period of the Republic (fourth century B.C.), can be seen—in the traditional home of Rome's largest stray cat colony, whose benefactors are numerous. Continuing on the same street, on the left is where *Tosca* begins: the **Church of Sant'Andrea della Valle**, designed by Carlo Maderno but publicized by Giacomo Puccini and, later, Franco Zeffirelli. Domenichino's contribution was considerable: the frescoes of the *Life of Saint Andrew*. The dome is the second highest and largest (after St. Peter's) in the city. A recently canonized saint of the family of Tommaso di Lampedusa (author of *The Leopard*) is buried here to the right of the high altar. Along corso Vittorio Emanuele II and off to the left on via Baullari (the trunkmakers' street) are the busy streets that surround piazza Campo dei Fiori.

The Campo dei Fiori Area

On sunny mornings there is no merrier market scene—a Medieval Covent Garden of cheeses and meats, fruits and flowers, greens and vegetables like none you've ever seen before, and all fresh from the fields, with the bakery **Il Forno** to provide fragrant bread and the **Enoteca campo dei Fiori** for wine. A fixture is the knife sharpener who sharpens as he pedals a stationary unicycle, flicking the knife or scissors with calm assurance. On gray or stormy days the campo is more fascinating and moody. Then the atmosphere of the Middle Ages at their most intense permeates the area around the statue of Giordano Bruno, who was burned as a heretic in 1600. **Da Francesco** on the piazza is a good trattoria for lunch; the crowded **Carbonara** rests on its shaky old laurels. The **Grotte del Teatro di Pompeo** on via Biscione is a favorite in the evening for its stylishly light dishes and the pizza from its wood-fired oven.

To the north of the campo is the lovely **Palazzo della Cancelleria**, whose court with a double loggia is a Renaissance masterpiece and is thought to be partly the work of Bramante. (A glimpse through the gate may be all you'll get, though its hallowed halls ring with chamber music during the Christmas season.) To the southwest of the campo, the next square is the **piazza Farnese**, reached from the via del Gallo. There stands one of the most influential of Renaissance palaces—it was reproduced all over Europe. The **Palazzo Farnese** was begun by Sangallo the Younger for Cardinal Alessandro Farnese, who would become Pope Paul III. Exactly what part Michelangelo played is disputed, but it appears that the central balcony, the cornice, and the third floor were his contribution. The palace is today the French Embassy; for admission, which may or may not be granted, apply to the French cultural attaché. The courtyard is sometimes open on Sunday mornings. While on the piazza, have a look at the tiles in the **Galleria Farnese** boutique. If you are antiques hunting, stroll along the via Giulia, which runs parallel to the Tiber.

Continue along via di Monserrato southeast to the **Palazzo Spada**, in piazza Capo di Ferro. The piazza was designed by Francesco Borromini, who built a wall to screen the palace's resident, Cardinal Spada, from prying eyes. Windows later broke the wall, however, and the fountain was replaced by a more modest one.

The palazzo's busy façade blends whimsy and artistry, and depicts heroes of ancient Rome fêted with garlands of stucco.

The palace was built about 1550, but Borromini wasn't called in until 1632. Because the Italian Council of State is the present occupant, access is not easily obtained, but the gallery and the garden are open. When you enter the courtyard—a fantasy of tritons, centaurs, and delicate garlands—stop at the custodian's corner office and ask him to show you the gardens (*giardini*) and the palace (*palazzo*). He often waits to assemble a small group—so you will know whether to stay there or head into the gallery, which has regular hours.

The garden has a charming secret—a colonnade that leads to a life-size figure . . . but no, it's an illusion created by diminishing columns; the figure is only about a foot tall in reality. We owe this fancy to the Augustinian priest Giovanni Maria da Bitonto (1653), not, as was thought until recently, to Borromini.

If you can enter the palace, you'll see the statue of Pompey under which Caesar was murdered (or a reasonable facsimile thereof). It's the "dread statue" to which Byron addressed this question: "Have ye been victors of countless kings, or puppets of a scene?" Borromini's stairway, the Corridor of Bas-Reliefs, and the state rooms are appropriately impressive.

The gallery is interesting partly because it is housed in its original setting, four rooms of the cardinal's palace. Of the artworks note especially Titian's *Musician,* the *Visitation* by Andrea del Sarto, and a portrait of Cardinal Spada by Guido Reni.

The Ghetto and Isola Tiberina

From piazza Mattei, south of the Area Sacra, via Sant' Ambrogio leads south to **via del Portico d'Ottavia**, named after the monument at the end of the block to the left. Augustus rebuilt the second-century B.C. portico of Cecilius Metellus, which surrounded the temples to Jupiter and Juno, and created two libraries—one Greek and one Latin—dedicating the portico to his sister, Octavia. It became a fish market (*pescheria*) during the Middle Ages, and now houses the fishmongers' church, Sant'Angelo in Pescheria, named in the fishmongers' honor.

Today, via del Portico d'Ottavia is the main street of what was Rome's Jewish **Ghetto**, one of the least touristed and most evocative sections of Rome. Formerly residents of Trastevere, the Jews of Rome moved to the Isola Tiberina following the pillage of Rome in 1084. Then, crossing over the ponte Fabricio (which was once known as the pons

Iudeorum, or the Bridge of the Jews), they moved into the area next to the Portico d'Ottavia, ironically the very site where Vespasian and Titus had convened the senate the day Rome conquered Jerusalem. Paul IV officially confined the Jews to the Ghetto in 1555, and although much of it was razed in 1885 to destroy what had become a crowded and insalubrious district over the centuries, many of Rome's Jews chose to remain here. People still come to the area for its characteristic cuisine, which may be sampled at **Da Luciano** on the via del Portico d'Ottavia, or more expensively at **Piperno** on via del Monte dei Cenci. There is also an excellent pastry shop, **Il Forno del Ghetto**, at number 119. Try the cheesecake.

Another unfortunate site nearby is the **Palazzo Cenci**, in piazza Cenci. Never a part of the Ghetto, the palazzo was the home of the bloody Cenci family. In a 16th-century scandal, the brutal and perverted Francesco Cenci was murdered by a killer hired by his wife and three of his 12 children. Although public opinion held that this was legitimate self-defense, his wife and daughter Beatrice were beheaded near the ponte Sant'Angelo, his son Giacomo was drawn and quartered, the other son was sentenced to life imprisonment, and the pope confiscated all the family property. The Cenci exploits inspired many literati, including Shelley and Antonin Artaud, and every year on the anniversary of their deaths a mass is celebrated for the repose of Beatrice's soul in the church of San Tommaso, next to the palazzo.

One block away is lungotevere dei Cenci, where, to your left, is the **Tempio Maggiore**, Rome's synagogue. Built in 1904, it also houses a museum of Roman Jewish memorabilia. Across from it is the boat-shaped island called the **Isola Tiberina**, reached by ponte Fabricio, Rome's oldest standing bridge, which dates from 62 B.C. (Farther downstream may be seen the remains of the older ponte Rotto, or Broken Bridge, which collapsed in 1598, the year Francesco Cenci was murdered.) The Isola Tiberina was sacred to Aesculapius, the god of medicine, and had hospitals on it long before the present-day Ospedale dei Fatebenefratelli (literally, the do-good brothers). The island's history will soon be commemorated in a museum to be opened by the American journalist Milton Gendel, a longtime resident. Until then it is pleasant enough to join the hordes of well-wishers from the hospital for a stroll along its embankment, where many before you have continued the longstanding Roman tradition of graffiti with declarations of love. From Isola Tiberina the ponte Cestio leads south into Trastevere.

Trastevere

After walking through the ever-rushing crowds in the center of the city, crossing the Tiber to Trastevere (tras-TAY-var-ay) can be like entering a country town (first the speedway along the Tiber must be bested; push buttons for lights are found about every 50 feet). Go to Trastevere late in the afternoon, when the light on the buildings glows rose and gold, and at night (money belt–only zone). You can stroll through lanes where green tufts of grass sprout from little cracks in thick-walled buildings; tiny shrines are lit to the Madonna; the smell of fresh bread entices; artisans repair statues, sand tables, solder tin pots; children play in long smocks and dark stockings; fountain steps harbor meetings; and on enviable roof gardens the long arm of gentrification is seen. The people of Trastevere consider themselves the true Romans and have made little accommodation to the "foreigners" who have adopted their quarter, although they themselves are warm and friendly by nature.

Start in the southern part of Trastevere at the **Church of Santa Cecilia in Trastevere**, whose large, tranquil courtyard is frequented by local mothers watching their *bambini* taking first steps. Life was far from tranquil for Santa Cecilia, however, who lived in a patrician villa on the site (excavations have been made of her rooms below ground; entrance from inside the church). Her husband, Saint Valerian, was beheaded because, as a Christian, he refused to worship the Roman gods. Cecilia was locked in the steam room of her house, which was then heated by a roaring fire; instead of dying, she was found singing in a heaven-sent shower. Three days of heat did not kill her, and even the blows of an ax failed. By the time she died, hundreds had converted, inspired by her courage. Thus armed with the legends, enter the church to see her statue by Stefano Maderno at the high altar, a figure lying down with her head turned away, as she was when her sarcophagus in the catacombs was opened. On November 22 concerts are held in her honor, and the Academy of Santa Cecilia in Rome, among the most prestigious of music academies, was named for her. During the late afternoon, you may hear the nuns singing mass from behind the grate.

In the nearby **piazza in Piscinula** (named for an ancient Roman bath) stands the 12th-century Palazzo Mattei (now private), once the home of the family that reigned over this neighborhood in Medieval days by force of intrigue and murder. Though both acts were common in the Middle Ages, apparently the Mattei went too far and were thrown out of Trastevere. They landed on their feet, however, amassing a great fortune and a cluster of palazzi at piazza Mattei across the river near the Fontana delle Tartarughe.

The spiritual side of the Middle Ages is also well represented at the piazza, with the church at the opposite side built above the house where Saint Benedict spent his childhood, and which he left to create one of the most widespread monastic organizations in the world. The tiny campanile (the smallest in Rome, with the oldest bell) can be seen to best advantage along via in Piscinula, leading from the piazza. Ceramics from all over Italy are beautifully displayed at the **Centro d'Arte** on via della Pelliccia, several blocks to the west and just north of piazza Santa Maria in Trastevere, a good place for gift buying.

Stop at nearby via dei Genovesi 12 and ring for the *custode* to see the *chiostro,* one of the loveliest small cloisters in the city. Follow via Anicia south from via dei Genovesi, past the church of Santa Maria dell'Orto, with the odd little obelisks on its façade, to piazza San Francesco d'Assisi. Here the **Church of San Francesco a Ripa** shelters Bernini's statue of *Blessed Ludovica Albertoni,* strikingly similar to his more famous Saint Teresa. Bernini was in his seventies when he made this statue but was still in command of his formidable powers. The chapel is a domed space, strangely illuminated over the body of the saint lying in her final agony. Howard Hibbard, in his book *Bernini,* describes it in terms that recall a host of Baroque scenes in Rome: "The waves of draperies in front echo her position, their heaving billows reflect her agony, their colors accentuate her pallor . . . the chiaroscuro of this drapery and the diagonal of Ludovica's arms, broken by [the position of] her hands, create an almost symphonic treatment of physical suffering and death . . . the frieze of bursting pomegranates below the painting signifies the immortality to which her soul is passing."

A living Baroque scene takes place daily (except Sundays) at the produce market in **piazza San Cosimato**, across the viale di Trastevere (a major bus artery) from the church of San Francesco. If the market doesn't have something to entice you, the streets that surround it are likely to. On **via di San Francesco a Ripa**, which runs from piazza Santa Maria to San Francesco, you'll find freshly made mozzarella and ricotta, banks of new cheeses to try, fresh bread, pizza squares, and pastries—the *bignè* (cream puffs) *con zabaglione* are rich with Marsala. On Sunday mornings the bakeries are open and filled with people seeking the traditional *cornetti,* *sfogliatelle* (a Neapolitan transplant), and their more sugary associates.

Come early (8:00 or 9:00 A.M.) on Sunday morning for the Porta Portese flea market, which extends for blocks and is filled with sometimes interesting antiques, old books and prints, stacks of jeans and shoes, fresh coconut and raw fava beans (*fagioli*) to munch on, and a liberal assortment of pickpockets. Roman authorities would close the market, but the *populus Romanus* yells a resounding no. Stop first at the bakeries on via di Francesco a Ripa (above) for fresh *cornetti* and coffee to fortify you. After 11:00 A.M. only the crowd-loving need apply—it's the thing to do on Sundays for many Romans. The entrance where the "antiques" dealers ply their trade, off via degli Orti di Trastevere, is the easiest. The section around Porta Portese, on the Tiber, is often mobbed by 11:00. (Remember that state museums are open Sunday mornings, however.)

From here to the famous **piazza Santa Maria in Trastevere** is only a short walk. Its dominant feature, the **Church of Santa Maria**, is enchanting, especially at night, when the façade mosaics glisten. By day it's a mini–piazza Navona, with crowds of local residents and visitors, soccer games, and entangled lovers on the fountain steps.

The church's portico, embedded with ancient relics, was built by Carlo Fontana in 1702. Its campanile (restored) has surveyed the piazza since the 12th century. Although the church we see dates from then, it was erected over what is traditionally thought to be the oldest church (first century) in Rome dedicated to the Virgin Mary. Inside is a gilded ceiling designed by Domenichino; the wonderful polychrome marbles and mosaics sparkle above the Cosmatesque pavement. In the mosaic of the *Madonna with Christ,* a very real woman sits with her son's arm about her in touching tenderness.

Sabatini's on the piazza is a popular place to dine, especially for the view, or stop at **Noiantri**, another landmark nearby. The English-speaking (or -learning) crowd in Rome turns out in force at the Pasquino, a second-run movie house on vicolo del Piede. **Vicolo delle Cinque** to the north is an attractive old street of stylish boutiques and trattorias. On via della Scala the **Pub della Scala** is the spot for jazz and drinks. Trastevere has several jazz clubs (Billie Holiday, Folkstudio, Big Mama) with American musicians in regular attendance. For a more elegant note, sit in the garden at the **Selarium** (just off via dei Fienaroli) and listen to live music. When it's late, the **Manuia** will follow up with Brazilian music and food, for a variation on Roman *cucina*.

Janiculum Hill

High above Trastevere to the northwest, and overlooking the Centro Storico on the other side of the river, the Gianicolo (Janiculum Hill) is frequently climbed (or driven) not only for the superb views of Rome it affords but also for the **Church of San Pietro in Montorio**, built over the spot west of Santa Maria in Trastevere where Saint Peter was once believed to have been crucified. In the courtyard is Bramante's lovely Tempietto, smug with Renaissance harmony. Beatrice Cenci is buried in the church, within sight of her place of execution.

If you walk farther west up via Garibaldi and then to the passeggiata del Gianicolo, you'll see the monument to Garibaldi, hero of a united Italy. The passeggiata continues past the statue of his wife, Anita, who fought and died at his side.

If you descend via Garibaldi almost to the river and turn left on via della Lungara, you'll arrive at the **Palazzo Corsini**, which houses an impressive collection of Renaissance and later masterworks from Fra Angelico to Poussin. Across the street, the **Villa Farnesina** contains several rooms frescoed by Raphael with voluptuous and dramatic tales of the gods. (The two museums are open mornings only, and can be left for another day.)

CAPITOLINE HILL TO AVENTINE HILL

An exhilarating walk (mostly downhill) leads with very few street crossings from the piazza Venezia to the Tiber (stopping off at the Capitoline museums, Santa Maria d'Aracoeli, and piazza Bocca della Verità) and then turns up the Aventine Hill, where during the warmer months the simple charms of early Christian basilicas are entwined with the scent of rose gardens and the orangery, exquisite in spring.

The monument to Vittorio Emanuele II, or the **Vittoriano**, as it is frequently called, has few redeeming architectural features, and its never-darkening white marble in a city of apricot and honey tones is a shock. But to the Italian tourists who come to Rome to see their capital of only a little more than a century, it is a powerful image of unity and durability. The Tomba del Milite Ignoto (Tomb of the Unknown Soldier), midway up the steps and guarded 24 hours a day by the military, adds to its nationalistic appeal. An oddity just in front on the left is a fragment of ancient wall—left there because, when the area was being razed for the monument, it proved to be the tomb of one Caius Publicius Bibulus, who died about 2,000 years ago. Since graves had to be outside the city limits, this provided a historical clue to the configuration of the first century B.C. city walls.

Around to the right as you face the monument are the steep steps that lead to the Aracoeli church. These are suitable for penitents, but if you feel guilt-free you might opt for Michelangelo's Cordonata, the sloped staircase on the right that leads to the Capitoline Hill's summit and piazza del Campidoglio.

The **Church of Santa Maria d'Aracoeli** (pronounced ara-CHAY-lee, or -SHAY-lee in Roman dialect) was built on the site of an ancient temple to Juno Moneta and to Jupiter—a holy place above the Forum where every Roman offered sacrifices. The earliest church on the site dates from the sixth century. In the ninth century a Byzantine monastery occupied the hill, and the present basilica was built around that time. Saint Bernard of Siena lived here, and his life is celebrated inside in a series of frescoes by Pinturicchio. The flight of 124 steps was built by the architect Simone Andreozzi, in gratitude for being spared from the plague in 1348; the parishioners contributed the funds. The church's name, which translates as Saint Mary of Heaven's Altar, is derived from the 12th-century *Mirabilia,* which tells of the time when the emperor Augustus consulted the sibyl about a problem: The senate wanted to deify him, but the idea didn't appeal to him as it had to his predecessor Julius Caesar. The sibyl prophesied that "from the sun will descend the king of future centuries." At that moment the Virgin Mary with the Christ Child in her arms descended from heaven and voices said to him: "This is the Virgin who will receive in her womb the Savior of the World—this is the altar of the Son of God." On that spot Augustus created the altar that was called the Ara Coeli. Later chroniclers mention the altar, which is now lost. A column in the church came from Augustus's bedroom in his palace on the Palatine Hill. It's marked *a cubiculo Augustoranum* and stands third on the left in the nave.

The sumptuous ceiling of gilt-coffered panels was built to honor the victory at Lepanto, which ended the Turkish fleet's rule of the Mediterranean—the papal fleet had taken part in the rout.

Pinturicchio's frescoes of Saint Bernard, painted in 1486, are among the best examples of the artist's work. In the right transept is a Roman sarcophagus festooned with fruit and flowers. Across from it at left is the octagonal tomb of Saint Helen, mother of Constantine. The altar beneath her burial urn is what was thought to be the Ara Coeli but is instead a fine 13th-century work that depicts the miracle. Also in this transept is the tomb of the 13th-century Cardinal Matteo d'Acquasparta, an exceptional work by Arnolfo di Cambio.

In the sacristy, or in the left aisle at Christmas, is the little gold- and gem-encrusted figure of the *Santissimo Bambino* (the Most Holy Child), whose intercession is still sought. Among the many legends surrounding the Bambino is one of a very wealthy woman who was so ill she wanted desperately to keep the Bambino with her through the night. In the morning she felt better but decided she couldn't part with him and had a replica made to return to the church. One Medieval night, stormy to be sure, the monks at the church were aroused by a loud knocking at the outer door. It was the Bambino come to his rightful home. At Christmas every year, children come to the church and recite poetry to him; and Christmas Eve mass here is among the most festive celebrations in Rome.

Piazza del Campidoglio

The adjoining piazza del Campidoglio is one of the most pleasant places in Rome to sit, and especially so in the evening. The museums here are open certain weeknights and Saturday evenings. Though you may have to make do with a bit of curbing to sit on, the beauty of the piazza and the lack of cars make it exceptionally conducive to a respite. Since Michelangelo was the planner, this is not entirely surprising. Even the approach along the Cordonata alerts the senses to something out of the ordinary at the top.

The Campidoglio (Capitoline Hill) is the smallest of Rome's famous seven hills, but it is the most imposing because it was the spiritual and political center of the Roman world—the Forum was built on its slope—and it remains the seat of city government to this day. It is especially brilliant each April 21, when the city celebrates its birthday by illuminating the Campidoglio with candles.

Although the equestrian statue of Marcus Aurelius that once graced the center of the piazza has been relocated to a side courtyard after restoration, the dramatic if less brilliant statues of Castor and Pollux stand at the top of the steps. At the right is the **Palazzo dei Conservatori**, in which the Conservators' Palace Museum is found. Its courtyard is unmistakably Roman; the enormous head and hand of Constantine, and odds and ends of muscles from the statue that was in his basilica in the Forum, line the warm apricot walls of the court.

On the stairs is the figure of Charles of Anjou, whose ambitions were ended by the Sicilian Vespers revolt; it is the only Medieval portrait statue in Rome. In this extensive Classical collection—the statues are mainly copies of Greek originals—the *Thorn Extractor* is notable, but the portrait busts from Augustus to Nero and Tiberius are the prizes. Here Roman art did not follow the Greek patterns but showed the rulers in unidealized portraits. The Etruscan bronze statue of the she-wolf with the nursing twins, Remus and Romulus, that Pollaiuolo added, is also here; its imprint is on everything in Rome, from state seals to sewer covers. The Museo Nuovo wing is devoted to the Renaissance: paintings by Bellini, the Carracci, Caravaggio, Lotto, Reni, and others.

Directly across the piazza, in the Palazzo Nuovo, is the **Museo Capitolino**, where the ancient god Marforio lies in seductive indolence in the courtyard. His name is assumed— he's one of the "talking statues" to which verses were attached, usually satiric poems directed at the celebrities of the time.

Hadrian's villa at Tivoli was awash with splendid mosaics, and some of them are now here, in the Room of the Dove. The theme is Love: Eros and his Roman counterpart, Cupid, with Psyche and the Capitoline Venus. Among the fine statuary are the poignant *Dying Gaul;* the *Marble Faun* (a satyr figure attributed to Praxiteles, and the faun of Hawthorne's last novel); and the *Wounded Amazon* (copy), which was sculpted for a competition at Ephesus, where the cult of Diana thrived.

The remaining building on the piazza is the Palazzo del Senatorio, where the local government meets. In back of it splendid views of the Forum unfold (by day and night).

Toward the Aventine Hill

To the west a couple of blocks on the via del Teatro di Marcello, in front of piazza del Campidoglio, is the **Teatro di Marcello**, Julius Caesar's first contribution to the dramatic world. Its impressive if fragmentary current state is enhanced by the oddity of its having apartments above. Known as the Palazzo Orsini, it is still inhabited by the Orsini family, who have perhaps the best view in Rome. (The stylish

Vecchia Roma restaurant is close by, and is recommended for lunch.)

Down via del Teatro di Marcello toward the Tiber, before piazza Bocca della Verità, stands the sturdy, newly restored **Arco di Giano** (Arch of Janus) in a valley (now behind a parking lot) where cattle dealers gathered in the days of the Empire, sheltering themselves inside the arch. On the far side of the arch is the delightful **Church of San Giorgio in Velabro**, named for the marsh in which Romulus and Remus were found. (The Palatine Hill is just beyond.) The church often bears the red carpet that awaits a wedding party, presided over by 13th-century frescoes.

The beautifully sculpted arch adjoining the church, erected in 204 in honor of Septimus Severus and his sons, is called the **Arco degli Argentari** (Arch of the Money Lenders). And again, after Caracalla murdered his brother, Geta, he removed Geta's name from the arch, as on the Arch of Septimius Severus in the Forum. On the pilasters contemporary views of the Forum provide the background.

As you turn back toward the Tiber, across the broad boulevard is the exquisite round marble **Tempio di Vesta** (second century B.C.), really a temple to Hercules, some think, and the so-called **Tempio della Fortuna Virile**.

At the end of the street is the Medieval **Church of Santa Maria in Cosmedin**, famous for the open mouth of truth, the *Bocca della Verità,* on the porch. Hordes of tourists wait in line to see if it will snap off their hand if they tell a lie. The face was a Medieval drain cover, but its appeal is not diminished by that knowledge. The sixth-century church was later enlarged and given to the colony of Greek refugees. The floor is a rare example of mosaics produced by the Cosmati themselves, most floors being only Cosmatesque; geometrical designs signal their work.

The Aventine Hill

Turn left at the corner by Santa Maria and walk to the next wide street, via del Circo Massimo. Across it, a winding road from the piazzale Romolo e Remo ascends the Aventine Hill; by following it you'll see the loveliest rose gardens in Rome (in season) and the orange trees of the **Church of Santa Sabina**—and the view of Rome from the balustrade in the little Savello park by the church. The church is an elegant example of a fifth-century basilica, wonderfully lit by clerestory windows and impressive-looking with its Corinthian columns, but the drama is in its simplicity. In 1222 it

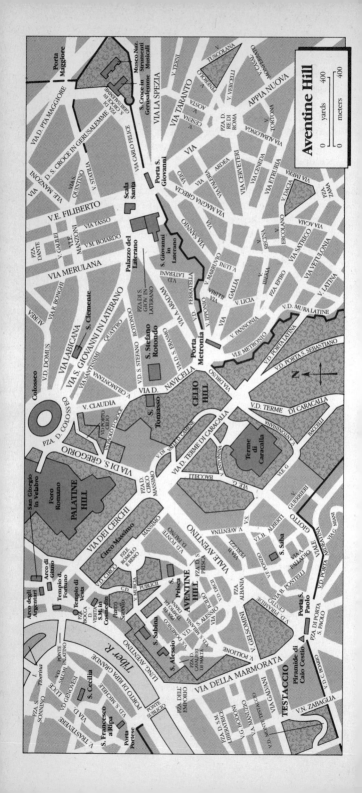

Aventine Hill

0	yards	400
0	meters	400

Porta Maggiore

Museo Naz. Strumenti Musicali

S. Croce in Gerusalemme

VIA NAZIONI

VIA D. PTA MAGGIORE

VIA D. S. CROCE IN GERUSALEMME

VIA CARLO FELICE

VIA STATILIA

VIA TASSO

VIA MANZONI

V.E. FILIBERTO

VIA S. QUINTINO

PZA DANTE

VIA MERULANA

VIA LABICANA

Colosseo

S. Clemente

Palazzo del Laterano

Scala Santa

S. Giovanni in Laterano

Porta S. Giovanni

VIA S. GIOVANNI IN LATERANO

S. Stefano Rotondo

VIA D. S. STEFANO ROTONDO

Porta Metronia

VIA AMBA ARADAM

VIA D. NAVICELLA

CELIO HILL

S. Tomasso

V. CLAUDIA

VIA DI S. GREGORIO

VIA LABICANA

VIALE METRONIO

VIA TARANTO

VIA TUSCOLANA

VIA LA SPEZIA

APPIA NUOVA

PZA D. RE DI ROMA

VIA SANNIO

VIA MAGNA GRECIA

VIA GALLIA

VIA LATINA

VIA D. MURA LATINE

V.D. PORTA LATINA

V.D. PORTA S. SEBASTIANO

Terme di Caracalla

VIA D. TERME DI CARACALLA

V.D. TERME DI CARACALLA

San Giorgio in Velabro

Foro Romano

PALATINE HILL

Arco di Giano

Arco degli Argentari

Tempio d. Fortuno

Tempio di Vesta

S.M. in Cosmedin

Circo Massimo

VIA DEI CERCHI

PZLE ROMOLO E REMO

PZA DI CIRCO MASSIMO

Parco Savello

S. Sabina

S. Alessio

Piazza Cavalieri di Malta

AVENTINE HILL

VIALE AVENTINO

S. Saba

Porta S. Paolo

Piramide di Caio Cestio

TESTACCIO

VIA DELLA MARMORATA

Tiber R.

S. Cecilia

S. Michele

San Francesco a Ripa

Portese

V. TRASTEVERE

PONTE SUBLICIO

was given to Saint Dominic, who was founding a new religious order, and the Dominicans still preside at the church. On the porch is a carved cypress door (under glass); the crucifix at the top left is apparently the oldest known representation of Christ on the Cross.

Continue southwest after Santa Sabina to **piazza dei Cavalieri di Malta**, a Piranesi-designed space most famous for the keyhole at number 3 that frames St. Peter's dome so beautifully. The Aventine is an obviously wealthy residential neighborhood (money belts advised), and it is a joy to stroll up and down its slopes, away from the hubbub of the city. If you have time, stop also at the ancient churches of Santa Prisca, built over a Mithraic temple (being excavated), and San' Saba, on the other side of piazza Albania to the southeast of the hill.

For lunch, go across via della Marmorata from the Aventine to the outskirts of **Testaccio**, an old neighborhood where the slaughterhouse once stood, and that is still famous for restaurants that specialize in cooking innards. Wonderful vegetables are also a specialty of the inexpensive trattorias that dot the area. **Perilli** is a favorite on via della Marmorata, which leads from the ponte Sublicio to the Porta San Paolo, but stop first up the street at **Volpetti** (number 47) to see one of the most marvelous shops for cheese and other delicacies, including a mortadella like no other. Try the very strong Pugliese *ricotta forte* and varieties of fresh mozzarella; tasting is encouraged.

ROME'S LEGACY OF FOREIGNERS

Begin one of your days in Rome early, at the **Museo Borghese** in the small palace of the **Villa Borghese** (not a villa but a large park built for Cardinal Scipione Borghese, the pleasure-loving nephew of Pope Paul V, on the Pincio Hill). Today the Villa Borghese, just north of the Spanish Steps/via Veneto area, is one of the greenest and most relaxing public places in Rome, a favorite spot for a picnic, a trip with the children to its modern zoo, or a promenade to its piazzale Napoleone I on the west side of the **Pincio** for a traditional view of Rome over piazza del Popolo.

For the purpose of this one early morning visit, however, go primarily for the museum, where the cardinal amassed, by patronage and plunder, an extensive collection of paintings (temporarily closed to the public) and sculpture. The display begins dramatically, if not scandalously, with the statue of

Napoléon's sister Pauline, who, when she married Prince Camillo Borghese, commissioned it as a wedding present for him from Antonio Canova. She insisted on posing as Venus, almost entirely in the nude. When asked how she could have done so, she replied, "Oh, there was a stove in the studio," anticipating Marilyn Monroe's remark about having a radio on in similar circumstances.

Scipione Borghese was an early patron of Bernini, a number of whose most outstanding sculptures are on display here, including *David, Apollo and Daphne,* and *Pluto and Persephone.* Upstairs are such paintings as Raphael's *Deposition* (stolen from a church in Perugia by the cardinal), Caravaggio's *Sick Bacchus* and *Boy with a Basket of Fruit,* and a roomful of Venetian paintings, including Titian's Neoplatonic allegory *Sacred and Profane Love.*

From the museum it is a pleasant walk (or, perhaps better for scheduling your time, taxi ride) to Villa Giulia at the northwest corner of the park, which actually *is* a villa, housing the **Museo Nazionale di Villa Giulia**—a vast collection of the art of the mysterious Etruscans who once inhabited central Italy. Highlights include the *Apollo of Veii,* found in the excavations there, and the *Bride and Groom,* a sarcophagus depicting a smiling, dreamy-eyed couple reclining as if at a banquet with an equality that shocked other ancient societies. Upstairs are attenuated bronze statues and other objects covered with drawings that, to our eyes, look strikingly modern.

If modern art is what interests you, head next to the **Galleria Nazionale d'Arte Moderna**, which you passed on your way from the Museo Borghese. It contains works of modern painters such as De Chirico, Boccioni, and Pistoletto, as well as some foreign works.

Piazza del Popolo Area

From Villa Giulia, ride or walk west to the ancient via Flaminia; turn south on it and you'll be entering Rome as travellers have traditionally for centuries, through the grand gate called the **Porta del Popolo**, at piazza del Popolo. One such arrival was Queen Christina of Sweden, who converted to Catholicism and came to Rome in 1655, an occasion for which Bernini decorated the inside of the great arch and Pope Alexander VII composed the arch's inscription: *Felici faustoque ingressui MDCLV.* Across the piazza are the twin churches of Santa Maria di Montesanto (on the left) and Santa Maria dei Miracoli (on the right), playful exercises in the art of illusionary design begun by Carlo Rainaldi. The church on the left is narrower than that on the right, so Rainaldi topped the left church with an oval dome and the right with a round one in order to make them look symmetrical—and they do.

Immediately to the left of the gate is the **Church of Santa Maria del Popolo**, which was constructed with funds from the *popolo* (people) and gives the piazza its name. It was built originally in the Middle Ages over what was thought to be Nero's grave, in order to exorcise his malign spirit. Best known for its two paintings by Caravaggio, *The Conversion of Saint Paul* and *The Martyrdom of Saint Peter,* it also contains the Cappella Chigi by Raphael and works by Pinturicchio, Annibale Carracci, Sebastiano del Piombo, and Bernini (who was responsible for the restoration of the church).

Between the twin churches runs the renowned **via del Corso**, named after the horse races that were run during Carnival along its entire length between piazza del Popolo to the north and piazza Venezia and the Vittoriano to the south. One new addition to the otherwise static street is the **Fondazione Memmo**, a private foundation that hosts art exhibitions in the Palazzo Ruspoli (via del Corso 418, Tel: 683-2177). Between shows, continue your tour by looking left (south) at via del Babuino (which leads to piazza di Spagna), and to the right at via di Ripetta. Either of the cafés at the beginning of these streets is a nice place to pause for some morning refreshment. Most evocative of the dolce-vita era is **Canova**, on the left, since it is modern in style and popular with employees of the nearby Italian television office, RAI. **Rosati**, on the right, with its original Art Nouveau decor, comes alive at night, when it is frequented by slick young lotharios on the prowl in noisy sports cars and motorcycles.

Follow the narrow **via di Ripetta**. For a look at the building where Antonio Canova once created his masterpieces, turn onto via Antonio Canova, the third street on the left. You'll find his former studio on the right, a low building with bits of classical sculpture set into its apricot-colored façade, which also has a bronze copy of a self-portrait bust of the artist.

Two streets ahead on via di Ripetta is the **Ara Pacis Augustae**, an altar finished in 9 B.C. to celebrate the Augustan peace, which not only brought peace to the Empire but ushered in the Augustan Age lauded by Virgil in the *Aeneid* and by other writers such as Livy, Ovid, and Horace. Much of

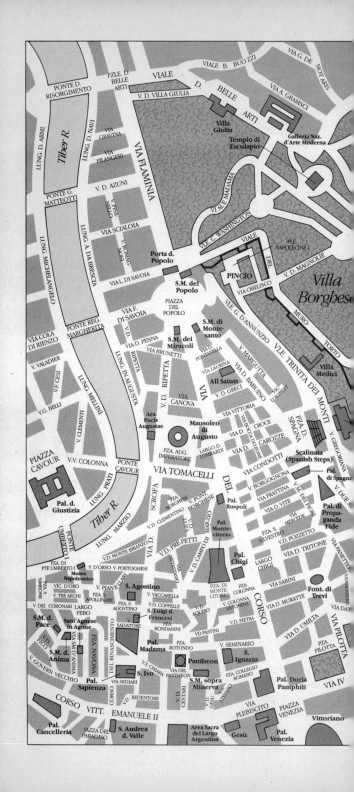

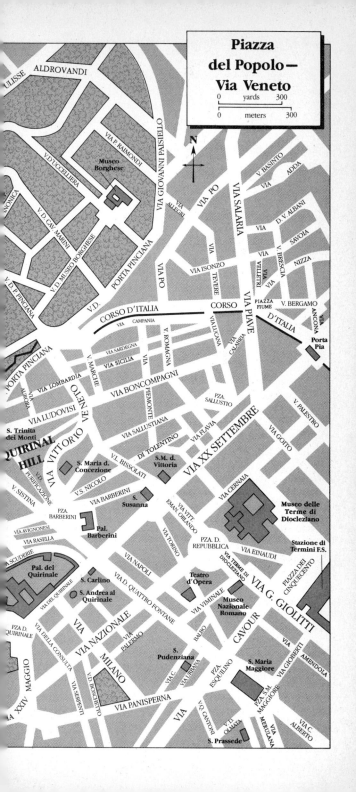

Piazza del Popolo — Via Veneto

0 yards 300

0 meters 300

N

the altar was rediscovered in Rome in the 1930s and transported to its present site, now covered with a protective piece of Fascist-era architecture. Missing segments were reclaimed from museums throughout the world or replicated.

On one side of the altar, Augustus walks first but remains, modestly, almost unseen in the procession. Sir Mortimer Wheeler wrote of the marble, "If we would understand the Augustan period—its quiet good manners and its undemonstrable confidence—in a single document, that document is the Ara Pacis Augustae." As a work of art it is brilliant, and as a portrait gallery it gives us an image of the Augustan *dramatis personae*. His daughter Julia (banished to the Tremiti Islands for her sexual exploits) and her husband, Agrippa, who built the Pantheon, are at the center. The scenes of everyday life here are superb: A child pulls at his mother's robe, and a woman silences a chattering couple with a finger to her lips. The child who wears the laurel crown would eventually be grandfather to Nero. The floral motifs on the far side are some of the finest examples of decorative art created in Roman times.

Across the street is the odd mound that is the **Mausoleum of Augustus**. Now stripped of its original travertine covering and obelisks, it was once counted among the most sacred places in Rome. Like Hadrian's tomb (Castel Sant'Angelo), it took the cylindrical Etruscan form, and Augustus's ashes and those of his family were buried within. At his funeral pyre, which was nearby, an eagle was released when the emperor's body was committed to the fire, symbolizing his immortal soul soaring to divine heights.

Continuing along via di Ripetta, the first piazza you will encounter is **piazza Borghese**. Here, in the morning, stalls are filled with antique books and prints, often of high quality and reasonably priced. Nearby on via della Lupa is **La Grapperia**, a bar dedicated to the consumption of hundreds of varieties of the Italian aquavit, grappa. Back at the beginning of the street, via del Clementino and via Fontanella Borghese lead to the Corso, across which begins via Condotti. Lined with designer shops, **via Condotti** is Rome's most famous shopping street, though the two streets parallel to it on the south—via Borgognona and via Frattina—are lined with equally luxurious shops. If you're interested in serious shopping (see Shops and Shopping, below), avoid the area on a Saturday, when the nearby Metro stop of piazza di Spagna disgorges hordes of young people from the suburbs who look but don't buy, much to the consternation of the owners of Gucci, Ferragamo, Fendi, and other shops in the area. Via Condotti goes straight to the Spanish Steps. Along the way, peek into number 68, the palazzo where the Sovereign Military Order of the Knights of Malta has its headquarters. Granted extraterritorial rights by the Italian state, it issues a limited number of passports and license plates with its S.M.O.M. insignia. If the Vatican is the world's smallest inhabited state, this is the only one entirely enclosed in a palazzo.

The Spanish Steps

Piazza di Spagna is laid out in the shape of a butterfly— without doubt a mellow subtropical species. The tall palms that greet you immediately and the languid crowds on the steps are beautiful reminders of how balmy Rome really can be. The piazza takes its name from the Palazzo di Spagna at number 57, the Spanish Embassy to the Holy See. Many other foreigners, however, have been active in the area. The Spanish Steps (Scalinata della Trinità dei Monti, in Italian), which rise in the middle of the piazza, actually were paid for by the French to create an easier access to the church of Trinità dei Monti, built by their kings at the top of the hill, and the piazza once was known locally as piazza di Francia. The whole area, in fact, was called *er ghetto del'Inglesi* by the Romans, assuming that all foreigners were English, just as the Greeks before them had referred to all outsiders as barbarians. Keats lived and died in the house at number 26 piazza di Spagna, and is commemorated with a death mask and cases full of memorabilia (as are Shelley and Byron) in the Keats-Shelley Memorial there, where you can purchase tiny volumes of the poets' works.

Goethe and Dickens also knew the Spanish Steps. In his *Pictures from Italy,* Dickens described the characters of the day who went to the steps to hire themselves out as artists' models. "There is one old gentleman, with long hair and an immense beard," he writes, "who, to my knowledge, has gone through half the catalogue of the Royal Academy. This is the venerable, or patriarchical model." He then goes on to describe other colorful types who posed as "the *dolce far niente* model," "the assassin model," "the haughty or scornful model," and writes that "as to Domestic Happiness, and Holy Families, they should come very cheap, for there are lumps of them, all up the steps; and the cream of the thing, is, that they are all the falsest vagabonds in the world, especially made up for the purpose, and having no other counterparts in Rome or in any other part of the habitable globe." The theatricality of the Italian street scene is nothing new. These days, though, you're likely to encounter all sorts of vendors as you climb the steps, for amid the pots of azaleas in the spring, the nativity scene at Christmas, and all over the steps throughout the year are the people selling crafts and offering modern-day Daisy Millers a coffee that turns out to be drugged, as the tale of her robbery will reveal in the next day's *Il Messaggero*. Like large metropolises everywhere, Rome is not immune to crime, and the Spanish Steps have been getting their share lately, particularly at night.

You'll need some sustenance to scale the 137 steps, however. Fortunately, the historical presence of travellers and the piazza's contemporary guise as a center for luxury shops (increasingly affordable, it seems, only to Italians) have ensured a number of cafés and restaurants in the area. If you're feeling fancy, try **Ranieri's** on via Mario dei Fiori, a remnant from the Grand Tour days. Otherwise, the pleasant outdoor courtyard of **Otello alla Concordia** on via della Croce is a fine spot for lunch. For a postprandial pickup, the old **Caffè Greco** on via Condotti has been offering coffee and other refreshment since the early 18th century. **Babington's**, to the left of the steps in the piazza, serves high-priced tea, and the bar at the Hotel D'Inghilterra, as well as **Baretto** at via Condotti 55, serve as watering holes for the elegant locals.

Or you may simply want a sip of water from the fountain called the Fontana della Barcaccia, at the base of the steps. Designed by Pietro Bernini, or possibly his son Gianlorenzo, it takes its shape from the boats that once came to the papal port of Ripetta, formerly nearby on the Tiber.

Before making your ascent up the steps, follow via del Babuino off the piazza to the left. Turn right on vicolo d'Alibert to the charming **via Margutta**, which is lined with an open-air art show every spring and fall (and art galleries yearround), and double back at via della Fontanella to via del Babuino, where amid the elegant antiques shops you'll notice the statue of Silenus, dubbed by residents "the baboon" and giving the street its name. The Anglican church of All Saints is at number 153; the English-language **Lion Bookshop** is at number 181, and, if you're in need of some refreshment, try the ultramodern **Café Notegen** at number 159. Cross piazza di Spagna to its southern triangle, where you'll see the column dedicated to the Immaculate Conception. Here each December 8 the pope crowns the statue of the Virgin with a garland of flowers; its height requires that the deed be performed by a member of Rome's trusty fire brigade from the ladder of a truck. The building behind the column is the Palazzo di Propaganda Fide (Palace of the Propagation of the Faith), the missionary center of the Catholic world. Bernini and Borromini both worked on its façades, but not at the same time. The side facing the piazza is the work of Bernini, and his rival's concave façade is to the right.

Perhaps braced with another sip of water from the Fontana della Barcaccia, you're now ready to climb the delightfully curving travertine steps to Trinità dei Monti, with its views of the shoppers below. In honor of the Trinity, the staircase is divided into three landings; each in turn is divided into three. The French occupy not only the church but the adjacent **Villa Medici**, just to the left as you face the church, on viale della Trinità dei Monti. It was here that Louis XIV established the Académie de France and the Prix de Rome in 1666. French artists still come to study at the academy within, which also hosts important art exhibitions. The street eventually leads to the view from the Pincio, but come back at sunset to enjoy that at its best, preferably from the **Casina Valadier** café-restaurant. Now is the time to turn around and head down via Sistina to piazza Barberini and the beginning of via Veneto. The centerpiece of the piazza is the Fontana del Tritone by Bernini, and at the corner of via Veneto is the Fontana delle Api (Fountain of the Bees), named after its numerous symbols of the Barberini family, who commissioned the work from Bernini. (The Palazzo Barberini here is the starting point of our Centuries of Christianity section below.)

Via Vittorio Veneto

The shady curves of via Vittorio Veneto recall the days when it was a cow path only a century ago but mask the more frenetic activity that has taken place there in recent years, most infamously in the 1960s, when it was the stage for the extravagances of international film stars working at Rome's film studio, Cinecittà. The way of life was dubbed *la dolce vita* (the sweet life) and fictionalized by Fellini in a movie of the same name. Before musing on that time, however, stop into the **Church of Santa Maria della Concezione** for a memento mori about where the sweet life eventually leads. Its five chapels were decorated in bizarre Rococo patterns formed by the bones of some 4,000 Capuchin monks.

The heady climate of la dolce vita was described by Italian journalist Lieta Tornabuoni: "Rome fills up with American divas," she writes, "the most mythical and the most restless.

"They live in the grand hotels of the Via Veneto. . . . Their wealth, flamboyance, temperament, hard drinking habits, and professional courtesy amaze Italian film people and journalists but don't shock them.

"They require spoken English. They animate the nights with amorous or alcoholic squabbles and fake suicides; they nourish journalism and photojournalism. . . . In Rome, Audrey Hepburn will find a husband and Anita Ekberg will find success with Fellini. Liz Taylor falls in love with Burton and poisons herself. Ava Gardner and Anthony Franciosa fight to the death over Walter Chiari, Anthony Quinn changes wives, Sinatra comes to blows over a performance. Everybody buys everything, everyone drinks."

These days the scene is quieter, interrupted occasionally by the clicking heels of the prostitutes who walk the street at night and the cars that screech to a halt to meet them. But the overall atmosphere is peaceful, and the street activity can be taken in over leisurely refreshment at **Café de la Paix**, the best-known café from the days of the sweet life.

CENTURIES OF CHRISTIANITY

Ever mindful of museum hours, begin one day's tour on via delle Quattro Fontane at the entrance to the **Palazzo Barberini**. Begun in 1625 for Pope Urban VIII (Maffeo Barberini) by Carlo Maderno, construction of the palazzo was taken over by Borromini, who was responsible for the oval stairs on the right, and then by Bernini, who designed the central façade and the rectangular staircase on the left. The palazzo remained in the hands of the Barberini family for years. Among its tenants was the American sculptor William Story, who entertained the Brownings, Henry James, and Hans Christian Andersen in his apartments here. In 1949 it was sold to the Italian government and now houses the **Galleria Nazionale d'Arte Antica**, which is not a gallery of antique art at all. The gallery contains paintings by such artists as Fra Angelico, Filippo Lippi, Bronzino, Caravaggio, Tintoretto, and El Greco, as well as Raphael's portrait of *La Fornarina,* the baker's daughter who was his mistress. The sumptuous Baroque and Rococo decoration of the rooms, especially Pietro da Cortona's ceiling fresco *Allegory of Divine Providence* (note the ever-buzzing Barberini bees in the center) in the salon, gives some idea of the splendor in which the popes lived.

Southeast up via delle Quattro Fontane, where it intersects via del Quirinale, are the four facing Baroque fountains for which the street is named. This is also the crossroads of the wide streets laid out under Sixtus V (1585–1590), with sweeping views leading to Porta Pia to the northeast and to the obelisks of the Quirinal Hill to the southwest, the Esquiline Hill to the southeast, and Trinità dei Monti to the northwest.

On the far corner of via del Quirinale is Borromini's **Church of San Carlo alle Quattro Fontane**, known affectionately as San Carlino, with a lovely adjacent cloister. The geometric complexity of the church's interior provides an obvious contrast (and convenient comparison) to the interior of Bernini's **Church of Sant'Andrea al Quirinale** just down the street, which is relatively simple in spite of its rich marble and gilt decor.

Farther down the street is the **Palazzo del Quirinale**. Designed by Maderno, Bernini, and many others, it was formerly a summer residence of the popes, and later used by the kings of Italy. It is now occupied by the president of the republic. Its rich decoration by such artists as Melozzo da Forlì and Pietro da Cortona can be seen only by permission (write the Ufficio Intendenza della Presidenza della Repubblica, via della Dataria 96, 00187 Rome). No appointment is necessary, however, to see the *corazzieri,* the presidential guard, all over six feet tall and dashing in their crimson and blue uniforms, gleaming boots, and shining helmets with tossing plumes.

Take via della Consulta south off piazza del Quirinale and turn left on bustling via Nazionale, where you'll pass the recently reopened **Palazzo delle Esposizioni** at number 194, where interesting art exhibitions are held, and the Neo-Gothic American church of St. Paul on the corner of via Napoli. The street leads to piazza della Repubblica, with its tall spray of water shooting out of the Fontana delle Naiadi, an 1885 bronze fountain by Alessandro Guerrieri of naiads cavorting with sea monsters. The piazza is commonly called piazza Esedra because the arcades of the two curving palaces around it are built where the *exedrae,* or semicircular benches, of the Terme di Diocleziano (Baths of Diocletian) once existed. (Coincidentally, the ring around the fountain is still a popular trysting place.)

Baths of Diocletian Area

Begun by Maximilian and completed by Diocletian, the baths (*terme*) were the largest of all such Roman facilities,

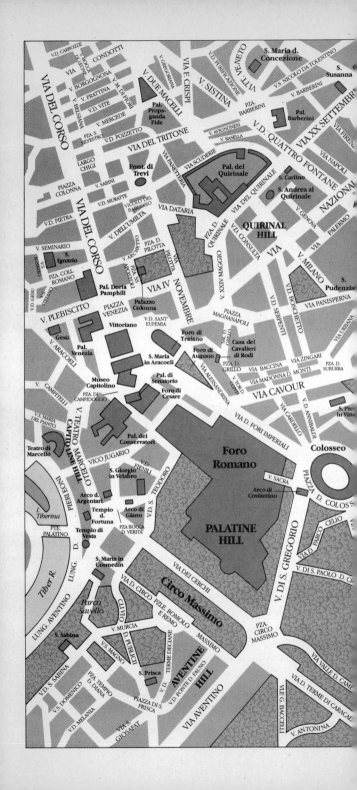

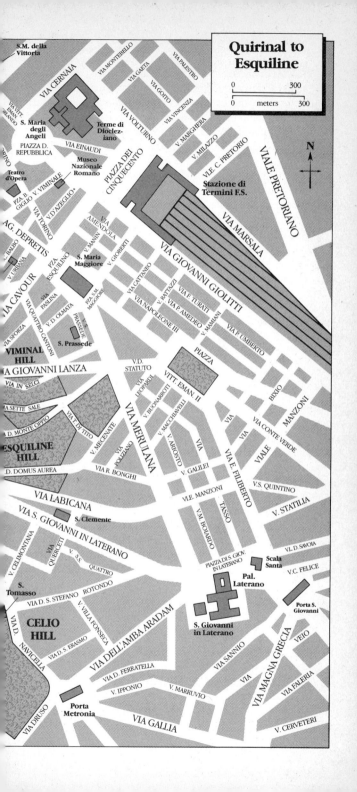

able to accommodate 3,000 people and covering an area of 32 acres. Today, the **Church of Santa Maria degli Angeli** is housed within the original Tepidarium. It was begun as a Carthusian church by Michelangelo, who converted the baths' vast central hall into the nave, but when Vanvitelli took over the design, he changed the nave into a transept. What has not changed is the sense of space, a uniquely Roman contribution to the course of architectural history. The church and its adjacent convent have just been restored to house the **Museo delle Terme di Diocleziano**, displaying art from the late Roman Republic.

Via Terme di Diocleziano leads to the **Museo Nazionale Romano**, newly installed in the Collegio Massimo on the corner of via Amendola. Best known for the chair-shaped Greek sculpture called the *Ludovisi Throne,* the museum also contains a copy of the Greek sculptor Myron's *Discobolus,* the *Daughter of Niobe,* the *Venus of Cyrene,* and a bronze *Boxer,* as well as mosaics, frescoes, stuccos, and portrait busts of Roman patricians. (Much of the museum is closed for restoration at present.)

Before leaving the area, stop into the **Church of Santa Maria della Vittoria** on via XX Settembre. (The American Catholic **Church of Santa Susanna**, with a magnificent façade by Maderno, is in the next block.) The simple interior of Santa Maria della Vittoria also was designed by Maderno in the Counter-Reformation style of the Gesù, and Bernini's theatrical Cappella Cornaro is Baroque at its most flamboyant. There, members of the Cornaro family are portrayed in marble as spectators in theater boxes to the statue of Saint Teresa of Avila, whose ecstasy seems decidedly secular. If her sensuality gets the best of you, cool off in front of the horned statue of Moses in the Fontana del Mose around the corner. The fountain was designed by Domenico Fontana, who allegedly died after seeing how badly his work compared to Michelangelo's statue of Moses in the church of San Pietro in Vincoli (see below), though the story is held to be apocryphal.

Better to sublimate your desires into lunch and take the five-minute taxi ride from piazza della Repubblica in front of the Terme di Diocleziano a few long blocks south to the simple setting of the restaurant **Cicilardone** at via Merulana 77. There you'll be able to sample the endless varieties of homemade pasta by ordering *assaggini,* or little tastes, which go a long way. (A less expensive alternative would be to buy provisions at the boisterous food market in nearby piazza Vittorio.)

If you haven't already done so on your travels, give a passing glance to **Stazione di Termini,** the railroad station often overlooked in the context of the city's more venerable architecture. Begun under the Fascists, as the neo-Roman side sections show, the construction of the station unearthed part of a wall built after the invasion of the Gauls in 390, the ruins of which in front of the station provide a stark contrast to the sweeping travertine curve of the entrance. Today the piazza serves as a gathering place for immigrants from Asia and Africa, a phenomenon reminiscent of the farthest-flung days of the Roman Empire.

Santa Maria Maggiore

From Cicilardone take via Merulana to the double-domed **Basilica of Santa Maria Maggiore,** one of the four so-called major basilicas of Rome, this one built on the Esquiline Hill. Many myths and legends surround the basilica, which was dedicated to the Virgin Mary after the Council of Ephesus in 431 affirmed that she was the mother of Christ. One of the most charming is that the Virgin appeared on this site on the night of August 4, 352, saying that her church should be built on an area she would cover—and did—with a snowfall the following morning. The event is commemorated each August 5 with a pontifical mass in the Cappella Borghese, accompanied by white flower-petal flurries from the dome of the chapel as well as much celebration in the piazza outdoors. (The chapel is also where the tiny coffin of Pauline Borghese lies.) The basilica preserves the relic (displayed each Christmas) of the Holy Crib in which the infant Jesus was laid, mentioned by Petrarch in a letter to Pope Clement VI in Avignon as one of Rome's sacred treasures to lure the papacy back.

The basilica has a magnificent vaulted ceiling covered with what is supposedly the first gold to have arrived in Europe from the New World, but even more precious are its mosaics, best seen with binoculars. The nave mosaics contain scenes from the Old Testament; the triumphal-arch mosaics depict the infancy of Christ; and the apse mosaics illustrate the Coronation of the Virgin. In the afternoon it is also likely you'll find a sacristan to admit you to the oratory of the manger beneath the Cappella Sistina, which houses the remains of Arnolfo di Cambio's original 13th-century decoration.

Outside, notice the campanile, which is the tallest in Rome. Its bells are said to speak in Roman dialect. When they ring, try to make out the words *Avemo fatto li facioli, avemo fatto li facioli* (We made the beans). The bells of San Giovanni in Laterano then ask, *Con che? Con che?* (With what?), and Santa Croce in Gerusalemme responds, *Co' le codichelle, co' le codichelle* (With *cotechino* sausage).

Nearby are Santa Prassede and Santa Pudenziana, two early Christian churches dedicated to sister saints, the daughters of a Roman senator named Pudens, who was once a Christian and a friend of Saint Peter. Off the piazza di Santa Maria Maggiore is the side entrance to the brick **Church of Santa Prassede**, on via Santa Prassede. The church was once a *titulus,* a private residence where Christians were sheltered and rituals took place during the time of persecution. In the apse mosaics the sisters are being presented by Saints Peter and Paul to the Redeemer, but the most spectacular Byzantine mosaics entirely cover the Cappella di San Zenone, which contains a column, brought from Jerusalem, on which the flagellation of Christ is believed to have taken place. Many relics are found in the church, among them a circular porphyry stone under which Santa Prassede is said to have placed the blood and bones of thousands of Christian martyrs.

On the other side of Santa Maria Maggiore, off piazza del Esquilino (with its obelisk that originally stood in front of the Mausoleo di Augusto), you'll find via Urbana, where the **Church of Santa Pudenziana** stands. Its apse contains one of the oldest mosaics in Rome, dating from the fourth century.

San Pietro in Vincoli Area

Follow via Urbana down the hill to piazza degli Zingari, which means gypsies in Italian, a reminder that bands of gypsy pickpockets roam the area (and much of Rome)—so be alert. The street then leads to piazza della Suburra, named after the most notorious district of ancient Rome—which today seems quite peaceful, even trendy, with restaurants and rents both rapidly on the rise. Taking the steps up to via Cavour (where you could slip into **Enoteca** at number 313 for an afternoon refresher), cross the busy street and, on your right, locate the steep staircase to the **Church of San Pietro in Vincoli**. The church preserves a relic said to be the chains (*vincoli*) that shackled Saint Peter during his imprisonment in Jerusalem as well as in Rome, but most people come here to see Michelangelo's statue of Moses. (The horns are an artistic convention meant to indicate the subject's status as a prophet.) The figure is part of Julius II's ill-fated tomb, originally intended for St. Peter's and supposed to contain some 40 statues but never finished; some of its statuary was dispersed to the Louvre and to Florence's Galleria dell'Accademia. The *Moses* was completed, however, and Vasari writes about how the Jews of Rome went there "like flocks of starlings, to visit and adore the statue." Many legends surround the statue: The mark on the knee supposedly comes from Michelangelo throwing his hammer at it, commanding it to speak.

Descend the Esquiline Hill on via degli Annibaldi and take the stairway that leads to piazza del Colosseo; around to your left, via San Giovanni in Laterano will bring you east to piazza di San Clemente. On the left is the fascinating **Basilica di San Clemente**, a three-level house of worship run by Irish Dominican brothers since the 17th century. Its upper level has a lovely 12th-century marble pavement by the Cosmati family, 12th-century mosaics, and 15th-century frescoes by Masolino da Panicale. Underneath, and reached by the right aisle, is the lower church, which has frescoes dating from the ninth century. Beneath it, and accessible at the end of the left aisle, are the remains of a first-century *domus* and third-century Mithraic temple, which has a bas-relief representing the sun god Mithras slaying a bull. And even farther below is another evocative phenomenon: If you listen carefully, you'll hear the Charonic sounds of an underground river, which leads to Rome's ancient Cloaca Maxima sewer.

San Giovanni in Laterano

Continuing along via San Giovanni in Laterano, lined with nondescript residential apartment buildings, you will soon come across another of the major basilicas of Rome, San Giovanni in Laterano. It is the cathedral church of Rome and the titular see of the pope as bishop of Rome; he usually celebrates Maundy Thursday services there. The basilica takes its name from the patrician family of Plautius Lateranus, whose huge estate on the site was confiscated by Nero but later was returned to the family and became the dowry of Fausta, wife of Constantine, who built the original basilica on the site. It subsequently underwent a series of disasters: a fifth-century sacking, a ninth-century earthquake, and a 14th-century fire; as a result, the present church has more historical than aesthetic appeal. The original Palazzo del Laterano next to the church was the residence of the popes until they moved to Avignon, and many important events in the history of the church took place there, including the 1123 Diet of Worms. (The current palazzo dates from the 16th century and is the seat of the Rome vicariate.)

Today you see an 18th-century façade on the church, crowned with gigantic statues of the saints surrounding Christ. Borromini designed the nave and aisles of the interior, which has a magnificent ceiling and statues of the apostles by followers of Bernini. Among the other sights of the church are a heavily restored fresco by Giotto in the Cappella Corsini; reliquaries containing (legend has it) the heads of Saints Peter and Paul and a piece of the table on which the Last Supper took place; and cloisters dating from the 13th century. The baptistery next door was built in the fifth century and is the only part of the complex remaining from its original incarnation.

The Scala Sancta, on the opposite side of the Palazzo del Laterano from the baptistery, contains the **Sancta Sanctorum**, the old private chapel of the popes, and, leading up to it, what are believed to be the steps Christ climbed in Pilate's house; today the faithful still climb them on their knees.

Farther on, at the other end of via Carlo Felice, is the **Church of Santa Croce in Gerusalemme**, one of Rome's seven pilgrimage churches. It contains two 15th-century works of art worth stopping for—an apse fresco, *The Invention of the True Cross* (the church was built to house the relics of the True Cross brought back from Jerusalem: three pieces of wood, a nail, and two thorns from Christ's crown), and a mosaic in the Cappella di Santa Elena—as well as another lovely marble floor by the Cosmati. The **Museo Nazionale degli Strumenti Musicali** next to the church, at piazza di Santa Croce in Gerusalemme 9A, houses an impressive collection of musical instruments from ancient times to the 19th century.

It is unlikely that the Diet of Worms attracted one of Rome's best fish restaurants, **Cannavota**, to the area, but nevertheless you can find it back in piazza San Giovanni in Laterano near the obelisk—Rome's oldest, dating from the 15th century B.C. The restaurant itself is worth a dinner reservation; Tel: (06) 77-50-07. If you need to cast about beforehand, have a look at the colorful street market outside Porta San Giovanni in via Sannio, or check out the local branch of Italy's Coin department-store chain.

THE VATICAN

If all roads lead to Rome, they soon after lead across the Tiber to the Vatican. Since 1929, when Benito Mussolini and Cardinal Pietro Gasparri signed the Lateran Treaty between Italy and the Holy See, Vatican City—the seat of the Roman Catholic church and the cradle of all Christendom—has been an independent state ruled by the pope, the only absolute sovereign in Europe. The Vatican, as it is most commonly known, has its own flag and national anthem, mints its own coinage, prints its own postage stamps (many Romans even have more faith in its postal system than in Italy's, and go to the Vatican just to mail their letters), has its own polyglot daily newspaper (*L'Osservatore Romano*), Latin-language quarterly (*Acta Apostolicae Sedis*), multilingual radio station, and plans for a television station. All these activities take place in an area just over 100 acres, a considerable part of which is taken up by St. Peter's, the world's greatest basilica in the world's smallest state. In addition to establishing the sovereign territory contained within the high walls of the Vatican, the Lateran Treaty granted special extraterritorial privileges to the churches of San Giovanni in Laterano, Santa Maria Maggiore, and San Paolo Fuori le Mura. Together with St. Peter's they constitute the four major basilicas of Rome.

Because of the limited visiting hours of many of the Vatican's attractions, you'll need careful planning to see the sights in the span of a day. *Begin early,* on Italian territory in piazza ponte Sant'Angelo across the Tiber from the Castel Sant'Angelo. You will be facing Rome's most beautiful bridge, the glorious ponte Sant'Angelo, which Bernini intended as the initial part of the approach to St. Peter's. Statues of Saints Peter and Paul greet you as you walk over the Tiber, virtually escorted by the ten statues of angels Bernini created to herald your visit.

Looming like a Medieval flying saucer over the other side of the Tiber is **Castel Sant'Angelo**. The ancient mausoleum of Hadrian, it was once landscaped, clad in travertine, covered with sculpture, and topped by a bronze statue of the emperor himself. In the Middle Ages it became part of the Aurelian Wall, and through a gate on the castle grounds called Porta San Pietro became the main point of entry to the Vatican for religious pilgrims. It also has served as a refuge for the popes, who entered it through a private passageway from the Vatican, and as a prison. One of its illustrious captives was the Renais-

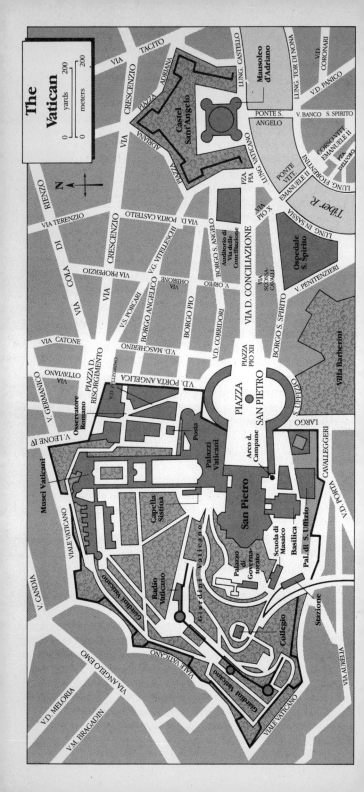

The Vatican

yards 200
meters 200

N

TACITO
VIA CRESCENZIO
VIA ADRIANA
PIAZZA ADRIANA
Castel Sant'Angelo
Mausoleo d'Adriano
LUNG. CASTELLO
V.D. CORONARI
LUNG. TOR DI NONA
PONTE S. ANGELO
V. BANCO
S. SPIRITO
PONTE VITT. EMANUELE II
CORSO VITT. EMANUELE II
PZA. D'ORO
V.D. PANICO
LUNG. FIORENTINI
Tiber R.
PZA. PIA
PONTE VITT. EMANUELE II
LUNG. VATICANO
VIA PIO X
LUNG. IN SASSIA

VIA RIENZO
VIA TERENZIO
VIA CRESCENZIO
VIA D. PORTA CASTELLO
COLA DI RIENZO
VIA PROPERZIO
VIA G. VITELLESCHI
VIA ORFEO
VIA OMBRONE
BORGO S. ANGELO
Auditorio di Via delle Conciliazione
VIA D. CONCILIAZIONE
VIA SCOSSA-CAVALLI
Ospedale S. Spirito
BORGO S. SPIRITO
V. PENITENZIERI

VIA CATONE
VIA GERMANICO
VIA OTTAVIANO
V. LEONE IV
PIAZZA D. RISORGIMENTO
V.D. PELLEGRINO
V.S. PORCARI
BORGO ANGELICO
BORGO PIO
V.D. MASCHERINO
V.D. CORRIDORI
V.D. PORTA ANGELICA
Osservatore Romano
BORGO PIO
PIAZZA PIO XII

V. CANDIA
VIALE VATICANO
Musei Vaticani
Posta
Palazzi Vaticani
Arco d. Campane
PIAZZA SAN PIETRO
LARGO
V.D. PORTA CAVALLEGGERI

V.D. MELORIA
VIA ANGELO EMO
Capella Sistina
Giardini Vaticano
Radio Vaticano
Palazzo di Governatorato
San Pietro
Scuola di Masaico
Basilica
Pal. di S. Uffizio
VIA AURELIA

V.M. BRAGADIN
VIALE VATICANO
Giardini Vaticano
Collegio
Stazione
VIALE VATICANO

sance goldsmith Benvenuto Cellini, whose escape is one of the most gripping moments of the dashing life he recounted with bravura, if not braggadocio, in his *Autobiography*. Bypass the castle's grim displays of weapons and prisons and opt for the sumptuous papal apartments on the top floor instead. From there take the staircase that, after a display of military paraphernalia, leads to the terrace familiar from the last act of *Tosca,* the one from which the heroine jumps to her death in the Tiber. (The river is actually too far from the castle for her to have made it; in fact, it would be physically impossible even for the sinewy-legged boys who play soccer on the land-scaped moat below, where she most likely would have landed.) The terrace has one of the best views of Rome and offers a close-up of Peter Anton Verschaffelt's 18th-century bronze statue of the Archangel Saint Michael, commemorating Pope Gregory the Great's vision during the plague year of 590, when Saint Michael appeared over Hadrian's tomb sheathing his sword, an act that signified the end of the plague and gave the castle its name.

In Bernini's day, a walk down the narrow Medieval streets from Castel Sant'Angelo directly west through the area known as the Borgo led to the delightful surprise of his expansive piazza at St. Peter's. Now, however, the grandiose **via della Conciliazione**, named after the Lateran accord, has ludicrously overextended the welcoming arms of Bernini's colonnade and ruined the dramatic element of turning into piazza San Pietro. In all fairness, a monumental boulevard had been planned since the middle of the 15th century; it was unfortunate that *domani* finally came in 1936 under Fascism. The wide swath, with double obelisks goose-stepping along either side, was completed in 1950, just in time for a Holy Year (they officially occur every quarter century but can be declared as often as the pope wishes, as seen in recent years). Walk quickly and fix your gaze on St. Peter's, heading straight for the tourist information office in the colonnade on your left as you face the basilica.

The **Vatican Gardens** are now open to guided tour groups only, so make the most of your time if not your money (the price of admission to most things at the Vatican is lofty) and get to the office no later than 10:00 A.M. to sign up for the daily tour. It begins at the Arco delle Campane (Arch of the Bells), watched over by the Swiss Guards, whose red-yellow-and-blue striped uniforms—supposedly designed by Michel-angelo—add a playful air to the increasingly serious job of protecting the pope. From there, guides escort visitors to a number of sights on the extensive grounds, given an occasional assist by a minibus. Included in the tour are sights most visitors to the Vatican have not seen—**Circo di Nerone**, where the first Christian martyrs (including Saint Peter) met their deaths; the 18th-century mosaic studio, which still sells stones as souvenirs; the train station (used primarily for the delivery of duty-free merchandise to fortunate employees and friends of the Vatican); the Palazzo del Governatorato, where the governor has his office; the radio station; and the prison. The most pleasant part of the tour is the gardens themselves, meticulously groomed and presided over by cypresses, umbrella pines, and—most magnificently—the only good views of the largest brick dome in creation, part of Michelangelo's original plan for St. Peter's.

The garden tour ends back at the tourist information office, and whether or not you've gone on it, this is where you should take the bus to a side entrance of the Vatican Museums. This bus also goes back through the gardens and is a pleasant alternative to the long walk from St. Peter's Square around the walls to the main museum entrance on the viale Vaticano to the north.

The Vatican Museums

The Vatican Museums have become so crowded that the authorities have had to resort to four color-coded tours to impose order. The only one that covers all the important sights is the yellow tour, which supposedly lasts five hours, but by following the yellow route and stopping only at the highlights listed below you can cut that time in half. (In general—check the exceptions—the museums close at 2:00 P.M. and on Sundays.)

The Egyptian Museum. Head straight for Room V, where the most impressive relics are the colossal granite statue of Queen Tuia, mother of Ramses II, and the sandstone head of Pharaoh Menuhotep across from it. Before leaving the room, peek through the door into the outdoor niche, which contains the giant bronze fir cone found near the Thermae of Agrippa, and to which Dante compared the giant's face ("just as wide as St. Peter's cone in Rome") in the *Inferno*.

Chiaramonti Museum. Rather than dwelling on any single work of art here, take a look at the display, which was laid out in the early 19th century by Neoclassical sculptor Antonio Canova. If you can't resist lingering just a little, concentrate on the realistically human portrait busts of ancient Romans.

Pio-Clementino Museum. Two of the most celebrated

antique sculptures in the world are exhibited in Room VIII. The undisputed star is the *Laocoön,* described by Pliny the Elder as "a work to be preferred to all that the arts of painting and sculpture have produced." The first original Greek work of art to be discovered in Rome (it was unearthed in 1506 on the Esquiline Hill), it depicts a passage from the *Aeneid* in which Virgil describes the wrath the gods released on the priest Laocoön for warning the Trojans about the horse, sending two serpents to destroy him and his two sons. In the same room is another famous work, the *Apollo Belvedere* (a Roman copy of a fourth-century B.C. Greek statue once displayed in the Agora in Athens), which influenced Canova's nearby Perseus. Other highlights of this museum are the *Apollo Sauroktonos* (Room V), the *Cnidian Venus* (Room VII), the *Belvedere Torso* (much preferred by the Romantics and Pre-Raphaelites to the Apollo Belvedere; Room III), the *Jupiter of Otricoli* (Room II), and the sarcophagi of Helen and Constantia (Room I).

Gregorian-Etruscan Museum. Highlights here are the Etruscan Regolini-Galassi Tomb (Room II) and *Mars of Todi* (Room III), the Greek *Head of Athena* and funerary stele (Room of Greek Originals), and the Greek amphora of *Achilles and Ajax Playing Morra* (Room XII).

Raphael Stanze. These four rooms were the official apartments of Julius II, who commissioned frescoes from Raphael, the masterpiece of which is *The School of Athens.* According to tradition it contains portraits of Leonardo as Plato, Michelangelo as Heraclitus, and Raphael himself as the figure in the dark cap second from the extreme right.

The Borgia Apartments. Here, Alexander VI had Pinturicchio paint frescoes, of which the richly decorated Room of the Saints is considered the major work.

Sistine Chapel. The chapel has been undergoing cleaning for a decade. Its most famous feature—the ceiling, which depicts scenes from the Book of Genesis—was uncovered last year to reveal the brilliant colors of Michelangelo's original palette. The scaffolding at the end wall covers his *Last Judgment,* the success of whose restoration will not be up for our judgment until completion in 1994.

The Vatican Library. Two paintings predominate here, the Greek Odyssey landscape series and the Roman *Aldobrandini Wedding.* In addition, temporary exhibits display the wonders of the library's rare book and manuscript collection.

Pinacoteca. Paintings by Giotto, Melozzo da Forlì, Raphael, Bellini, Reni, Domenichino, and Poussin will delight the retina still capable of retaining anything after having taken in the rest of the museums.

Before leaving, have a look at the museum gift shop, which, among its many reproductions and religious articles, sells men's ties patterned with papal coats of arms.

The sin of gluttony is not exactly catered to around the Vatican. However, take via del Pellegrino from the museum exit to **Borgo Pio**, the east–west street running parallel to via Corridori/via Borgo to the south, where you'll find a number of prim little restaurants, the nicest of which is probably **Marcello**. It has tables in a vine-covered courtyard during the warmer months and, like its neighbors, serves a standard Italian menu.

St. Peter's Square

After lunch, return to the immense oval of St. Peter's Square, which can now be enjoyed at a leisurely pace without having to worry about the pearly gates of the morning's attractions slamming shut. At noon on Sundays Pope John Paul II gives a blessing from his window in the Apostolic Palace, the second from the right on the top floor. At variable times on Wednesday mornings he holds an audience. In the summer, until the pope moves to his summer residence at Castel Gandolfo (see the Rome Day Trips chapter), it takes place in the piazza. In the winter the audience is held in the new audience hall designed by Pier Luigi Nervi in 1971, for which permission must be received by writing to the Prefect of the Pontifical Household, Città del Vaticano, 00120 Rome, or applied for in advance and in person at the bronze door to the right of the piazza.

On audience days the square is filled with religious pilgrims, often grouped together and carrying banners announcing their places of origin. Even at other times the square is bustling with large-scale activity, as befits a monumental space. Tight phalanxes of black-clad nuns and priests scuttle back and forth on official Vatican business. Schoolteachers lead groups of their uniformed charges and try to distract them from the surrounding grandeur with lectures. Fatigued tourists squint at the immensity of the piazza and the façade of St. Peter's. And the occasional self-contained honeymoon couple from the provinces wanders dazedly toward the basilica. Keeping watch upon it all are the 140 stone saints above Bernini's colonnade and the 13 giant statues over the façade of St. Peter's. For aerial variation, flocks of pigeons swoop freely to and fro, and if you're especially fortunate, it's all topped off by the colossal clusters of cumulus clouds that God seems to have designed especially for Baroque Rome.

The focal point of Bernini's oval piazza is the obelisk at the center, originally from Alexandria, where it had been erected by Augustus, and brought to Rome by Caligula. Not until much later was it erected on its present site; in 1586, chroniclers tell us, 900 men, 140 horses, and 44 winches accomplished the feat. Another account tells of a Ligurian sailor who, defying the papal order to remain silent during the dangerous enterprise, saw that the ropes were about to give out and cried, "*Aigua ae corde!*" an admonition to wet the ropes. He thus saved the day and Pope Sixtus V not only spared his life but rewarded him by starting the tradition of supplying the palms for Palm Sunday from his native port of Bordighera. Apocryphal as the tale may be, it is a charming example of the innumerable secular legends that surround the Vatican.

On either side of the obelisk spout the jets of two Baroque fountains, and between the two fountains and the colonnades is a circle of black marble in the pavement. If the squealing schoolchildren will allow you to stand on it, look toward the colonnade and you'll see the four rows of columns blend into one.

St. Peter's Basilica

Built under Constantine on the site of the tomb of Saint Peter, the original St. Peter's basilica, constructed in 326, was a sumptuous early Christian edifice almost as large as the present one. When the basilica began showing signs of age, the popes decided to build a new one and appointed a succession of architects to supervise the project. Bramante, Raphael, Sangallo, Michelangelo, and others were involved at one point or another, and their designs alternately called for Greek- and Latin-cross plans. Michelangelo's design for a Greek cross and dome was being carried out at the time of his death in 1564, but under Paul V it was decided to extend the front portion to conform to the outlines of Constantine's original basilica. This unfortunately makes Michelangelo's dome appear to sink as you approach the entrance, although it is the glory of the Roman skyline from elsewhere in the city. Carlo Maderno designed the façade and portico (where Giotto's *Navicella* ceiling mosaic from the old basilica was installed) in an early Baroque style.

As you step inside (you will not be admitted wearing

shorts, skirts above the knees, or sleeveless dresses—St. Peter's dress code is stricter than Lutèce's or Claridge's, but the ambience is worth it), the effect is as dazzling as was intended. Perfect proportions mask the vastness of St. Peter's, but spotting the minuscule forms of other visitors beneath the gigantic statues, or a look at the comparative lengths of other European churches—traced in metal on the floor of the nave—confirm its enormous size. The immensity of history is also immediately present at the round porphyry slab set into the pavement in front of the central door: On this stone, on Christmas in the year 800, Leo III crowned the kneeling Charlemagne the first emperor of the Holy Roman Empire.

In the first chapel on the right, Michelangelo's **Pietà** stands behind the glass erected after the sculpture was assaulted in 1972. At the right end of the nave is Arnolfo di Cambio's bronze statue of *St. Peter Enthroned,* its foot worn by the touches and kisses of the faithful over the centuries. Over the high altar soars Bernini's gilded bronze **baldacchino**, its four fluted columns spiraling up to support a canopy crowned by an orb and cross a hundred feet above the floor. Be sure to note the more down-to-earth, human dimension of the carvings of a woman's features in the marble pedestals that support the columns; the facial expressions become progressively more contorted, culminating in the smiling visage of a newborn infant. Legend has it that Pope Urban VII asked Bernini to add the sequence in gratitude for his favorite niece surviving a difficult childbirth.

Bernini was entrusted with the decoration of the interior of St. Peter's, and his works abound throughout. In the apse behind the *baldacchino* is his reliquary of the throne of Saint Peter, topped by a stained-glass representation of the Holy Spirit. His tomb of Alexander VII in the passage leading to the left transept is but one highlight among many magnificent monuments in the church by other artists. The Treasury, reached from the left aisle near the transept, houses a valuable collection of sacred relics. Room III contains Pollaiuolo's tomb of Sixtus IV.

Back near Arnolfo's statue of Saint Peter is the entrance to the **Vatican Grottoes**, a dimly lit church containing a number of chapels and tombs. Beneath them (visitable, again, by written permission from the Prefect of the Pontifical Household) are the famous excavations of what is held to be the original tomb of Saint Peter, where in the 1940s an ancient crypt containing bones and the remains of a garment fitting the description of Saint Peter's were discovered by archaeologists.

For a final survey of your visit to the Vatican, take the elevator at the front of the left aisle for a walk on the roof. Inspired souls may then continue up the 537 steps to the lantern for a last inspirational view of the Vatican, Rome, the Alban Hills, and the surrounding blessed countryside.

GETTING AROUND

International flights generally land at Leonardo da Vinci airport in Fiumicino, about 30 km (20 miles) southwest of Rome. Taxis are available at the airport, and although the trip is expensive (60,000 lire, around $50), it is the most reliable and convenient way of getting into the city. There is limited bus service to the Stazione di Termini railroad station in Rome, and there are trains to the Stazione Ostiense. See the "Useful Facts" section of the Overview for more suggestions.

Ciampino airport, about 16 km (10 miles) southeast of the city, is used mainly by charter flights. ACOTRAL buses provide service to the Cinecittà metro stop; from there you can take the subway to Rome, but unless you know the system, taxis are your best bet.

International (and most national) trains arrive at Rome's central station, Stazione di Termini, from where you can take taxis, buses, or the subway. Some trains arrive at Stazione Tibertina, less central but still served by taxis and buses.

Though construction of Rome's subway line often screeches to a halt when digging unearths some ancient relic, the *Metropolitana* (marked by a large M at the entrances) connects many of Rome's main tourist sights. Tickets may be purchased with exact change, in coins only, in the subway stations. Tobacconists, newsstands, and bars are also supposed to sell subway and bus tickets, but don't count on them.

Rome's bus system is extensive, and various types of tickets—and a valuable map—are available at the ATAC booth in piazza dei Cinquecento across from Stazione di Termini. (Telephone information is available by dialing 46-95.) Those traveling on a tight budget should take a good look at the bus map, since many routes pass major sites. If you buy the week-long tourist pass, you have the advantage of entering the bus from the front during crowded rush hours; watch your belongings. Tickets for single rides are also available at most tobacconists, newsstands, and bars. With these tickets you must board from the back of the bus and put the ticket into a machine that stamps it. The same applies to the city's more limited tram service. The main office of ACOTRAL, which serves the surrounding area, is at via del Telegrafisti 44; Tel: 575-31. A special sightseeing bus, no. 110, leaves from the front of Stazione Termini at 3:30 P.M. in summer and 2:30 P.M. in winter.

Another unusual (if erratic) way of seeing Rome is by boat on the Tiber. The Acquabus service runs the length of the river in the city; for information, call 686-9068. The *Tiber II* goes to the excavated city at Ostia Antica; call 446-3481.

Taxis are found at numerous stands throughout the city, or may be called by dialing 35-70, 38-75, 49-94, or 84-33. There are extra charges, such as for baggage, night service, and holidays, but the additional fee should never be more than a few thousand lire. Tipping is optional.

ACCOMMODATIONS

The rates given below are projections for 1992; always check for up-to-date information before making reservations. Wide ranges may reflect the differences between low- and high-season rates. Unless otherwise indicated, the figures indicate the cost of a double room (per room, not per person). However, half-board (*mezza pensione*) rates, which include breakfast and one other meal per day, are per person. Most hotels will add a service charge of 10 to 15 percent.

The telephone and fax area code for Rome is 06. When telephoning from outside the country, omit the zero in the city code.

"We were well accommodated with three handsome bedrooms, dining room, larder, stable, and kitchen, at twenty crowns a month," wrote Montaigne's secretary of their lodgings in Rome in 1580. "The inns are generally furnished a little better than in Paris, since they have a great deal of gilt leather, with which the lodgings of a certain class are upholstered. We could have had lodging at the same price upholstered with cloth of gold and silk, like that of kings. But Monsieur de Montaigne thought that this magnificence was not only useless but also troublesome on account of the care required by this furniture, for each bed was worth four or five hundred crowns."

Then as now, lodgings in Rome range from the simple and efficient to the unabashedly luxurious, for the city has a tradition of taking care of strangers that goes back to the days when Greeks and Romans first exchanged visits, giving rise to the word *ospite,* which means both guest and host, and is the root of our own *hospitality.*

Most Roman hotels are conveniently clustered into neighborhoods, so you can choose accordingly. The Centro Storico (Old Rome) area offers proximity to major monuments; Villa Borghese affords welcome glimpses of green park; piazza di Spagna is close to Rome's most elegant shops; via Vittorio Veneto has the city's highest concentration of luxury hotels and an active nightlife; and the area near Termini (the train station) is convenient for those travelling with lots of luggage or who need to come and go in a hurry. Hotels in other areas also have their advantages, which are described below.

Centro Storico

An inexpensive option near the piazza of the same name is the **Campo di' Fiori.** A walk-up, its first-floor rooms have been gussied up to include Neo-Baroque ceiling frescoes; the rest of the rooms were all given new baths. Those who make it to the sixth floor can enjoy the rooftop terrace. Via del Biscione 6, 00186; Tel: 654-08-65. £66,000–£85,000.

Montaigne would have felt right at home at the expensive **Cardinal,** appropriately decorated in red fabrics with a heavy touch of leather. Housed in a palazzo attributed to Bramante on Rome's most famous Renaissance street (the rooms on the upper floors offer great views of the whole Renaissance quarter), the hotel possesses antiques that include cardinals' chairs donated by the Vatican and huge stones from the Forum, taken in the days when the site was considered a quarry and now displayed behind the bar. Via Giulia 62, 00186; Tel: 654-27-19. £193,000.

A Borromini palazzo is the unlikely setting for **Navona,** one of the least expensive options in a prime accommodations area. The down-under Australian owners give the atmosphere a downright friendly air and the rooms a down-home Anglo touch. Via dei Sediari 8, 00186; Tel: 686-42-03. £44,000–£78,000.

Spacious light-filled rooms (some with views of St. Peter's) are the hallmark of the **Ponte Sisto,** a reasonably priced option near the bridge of the same name. Via dei Pettinari 8, 00186; Tel: 686-8843; Fax: 654-8822. £127,000.

The 150-year-old **Portoghesi,** located in one of Rome's priciest neighborhoods for hotels, is small and inexpensive, and recent efforts to update it have hardly touched its slightly bohemian atmosphere. Depending on your point of view, the service is laissez-faire or lackadaisical. Via dei Portoghesi 1, 00186; Tel: 686-42-31; Fax: 687-69-76. Ł73,000–Ł115,000.

The tiny (13-room) **Teatro di Pompeo**, built above the ruins of the Theater of Pompey (where Julius Caesar was assassinated), offers reasonably priced accommodations on a small piazza. Largo del Pallaro 8, 00186; Tel: 687-2812; Fax: 654-5531. Ł127,000.

Discretion is the rule at the vine-covered **Raphael**, a favorite of jet-setters and Italian politicians. The lobby, an interior decorator's tour de force, blends antiques with modern marble, and though the rooms are small, the views from the upper floors and rooftop terrace are quite expansive—and expensive. Largo Febo 2, 00180; Tel: 650-88-52. Ł284,000–Ł325,000.

Dating from 1493, **Sole al Pantheon** is considered the oldest hotel in Rome; its façade displays plaques attesting to the stays here of Ariosto (author of *Orlando Furioso*) in 1513 and Pietro Mascagni (composer of *Cavalleria Rusticana*) in 1890. Opening the shutters onto Western architecture's most venerated monument—the Pantheon—makes it worth the price. Piazza della Rotonda 63, 00186; Tel: 678-04-41. Ł280,000–Ł330,000.

Even closer to the Pantheon and more moderately priced than the Sole is the **Hotel Senato**. Its jazzy but narrow postmodern lobby leads to less jazzy but serviceable rooms. The tiny elevator is an appropriate prelude to the size of the rooms, but when you open your window on the Pantheon, who's counting square feet? Piazza della Rotonda 73, 00186; Tel: 679-32-31; Fax: 684-02-97. Ł165,000.

On the other side of the Pantheon, the **Holiday Inn Crowne Plaza Minerva** recently opened after the property, once a hotel where George Sand and Marie-Henri Beyle (Stendhal) slept on different occasions, was renovated and modernized by noted architect Paolo Portoghesi. You'll pay handsomely for handsome business-traveller-style amenities such as non-smoking rooms and satellite TV. Piazza della Minerva 69, 00186; Tel: 684-1888; Fax: 679-4165. Ł428,500–Ł478,500.

An alternative just across the street is the **Hotel Santa Chiara**, where the antiques-furnished rooms (with and without bath) were completely renovated by a less expensive architect, if the more affordable prices are any indication. Via Santa Chiara 21, 00186; Tel: 654-01-42; Fax: 687-31-44. Ł60,000–Ł127,000.

Villa Borghese

The **Eden** is located in the chic Ludovisi area off via Veneto, and is one of the best values in the luxury price range, with views of more green per lira than any hotel in Rome. Built at the turn of the century, the hotel gives guests a choice of antique or modern accommodations, and its roof-garden bar and restaurant is a favorite Roman rendezvous spot (see the Dining and Nightlife sections). Via Ludovisi 49, 00187; Tel: 474-35-51; Fax: 482-15-84. £476,000–£530,000.

For a view of the green expanses of the Villa Borghese (albeit jaundiced by the gold-tinted windows), ask for a room facing the gardens at the **Jolly Vittorio Veneto**, a somewhat expensive modern hotel convenient to both the park and via Veneto. Corso d'Italia 1, 00198; Tel: 84-95; Fax: 884-11-04. In U.S., Tel: (212) 213-1468 or (800) 221-2626; Fax: (212) 213-2369. In U.K., Tel: (923) 89-62-72 or (0800) 28-27-29; Fax: (923) 89-60-71. £255,000–£375,000.

Also near both the Villa Borghese and via Veneto is the **Golden Residence**, whose windows are *not* golden and which offers modern, comfortable accommodations at a rather more modest price; in addition, each room comes equipped with heating, air conditioning, mini-bar, telephone, and radio. Via Marche 84, 00187; Tel: 482-16-60; Fax: same. £139,000.

Perhaps because of its past as a house of ill repute, the luxury-class **Valadier** has some of the largest bathrooms in Rome. Located just below Pincio Hill, the marble-clad Art Nouveau villa also has spacious rooms and lounges, and has just opened a restaurant. Via della Fontanella 15, 00187; Tel: 361-05-92; Fax: 320-15-58. £370,000.

Marvelous views of the park may be had from the upper floors and roof garden of the **Victoria**, on the via Veneto side of the Villa Borghese. Its facilities are chic and modern, and are among the few in Rome with good services for the handicapped. Via Campania 41, 00187; Tel: 47-39-31; Fax: 494-13-30. £220,000–£350,000.

Piazza di Spagna

The **Carriage** is named after the street where the touring carriages of yesteryear used to stop for repairs. That atmosphere is preserved in this small hotel furnished in antique style with modern bathrooms. The best rooms are clustered around a terrace on the top floor. Via delle Carrozze 36, 00187; Tel: 679-33-12; Fax: 678-82-79. £210,000.

Rooms with views of the surrounding area may also be had at **Condotti**, located just off Rome's chicest shopping street. The accommodations are likewise drop-dead chic, but what you spend on leather goods you'll save on shoe leather and the bill in this establishment, recently taken over by new owners and made even more pristine. Via Mario dei Fiori 37, 00187; Tel: 679-46-61. ₤203,000.

With its Oriental rugs, crystal chandeliers, and marble tables, the **De La Ville Inter-Continental** is for many the quintessence of Old World charm—and you pay for it. Located at the top of the Spanish Steps close to the Hassler, its upper floors and roof garden (which offers Sunday brunch) share the same views as its even more expensive counterpart, while the rooms on the lower floors overlook a central courtyard. Via Sistina 69, 00187; Tel: 673-31; Fax: 678-42-13. ₤371,000–₤492,000.

The now pricey **D'Inghilterra** was a refuge for writers (Henry James, Mark Twain, Anatole France, Ernest Hemingway), musicians (Franz Liszt, Felix Mendelssohn), and royalty (the king of Portugal) for over a century. Its prices have placed it beyond most writers' means, however. Whether or not you're a guest (and if you are, request an upper room with a terrace and a view), its bar and newly opened restaurant, the Roman Garden, make refreshing stopovers while shopping the streets in the nearby via Condotti area. (See Dining.) Via Bocca di Leone 14, 00187; Tel: 67-21-61; Fax: 684-08-28. ₤333,000–₤404,000.

The small and stylish **Gregoriana** was decorated by Erté, and the rooms bear his anthropomorphic letters rather than numbers. Located in the area at the top of the Spanish Steps in a former convent on the appealing street of Rome's *haute couture* houses (take a look at the amusingly grotesque palazzo façade at number 30) that also attracts a fashion-world crowd, the 19-room hotel does not take credit cards. Via Gregoriana 18, 00187; Tel: 679-42-69. ₤120,000–₤185,000.

The sumptuous **Hassler–Villa Medici** is the preferred hotel of many of Rome's most distinguished visitors, from American presidents to movie stars, whose presence seems to lend it an air of prewar luxury reminiscent of an ocean liner. Firmly moored at the top of the Spanish Steps, it is crowned with one of the city's most elegant restaurants, which also serves Sunday brunch. At these prices, ask for a room with a view of the city or the gardens behind the hotel. No credit cards accepted. Piazza Trinità dei Monti 6, 00187; Tel: 679-26-51; Fax: 678-99-91. In U.S., Tel: (212) 838-3110 or (800) 223-6800; Fax: (212) 758-7367. In U.K., Tel: (0800) 18-11-23; Fax: (071) 353-1904. ₤470,000–₤560,000.

A reasonably priced alternative for those who want to stay in the neighborhood is **King**, just down the street from the Hassler. Its sparsely decorated rooms are comfortable, and the rooftop terrace has more of those wonderful views. Via Sistina 131, 00187; Tel: 474-34-87; Fax: 49-10-47. Ł130,000–Ł185,000.

Another reasonably priced hotel in the area (nearer piazza del Popolo) is **Margutta**, decorated in bold colors that reflect the artistic spirit of the nearby street from which it takes its name. Two of its 21 rooms are on the roof and come with fireplaces and terrace. Via Laurina 34, 00187; Tel: 361-41-93. Ł105,000.

Reservations are also required for the moderately priced **Scalanita di Spagna**, opposite the Hassler at the top of the Spanish Steps, and sharing those gorgeous views. It too has a roof terrace for even better views to go with your breakfast. Piazza Trinità dei Monti 17, 00187; Tel: 684-05-98; Fax: 679-95-82. Ł213,000.

Reflecting its name, the **Suisse** is efficiently run, with rooms furnished in a choice of antique or modern style, a charming roof terrace characteristic of the area, and a clientele loyal enough (and rates low enough) to require reservations well in advance. Via Gregoriana 56, 00187; Tel: 678-36-49. Ł118,000.

The frugal option on a street lined with grand hotels, **Venier** manages to maintain an old-fashioned room-with-a-view *pensione* character (though few of the rooms *do* have views) in the old-fashioned foreigners' quarter. Via Sistina 42, 00187; Tel: 679-17-44. Ł66,500–Ł85,000.

Via Vittorio Veneto

Set in a 19th-century mansion, the reasonably priced **Alexandra** is a fourth-generation family-run establishment where the rooms have recently been renovated; the breakfast room was designed by architect Paolo Portoghesi. Via Vittorio Veneto 18, 00187; Tel: 488-1943; Fax: 487-1804. Ł120,000–Ł127,000.

Opposite the American Embassy, the **Ambasciatori Palace** offers large and luxurious accommodations in a modern setting, and has a lively bar popular with embassy types and their guests, as well as one of the better restaurants if you happen to be in the vicinity, the **ABC Grill Bar**. Via Vittorio Veneto 70, 00187; Tel: 474-93; Fax: 679-93-03. Ł300,000–Ł400,000.

Despite its monotonous marble façade, the **Bernini Bristol**, at the foot of via Veneto, has luxurious rooms furnished in a modern style reminiscent of the dolce vita days. All rooms are soundproofed to keep out the constant traffic noise, and the ones on the upper floors, like the roof terrace, have pleasant views of the surrounding area. Piazza Barberini 23, 00187; Tel: 46-30-51; Fax: 482-42-66. £280,000–£550,000.

The pricey **Boston**, decorated in velvet and reproductions of Grand Tour–era furniture, lives up to the Jamesian implications of its name and is popular with American visitors. Ask for rooms with views of the Villa Borghese. The bar, downstairs, has the intimacy of a private club where American businessmen often meet their Italian counterparts for *un drink*. Via Lombardia 47, 00187; Tel. 47-39-51. £189,000–£234,000.

The **Excelsior** excelled as the residence of Liz Taylor and other Hollywood stars during the dolce vita era, and its roomy, luxurious suites and well-appointed rooms decorated in the French Empire style live up to the hotel's glorious past. Via Vittorio Veneto 125, 00187; Tel: 47-08; Fax: 482-62-05. In U.S., Tel: (212) 935-9540 or (800) 221-2340; Fax: (212) 421-5929. In U.K., Tel: (071) 930-4147 or (0800) 28-92-34; Fax: (071) 839-1566. £323,000–£569,500.

Offering the most discreet service of the via Veneto hotels, **Flora** has Old World decor to match. Its location just inside the Aurelian Wall on the other side of the Villa Borghese gives the upper floors great views of the park, and its Empire Bar is a popular via Veneto watering hole. Via Vittoria Veneto 191, 00187; Tel: 49-78-21; Fax: 482-03-59. £242,000–£396,000.

Quirinal

The name of the **Anglo-Americano** has served to draw a proper Anglophone clientele to its modern facilities, an upholsterer's apotheosis. Set next to Palazzo Barberini, its rooms have a tranquil air, especially the ones facing the palazzo's gardens. Via delle Quattro Fontane 12, 00184; Tel: 47-29-41; Fax: 474-64-28. £125,000–£227,000.

Originally built during the Renaissance with material taken from the nearby Imperial and Roman forums, the **Forum**, luxuriously appointed with antique furnishings and modern fixtures, overlooks both sites in a setting that transcends time; a meal or drink in its roof restaurant is one of the most relaxing ways to appreciate ancient and contemporary Rome, with an enchanting view of its namesake. Via Tor de' Conti 25, 00184; Tel: 679-24-46; Fax: 678-64-79. £296,000–£370,000.

The expensive **Quirinale** was designed by Achille Sfondrini, the architect of the adjacent Teatro dell'Opera and the passageway that leads to it from the hotel lobby. Its rooms are modern, and the ones that face the garden are preferred by its substantially North American clientele. Verdi's sojourn here in 1893 for the premiere of *Falstaff* set the stage for the hotel's bar becoming a popular place for a drink before a night at the opera. Via Nazionale 7, 00184; Tel: 47-07; Fax: 482-00-99. ₤242,000–₤330,000.

A moderately priced option is the **Trevi**, overlooking the fountain of the same name. If you'd rather avoid the excitement of the bustling piazza, ask for one of the inside rooms (be warned, they're rather small), which recapture the quietude of the building's original function as a Medieval monastery. A small rooftop garden completes the experience. Vicolo del Babuccio 21, 00187; Tel: 678-95-63; Fax: 68-41-40. ₤127,000.

Also near the opera is the **Viminale**, a small, moderately priced hotel offering modern accommodations and a rooftop terrace with a view of the twin domes of the basilica of Santa Maria Maggiore. Via Cesare Balbo 31, 00184; Tel: 488-19-80; Fax: 474-47-28. ₤140,000.

Near the Station

The grandness of **Le Grand Hotel et de Rome** is not diminished by its location near piazza della Repubblica, which has fallen from the glory it once enjoyed at the turn of the century. The hotel boasts rooms and suites whose elegance is matched by the appointments of the expansive public areas, where an elaborate tea is served in the afternoon accompanied by live music. Its romantic apricot-colored **Le Grand Bar** is still the place for a business or romantic rendezvous, and its **Le Restaurant** is a viable part of the Roman gastronomical scene (see the Dining section). Via Vittorio Emanuele Orlando 3, 00185; Tel: 47-09; Fax: 474-73-07. In U.S., Tel: (212) 838-3110 or (800) 223-6800; Fax: (212) 758-7367. In U.K., Tel: (0800) 18-11-23; Fax: (071) 353-1904. ₤325,000–₤594,500.

Moderately priced, the tastefully modern **Marcella** is another option in the area between the train station and via Veneto, and has a roof garden with panoramic views stretching from St. Peter's to the Alban Hills. Via Flavia 96, 00187; Tel: 474-64-51; Fax: 481-58-32. ₤140,000–₤210,000.

Large rooms and a location convenient to the train station and public transportation make the **Massimo d'Azeglio** popular, while the service somehow manages to remain courteous. Begun as a restaurant over a century ago by the great-grandfather of the present owner, the hotel maintains its reputation for Old World courtesy, and its restaurant (see the

Dining section) is still among the best in Rome. Via Cavour 18, 00184; Tel: 488-06-46; Fax: 482-73-86. In U.S., Tel: (212) 599-8280 or (800) 223-9832; Fax: (212) 599-1755. £142,000–£284,500.

Like its sister hotel the Massimo d'Azeglio, the **Mediterraneo** does a brisk business in tour groups, and also has in common with its counterpart an efficiency and courtesy that make it an elegant oasis in a nondescript but well-located area. Its roof garden is a veritable Eden, providing extensive views of the city. Via Cavour 15, 00184; Tel: 488-40-51; Fax: 474-41-05. In U.S., Tel: (212) 599-8280 or (800) 223-9832; Fax: (212) 599-1755. £232,000–£326,500.

The friendly and helpful English-speaking management and the recent refurbishment of the **Morgana** set it apart from the other options on this otherwise undistinguished street a block from the train station. Via Filippo Turati 37, 00185; Tel: 446-72-30; Fax: 731-65-47. £95,000–£127,000.

Located opposite Le Grand is the **Sitea**, whose eclectic decor and sprawling layout reflect the character of its Italian owner and his Scottish wife. The reception desk is made from an antique altar, and other period pieces are displayed in showcases scattered about its five rambling floors. Topping it all off is a display of 18th-century Neapolitan nativity scenes on the roof terrace and bar. Via Vittorio Emanuele Orlando 90, 00185; Tel: 482-75-60; Fax: 481-76-37. £160,000–£242,000.

A quiet oasis through a courtyard on a street that is making a concerted effort to improve on its admittedly somewhat squalid present state is **Di Rienzo**. The friendly family-run establishment has the pleasantly worn feeling of having been around for years, though its simply furnished rooms are maintained with pride. Via Principe Amadeo 79/a, 00185; Tel: 73-69-56. £55,000.

A former private villa is the setting for the **Villa della Rose**, a quiet hotel in a still-residential quarter behind the station. Besides convenience to transportation, it also has a getaway garden. Via Vicenza 5, 00185; Tel: 445-17-88. £83,500–£115,000.

Accommodations in monasteries and convents are scattered throughout town; clearinghouses for such religious institutions, called **Protezione della Giovane**, are located inside Stazione Termini (Tel: 475-15-94) and nearby at via Urbana 158 (Tel: 46-00-56). Curfews of anywhere from 10:30 P.M. to midnight are usually imposed, but for non-night-owls, these clean, inexpensive rooms are a bargain. £30,000.

The Vatican

Housed in a Renaissance palazzo with appropriately splendorous lobby decor, the **Alicorni** is moderately priced if inconsistent in the size and amenities of its rooms. Ask to see one first. Via Scossacavalli 11, 00193; Tel: 687-52-35; Fax: 686-50-78. ₤94,000–₤127,000.

Immaculate is the word for **Alimandi**, a surprisingly high-concept (jazzy public rooms including a piano bar) though low-priced former *pensione* convenient to the Vatican Museums and peacefully providing its own terrace and garden. Via Tunisi 8, 00192; Tel: 679-93-43; Fax: 31-44-57. ₤65,000–₤95,000.

The unabashedly modern, expensive **Atlante Star** has a roof-garden restaurant, **Les Etoiles** (see Dining), with unusually close-up views of St. Peter's, and the unique policy in Rome (which it shares with its sister hotel, the Atlante Garden) of picking up its guests, largely business travellers, at the airport free of charge. Via Giovanni Vitelleschi 34, 00193; Tel: 687-95-58; Fax: 687-23-00. ₤395,000–₤420,000.

The **Atlante Garden** is the proper older sister of the Atlante Star, offering tastefully renovated Old World–style accommodations at the same rates along with its free airport service. Via Crescenzio 78/a, 00193; Tel: 687-23-61; Fax: 687-23-15. ₤250,000–₤295,000.

Formerly the Renaissance palazzo of Pope Julius II, the moderately priced **Columbus** maintains some of its sumptuous trappings in the lobby and public rooms, though management has opted for simplicity in the private rooms. The combination, and the fact that the hotel is a block from St. Peter's, might account for the large numbers of clergy among its clientele. Via della Conciliazione 33, 00193; Tel: 686-54-35; Fax: 686-48-74. ₤155,000–₤210,000.

Other Places in Rome

With pool, tennis courts, bars, and restaurants (see the Dining section), the luxurious **Cavalieri Hilton** is such a self-contained unit that many of its guests never get into the city. Nevertheless, its privileged position high atop Monte Mario (north of the Vatican) gives it some of the best views of Rome, and a bus regularly shuttles guests to the Spanish Steps and then returns them—usually laden with luxury goods—to the hotel. Via Alberto Cadlolo 101, 00136; Tel: 315-11; Fax: 31-51-22-41. ₤350,000–₤520,000.

Located in the quiet Prati quarter just north of the Vatican, the inexpensive and functionally furnished **Forti's Guest**

House is a block from the Tiber and convenient to all forms of public transportation; the Italian-American management is friendly and helpful as well. Via Fornovo 7, 00192; Tel: 320-07-38. ₤43,000–₤57,000.

The imperially priced **Giulio Cesare** is located in a quiet residential neighborhood on the Vatican side of the Tiber, not far from Castel Sant'Angelo. All rooms are fitted with tasteful old-fashioned furnishings and modern bathrooms; particularly restful are the rooms (many with balconies) overlooking the tree-filled garden. Via degli Scipioni 287, 00192; Tel: 321-07-51; Fax: 321-17-36. ₤260,000–₤370,000.

Located in a residential area between piazza del Popolo and the Tiber, the **Locarno** offers small, comfortable rooms and an attractive bar and roof terrace in a relatively untrafficked spot ideal for romantic walks along the river and café-sitting in piazza del Popolo; it's not too far from the Borghese Gardens or the shopping district near the Spanish Steps, either. Via della Penna 22, 00186; Tel: 361-08-41; Fax: 321-52-49. ₤127,000.

In the exclusive residential neighborhood of Parioli behind the Villa Borghese, the luxurious **Lord Byron**, decorated in subtle tones and bursts of fresh flowers that attract a well-heeled clientele, is one of the quietest hotels in town; its restaurant (see the Dining section) is also one of the city's best. Via Giuseppe de Notaris 5, 00197; Tel: 322-45-41; Fax: 322-04-05. In U.S., Tel: (212) 838-3110 or (800) 223-6800; Fax: (212) 758-7367. In U.K., Tel: (0800) 18-11-23; Fax: (071) 353-1904. ₤430,000–₤480,000.

—*Dwight V. Gast*

DINING

Rome's penchant for the table is legendary. Its roots go back to the Lucullus-style banquets satirized by Petronius in his *Satyricon* and re-created by Fellini for the cinema in our time. Even today, nothing gives a Roman more pleasure than an outing at the local *osteria*—the simple neighborhood eatery more abundant in Rome than anywhere else in Italy—for a loud and lengthy meal accompanied by many a *fujetta* (the glass carafe introduced by the ever-efficient Pope Sixtus V) of Colli Albani wine.

The *osteria* is the essence of Roman dining, for the best restaurants in town are neither trendy nor fussy. The *osteria* traditionally serves such regional Roman dishes as *coda alla vaccinara* (oxtail stew), *rigatoni e pajata* (tubular pasta prepared with veal intestines), tripe, and sweetbreads, but if you have a weak stomach (or are not particularly fond of eating one), there are a number of other Roman specialties found in *osterie* and in the more formal Roman restaurants.

A complete Roman meal begins with *antipasti* of everything from vegetables to salami and shellfish, often selected from a large table set up as a lure near the entrance of the restaurant, or *bruschetta,* a garlic bread topped with tomato sauce. The most popular pasta dish is spaghetti, served *alla carbonara* (with bacon, egg, cheese, and pepper), *all'amatriciana* (in a tomato sauce with onions, bacon, and cheese), *all'arrabbiata* (with a peppery tomato and garlic sauce), or *alla puttanesca* (with a sauce made from tomatoes, capers, and black olives). The hollow spaghetti called *bucatini,* the quill-shaped pasta called *penne,* and *fettuccine* are also popular forms of pasta, and on Thursdays restaurants in Rome offer *gnocchi* (potato dumplings) as a first course.

An increasingly popular choice for a light main course is grilled *scamorza* cheese (due to inevitable changes in eating habits and the profusion of cooks from Abruzzi, where the cheese originates), but meat dishes are as abundant as ever. The best-known is *saltimbocca alla romana* (sliced veal prepared with prosciutto, cheese, and sage); other typical entrées are *abbacchio* (baby lamb), *capretto* (kid), and *porchetta* (suckling pig roasted with herbs), which are often eaten with a salad of one of the local greens unknown outside the Rome area, such as the crunchy *puntarelle,* served with a dressing made with anchovies and garlic, or the more traditional arugula or roast peppers.

Accompany your meal with the local Colli Albani, Frascati, or Marino wines, or try the Latium Est! Est!! Est!!!, the wine that was considered so good by the servant and wine scout of a certain 12th-century Bishop Fugger that an establishment selling it was enthusiastically marked with those words (they mean "it is" in Latin) for the good bishop. Traditional Roman digestives are sambuca (an elder-flavored liqueur—reminiscent of anise—in which you are supposed to place three coffee beans, referred to as *mosche,* or flies), the sweet, saffrony Strega, or the ever-popular grappa.

Rome's role as the country's seat of government has brought one good side effect along with the nightmarish bureaucracy. There is a profusion of regional restaurants in the city, perhaps a better argument for making Rome the nation's capital than Garibaldi could ever have made. In fact, you can become acquainted with some of the best culinary aspects of the entire Italian peninsula in a taxi ride just a few minutes long.

Though *cucina nuova,* the Italian counterpart of nouvelle cuisine, has proved to be antithetical to the nation's way of eating, it did serve to foster experimentation among restaurateurs. *Cucina creativa* (creative cuisine) is one manifestation of their efforts, and may best be sampled at some of the restaurants listed below.

Romans eat late (lunch is usually served between 1:00 and 3:00 P.M.; dinner begins at 8:00 P.M. at the earliest), a practice often attributed to their need to discuss restaurant candidates for the meal ad infinitum before deciding where to settle in. This habit may leave some visitors hungry early; however, there are a number of snacks that are often available in neighborhood coffee bars between restaurant hours. *Tramezzini* are the finger sandwiches found throughout Italy, but peculiar to Rome are *supplì,* rice croquettes stuffed with a dollop of mozzarella cheese, then breaded and fried; *filetti di baccalà,* strips of dried cod batter-dipped and fried; and sandwiches made of *porchetta.*

The following restaurants, organized in the same neighborhood order as our narrative, should guide but not limit your dining choices. Don't forget to note the weekly closing days and the summer and Christmastime holiday schedules, and remember that the loyalty of the regular clientele usually makes reservations necessary.

If you find it difficult to get a reservation, remember that Rome has some five thousand such establishments, and the joy of discovery that characterizes the city also applies to its eateries. As a rule of thumb, to ensure quality when choosing an unfamiliar restaurant, look for a handwritten daily menu, a fresh display of antipasto, and an appreciative local crowd. Once you've sat down, don't expect to get up for some time, for you'll have become part of Rome's time-honored ritual of *sapersi contentare*—that distinctively Roman knack for knowing how to enjoy oneself.

Ancient Rome

The owner of **Alvaro al Circo Massimo,** at via dei Cerchi 53, is shaped like the Circus Maximus, from which his place takes its name. The fish dishes are generally the better choice here during the summer, when there are a few outdoor tables for alfresco dining, and game is appropriate during the winter, but let Alvaro order for you if money is no object. Closed Mondays and August. Tel: 678-61-12.

Located at piazzale del Colosseo 15, **Hostaria Il Gladiatore** is best appreciated during the warm weather, when outdoor tables spill out onto the street. Abundant portions of Roman food are served here. Closed Wednesdays and national holidays. Tel: 73-62-76.

Located in the former stable of a Medieval palazzo near the Foro di Traiano at salita del Grillo 6, **La Tana del Grillo** is one of the few restaurants in Rome to feature the cuisine of Romagna. Spicy sausage antipasti, pasta with meaty ragù sauce, and rich desserts are the order of the day here, to be downed with sparkling red Lambrusco wine and finished with *nocino,* a digestive liqueur made from walnuts. Closed Sundays and August. Tel: 679-87-05.

A unique marriage of a Sicilian and an Emilian makes the cuisine of the tiny and quiet **Ai Tre Scalini Rossana e Matteo**, at via Santissimi Quattro 30, a side street near the Colosseum, one of the most unusual dining experiences in Rome. This, as they say in Italian, is a *ristorante serio,* a serious restaurant, and the devotion both owners have to creating original and refined dishes based on simple Italian ingredients is apparent to the eye, palate, and pocketbook. Closed Mondays and holidays. Tel: 709-63-09.

Ulpia overlooks the basilica of the same name in the Foro Traiano. Its menu is standard Italian, but if it's food with a view you want (with a decided emphasis on the latter), this is the place. You'll be sharing both with the legions of cats that inhabit the grounds of the forum below, waiting for scraps; the forbidding statue of the goddess Ulpia indoors might force you to make just such a sacrifice. Closed Sundays. Tel: 679-99-80; Fax: 679-62-71.

Pantheon

Though located in a frescoed 16th-century palazzo, **Le Volte**, at piazza Rondanini 47–47/a, serves chic and simple pizza along with an equally understated version of Roman cuisine. The owner is justly proud of his dessert *ciambelle,* ring-shaped cookies made with (and to be dunked in) white wine. Closed Tuesdays. Tel: 687-74-08.

On the street of the same name, **La Rosetta** ranks high among Rome's fish restaurants, with the catch from Sicily arriving fresh daily. Everything is prepared simply, out of respect for the taste of the fish, but the Sicilian influence becomes evident in pasta dishes accompanied by sardines, grapes, or fennel, as well as in the deeply chilled Corvo wine. Closed Sundays, Monday lunch, and August. Tel: 656-10-02.

On the other street leading to the Pantheon is **Da Fortunato**, which serves classic Roman cuisine popular with politicians and North Americans who can afford it. The Saturday-night special is *trippa alla romana,* tripe served in a tomato sauce with ham, garlic, parsley, and mint. Closed Sundays and national holidays. No credit cards. Tel: 679-27-88.

Piazza Navona

The Venetian-inspired menu and glamorous, discreet surroundings make **El Toulà** on via della Lupa one of the best of this Italian chain—for those who can afford it. Stick with the simpler items on the menu if you're here for the food. Most people aren't: Italian politicians and movie stars like to be seen dining here, sometimes together. Closed Saturday lunch, Sundays, and August. Tel: 687-34-98; Fax: 687-11-15.

If you eat in one non-Italian restaurant in Rome, make it **Chez Albert**, at vicolo della Vaccarella 11. The French owner-chef of this small establishment serves the Gallic standards (nothing *nouvelle* about this cuisine) in such classic fashion that local French clubs make field trips here. At Christmastime, if you absolutely have to have stuffed turkey, *voilà*. Closed Sundays, Monday lunch, Tuesdays, and Wednesdays. Tel: 656-55-49.

A relative newcomer on via dei Coronari, **Il Giogo**, at number 233, offers Roman classics along with the still-trendy pasta *alla vodka* (with a vodka-based tomato sauce) and risotto *allo champagne* (with a Champagne-based sauce), all in a smallish and sophisticated setting in keeping with the upscale theme of the antiques shops that surround it. Closed Sundays. Tel: 686-58-90.

L'Orso Ottanta, at via dell'Orso 33, passes the antipasto test with flying colors. There's a generous table of it at the entrance, and the husband-and-wife team from the Abruzzi sees to it you eat your fill. The pasta dishes and main courses are equally abundant, but after all that antipasto, you'll probably just want a pizza. Closed Sunday evening, Mondays, and August. Tel: 686-49-04.

More Abruzzese specialties are to be had at **La Majella**, piazza Sant'Apollinare 45, a favorite with the Roman rich and famous. *Maccheroni alla chitarra* (pasta sliced thin on a guitarlike instrument), various types of risotto (with everything from zucchini flowers to Champagne), *abbacchio* (baby lamb), *porchetta* (roast pig), and game dishes are all highly recommended here. Closed Sundays and one week in August. Tel: 656-41-74.

The view of piazza Navona is the drawing card of **Mastrostefano**, where you'll eat practically in the mist from Gian Lorenzo Bernini's *Fontana dei Quattro Fiumi* (Fountain of the Four Rivers), which overlooks the considerable activities of the piazza. As if that weren't enough in itself, some of the food—especially the Roman dishes such as *porchetta* and *abbacchio* (lamb)—isn't bad either. Closed Mondays and the last two weeks in August. Tel: 654-28-55.

Osteria dell'Antiquaro serves highly refined Italian cuisine such as *lasagne con melanzane al sugo di anatra* (lasagna with eggplant in duck sauce) and *coscio di anatra alle erbe in casseruola* (herbed thigh of duck in casserole) in the tiny piazza San Simeone, which makes it one of the most intimate summer dining experiences in Rome. Dinner only. Closed Sundays and one week in August. Tel: 687-96-94.

For those to whom dining must be an educational experience, **Papà Giovanni**, at via dei Sediari 4, is a tasteful classroom. The owner-chef takes great pains to create highly personal gastronomic statements that vary with the vagaries of the market and the chef, but *vermicello cacio e pepe* (thin spaghetti with cheese and pepper) is available year-round. On the wine list, pay attention (and pay you will, for everything) to the ones from Latium. Reservations are a must at this Roman temple of gastronomy. Closed Sundays and August. Tel: 686-53-08.

With a number of changes of management in recent years, **Pino e Dino**, at piazza di Montevecchio 22, has retained its name and maintained its fame. The inventive seasonal menu (you'll pay for the creativity) includes strudel of funghi, boar with blueberries, and other rich variations on a basically Italian theme. Closed Mondays, one week in August, and three weeks in January. Tel: 686-13-19.

Pizzeria Baffetto, at via del Governo Vecchio 114, is an active and inexpensive location filled with young Romans. Outdoor tables right on the busy street enliven the festivities. Closed Sundays and August. Tel: 686-16-17.

An even less expensive alternative is **Monte Carlo** at vicolo Savelli 11-13, another popular spot where you can sample pizza that some say rivals Baffetto's, or choose from a groaning antipasto table. Closed Mondays and August. Tel: 686-18-77.

Once a not-so-simple inn that hosted Dante and Rabelais, **Hostaria dell'Orso**, at via dei Soldati 25, has retained its palatial look, with cuisine and prices to match. Many diners go from the table to the **Cabala Discotheque** upstairs. Dinner only. Closed Sundays. No credit cards. Tel: 686-42-50.

On via de Baullari, near campo dei Fiori, **Filetti di Baccalà** is always filled with young people, especially on Friday evenings when they come from all over Rome to taste the specialty for which the restaurant is named— fried cod, served at paper-covered communal tables and accompanied by the strong house white. Closed Sundays and August; Tel: 686-4018.

Campo dei Fiori

Roman specialties are the rule at **Il Cardinale**, a palatial establishment at via delle Carceri 6, on the corner of via Giulia. Run by the wife of Papa Giovanni, it, too, is noted for its fresh vegetables selected daily from campo dei Fiori, as well as for its refined sorbets. The Jewish aspect of Roman cuisine is also featured here, with excellent artichokes along with *rughetta* and *pecorino romano*. Closed Sundays, holidays, and August. Tel: 686-93-36.

As if it weren't enough to dine in the entrance of the Theater of Pompey, where Julius Caesar was assassinated, how nice to be able to sample some classic local cuisine. **Costanza**, at piazza del Paradiso 65, offers some of the best Roman cuisine in town. All the grilled meats and fish are highly recommended, and the influence of the nearby Jewish ghetto may be tasted in the *carciofi alla giudia,* artichokes fried Jewish-style. Closed Sundays and August. Tel: 686-17-17.

Il Pianeta Terra di Patrizia e Roberto, at via Arco del Monte 94, is another rarity in Rome, run by a Tuscan rugby player and his Sicilian lawyer wife. Its inventive menu includes such dishes as *ravioli d'oca al Barolo* (ravioli stuffed with goose prepared with Barolo wine) and *petto d'oca in salsa di prugne* (breast of goose in plum sauce). French wines have made inroads here, too, as have prices that would hold their own on the international market. Dinner only. Closed Mondays and August. Tel: 686-98-93.

The dowager of campo dei Fiori, **La Carbonara** has been going strong since it was founded by the daughter of a coal merchant in the early 1960s as a place for local food sellers to have their early morning meal. Though now few workers can afford it, those who can are particularly fond of its specialty, *penne alla carbonara.* Closed Tuesdays. Tel: 686-47-83.

To call **Il Drappo** (at vicolo del Malpasso) "Sardinian-inspired" is missing the mark. The cuisine here is inspired, period. Sister Angela recently joined the original brother-and-sister team of Paolo and Valentina, and together they produce loving variations on the hearty cuisine of their native island. The menu is seasonal, but try any one of their risottos or their *maialino arrosto* (roast pig), accompanied by *carta di musica* (sheet music) bread and a strong Sardinian wine such as Malvasia. Closed Sundays and two weeks in August. Tel: 687-73-65.

The numerous small dining rooms of **Vecchia Roma**, at piazza Campitelli 18, are an intimate setting for classic Roman cuisine or the restaurant's specialties of *gnocchi Vecchia Roma,* served with cheese sauce, or the *fantasie di polenta* menu, on which all entrées are made with the cornmeal mush called *polenta.* Closed Wednesdays and two weeks in August. Tel: 686-46-04.

Ghetto

Rome's artichokes are famous, and the most famous artichokes in Rome may be found at **Evangelista**, via delle Zoccolette 11, where they are prepared in a variety of appetizing ways for a variety of diners from the ranks of Rome's worlds of politics and entertainment. Also noteworthy is the rest of the menu, which consists of Roman classics finished off with homemade desserts. Dinner only. Closed Sundays and August. Tel: 687-58-10.

Da Giggetto, at via del Portico d'Ottavia 22, is the least fancy of the ghetto restaurants, and the most reasonably priced. It serves all the specialties in the Roman Jewish *cucina povera* (poor man's cuisine) tradition, such as *carciofi alla giudia* (fried artichokes) and *filetti di baccalà* (fried batter-dipped dried cod), along with basic Roman fare. Closed Mondays and July. Tel: 686-11-05.

The liveliest of the ghetto restaurants, on via del Portico d'Ottavia, is **Da Luciano**, another reasonably priced choice in the area. Closed Wednesday lunch. Tel: 687-47-22.

The most established of the ghetto restaurants, **Piperno** is also the most pricey; but if you want exemplary (though non-kosher) versions of the Jewish classics in a setting slightly removed from the hustle and bustle of the ghetto's main street, this is the place (Monte de' Cenci 9). Closed Sunday dinner, Mondays, Christmas, Easter, and August. Tel: 654-06-29.

Trastevere

If you prefer your fish on the refined side, try **Alberto Ciarla** (piazza San Cosimato 40), locally famous for its international menu featuring everything from Maine lobster to Scottish salmon, and a wine list to match. The freshest catch is usually local, however, and the same goes for the olive oil and the Bianco di Velletri Vigna Ciarla white wine, both produced by the owners. Dinner only. Closed Sundays. Tel: 581-86-68; Fax: 688-43-77.

The ultimate tourist experience, **Da Meo Patacca**, piazza dei Mercanti 30, advertised up and down the streets of Rome, puts on a kitsch dinner show of singing minstrels who encourage the tables full of North Americans and Germans to sing along. Though its authenticity is reflected in its name (*patacca* is Roman dialect for fake), the experience can be good fun if you're in the right mood. Dinner only. No credit cards. Tel: 581-61-98.

The most popular spot for pizza in Trastevere is **Pizzeria Panatoni** at viale Trastevere 53-59, where simple surroundings are a foil to a people-watching parade of boisterous young and a seemingly endless supply of pies. Closed Wednesdays and two weeks in August. Tel: 580-09-19.

On a quieter street than the above, but no less bustling inside (and out, during the warmer months), is **Pizzeria Ivo** at via Francesco a Ripa 157-158. Closed Tuesdays and August. Tel: 581-70-82.

To many, dining in Trastevere still means **Sabatini I**, in the piazza facing Santa Maria in Trastevere. The main dining room reeks of atmosphere, with beamed ceilings and frescoed walls, but even better are the crowded and noisy outdoor tables overlooking the church (and watched over by the local pickpockets). Closed Wednesdays and two weeks in August. Tel: 58-20-26.

Sabatini II absorbs the spillage from its namesake listed above, and for those who prefer less boisterous surroundings, this is the place. Located next door, it has the same menu and prices as Sabatini I. Closed Tuesdays, and for two weeks in August when the other is open. Tel: 581-83-07.

The full name of **Tentativo** (via della Luce 5) reads like the title of a Lina Wertmuller film: Tentativo di Descrizione di un Banchetto a Roma (Attempt at a Description of a Banquet in Rome). The creative and pricey attempts here, such as *ravioli d'anatra* (duck ravioli) and *filetto di manzo affumicato con funghi porcini* (fillet of smoked beef with porcini mushrooms), are usually quite successful, with an increasingly international flavor. Closed Sundays and August. Tel: 589-52-34.

Piazza del Popolo

The late Roman restaurateur Alfredo, self-proclaimed King of Fettuccine and creator of *fettuccine all'Alfredo,* was popular with Americans from the day he served fettuccine to Douglas Fairbanks and Mary Pickford with a golden spoon and fork. **Alfredo all'Augusteo l'Originale** continues his tradition at piazza Augusto Imperatore with what they say are the original utensils, and the drama is enhanced by live music, which makes this place an enduring character in the cast of Roman street theater. Closed Sundays. Tel: 687-86-15.

Dal Bolognese, in the piazza del Popolo, specializes in the cuisine of Bologna, considered the gastronomical capital of Italy. The pasta is all homemade, and any such dish should properly be ordered *al ragù,* with the meat sauce typical of Bologna. Though *cotolette alla bolognese* (breaded veal cutlet with ham) is the most characteristic dish, the *bollito misto* (boiled meats accompanied by a green sauce of parsley, capers, and onions) is an equally good choice. Closed Sunday dinner and Mondays. Tel: 361-14-26.

The setting on Pincio Hill in Villa Borghese is what sells **Casina Valadier**, best for a light alfresco lunch, with plenty of room to let the kids loose while you engage in pleasant people-watching. Closed Mondays. Tel: 679-20-83.

One of Rome's most creative fish restaurants, **Porto di Ripetta** is run by Maria Romani, the daughter of a fisherman. Impulsively, imaginatively, and impeccably, she works her magic on the catch of the day in this quiet and chic restaurant a few steps from piazza del Popolo, at via di Ripetta 250. Closed Sundays and three weeks in August. Tel: 361-23-76.

Piazza di Spagna

A Roman institution, **La Campana** (located on the street of the same name) traces its origins to an *osteria* sited here more than 500 years ago that later became a front for a house of ill repute on the other side of the courtyard. It now serves, impeccably, a classic Roman menu to a lively and sophisticated crowd largely composed of journalists and Italian television personalities, all at moderate prices. Closed Mondays and August. Tel: 687-52-73.

One of the happiest mediums between the generally pricey restaurants and McDonald's in the area is **Al Piccolo Arrancio** at vicolo Scanderberg 112, which serves all the seasonal Roman specialties in a no-nonsense setting. Closed Mondays and August. Tel: 678-61-39.

Pizzeria La Capricciosa (largo dei Lombardi 8) credits itself with the invention of pizza *alla capricciosa,* a capricious blend of just about everything, and the version in this lively, reasonably priced place is certainly as good as any. Closed Tuesdays. Tel: 679-40-27.

One of the most popular spots for pizza in the vicinity is **Pizzeria Al Leoncino** at via del Leoncino 28. Its pies are authentically prepared by hand and baked in the traditional wood-burning oven. Closed Wednesdays and August. Tel: 687-63-06.

Nino, at via Borgognona 11, is one of the nicest Tuscan restaurants in town, serving *pappardelle al sugo di lepre* (wide pasta noodles in a hare sauce), *bistecca alla fiorentina* (thick Florentine steak), and *cannellini* beans—to be eaten with Chianti *a consumo,* meaning you pay only for what you drink from the carafe on the table. Closed Sundays and August. Tel: 679-56-76.

Otello alla Concordia, at via della Croce 81, provides simple meals in a trattoria-type indoor setting decorated with paintings, or beneath a vine-covered pergola during the warmer months. Closed Sundays and two weeks at Christmas. No credit cards. Tel: 679-11-78.

Ranieri 1843, at via Mario de' Fiori 26, has been around at least as long as the date in its name. Giuseppe Ranieri was the restaurant's original owner and chef to Queen Victoria. A classic stop on the Grand Tour itinerary, some find its Old World ambience a bit stuffy, but the ingredients that go into its venerable fish and meat dishes are as fresh as any in town. Closed Sundays. Tel: 679-15-92.

Via Veneto

Andrea is considered one of the best restaurants in Rome, and such dishes as *gamberetti con rughetta* (shrimp with rughetta greens) and *stracetti di manzo con porcini e tartufi* (strips of beef with porcini mushrooms and truffles) certainly uphold any such claims. Flawless service and an intelligent list of Italian wines enhance the pleasures of Andrea's pricey tables; at via Sardegna 26. Closed Sundays, Monday lunch, and three weeks in August. Tel: 482-18-91.

The hearty specialties of Emilia are served in a trattoria-type setting at **Colline Emiliane**, via degli Avignonesi 22, near piazza Barberini. Homemade pasta (made in front of your eyes), *culatello* (a mouth-watering type of prosciutto from Parma), and *l'anitra all'arancia* (duck with orange sauce) are the dishes to order here. There is an excellent selection of Lambrusco and other Emilia-Romagna wines as well. Closed Fridays and August. Tel: 481-75-38.

Osteria Marcello, at via Aurora 37, attracts a crowd (and it *is* crowded) of dolce vita–era actors and other movie industry types, with its numerous pasta-and-vegetable combos and its *brasato* (pot roast simmered in wine). Closed Sundays and August. Tel: 481-94-67.

For those looking for an "international" atmosphere, **Sans**

Souci, at via Sicilia 20, is the expensive answer. Black and gold decor sets the chic scene for elaborate Italian-based dishes, often heavy-handed, such as *ravioli di pesce* (fish ravioi swimming in heavy cream). Dinner only. Closed Mondays and August. Tel: 482-18-14.

Near the Station

At via Merulana 77, **Cicilardone** is inexpensive and extensive in its selection of pasta, various types of which can be sampled all at once if you ask for *assaggini* (little tastes), but the other light selections on the menu make it perfect for lunch if you're in the Santa Maria Maggiore area. Closed Sunday dinner, Mondays, and late July to early August. No credit cards. Tel: 73-38-06.

One of Rome's least expensive fish restaurants, **Cannavota** (piazza di San Giovanni in Laterano) is of the old school in that its owners believe in copious portions and generous amounts of house wine served in hand-painted Faenza pitchers. Large dining rooms and a quick turnover keep things hopping, but the atmosphere is festive, never pressured. Closed Wednesdays and the first three weeks in August. Tel: 77-50-07.

The pizzeria **Est Est Est** claims to be the oldest in Rome. Its copious pies are quite inexpensive and good, and are served in a plain but boisterous setting at via Genova 29 that encourages sampling the ancient wine for which this place is named. Closed Mondays and August. Tel: 46-11-07.

Don't be fooled by the stage-set Neapolitan trappings of **Scoglio di Frisio**, at via Merulana 256, decorated as it is with fishnets and murals of Vesuvius. The food is genuine, largely made up of fish but including such meat dishes as *bistecca alla pizzaiola* (beef stewed in a spicy tomato sauce). Musicians lead diners in rousing choruses of "O Sole Mio" and other Neapolitan standards, adding to the theatrical atmosphere. Closed Sundays in spring and summer, and Mondays in fall and winter. Tel: 487-27-65.

The Vatican

Taverna Giulia specializes in Ligurian cuisine such as pasta *al pesto* (a sauce made from basil), and serves a large number of fish dishes and wines from the same area in the sumptuous setting of a Renaissance palace (vicolo dell'Oro 23). Closed Sundays and August. No credit cards. Tel: 686-97-68.

At borgo Pio, **Marcello** is one of the most pleasant of the rather standard restaurant offerings near the Vatican, but its courtyard, open during the warmer weather, sets it apart from its otherwise indistinguishable neighbors. Closed Fridays and August. Tel: 686-44-62.

Other Places in Rome

Located at via Ancona 14, just outside Porta Pia (north of Termini where the corso d'Italia and via Nomentana meet), **Coriolano** offers outstanding versions of Italian classics, including *ravioli di ricotta e spinaci* (ravioli pasta stuffed with ricotta cheese and spinach) and such Roman dishes as *abbacchio* (lamb) and *capretta* (kid). Closed Sundays, Saturdays in July, and August. Tel: 855-11-22.

The chic place to eat the Roman specialties of various animal innards is **Checchino dal 1887**, at via di Monte Testaccio 30, across from an old slaughterhouse in the neighborhood of Testaccio near the Ostiense train station. The original Checchino invented *coda alla vaccinara* (oxtail stew), which is the most palatable item on the menu for the squeamish. The house Frascati is quite good, and is kept cool in wine cellars carved out of the mountain of broken pottery that is Monte Testaccio. Closed Sundays, Mondays, August, and one week at Christmas. Tel: 574-38-16.

More conventional Roman specialties may be sampled at **Severino a Piazza Zama**, piazza Zama 5, beyond the Terme di Caracalla, which serves excellent *bucatini* and *tagliatelle* pasta, as well as *saltimbocca* and *abbacchio alla romana* (baby lamb). Closed Sunday dinner, Mondays, and August. Tel: 700-08-72.

Hotel Restaurants

Charles Roof Garden at the Eden Hotel (via Ludovisi 49) has the greenest views in Rome, made all the more enjoyable by the simple, fundamentally Roman cuisine of this exclusive restaurant, which offers seasonal specialties in an incomparable setting. Lunch overlooking the city skyline is lovely, while in the evening the night light of the city is further softened at the bar. Closed Sundays and August. No credit cards. Tel: 474-35-51; Fax: 482-15-84.

Les Etoiles, the rooftop restaurant of the Hotel Atlante Star (see Accommodations), combines stellar views of St. Peter's with a refined cuisine based on Italian ingredients. Pastas such as gnocchi with funghi porcini and main courses such as pheasant breast with chestnuts are remarkably light; not so such desserts as Bavarian cream torte with strawberries and kiwi. Open seven days. Tel: 687-95-58; Fax: 687-23-00.

A rapidly disappearing Old World elegance is still in evidence at the **Massimo d'Azeglio**, via Cavour 14, which dates from the days when Rome was capital of a newly united Italy. Its copious antipasto wagon rivals anything from the most lavish neighborhood trattoria, and the pasta and main courses are equally generous. Closed Sundays. Tel: 488-06-46.

La Pergola, in the Cavalieri Hilton (via Cadlolo 101), is another restaurant for which Romans go out of their way. Besides the magnificent view of Rome from its setting high above the city on the Vatican side of the Tiber, its menu has a heavy international Italian accent, with dishes such as *carpaccio* (thinly sliced uncooked beef) and seafood with balsamic vinegar. Try the *degustazione* menu, a sampling of house specialties. Dinner only. Closed Sundays and the first three weeks in January. Tel: 315-11; Fax: 315-122-41.

Le Relais La Piscina recently opened a separate entrance in its home at the Aldovrandi Palace Hotel (via Mangili 6), symbolizing its status as an establishment in its own right. A demanding hotel clientele and a French-Sicilian husband-and-wife team in the kitchen keep the basically Italian menu fresh and up to international standards. It also boasts one of the largest selections of grappa in Rome. Closed Sunday evenings. Tel: 321-61-26; Fax: 322-14-33.

Considered by many locals to be Rome's best restaurant, **Relais Le Jardin** in the Lord Byron Hotel (via Giuseppe de Notaris 5) has a menu that leans heavily toward the nouvelle cuisine implied by its name, though the inventive dishes are all inspired by authentic Italian ingredients. The quiet indoor setting, decorated in cool pastels, attracts upscale neighborhood types from nearby Parioli as well as a crowd of wealthy Romans and foreigners. Closed Sundays. Tel: 322-04-04; Fax: 360-95-41.

Le Restaurant del Grand Hotel (via Vittorio Emanuele Orlando 3) boasts an opulent setting straight out of Scarpia's apartment in *Tosca,* with gilded furnishings and private banquettes. The menu is international Italian, with some elegant touches such as the truffle-oil marinade on its *carpaccio.* Closed August. Tel: 47-09; Fax: 474-73-07.

The Hotel d'Inghilterra has opened its own restaurant, **Roman Garden** (via Bocca di Leone 14), which has quickly become a popular spot for business lunches. Among the refined creations on the menu are *insalitina di sogliola e salmone con spinaci* (sole and salmon salad with spinach) and *tortelli di anatra al tartufo di Norcia* (duck tortelli with truffles). Open seven days. Tel: 67-21-61.

—*Dwight V. Gast*

NIGHTLIFE

Nightlife is the most fleeting aspect of life anywhere, though it's not nearly as trendy in the Eternal City as in many other capitals. Rather than looking at the after hours as a time for boisterous partying, the Romans take the opportunity to put on their most civilized airs—dressing to the nines, posing, posturing, speaking in hushed tones with knowing expressions—in short, pursuing the night in a characteristically classical way. This practice has given rise to a larger proportion of reliable and regular establishments than elsewhere. When the sun goes down, the Roman expression "One life is not enough" becomes "One nightlife is not enough."

Not that Rome is devoid of cultural activities to be taken in during the evening. Its opera (box office, via Nazionale 64; Tel: 46-17-55) mounts productions outdoors in the summer at the Terme di Caracalla; the season at the Teatro dell'Opera (piazza Beniamino Gigli 1; Tel: 46-17-55), while not on a par with that of Milan, Naples, or Bari, runs from November through January. Concerts are given by the Accademia di Santa Cecilia orchestra (Tel: 654-10-44) in piazza Campidoglio in July and August, and in the Auditorio di Via delle Conciliazione, near the Vatican, from October through June. Plays and concerts are listed in the Tuesday edition of *Il Messaggero,* Rome's local newspaper; same-day half-price tickets for many events are available at the TKTS office at the Teatro Ateneo (Città Universitaria; Tel: 49-91). Another good source for what's on is the English-language biweekly *Wanted in Rome,* free at many hotels.

Film and performing arts events take place all over town during the summer festival called L'Estate Romana, which is widely publicized in the local papers.

Since most foreign films in Italy are dubbed, English speakers in Rome like to congregate at the English-language Pasquino Cinema in Trastevere (vicolo del Piede; Tel: 580-36-22) or at such cinemas as the Alcazar (via Cardinale Merry del Val); Capranichetta (piazza Montecitorio 125), Tel: 679-69-57; Fiamme (via San Nicola di Tolentino 5), Tel: 475-11-00; and Majestic (piazza Santi Apostoli 20), Tel: 679-49-08, all of which recently began showing films in original-language versions. Follow the movies with an ice cream at one of the many *gelaterie* around town.

There are many other possibilities for an evening's entertainment. From an after-dinner *espresso* coffee or *prosecco* sparkling wine in a café or bar, on to live music in a piano bar or club, and through to dancing and perhaps a late-night supper in one of many specialized nightclubs around town, the Roman night can easily extend into the wee hours. Each step of the way there are ample chances to observe—and perhaps participate in—the mating game *alla romana*. Also, Anglophones have an automatic advantage in the stakes, since speaking English is considered as sophisticated as taking part in the nocturnal circuit. But communication is hardly a problem under the circumstances.

Activity in cafés and bars starts picking up after dinner, at around 9:00 P.M. Piano bars and live-music clubs begin to get lively a couple of hours later, and nightclubs don't get into full swing until after midnight, though all open sooner. Most of the clubs charge a cover to get in, and some may even require a membership fee. In true international style, the more exclusive ones may make you wait at the door and even then may not let you in.

Cafés and Bars

Many Romans follow their meals with a coffee or ice cream at one of the places in the Centro Storico. **Sant'Eustachio** (piazza Sant'Eustachio 82) and **Tazza d'Oro** (via degli Orfani 84) are both equally famed for their coffee as well as for their *granita al caffè* (coffee ice). **Giolitti** (via degli Uffici del Vicario 40) and **Tre Scalini** (piazza Navona 30) are the best known among the many *gelaterie* in the area. In Trastevere, **Caffè-Bar di Marzio** (piazza di Santa Maria in Trastevere 14/b) serves coffee at the bustling center of the action in the area's main piazza.

Those looking for action still go to **Rosati** and **Canova**, facing cafés in piazza del Popolo. Rosati is currently the more chic of the two, its motorcycles and sports cars winning hands down in the mating display department, often even over their owners. The men here tend to be Roman, the women foreign. The reverse is true of the cafés of via Veneto. **Café de Paris** (No. 90), **Gran Caffè Doney** (No. 145), and **Harry's Bar** (No. 150) have faded from their heyday during the dolce vita era, and tend to fill up with foreign men and domestic ladies looking to keep them company— usually for a price.

Piano Bars and Live-Music Clubs

Via Veneto also has some of Rome's nicest piano bars. Practically every hotel in the area has its own, but the **Roof Garden Bar** of the Eden Hotel (via Ludovisi 49) has the most romantic view of all.

For live music the choices are even wider and are scattered

throughout the city. **Big Mama** (vicolo San Francesco a Ripa 18, in Trastevere), true to its name, is the leading jazz club in Rome, but there are many others. The **Mississippi Jazz Club** (borgo Angelico 16, near the Vatican), **Music Inn** (largo dei Fiorentini 3, off via Giulia), and **Billie Holiday Jazz Club** (via degli Orti di Trastevere 43, in Trastevere) are all just as well established. **Saint Louis** (via del Cardello 13/a, near the Colosseum) is still enormously popular, but lately has been displaced by **Caffè Latino** (via di Monte Testaccio 96, in the trendy Testaccio neighborhood) as the current favorite.

For other kinds of music, there's **Four Green Fields** (via Morin 40, near the Vatican) for Irish music; **Yes Brazil** (via San Francesco a Ripa, in Trastevere) for Brazilian; **Makumba** (via degli Olimpionici 19, near the ponte Flaminio) for African reggae and salsa (weekends only); and **Folkstudio** (via Sacchi 3, in Trastevere) for folk.

Nightclubs

Nothing is eternal about Rome's nightlife, which has become increasingly trendy. Jaded jet-set types still frequent **La Cabala** and the **Blue Bar** (via dei Soldati 25), both upstairs from the Hostaria dell'Orso restaurant near piazza Navona. More in at the moment, however, are **Gilda** (via Mario de' Fiori 97, near the Spanish Steps) and, especially, the recently opened **Alien** (via Velletri 13/19, near Piazza Fiume), both frequented by beautiful people from the worlds of politics and entertainment. The poor rich kids of the Parioli residential district north of Villa Borghese—so much a cultural phenomenon that *pariolini* has become the Roman term for "gilded youth"—are dragging themselves to the new **Krypton** (via Luigi Luciani 52) with renewed lack of enthusiasm. And the latest gay hangouts for both sexes are **L'Angelo Azzurro** (via Cardinal Merry del Val 13, in Trastevere) and **Hangar** (via in Selci 69/A, near Santa Maria Maggiore). But who knows when the new emperors of entertainment will turn their thumbs down on what Cicero called the *aura popularis,* or popular breeze, of these "in" establishments. Before you go, you'd better have your hotel check to make sure they're still in business.

—*Dwight V. Gast*

SHOPS AND SHOPPING

Though T. S. Eliot's women may "come and go, talking of Michelangelo," when shoppers come and go in Rome today the talk is more likely to be of Valentino, Fendi, and other designers who keep their ateliers here. For despite Milan's prominence in the ready-to-wear fashion world, Rome still reigns supreme for *alta moda*.

Rome's sartorial splendor extends to men as well. The fabrics of made-to-measure shirts rival anything you'll see on Savile Row, and the tailoring is often superior. Quality, and the traditions of pomp and circumstance running from the ancients through the popes and now to the headquarters of Italy's major television networks and film industry, are what distinguish shopping in the capital. Thus clothing, antiques, engravings, jewelry, fabrics, and crafts remain the best buys in Rome, fluctuating exchange rates notwithstanding.

Shops in Rome generally are open from 9:00 or 10:00 A.M. to 1:00 or 1:30 P.M., and unless they're on *orario no-stop* (chic Italian for nonstop schedule), they reopen between 4:00 and 5:00 P.M. and stay open until between 7:00 and 8:30 P.M. All shops are closed Sundays and Monday mornings, except around Christmas, and food shops close Thursday afternoons. In addition to national holidays, many shops close on Rome's birthday, April 21.

Most of the shops listed below accept credit cards, but if you find that you need cash outside of normal banking hours, try the American Service Bank (piazza Mignanelli 15, within the piazza di Spagna; Tel: 544-21) or the Banca Nazionale del Lavoro (via Veneto 11; Tel: 475-04-21), both of which stay open *no-stop* until 6:00 P.M.

Spanish Steps

The most elegant shopping in Rome can be found in the area around the Spanish Steps. Off the top of the steps themselves runs via Gregoriana, where top designers such as Valentino have their studios. (It was he, in fact, who was outraged over the opening of Rome's first McDonald's a few years back on the grounds that the hamburger fumes would taint his couture, but he has since quieted down.) At the bottom of the steps, directly in front of Bernini's *Fontana della Barcaccia,* is **via Condotti**, where the traffic has been closed off to make way for some of Italy's biggest names in clothing and jewelry. Before you make a beeline for it, have a look around piazza di Spagna, where you'll find the **American Express** office handy for a quick fix of cash at number 38.

Italy's leading linens may be purchased at **Pratesi**, at number 10, while Rome's most exclusive jeweler, **Petochi**, is at number 23. The Missoni men's shop, **Missoni Uomo**, is at number 78, and next to it is the natty women's clothier **Krizia**, at number 77. Artsy types might then want to wander up **via Babuino** to the north off the piazza, where besides

Armani's (number 102) and the inexpensive boutique Emporio Armani (number 140), some of the city's leading antiques dealers are located. **Antonacci** (number 146) and **W. Apolloni** (number 133–134) are the most famous, and expensive, but you can still pick up the inexpensive gift item at **Il Granmercato Antiquario Babuino** (number 150). If trattoria-type painting appeals, double back down **via Margutta** and have a look at Rome's highest concentration of commercial art galleries. A recent addition is the more contemporary **Galleria Apollodoro**, at piazza Mignanelli 25, within piazza di Spagna.

Return to piazza di Spagna and head down via Condotti, where you'll immediately recognize Richard Ginori, Gucci, Cartier, Bulgari, Beltrami, Buccellati, and Hermès, and may want to stop to see how their Rome inventories vary from those of the other cities where they sell their pricey wares. There are certain stores, however, to which you should pay particular attention, since they do not exist outside Rome. **Barilla** (number 29) makes classic hand-sewn shoes for men and women, while **Capuano** (number 61) sells custom-made jewelry to the stars, and **Battistoni** (number 61/a), made-to-measure menswear. Before heading south to the parallel luxury shopping streets, aficionados of elegantly designed office supplies might want to venture two blocks north to the two **Vertecchi** stores on the via della Croce (numbers 38 and 70). Also nearby is **Artigianato del Cuoio** (via Belsiana 90), a leather-goods shop whose low-key atmosphere conceals high-quality merchandise.

Via Borgognona and via Frattina are filled with more famous-name designers. **Fendi** virtually owns the former venue, its women's shop at number 36 dominating the street (though **Gianni Versace** has his men's shop at number 29, and **Gianfranco Ferrè** has his men's shop at number 6 and women's shop at number 42/b; the ever-effete **Franco Maria Ricci** sells the most esoteric cards and books on the face of the earth at number 4/d).

Via Frattina is home to **Mario Valentino** (number 84), who also has a women's store at via Bocca di Leone 15 and via Mario de'Fiori 22. More designers line the cross streets: **Basile** has a store for both men and women at via Mario de'Fiori 29, and **Gianni Versace** has a women's store at via Bocca di Leone 26. If it's cheap Italian woolens you want, go to **Anticoli** at via della Vite 28 before leaving the area. You can mail them, or any other purchases weighing less than two kilograms, from the post office in nearby piazza San

Silvestro, open *no-stop* from 8:00 A.M. to 8:00 P.M. weekdays, and 8:00 A.M. to noon on Saturdays.

Specialty Shops in Centro Storico

The area just to the west across the Corso from the via Condotti is filled with specialty shops. Since it encompasses the Pantheon, piazza Navona, and campo dei Fiori, it's a good place to wander aimlessly. Therefore the following shops are listed by the type of merchandise they sell.

Antiques and engravings. The auction house **Christie's** has its Italian headquarters in Palazzo Lancellotti (piazza Navona 14; Tel: 656-40-32). Besides the open-air print market in piazza Fontanella di Borghese, which sells antique prints, there are a number of dealers who keep shops in this part of town. **Via dei Coronari** is almost completely lined with antiques dealers, and if you're there in May or October you'll see the street decked out for the antiques fair called the Mostra Mercato di Antiquariato. Some exceptions to the rule of 19th-century English furniture sold in the street's shops are **Metastasio** (at number 33–34), which boasts the unusual specialty of nautical paintings; **Mario Morisco** (number 136), which sells French Empire furniture; and **La Mansarde** (number 202–203), which deals in Piedmontese furniture. Dealers along **via Giulia**, considered the heart of Renaissance Rome, specialize in Italian antiques. Among the nicer ones are **La Chimera** (at number 122), which deals in 19th-century Italian furniture, and **La Pinacoteca di Via Giulia** (at number 188), which handles Italian painting from the same period. Scattered around the area are **Roberto Boccalini** (via del Banco di Santo Spirito), who deals in old prints, books, and engravings, as do **Casali** (piazza del Pantheon 81/a), **Cascianelli** (largo Febo 14), **Nardecchia** (piazza Navona 25), and **Galleria Carlo Virgilio** (via della Lupa 9).

Contemporary art galleries. Rome has been undergoing a renewed importance as a center for contemporary art in recent years, and although there's no one distinct area for them as in other cities, many of the galleries are in Centro Storico. Among the ones to watch out for here are **Galleria Giulia** (via Giulia 148), **Galleria Mara Coccia** (via del Corso 530), **L'Attico** (via del Paradiso 41), **Planita** (via di Ripetta 22), and **Monti** (via di Ripetta 41).

Crafts. **Via dell'Orso**, just off the ponte Umberto, holds a crafts fair every October; there are quite a few artisans working along it and its side streets. For do-it-yourselfers, **Canguro** (via di Campo Marzio 45) sells some of the best yarns in town, as does **Le Vie Delle Lane** (via dei Banchi Vecchi 116). The antique craft of tile making is still practiced at **Galleria Farnese** (piazza Farnese 50), which makes reproduction and original designs. Mosaic tiles may be made to order at **Opificio Romano** (via dei Gigli d'Oro 9–10), reproducing Pompeiian floors or following your own design. If you thought candle making was a lost art, step into **Cereria Pisoni** (corso Vittorio Emanuele 127–129), which has kept the popes enlightened since 1803 and will make any size, color, and quantity of candle to order. They are also the exclusive manufacturers of the saucer-shaped candles called *torcie a vento,* typically Roman street illuminations found along the city's streets on festive occasions. To have your travel journal or other favorite book bound for glory, take it to **Mario Rossini** (via dei Lucchesi 25), bookbinders par excellence.

Housewares. **Croff Centro Casa** has two stores filled with their well-designed housewares in the area, one at via Tomacelli 137 and the other at via del Corso 316.

Men's made-to-order. **Caleffi** (via Colonna Antonina 53) has been making men's shirts, suits, and ties for three generations. **Caraceni** (via Marche 1/3 and via Campania 61/b) is another respectable family dynasty in custom tailoring. **Camiceria Piero Albertelli** (via dei Prefetti 11) specializes in men's nightwear.

Unusual shops. The entire street of **via dei Cestari** specializes in sacred vestments and accoutrements, from the chasubles at Luciano Ghezzi (number 32–33) to the ornamental reliquaries and monstrances at Statuaria Arte Sacra (number 2). For something more *urbis* than *orbis,* **Art'è** (piazza Rondanini 32) sells witty replicas of urban architecture. Rome's only magic shop is **Curiosità e Magia** (via Aquiro 70). **La Gazza Ladra** (via dei Banchi Vecchi 29) has an extensive stock of 19th-century walking sticks. **Ai Monasteri** (corso del Rinascimento 72) sells liqueurs, perfumes, honeys, and other products made by monks and nuns throughout Italy's monasteries and abbeys. **Olfottoteca** (piazza della Concelleria 88) mixes perfumes to order. For the young at heart, try **Mondo Antico** (via dei Pianellari 17), where miniature stage settings and puppets are the stars. **Zanon** (via Santa Maria dell'Anima 18) continues the venerable Roman art of *tarsia,* or marble inlay, with a vast array of objects such as lamps and tabletops.

More stores in the area. Rome's most central bookstore is **Rizzoli** (largo Chigi 15), which sells the city's largest selection of art and travel books, many of which are in English.

Finally, cross back over the Corso to stop for a snack at Rome's oldest chocolate store, **Moriondo & Gariglio** (via della Pilotta 2).

Other Shopping Streets

Via del Tritone, which leads from largo Chigi into the via Veneto area, offers inexpensive clothing and expensive fabrics; Galtrucco, at number 18–23, has the most luxurious of the latter. While in the area, stop by **Pineider**, the elegant Florentine stationers, at via Due Macelli 68–69. More inexpensive clothing and shoes are sold along the entire length of **via Nazionale**, off which you'll find a designer-seconds outlet called **Discount System** on via Napoli. While in the neighborhood, check out the **Economy Book & Video Center** at via Torino 136, which now rents English-language videos (they're on a different system, but may make a nice gift for a Roman friend) in addition to its vast selection of English-language books on every subject. Also nearby is Rome's leading wine and olive oil shop, **Trimani** (via Goito 20), behind the Terme di Diocleziano.

If you're feeling adventurous, at the opposite extremes of the middlebrow via Nazionale (and at opposite ends of town) are **via Sonnio** (near San Giovanni in Laterano), an open-air street market specializing in used clothing, and **via Cola di Rienzo** (near the Vatican), a tree- and boutique-lined street where the Romans do their shopping. All the respectable names are here, but for a touch of the unusual go to **F.A.M.A.R.** (piazza dell'Unità 51–52), at the end of the street, where you'll be able to buy such unusual items as blazer buttons with designer logos on them. If you must have a suburban shopping experience, go to viale Europa in E.U.R., where major designers all have stores.

More unusual items may be found at **Galleria del Batik** (via della Pelliccia 29–30), which carries a full range of highly original crafts from throughout Italy. Finally, don't leave Rome without spending a Sunday morning at Trastevere's **Porta Portese**, the open-air flea market. Everything from *porchetta* sandwiches to vintage postcards to stolen car parts and fake antiques is on sale here. The place is also rife with pickpockets—the common dictum is that if your wallet is stolen on the way in, you'll find it for sale on the way out—but if you take precautions accordingly you should have a great time.

—*Dwight V. Gast*

LAZIO
DAY TRIPS FROM ROME

By Dwight V. Gast and Barbara Coeyman Hults

Lazio (LA-dzio), a land of forests, castles, and ancient abbeys, is rarely experienced by tourists, except when they hurry along the crowded major arteries to Rome. Besides visiting Rome, a day or evening trip to the Villa d'Este is apt to be the only part of the region visited. (The Roman name, Latium, is sometimes used in English.)

This has been a great boon to Lazio, for it has been able to go its own way, for the most part without the click of cameras or the exclamations of the adoring to make the region self-conscious. Actually, Lazio is one of the most beautiful parts of Italy, with a rare mystical quality all its own, born of monasticism and pine forests, mountain grottos worn deep in the porous tufa rock, lakes and spas, and quiet towns. As to its superlatives, Lazio has more lakes than any region of Italy—still, shadowy volcanic lakes in the midst of thick forests.

Lazio's boundaries extend north to Viterbo and the borders of Umbria and Tuscany, south beyond Anzio and Gaeta to the border of Campania, and east to the mountainous Abruzzi.

Its castles and abbeys are often rugged and isolated on mountaintops covered with pine and *macchia,* the pervasive Mediterranean shrub. Its gastronomy has the same simple, fresh, and hearty character: rice or pasta with beans, pasta *all'amatriciana* (with *pancetta* and the local pecorino cheese) or *all'arrabbiatta* (in a tomato sauce made "angry" with hot peppers), lamb or pork roasted outdoors, chicken done in hundreds of ways, roasted artichokes, oxtail stew, tripe, and Rome's famous *saltimbocca* (slices of veal, cured ham, and sage leaves in a tangy sauce).

134

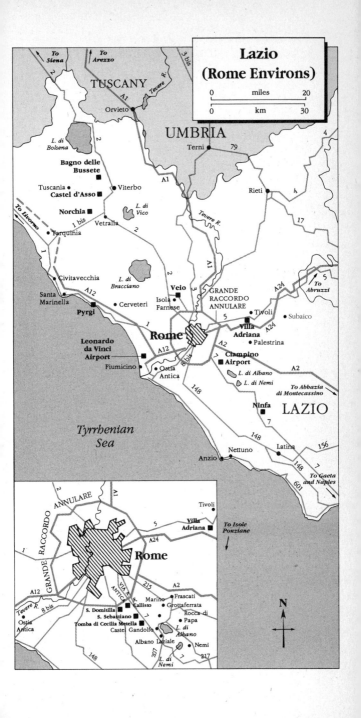

Lazio
(Rome Environs)

miles 0 — 20

km 0 — 30

To Siena
To Arezzo

TUSCANY

Tevere R.

A1

Orvieto

UMBRIA

L. di Bolsena

Terni 79

4

Bagno delle Bussete

A1

Tuscania • Viterbo
Castel d'Asso ■

Rieti 4

Norchia ■

L. di Vico

17

1 bis Vetralla

To Livorno

• Tarquinia

2

Tevere R.

A1

Civitavecchia

L. di Bracciano

2

A12

Santa Marinella

1

Pyrgi ■

• Cerveteri

Isola Farnese

Veio ■

3

GRANDE RACCORDO ANNULARE

A24

To Abruzzi 5

Tivoli • Subaico

5

Villa Adriana ■

A24

Rome

A12

Ostia Antica

8 bis

• Palestrina

Leonardo da Vinci Airport —

Fiumicino

A2

Ciampino Airport ■

7

L. di Albano

L. di Nemi

A2

To Abbazia di Montecassino

148

Tyrrhenian Sea

Ninfa ■

LAZIO

7

148

Latina 156

148

Nettuno

Anzio •

601

To Gaeta and Naples

GRANDE RACCORDO ANNULARE

A1

Tivoli

Villa Adriana ■

To Isole Ponziane

5

A24

Rome

1

A12

Tevere R.

8 bis

• Ostia Antica

215

A2

S. Marino • Frascati

VIA X. ANTICA

S. Callisto ■

• Grottaferrata

S. Domitilla ■

7

S. Sebastiano ■

Rocca di Papa

Tomba di Cecilia Metella ■

L. di Albano

Castel Gandolfo

Albano Laziale • Nemi

148

207

217

L. di Nemi

7

N

Autumn is Lazio's season, when a cool breeze picks up the scent of wood fires and the red wine is uncorked.

MAJOR INTEREST

The Catacombs
Archaeological excavations at Ostia Antica and
  Palestrina
Tivoli for Villa d'Este and Villa Adriana: frescoes,
  gardens, fountains
The Castelli Romani, castles and villas in the Alban
  Hills: Frascati, Castel Gondolfo, and others
Viterbo
Major Etruscan sites: Tarquinia, Cerveteri, and Tus-
  cania
The ancient Benedictine Abbey of Montecassino
The gardens of Ninfa
The island of Ponza

THE CATACOMBS

Shaded with cypress trees, the graceful symbol of death, numerous elaborate tombs of wealthy ancient Romans border the Appian Way (*Via Appia*), the consular road opened in 312 B.C. to link Rome with the south. In the early years of Christianity, the bodies of several saints were buried in the tombs for safety, and soon others wanted to be interred alongside them. During the years of persecution these long caverns sheltered the followers from Roman authorities, and some symbols from that time, such as the fish and the dove, can still be seen there.

Catacombs are systems of underground galleries on several levels, extending often for miles. The openings to the tombs were closed with slabs of marble, and a name— originally in Greek, later in Latin—was carved into them. Over the centuries the tombs have been opened by invaders and local thieves, but much of interest remains.

Many of the catacombs are dark, most of the steps are uneven, skulls and bones are quite visible, and retreat is often impossible once inside—and some people do want to retreat.

The **Catacomb of San Callisto** is the most important of all. Named after Saint Calixtus, who was appointed guardian of the site by Pope Zephyrinus (199–217), it constituted the first specifically designated cemetery of the early Christians, and was the burial place of the early popes as well as Saint Cecilia, who is commemorated by a copy of the Carlo Madreno statue in the crypt. It is also the most extensive of the catacombs, stretching some 15 miles underground, and has not yet been fully explored. Just behind the catacomb of San Callisto is the **Catacomb of Santa Domitilla**, which contains the fourth-century basilica of San Nereus and San Achilleus, as well as some beautiful paintings, including the first known representation of Christ as the Good Shepherd, painted in the second century.

The **Catacomb of San Sebastiano**, a few minutes away, developed around the spot where Saint Stephen was martyred, and is also where the bodies of Saint Peter and Saint Paul were once buried. It is the oldest known catacomb, and consequently has been visited heavily over the centuries and damaged by pilgrims as a result. Nevertheless, the tunnels, covered with ancient graffiti, and the nearby **Basilica of San Sebastiano** (one of Rome's seven pilgrimage churches) are the most impressive examples of catacombs in Rome.

Along the Appian Way at number 119A is the entrance to the Jewish Catacombs, where names and symbols can still be seen on the tombs. For permisssion to visit, ask at the Synagogue in Rome, Lungotevere Cenci 9.

The best-known of the Roman burial monuments is the **Tomb of Cecilia Metella**, a vast circular shape created for the mother of the triumvir Crassus. The crenellated top was part of a fortified castle built around it during the 14th century. Unlike most monuments of the period, it has been preserved with much of its marble facing intact, and is decorated with charming relief scenes. Nearby is the restaurant **Cecilia Metella** (via Appia Antica 125; Tel: 06-513-67-43; closed Mondays), which makes for a pleasant outdoor lunch or dinner during the warm weather.

The number 118 bus from the Colosseum stops at the catacomb of San Callisto; the other sites are all within walking distance from San Callisto.

OSTIA ANTICA

The extensive excavations of the ancient seaport of Ostia are most important to archaeologists for their examples of Roman residential architecture, ranging from the patrician villa, called the *domus* (much more common at the wealthy resort town of Pompeii), to the apartment block called the *insula*. Set in a park unbothered by the intrusions of the centuries and pleasantly planted with cypresses and umbrella pines, the site gives a more vivid picture of everyday life in the Empire than anything in Rome does. From the entrance at Porta Romana, follow the Decumanus Maximus, the town's main street, to the **Terme di Nettuno** (Baths of Neptune), which contain some interesting marine mosaics. Continue on to the theater and the tree-shaded piazzale delle Corporazioni, the former business district, where the mosaic pavement in front of the various offices depicts the nature of the businesses inside. Several blocks later you'll reach the **Capitolium**, a large temple dedicated to Jupiter, Juno, and Minerva. Behind it is the **Museo Archeologico Ostiense**, housing well-displayed sculptures from the excavations, noteworthy among them *Cupid and Psyche, Family of Marcus Aurelius,* and *Lion Attacking a Bull.* Farther on are some remarkable mosaics in the ancient residences called the **Casa delle Muse** (House of the Muses) and the **Domus dei Dioscuri** (House of the Dioscuri). At the farthest end of the excavations are the remains of one of the oldest synagogues yet discovered, dating from the first century.

The most picturesque way of getting to Ostia is on the boat sponsored by the Amici del Tevere, which leaves from the ponte Marconi in Rome. Otherwise, the trains that leave from Stazione di Termini for Lido di Ostia stop at Ostia Antica; the trip takes about half an hour. There is also a subway line from Rome to the popular and crowded beach of Lido di Ostia, a short walk from Ostia Antica. Lido di Ostia also has a number of seafood restaurants, of which **Da Negri** is among the nicest (via Claudia 50; Tel: 06-562-22-95; closed Thursdays).

TIVOLI AND VILLA ADRIANA

Medieval in appearance, the town of Tivoli (30 km/19 miles east of Rome) is the bastion of the Renaissance **Villa d'Este**, built for Cardinal Ippolito II d'Este by Pirro Ligorio. The villa itself contains frescoes by 16th-century artists, but more noteworthy are its gardens, awash with hundreds of fountains. Though the *giochi d'acqua,* the sprays of water that surprised unsuspecting visitors, are no longer in use, the fountains themselves are just as wondrous. (The Organ Fountain, Terrace of the Hundred Fountains, Ovato Fountain, Rometta Fountain, and Dragon Fountain are but a few.) Dry for centuries, the fountains have been restored by the

Italian government, which also illuminates them at night during the summer.

Tibur (Tivoli's ancient name) was founded, some say, by the Siculi, and later became an important resort for wealthy Romans. It was here that the Sybil Albunea was consulted, whose shrine was sacred to her cult.

The most pleasant warm-weather dining option in the area is **Sibilla** (via della Sibilla 50; Tel: 0774-202-81), a regional restaurant whose outdoor garden overlooks the temples of Vesta and Sibilla. Seeing the fountains at Villa d'Este is perhaps best combined, however, with a surreptitious picnic dinner at **Villa Adriana** (Hadrian's Villa), 4.5 km (3 miles) south of Tivoli. Now in ruins, it was once the largest villa in ancient Rome. The Emperor Hadrian built it for his retirement, reconstructing some of his favorite sights from around the world to keep him company. Among them were the entrance colonnade, called the Poikile, from Athens, and the Canal of Canopus from Egypt. Other monuments include the Lyceum, the Maritime Theater, and the Academy. The extensive grounds serve as an ideal backdrop for a discreet meal, which might be taken as lunch after a visit to the Villa d'Este (if you are unable to see its fountains at night); or try the **Antico Trattoria del Falcone** (via del Trevio 34; Tel: 0774-223-58; closed Mondays), where Lazio's dishes—such as chick-pea soup, baccalà, and fresh fruit pies—as well as pizza are featured.

ACOTRAL provides regular bus service from Rome (via Gaeta, near the piazza dei Cinquecento) to Tivoli, depositing passengers near the entrance to the Villa d'Este; buses stop about a mile from the entrance to the Villa Adriana. The local CAT bus in Tivoli goes near the Villa Adriana stop as well. Taxis from the town of Tivoli go to the door.

PALESTRINA

Known to the ancient Romans as Praeneste, Palestrina was founded, according to legend, by the son of Ulysses and Circe. Then the site of the oracle at the **Temple of Fortuna Primigenia** (the first daughter of Jupiter), one of the richest and most elaborate sanctuaries of antiquity, today the town is visited for the archaeological excavations surrounding the temple, magnificently located on the slopes of Monte Ginestro, 37 km (23 miles) east of Rome. Its adjacent museum, the **Museo Archeologico Prenestino** (in the Palazzo Barberini), houses material from the excavation, the highlight of which is a first-century B.C. mosaic depicting the floodwaters of the Nile.

Music lovers might want to have a look at the monument to the town's most famous native son, 16th-century composer Giovanni Pierluigi da Palestrina, in the main piazza. Just outside town (via del Piscarello, Tel: 06-955-77-51) is the restaurant **Trattoria del Piscarello**, where you can enjoy a classic Roman menu—in an outdoor setting in fair weather.

ACOTRAL buses leave Rome regularly for Palestrina from Piazza dei Cinquecento; there is also train service from Stazione Termini to the Palestrina station, from which a local bus takes you to the town center.

East of Palestrina, the abbeys of Santa Scolastica and San Benedetto at **Subiaco** merit a visit.

CASTELLI ROMANI

The Castelli Romani (Roman castles) are, collectively, the 13 towns about 21 km (13 miles) southeast of Rome where wealthy Romans built castles and villas in the Colli Albani, or Alban Hills, best known for their crisp white wine.

Frascati is the most popular of the Castelli Romani, and though its lovely 16th-century **Villa Aldobrandini** has spectacular views of Rome, it is best known as a gathering place for *fagottari,* people who buy or bring bundles of *porchetta* (pork roasted with herbs) and other delicacies to enjoy on open-air terraces next to the wine shops while drinking healthy amounts of the Frascati wine. **Cacciani** (via Armando Diaz 13; Tel: 942-03-78; closed Tuesdays) is an excellent restaurant here, with an expansive outdoor terrace from which to enjoy the scenery; reservations are recommended.

The woods and vineyards of **Grottaferrata** shelter the Abbazia, a Basilian abbey founded in 1004, where the Greek Orthodox rite was reinstituted with the pope's permission during the last century. The monks will show you around the grounds and the museum of religious artifacts, and also sell olive oil and a good local wine.

The elegant **Villa Fiorio**, in its park of pine trees, is the place to stay and to dine, an ideal retreat (viale Dusinet 28; Tel: 06-945-92-76; Fax: 06-945-92-79). Ask in advance, however, if it's to be a wedding-party weekend. In the town, the **Taverna dello Spuntino** is a charming spot to relax in over homemade pasta, veal with arugula, roast pig, and homemade desserts (via Cicerone 22; Tel: 06-945-93-66; closed Wednesdays).

The wine of **Marino** is considered the best of all the Colli Albani whites, and is especially celebrated during the Sagra dell'Uva (Festival of the Grape) on the first Sunday in October, when, after a procession and an offering to the Madonna, the Fontana dei Mori flows with wine.

Castel Gandolfo is believed to be the location of Alba Longa, the most powerful city in ancient Latium, founded by the son of Aeneas and destroyed by the Romans. The current town contains the **Church of San Tommaso da Villanova** and a fountain, both by Bernini, in its main square. Its **Palazzo Pontificio** is part of the Vatican State and serves as the summer residence of the pope, who gives addresses here on Sundays and holds audiences on Wednesday mornings (apply for admission at the Vatican). **Albano Laziale** is on a lake on the site of the Castra Albana, which was built by Septimius Severus for a Roman legion in the second century. Ruins of the ancient town and subsequent Medieval additions may be seen.

The Nemus Dianae, or Grove of Diana, sacred to the primitive cult with which Frazer opens *The Golden Bough,* gave its name to the town and lake of **Nemi**, today famous for its strawberries. Though very few of them are wild, they are all celebrated in the Sagra delle Fragole, or strawberry festival, in June. **Rocca di Papa**, named after the castle, or *rocca,* built by the popes, is the highest of all the Castelli Romani. The upper portion of the town is Medieval, and if you ascend Monte Cavo above that (as did the Roman legions when the Temple of Jupiter Latialis was located here) you'll be treated to magnificent views of the Castelli, the lakes of Albano and Nemi, and the surrounding countryside as far as the coast.

The most convenient way to see the Castelli Romani in a day is undoubtedly by car, beginning on the Roman via Tuscolana (route S 215) and following signs for the individual towns; otherwise, select the one or two towns that appeal most to you and check train and bus schedules. Trains from Stazione di Termini serve Albano, Marino, and Frascati. ACOTRAL buses from Cinecittà (a stop on the Metropolitana Line A) serve all the towns.

The **Gardens at Ninfa**, south of the Castelli, exude a melancholy magic from the 12th century, when the overgrown ruins were a prosperous town. The Botanical Gardens, with plants brought from all over the world, and the Zoological Gardens come to life, like *Brigadoon,* the first Saturday and the first Sunday of every month from April to October. For admission, contact the Amministrazione Cae-

tani, via delle Botteghe Oscuri 32, Rome (Tel: 06-68-66-101),
or the Oasi di Ninfa (Tel: 0773-432-31).

VITERBO

Few Medieval cities convey their era as dramatically as
Viterbo. The priorities of the Middle Ages—defense, defense, and prayer—are met in Viterbo's massive walls and
brooding introspection. This mood doesn't extend, however, to the young soldiers in today's town, putting in their
year of compulsory military service at the Viterbo base.
Their preoccupations are predictable, and not very militant.

On rainy days the city seems too dour for some travellers,
like many cities of its time, but when the weather is fair it is
superb, flourishing at the foot of the Cimini hills. The tufa, a
soft, porous volcanic stone typical of central Italy, changes
color with the weather, absorbing foggy grays and warm sun
tones with equanimity.

The capital of its province, Viterbo is 104 km (50 miles)
northwest of Rome. It has been a city to be reckoned with
since the 13th century, when it was the papal seat during
strife between the papacy and the empire, and the place
where the first Conclave in Catholic church history was held.

The heart of Viterbo is the **Piazza del Plebiscito**, where
yesterday and today vie for supremacy, overlooked by tufa
lions. Here the **Palazzo dei Priori**, or Communale (town
hall), begun in 1460, still maintains the city's records. Its fine
Renaissance courtyard and loggia are usually open to visitors, and you can glimpse the current powers of Viterbo as
they pontificate. The building with the clock tower is the
13th-century Palazzo del Podestà (Mayor), the secular authority of its time.

Across the square, near the door of the church of
Sant'Angelo, a Roman sarcophagus has been set into the
wall. It is called the tomb of the beautiful Galiana, who was
killed with an arrow by a Roman officer whom she'd refused, thus sparing the city from seige, we're told.

Along the **via San Lorenzo**, a twisting street through the
ancient city, stands the imposing Renaissance form of the
Palazzo Chigi, enhanced with a lovely court and loggia.
Beyond it is what is now the Jesuit church of the **Gesù**, a
simple 11th-century structure, but restored. Inside, it seems,
two brothers of the Monforte family beat up Prince Henry of
Cornwall during Mass, avenging the death of their father,
which had been ordered by King Richard.

At the triangular **Piazza della Morte**, probably the site of executions yet today green and cheerful, the vicolo Pellegrini leads to the **Ponte del Duomo**, set on an Etruscan base that can be seen if you descend the stairs at the bridge's side. The bridge united the city with an ancient castle.

The beautiful 14th-century **Palazzo Farnese**, birthplace of the Farnese pope Paul III, has a stylish courtyard.

The **cathedral of San Lorenzo** is a 12th-century Romanesque building, with a splendid campanile in Gothic form. The interior was severely damaged during World War II. In the left apse the *Madonna della Carbonara,* and in the sacristy the painting of *Christ Blessing the Saint,* both by Girolamo da Cremona, are among the treasures. On the altar, *Saint Laurence in Glory* is the work of the Baroque artist Giovanni Romanelli, who also painted the *Holy Family,* in the right aisle.

In the piazza, the **Palazzo dei Papi**, with its open loggia, is the true cornerstone of the city. It was built between 1257 and 1266, and soon after was used to house the first Conclave. Even the recent Second Vatican Council is unlikely to have had a stormier session, or certainly a longer one (1268–1271). To end the impasse over the election of Gregorio X as pope, the Viterbese removed the roof of the congress hall. The Princes of the Church, sequestered beneath, erected tents and continued, until their subjects resorted to stones; holes can still be seen where they hit the floor. Gregory was thus pelted in, and despite this electoral process four more popes were elected here.

Returning to the piazza della Morte: The little street in front of the fountain will take you through the beautifully preserved 12th-century **Medieval Quarter**, with its pinnacle, the **Piazza San Pelligrino**, considered the most comprehensive Medieval piazza in Italy. The **Palazzo degli Alessandri** is a typical example of an austere private palace. This section is the place to wander, on the lookout especially for the superb fountains that are typical of Viterbo and for other signs of the Middle Ages—towers, covered passageways, gently arched bifurcated windows, and dark streets. The **Fontana Grande**, off the via Cavour (near where you began), is one of the city's finest.

The **Museo Civico** at piazza Crispi is housed in the convent of the church of Santa Maria della Verità. The Etruscan objects on the ground floor reflect Viterbo's other dominant influence. To the west of Viterbo are some of Italy's most important Etruscan sites, notably at Tarquinia, Cerveteri, and Tuscania; they are described below. In the gallery, the star is

Sebastiano del Piombo's *Pietà,* based on a lost drawing by Michelangelo. There is also a lovely cycle of frescoes on the life of the Virgin by Lorenzo da Viterbo (1469).

The **church of San Francesco**, near the northern city walls and close to the Public Gardens, houses the tombs of Pope Clement IV and Hadrian V, the latter attributed to Arnolfo da Cambio.

Viterbo has one notable restaurant, **Il Richiastro**, which is open only Thursday through Sunday. The Scappucci family restored a 12th-century building for the atmosphere they wanted, and in 1981 opened this delightful trattoria. Here traditional recipes have been carefully researched, and the best of Lazio emerges. Hearty soups of beans and grains, steaks, and the less popular (in America) cuts of meat, the offals, are done to perfection. Many of the products, including the olive oil, are home-grown or homemade. Call to reserve (via della Marrocca 16–18; Tel: 0761-22-36-09; no credit cards, closed in August).

As to hotels, the best-appointed are the **Mini Palace** and the **Balletti Palace**. The **Tuscia** is fine for an overnight and within most budgets.

Rome's transit authority, again in its infinite wisdom, has changed things around so that getting to Viterbo is a project. We can only hope that the situation will be changed by the time you want to go.

At present the way to get there is to go to Saxa Rubra, near Prima Porta, a stop on the Roma Nord line that starts near the Flaminia metro stop, just beyond (outside the gate of) piazza del Popolo. (To save time and frustration, take a taxi to Saxa Rubra.) At Saxa Rubra a bus will take you on to Viterbo. The train will too, but the trip is long, although a nice way to see the countryside (unless you get one of the old wooden-seaters). In any case, leave as early as possible if you're making a day trip. In Viterbo, cars can be left outside the walls at piazza Martiri d'Ungheria.

On the way back you might want to dine in Saxa Rubra at the **Grotte di Livia,** a pleasant family-run restaurant on the grounds of a villa that Livia and Augustus shared during Rome's imperial golden age. Their homemade pasta is superb, and the steaks are excellent. On a hot evening in Rome, its outdoor dining is the right choice (piazza Saxa Rubra 9; Tel: 06-691-12-53; closed Mondays).

ETRUSCAN SITES

Most of the beautiful removable objects—sculpture, vases, and gold artifacts—unearthed from Etruscan necropolises over the last century are on display at museums such as the Museo Nazionale di Villa Giulia and the Musei Vaticani in Rome. The tombs themselves, however, which so fascinated D. H. Lawrence (he wrote about them in *Etruscan Places*) and others, are easy to visit from Rome, and a look at their faded frescoes and homelike arrangement makes the ancient civilization seem both closer and more distant.

The area west of Viterbo is one of the richest parts of Italy in Etruscan excavations. The principal sites, from northern Lazio to near Rome, can be seen in a day trip from Rome.

Begin at the site farthest from Rome, the Medieval-looking town of **Tarquinia**, about 90 km (56 miles) up the coast, where the **Museo Nazionale Tarquiniese** has an extensive collection of Etruscan art from the nearby necropolises (about 3 km/ 2 miles west of town)—only a few of which are also open to the public (apply at the museum) on any given day because of their delicate condition and to protect them from grave robbers (*tombaroli*). The unrivaled collection of wall paintings give a vivid impression of the partying afterlife that the Etruscans anticipated—perhaps the reason they are always smiling. Tarquinia today is home for hundreds of refugees from Eastern Europe, an unsettling experience for all concerned.

Toward Viterbo, more necropolises are to be seen surrounding the hill town of **Tuscania** as well as farther along the road at **Bagno delle Bussete**. **Castel d'Asso**, on a small road southwest of Viterbo, has a large cliffside necropolis, as does **Norchia**, to the west of Vetralla. From there, after returning to Tarquinia, the coastal road is dotted with both Etruscan and Roman sites at Civitavecchia, Santa Marinella, and Pyrgi. **Cerveteri**, perched on a spur of tufa, was once the most flourishing of the Etruscan cities, and its Banditaccia necropolis about a mile outside of town gives the best idea of the extent and luxurious furnishings of that civilization's cities of the dead. Nearby is **Nazareno** (Località San Paolo; Tel: 06-995-23-82), which offers excellent dishes featuring local meats and seafood. Closest to Rome, off route S 2, is the necropolis at **Veio**, near the hill town of Isola Farnese.

Since many of the Etruscan sights are tombs in the open countryside, the best way to visit them is by car. Depending on how long you want to stay at the individual sites, this can take one lengthy day or two leisurely days, with the best accommodations for a stopover at Tarquinia's **Tarconte e Ristorante Solengo**, via Tuscia 19; Tel: (0766) 85-61-41; closed Wednesdays. Otherwise, buses leave from via Lepanto in Rome for Tarquinia and Cerveteri, and Veio is on Rome's number 201 bus route from the piazza Mancini.

ANZIO AND NETTUNO

Anzio was the birthplace of both Caligula and Nero, a bloody legacy continued more recently by the landing in World War II of American and British troops. Today it and Nettuno are modern seaside resort towns with decent beaches and family-style accommodations, about 60 km (37 miles) south of Rome. In addition, Anzio boasts the excavations of the **Villa di Nerone** (Nero's Villa). Both are of particular interest for their cemeteries: The British Military Cemetery is located at Anzio, the American at Nettuno. Anzio also has a panoramic seafood restaurant, **All'Antica Darsena** (piazza Sant'Antonio 1; Tel: 06-984-51-46; closed Mondays); Nettuno's is **Il Gambero II** (via delle Liberazione 50; Tel: 06-985-40-71; closed Mondays and from September 15 to June 15).

ACOTRAL buses leave for Anzio from Rome at Cinecittà, at Osteria del Curato; trains from Stazione Termini.

ABBAZIA DI MONTECASSINO

The **Abbey at Montecassino** was one of the most important outposts of Christian culture during the Middle Ages, when much of the world was dark. Begun in the sixth century by Saint Benedict, founder of the Benedictines, it existed for more than 13 centuries, despite destruction by an earthquake in 1349 and the Allied bombardment of 1944, in which hundreds of tons of bombs were dropped to destroy a German stronghold. After the war an inspired work of reconstruction was begun, and today the monastery is almost identical to the original.

The abbey commands as dramatic a position as nature allows, atop a high peak that overlooks a breathtaking panorama of rolling hills and valleys. To reach it, hairpin curves must be executed along a 9 km (5 mile) road.

Saint Benedict, who had been living as a hermit in nearby Subiaco, was asked by a group of monks to be their abbot—but apparently things didn't work out, as they tried to poison him. When he returned to Subiaco, he attracted a great number of disciples. An orderly man, he divided the monks among 12 monasteries, appointed a prior for each one, and made manual work a part of the program. Subiaco quickly developed as a center of spirituality and learning. Benedict left suddenly, apparently because of bad rapport with a prior, and settled at Montecassino, destroying the temple to Apollo on the mountaintop and constructing an altar on the site. In about 530 he began to build the monastery, attracting many disciples, whom he organized into a monastic community. He then wrote the Rule of Saint Benedict, prescribing a life of moderation in asceticism and a program of prayer, chastity, study, and work, in community life with one superior. Obedience, stability, and zeal were the watchwords, and his Rule has affected monastic life throughout the centuries since.

At the abbey's entrance, three cloisters lead to the Loggia del Paradiso, from which the view of the valley is superb. The original loggia, which has been reconstructed exactly, was designed by Sangallo (who designed Orvieto's famous well). The basilica's altar, originally the work of Fanzago, has also been duplicated, as has Sangallo's tomb of Pietro de'Medici, the son of Lorenzo. The original crypt remains, where Saint Benedict was buried. A museum is open but the library, with thousands of the original books and manuscripts, is available only to those with requests for serious study.

Among nearby restaurants are **Boschetto**, via Ausonia 54 (Tel: 0776-30-12-27), with good local cooking, and **Canguro**, via Appia Nuova 8500 (Tel: 0776-442-59; closed Mondays). Both are inexpensive.

PONZA

Lazio's dramatically beautiful island of Ponza, off the coast of Anzio south of Rome, had been kept in the family until recently; foreigners didn't flock there, except perhaps in August when every puddle in Italy speaks a different language. In recent years, easier transit, including hydrofoils, has changed all that, facilitating weekend trips. Yet despite it all, Ponza maintains a striking individuality.

The Pontine Islands (Isole Ponziane), of which Ponza is the largest and most important, are volcanic islands whose past extends to the Paleolithic era. Their early history followed the course of their supply of obsidian, the hard stone best suited for knives. Used first as a trading post, Ponza became a convenient isle for receiving those who'd fallen out of favor with the Roman emperor Tiberius. Monks lived on the island through the Middle Ages, and colonists arrived during a tax-incentive program of the Bourbons in Naples. During World War II the island was again used for exiles— and also for Mussolini during a short period after the war.

The island's charm is its 6 miles of amazing configurations: jagged, pale tufa cliffs rise high above the sea, and beaches and grottos soften the rocky shoreline. The principal town, also called **Ponza**, is pastel-colored and simple. The island's interior is usually reached through tunnels, like the one the Romans dug to the **Chiaia** (kee-AY-ya) **di Luna** (Moonlight Bay), where a 300-foot-high crescent of cliff shelters a beach below (at low tide). A boat trip around the island circles grottoes and beaches, but the real joy is the drama of the island itself against the sea. If you climb **Monte Guardia** to Punta della Guardia (1 hour) you will discover extraordinary, bizarre rock formations. At sea, scuba divers may find coral and sunken ships amid the sea creatures.

The **Chiaia di Luna**, on a cliff that overlooks the bay, is an unusual hotel complex of small buildings united by terraces and stairways. The beach is reached through a Roman tunnel, but the pool and bar, solarium and restaurant are close at hand. The **Torre dei Borboni** takes a bit of walking to get to (they'll send a porter); the hotel and its site in an old Bourbon fort are worth the effort, especially if your room is in the 18th-century castle that overlooks the port. Ponza's lobster (*aragosta*) is served in the sea-view dining room, and their private beach is down a stairway. The good budget choice on Ponza is **Gennarino a Mare**, with balconies overlooking the sea.

Ponza's festivals occur on the last Sunday in February and on June 20, both commemorating San Silverio, the pope who drew the wrath of the Byzantine empress Theodora, who backed another candidate. Legend has it that he was murdered on Ponza on June 20.

To arrive at Ponza from the port of Fiumicino (near Rome's airport), take the Medmar hydrofoil or ferry (about 40,000 lire); the trip takes about 6 hours. Reserve well in advance during the summer (piazza Barberini 5, 00187 Rome; Tel: 06-482-85-79; Fax: 06-481-45-01). Helios runs ferries from Anzio and Formia on the Lazio coast (Anzio: 06-984-50-85; Formia: 0771-70-07-10).

If you're held up at Fiumicino (the airport or the nearby harbor town), or if you need a respite between flights, stop at the **Ship Museum** near the airport on via Portuense at km

5, and at the **Isola Sacra** excavations of ancient Roman tombs, on the road to Ostia at km 3.5. For lunch at Fiumicino's port, stop at **Il Pescatore**, via Torre Clementina 154 (Tel: 06-644-01-89), or at the famous **Bastianelli al Centro**, on the same street at number 88 (closed Wednesdays; Tel: 06-644-00-95).

ACCOMMODATIONS REFERENCE

The rates given below are projections for 1992; always check for up-to-date information before making reservations. Wide ranges may reflect the differences between low- and high-season rates. Unless otherwise indicated, the figures indicate the cost of a double room (per room, not per person). However, half-board (mezza pensione) rates, which include breakfast and one other meal per day, are per person. Most hotels will add a service charge of 10 to 15 percent.

► **Balletti Palace.** Viale Trento 100, 01100 **Viterbo**. Tel: (0761) 34-47-77; Fax: same. ₤88,000–₤135,000.

► **Chiaia di Luna.** Via Chiaia di Luna, 04027 **Ponza**. Tel: (0771) 801-13; Fax: (0771) 89-98-21. Open May 15–October 10. ₤200,000.

► **Mini Palace.** Via Santa Maria della Grotticella 2, 01100 **Viterbo**. Tel: (0761) 23-97-42; Fax: (0761) 23-97-44. ₤100,000–₤165,000.

► **Torre dei Borboni.** Via Madonna 1, 04027 **Ponza**. Tel: (0771) 801-09. ₤60,000.

► **Tuscia.** Via Cairoli 41, 01100 **Viterbo**. Tel: (0761) 22-33-77; Fax: (0761) 34-59-76. ₤55,000–₤90,000.

► **Villa Fiorio.** Viale Dusmet 28, 00046 **Grottaferrata**. Tel: (06) 945-92-76; Fax: (06) 945-92-79. ₤160,000.

► **Gennarino a Mare.** Via Dante 64, 04027 **Ponza**. Tel: (0771) 800-71; Fax: (0771) 800-98. ₤70,000.

THE ABRUZZI

By Joanne Hahn

There are few world capitals you can leave and, within a couple of hours, find yourself in a region as high, as wild, and as spectacular as the Abruzzi (actually the regions of Abruzzo and Molise joined). Rome is such a capital, and the province to its east, which until recent times was known for being both primitive and remote, has suddenly been brought into the orbit of every traveller, thanks to the miracle of Italy's roads. The same autostrada that skirts Hadrian's Villa, A 24, soon enough delivers you into the center of a mountain world once known for its witches, its superstitions, its wolves, and, just to help things along, its werewolves, or *lupi mannari*. You'll glimpse men and women in colorful peasant dress, see farmers making cheese in their backyards, marvel at barns constructed of reeds, and at times believe you have just encountered the beginnings of civilization. The region is not without its learned men, however, for three stellar minds were born here: Ovid, Gabriele D'Annunzio, and Benedetto Croce.

The breathtaking mountains—the highest of the Apennines—were largely responsible for cutting the Abruzzi off from the north and directing its traffic toward Apulia and the south as well as to the port of Pescara on the Adriatic. These peaks are high enough to be snow-covered year-round and can be seen from every side: From the seacoast they form a silhouette the natives call "The Sleeping Beauty," and from Abruzzo's capital, L'Aquila, the white crests of the Gran Sasso form a barrier 9,000 feet high. Natives claim that the weather is best here, with 11 cool months and only one cold one.

The well-constructed roads to L'Aquila from every direction glide through a landscape that never fails to delight: lush valleys, rushing streams, and Medieval towns perched on terraced hills. Voyagers who arrived at these villages were once in for a rough night in whatever passed for lodgings; inedible food and beds crawling with "little strangers" were commonplace. Now there are modern hotels not only in the larger towns but in the mountains as well—the latter opened up as ski resorts in the winter and as havens for nature and wildlife lovers in the summer. For those who ski there are outposts in every direction—Campo Imperatore, Campo Felice, Campo di Giove. If you're searching for interesting flora and fauna, head toward the south, where the hills below Sulmona and Scanno lead to the Parco Nazionale d'Abruzzo.

MAJOR INTEREST

Wild, mountainous landscape
Medieval villages
Rustic, strongly flavored food

L'Aquila

Churches of Santa Maria di Collemaggio and San
    Bernardino
Castello and its Museo Nazionale d'Abruzzo
Fontana delle 99 Cannelle
Tre Marie restaurant

Teramo (mountain town)
Gran Sasso d'Italia and its ski resorts
Scanno (jewelry in Roman style)
Sulmona (Medieval hill town)
Parco Nazionale d'Abruzzo
Chieti (Roman ruins)
Saepinum (preserved ancient Roman town)

L'Aquila

From its Romanesque and Renaissance churches to its perfect Spanish **Castello**, a fine example of military architecture (complete with moat) built by Don Pedro of Toledo during the reign of Charles V to protect the northern outpost of the Kingdom of Naples and keep tight reins on its rebellious citizens, L'Aquila is a town of architectural treasures. From its ramparts you can see the snow-capped peaks of the Gran Sasso. There are many parks and piazzas that weave among lovely Medieval homes and finely decorated churches. The

MARCHE

UMBRIA

*To Rimini
and
Bologna*

A14

80

Teramo

150

Atri

A14

A24

491

Castelli

Albe

553

Il Gran Sasso d'Italia

Assergi

Corno Grande

Forte Cerreto

Campo Imperatore

Amniterium

L'Aquila

Bazzano

Campo Felice

Castelnuovo

17

San
Clemente

Caporciano

Aterno R.

*Mt.
Rotondo*

San
Felino

*Mt.
Morrone*

Sulmona

*Tav
Rotor*

5 bis

A24

A25

Albe

Cocullo

479

Gizio R.

Sagittario R.

17

5

Avezzano

Colle Rotondo

Scanno

82

Balsorano

Pescasseroli

83

Sora

N

A2

*To
Rome*

**Parco
Nazionale
d'Abruzzo**

LAZIO

E1

**The
Abruzzi**

0   miles   15

0   km   15

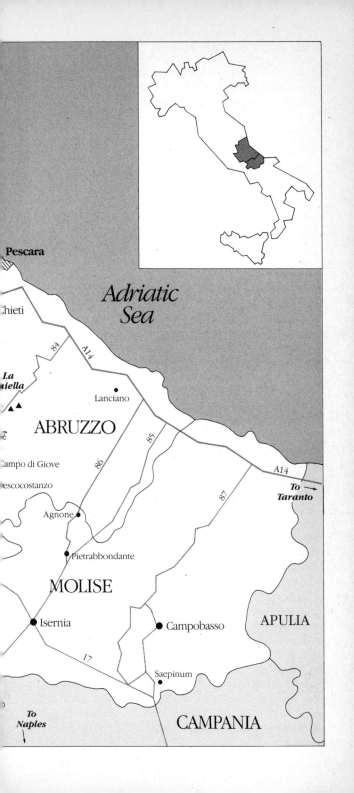

Spanish were here for some time, and they must have felt at home. The spectacle of L'Aquila's buildings, often subtle yet colorful, in contrast with the drama of their background is reminiscent of Granada, another town favored by Emperor Charles, even though here the streets are laid out in a more rectilinear manner. Set in a sprawling park with lovely paths, the Castello has been turned into a very well designed museum, the **Museo Nazionale d'Abruzzo**, with collections of archaeological treasures, Medieval art, and Renaissance sculpture. The ground floor contains some of the most interesting exhibits, including the overwhelming *elephas meriodinales,* a marvelously reconstructed skeleton of a 1.5-million-year-old pachyderm, as well as numerous Roman portraits, statues, and a wonderful polychrome wooden statue by Silvestro d'Aquila. During July and August, concerts sponsored by the Societa Aquilana Concerti are held in the castle's auditorium. (An attractive modern hotel, appropriately named the **Castello,** is conveniently located opposite the castle in the piazza Battaglione Alpini and marks the entrance to the main street, via Vittorio Emanuele. It's a bit noisy here, so ask for a back room.)

The natural daughter of Charles V, Margaret of Parma, retired to L'Aquila after two not very happy marriages: one to a Medici (murdered), the other to a Farnese. She was an *amazone* and, by all accounts, was a kindred spirit to Christina of Sweden, often riding forth from her palace (now the Palazzo di Giustizia) dressed as a man. The streets of L'Aquila have hardly changed since then, and it is thanks to them, and the inviting promenades they offer, that the town can be best enjoyed if you stay over—to search for the rare *tombola* lace, one of Abruzzo's treasures; to see the *passeggiata* down the corso Federico II at sunset or stop at the **Magic** shop for a winning *tiramisù* and coffee, or their delicious *gelato* (via dell'Indipendenza 25); to see its small piazzas with their fountains in the evening under the stars; and then to witness the hubbub of the market in front of the Duomo the next morning. A perfect stand-up lunch can be had here, with stands offering chickens roasted on a spit and a wonderfully spicy *porchetta* sandwich.

At the end of Federico II and the juncture of via Rendina is the **Grand Hotel del Parco,** an excellent choice for lodging, with formal furnishings, marble lobby, fine antiques, excellent rooms (the quietest are in the back), and a fine restaurant, **La Grotta di Aligi** (reservations needed; Tel: 0862-652-60; closed Mondays). On a grander scale, although the atrocious façade belies the comforts within, is the **Duca degli Abruzzi**, viale Giovanni XXIII 10, with a lovely roof garden and a splendid restaurant offering super-lative mountain views. Ask for a room on the third floor, which seems to be the quietest.

The cathedral, due to the earthquakes that plague the Abruzzi, has fared badly; but it never did compare with the two outstanding churches of L'Aquila. One, **Santa Maria di Collemaggio**, is on the edge of town and reached via a tree-lined avenue. It has a boldly designed façade of pink-and-white stone, and its patterned polychrome is interrupted by three Romanesque portals and three rose windows. Santa Maria was founded by an aged hermit named Pietro Angeleri at the end of the 13th century, to honor a miraculous appear-ance of the Virgin. Later, when Pietro was living in Monte Morrone, the College of Cardinals, which had reached an impasse, almost dragged him from his mountain retreat to become pope. Pope was the last thing that the naïve Pietro wanted to be, and once his ill-suitedness for the job was recognized he abdicated, only to be imprisoned by the suc-ceeding pontiff, Pope Boniface VIII, who wasn't naïve at all. Pietro was kept in a castle at Fumone until he died at the age of 81, and only then was it considered safe to bring his remains back to his own church, to canonize him as Saint Celestine, and later to build him the fine Renaissance tomb that graces the church.

The other saint who ended up in L'Aquila was Saint Bernardino of Siena, the great revivalist preacher who ar-rived at the Franciscan convent in L'Aquila just in time to die—to the everlasting fury of the Sienese, who never got his body back. The people of L'Aquila gave him a superb Renaissance church, however: The **Church of San Bernar-dino** has one of the most elegant and balanced façades, with an imposing mausoleum sculpted by Silvestro dell'Aquila, the master Abruzzeso sculptor who created one almost equally fine for Maria Pereira in the north chancel. And don't miss the Della Robbia altar.

Very much the point of visiting L'Aquila are the smaller churches and their respective piazzas, which are scattered all over town: San Giusta and San Flaviano (Romanesque); Santa Maria di Paganica, surrounded by Gothic palaces; San Silvestro, with its frescoes; and San Giuseppe, with its Gothic tombs. Near the Porta Rivera is San Vito, and below it is the **Fontana delle 99 Cannelle**, built in 1272, where 99 sculpted masks of humans, animals, and grotesques spout water—today a lamentable sight with bits of garbage floating in its trough. According to legend, L'Aquila rose from the earth, like Athena from the brow of Zeus, with 99 of everything: quarters, fountains, churches, and 99 villages around it to come to its rescue in time of need. The truth is that the city was founded in 1240 by Emperor Frederick II as yet another bastion against Rome. Near the fountain is the hotel **Le Cannelle**, on via Tancredi da Pentina, with 115 modern rooms, a pool, tennis courts, and other amenities.

L'Aquila is an excellent base from which to explore the area's archaeological collections, Medieval villages, and monastic sites. By taking scenic route 17 east, which cuts through fields of lavender and saffron, past Bazzano— where the 13th-century church of Santa Giusta with its vaulted campanile and frescoes is worth a visit—you'll come to the small hill town of **Castelnuovo**. Beyond it lie the ruins of Peltuinum, an important city in Roman times. Amid the remains of a theater and town walls rises the **Church of San Paolo**, erected in the eighth century. Threaded through these grassy fields is the ancient *Tratturo Magno,* a ribbon of white stones and part of a larger network of *tratturi,* migration paths used by shepherds to herd their flocks from summer pastures in the mountains to winter ones along the Adriatic. In just a short distance you'll see the turnoff for the little town of **Caporciano**, beyond which is the tiny hamlet of Bominaco, perched on a hill and dominated by the ruins of a castle above. Here are two of the most celebrated monuments in Christendom, the churches of **Santa Maria Assunta** and the small **San Pellegrino**, founded by Charlemagne. The primitive oratory of San Pellegrino has fascinating colorful naïf frescoes. The upper church, Santa Maria, has none of the delicate charm of the oratory but is a handsome Romanesque basilica richly endowed with carved doors, an outstanding pulpit, and a giant Paschal candelabrum. A spirited custodian who lives right across from the churches will admit you and fill you in on the details.

Retracing route 17 through L'Aquila and then travelling route 80 for a few miles, you will come to the ruins of Amniterium, the Sabine city that was the birthplace of the Roman historian Sallust.

The Food of L'Aquila
and the Abruzzi

Frederick did a great deal for the cuisine of Apulia and his other domains to the south, and it is possible that a whiff of the East inherited from his childhood in semi-Saracen

Palermo affected the food of the Abruzzi, too. And varied that food is, originating as it does in the five provinces that make up this region of the Abruzzi, in the plural. The region's red-hot pepper, *diavoletto,* is thrown around with an almost Moroccan abandon, and little jars of fire and oil grace every tabletop. Every aromatic herb at hand is used as well, including tarragon (supposedly introduced to the French by the Abruzzese chef of Caterina de' Medici). Meats are almost always treated with rosemary, white wine, and olive oil, and saffron and capers turn up in many dishes. The various cuisines of the province—mountain, hill, and sea—were once more separate than they are now, and renowned cheeses appear in every area: *Pecorino* is often used in cooking, and the pear-shaped *scamorza,* made from the milk of cows that graze high in the mountains, is exported on a large scale. Vegetables are prepared with great care, and those of the spring, such as peas and fava beans, are thrown—along with lentils—into a *minestra* known as *le virtù.* (The key to the dish is the number seven—referring to the seven virtues; tradition dictates that seven types of meat, vegetables, seasonings, and pasta must go into the soup.)

In L'Aquila, you can sample some of the best regional cuisine (without bankrupting yourself) at the venerable **Tre Marie** restaurant, tucked away at number 3 on via Tre Marie, off piazza del Duomo (Tel: 0862-201-91; closed Sunday evenings and Mondays). Even in the story of its inception, the Tre Marie is typical of L'Aquila's past. In the 19th century the great-grandfather of the present owner went off to the hills to buy cheese and lamb for his inn. He was killed by bandits, and his widow was left with three daughters to raise. The widow taught her daughters to cook, and a restaurant was started when they passed on her recipes to their children. The menu changes with the season, of course, but quite conveniently always includes the basic local dishes. For soups there is a *minestra* of vegetables, or a chicken broth served with light crêpes—*scrippelle M'Busse*—and sprinkled with Parmesan. Most diners will opt for the Abruzzi's favorite pasta: *maccheroni alla chitarra,* also called *tonnarelli.* Pressed into very thin strips through the strings of the wood-and-steel harp once found in every household here, the pasta is then served with either a sauce of tomato or one of diced meat and *pecorino.* Polenta with chopped sausage is an alternative, and so are the short, flat *fusilli* served with a game sauce. All the local cheeses are on the menu of the Tre Marie, with the *scamorza* prepared *allo spiedo* (on a skewer). The best of the desserts are the *dolcetti paesani di mandorle,* a selection of every sort of almond sweet, from the rich soft marzipan made in the southern hills of Maiella to a crisp variation of Spanish *turron.* In the midst of this gustatory ecstasy, don't forget to look up at the pretty antique majolica plates on the wall.

The ham of L'Aquila was certainly a Spanish innovation— cured here but resembling that of Serrano. Fresh mountain river trout are served at the Tre Marie on a bed of potatoes and black olives; also from the mountains come the truffles, sliced and served with breast of chicken. The two favorite local meats are roast lamb and pork, both cooked with herbs. For the spring festivals, pork is served out on the piazzas, and roast suckling pig is sold at stands with accompanying slabs of bread.

More modest dining can be found at **Trattoria San Biagio**, in the piazza of the same name, number 4. Simple furnishings pair well with honest cooking such as grilled meats, a delicious side dish of bitter greens called *agretti,* and fresh fruit for dessert. Closed Sundays. Tel: (0862) 221-39.

The wines of the Abruzzi have recently improved: the rosé (Rosatello) has always been worthy of export, but it has now been joined by a red Montepulciano d'Abruzzo and a white Trebbiano.

The cuisine of the Abruzzi has come very much into its own in the past decade, and apart from L'Aquila there are two other centers for sampling it. One, the mountain town of **Teramo**, 75 km (45 miles) to the northeast and reached by beautiful roads (route 80), is the capital of its own province within a province. A picturesque place, it is a Roman town in origin, though much of the city is Medieval and Renaissance in appearance. Its heyday occurred during the Angevin reign, and there are many fine buildings dating from this period. Eventually the city was incorporated into the Kingdom of Naples. In the 12th-century red-brick **Duomo**, there is a silver altar consisting of 34 panels depicting scenes from the Bible, by Nicola da Guardiagrele (1448). Located in the old part of town, the Duomo also has a stunning Cosmati portal, good Romanesque statues of saints, and a swallowtail crenelated roofline indicating its Ghibelline allegiance. Roman ruins have been excavated near the center of town.

At the **Church of Madonna della Grazie**, in the east end of town, there is a good 15th-century Virgin made of wood, the work of Silvestro dell'Aquila. The Villa Comunale houses a museum with artworks by local and Neapolitan artists. In Teramo, the restaurant **Duomo**, via Stazio 9 (Tel: 0861-32-12-74; closed Mondays), has been turned by its proprietor, Elio

Pompa, into a place for both traditional dishes and some of his own creations, such as rigatoni *alla Candida,* an aromatic dish with olives, herbs, and prosciutto. Lamb or roast kid can follow, and the wines here are particularly good.

The best hotel in Teramo is the **Sporting,** via De Gasperi 41, which is sited on a gorge acoss from the old city. Offering not much in the way of architectural appeal, the hotel does have a host of modern conveniences, such as an indoor pool, air-conditioning, sauna, and gym. And a pretty good restaurant, **Il Carpaccio** (closed Mondays). One annoying detraction is noise: The walls are thin in this hotel, and every sound reverberates.

The road south from Teramo, along route 80, which connects to route 491, requires some careful driving through twisting roads and culminates at the dramatically situated village of **Castelli,** set high on a hill of the Gran Sasso. The town is a haven for pottery lovers and, as one of the oldest ceramic capitals in Italy, contains an impressive collection, which you can see in the **Museo delle Ceramiche di Castelli.** Don't miss the ceiling of the **Church of San Donato** (just outside of town), covered with more than 1,000 beautifully painted tiles and appropriately called the Sistine Chapel of Italian Majolica.

Another worthwhile detour from Teramo is to the little town of **Atri,** reached by scenic route 150 east, and then 553 south. Along the way there are two Romanesque gems of churches to see, both near the juncture of route 553. The first, **San Clemente al Vomano,** is a sweet stony quilt made up of bits of Roman ruins. Built in the ninth century and rebuilt in the 12th, it contains a highly original ciborium and a statue of (who else?) Saint Clement. A few miles beyond is the Romanesque-Gothic church and abbey of **Santa Maria de Propezzano,** which has 12th-, 13th-, and 15th-century frescoes, and 17th-century frescoes by the Polish artist Sebastiano Majewski, in the spacious cloister. (Obtain keys from the nearby house.)

A good stop for lunch in Guardia Vomano is **Tre Archi,** a simple place serving good regional cuisine (closed Tuesdays and November; Tel: 085-89-81-40).

Atri, the legendary Hatria, which stands on the site of the ancient Sabine city, became a Roman colony in 282 B.C. Vain and somewhat of a big deal during its checkered past, it is credited by some for giving its name to the Adriatic—although another proud contender for this distinction is the Veneto town of Adria, whose name does sound a bit closer to Adriatic. Ancient scholars such as Pliny and Livy hotly debated these claims. Atri even went so far as to engrave the claim on its coins, thus realizing the even greater prestige of having the heaviest minted coins in Western Europe (exceeding in weight the oldest Roman coins). Controlled intermittently during the Middle Ages and Renaissance by the Acquaviva dukes, whose **Palazzo Ducale** is now the city's municipal and post office, the city has recently unearthed some Roman remains, particularly in the piazza and under its fine Duomo. The 13th-century Romanesque-Gothic **Duomo**, with its graceful campanile and elegant façade, contains beautiful 15th-century frescoes by Andrea Delitio on the life of the Virgin. It also contains the largest church organ in Abruzzi (6,000 pipes). In the crypt you'll see the remains of a Roman *piscina,* and mosaics under the altar.

The **Museo Capitolare** (open mid-June to mid-September; reserve in advance at other times) has an excellent collection of jewelry, ecclesiastical items, and wooden sculptures. There's a pretty good restaurant in town, too: the **Campana d'Oro**, piazza Duomo 23 (closed Tuesdays; Tel: 085-87-01-77).

The Gran Sasso

With nature at its most awe-inspiring and views at their most thrilling, an excursion to **Il Gran Sasso d'Italia**, a snow-capped ridge of limestone 22 miles long and bare but for the snow, is one of the most compelling reasons for visiting the Abruzzi. The highest peak, the Corno Grande (9,554 feet), is higher than any peak in southern Italy except Sicily's Etna. Consisting of two chains, almost parallel and separated by a depression, the Gran Sasso divides the Abruzzi from the Marches to the north. Hikers equipped with good maps, which are available at newsstands, can walk to *rifugi* (inexpensive inns). The Club Alpino Italiano, via XX Settembre 8, L'Aquila, is the best source of information, but a knowledge of Italian is essential. To make the trek to the top of the massif from L'Aquila, take a city bus to Fonte Cerreto, near the village of Assergi (or travel route 17 *bis* north), and from there take the cable car to Campo Imperatore (about a 15-minute ride), at the foot of the Corno Grande. The hike to the top will take you about seven hours. **Campo Imperatore**, at 7,029 feet and once the bed of a prehistoric lake, is also connected by bus with L'Aquila (about 25 km/15 miles away) and is a lively ski and hiking resort that brims with flowers in spring and sleek skiers in winter. There are three ski lifts at Campo Imperatore and nearby Monte Cristo, with runs rivaling the best the Alps have to offer and cross-country ski trails, too. **Campo Felice**, south of L'Aquila, off route 5 *bis,* also has good skiing and bobsledding. From here you can visit the picturesque village of **Rocca di Cambio**, the highest in the Abruzzi.

The Gran Sasso is certainly more accessible to present-day travellers than it was to Otto Skorzeny, who was sent to these mountains by Hitler in 1943 to rescue Mussolini. After his arrest, Il Duce had been shifted from one isolated prison to another, and it took two months for the Germans to discover where he was. Once found, the hideaway—a hotel on the Gran Sasso—was surrounded by German commandos who had been landed by glider. The Italian guards put up no resistance, and Skorzeny rushed to the room where Mussolini was lodged, explained what was happening, and with the help of a crack aviator named Gerlach managed, in a damaged plane, to get the dictator to Vienna that very evening.

The Southern Ranges

Many travellers will want to head southeast to the range of La Maiella and Monte Morrone above Sulmona, or to the Colle Rotondo above Scanno, because this southern region culminates in the **Parco Nazionale d'Abruzzo**, 150 square miles of scenic splendor inhabited by chamois, bears, and golden eagles, much of it crisscrossed by excellent roads. Most people begin their excursion at **Pescasseroli**, the largest village in the park, where you'll find a museum, gardens, and a small zoo, as well as a reception center that can provide excellent hiking itineraries. The trails to the Camosciara, a superb mountain area embracing woods, waterfalls, and the Val Fondillo, which is thick with beech, pines, and crystalline waters, are the most favored. A lovely trail of moderate difficulty is the two-hour hike up to the Valico di Monte Tranquillo. The less ambitious may take the *funivia* to the summit of Monte Vitelle. The grandest hotel in the Pescasseroli area is the **Grand Hotel del Parco**, which is beautifully situated and has a garden and pool.

The roads south to the Parco Nazionale, however, also pass through or near places of interest: **San Pelino**, with its Romanesque church, and **Pescocostanzo**, off route 84 near route 17, a gabled Medieval town of artisans and once famous for its delicate lace. The church of **Santa Maria del Colle** is noteworthy, with an exceptionally fine ceiling in the nave and a lovely painting of the *Madonna and Child* on the high altar.

Situated between routes 83 and 17 and reached by route 479, **Scanno** is a dreamy city perched on a hill and dusted with antiquity; on Sundays the town's matrons don traditional headdresses and long black Middle Eastern dresses that seem frightfully cumbersome. Any attempts to snap a shot of these ladies should be suppressed, for they take none too kindly to gawking tourists and "the sight of a camera is enough to send the old women in black scurrying into archways and vanishing from balconies," as H. V. Morton says in his superb book *A Traveller in Southern Italy*. The town is a center for jewelers whose designs have changed little since Roman days. There are hotels aplenty, thanks to winter sports, both in town and on the lake, where a rain-bringing Virgin has her shrine. In the first week of May, the little statue, no more than a foot high, draped in fancy Spanish vestments and dripping with gold and other gifts, is carried the two-mile run into town and is then placed in the altar of the village church, where she remains for a month.

The best hotel is the inexpensive **Mille Pini**, simple, neat, Alpine in style, and, as the name suggests, surrounded by pines. It is situated at the foot of the chair lift to the small winter resort of Monte Rotondo. If you don't mind staying a five-minute drive outside of town, the rustic **Hotel del Lago** sits right on tiny Lago di Scanno and offers simple but comfortable lakeside rooms, as well as enclosed terrace dining and boating facilities. And across the lake is the little frescoed chapel of the Madonna del Lago, where the presiding Virgin of the rain stands. Scanno's top restaurant is **Gli Archetti**, a wonderful old-fashioned tavern in a 16th-century cellar tucked away on a quiet back street, serving excellent bean dishes and grilled trout (via Silla 8; Tel: 0864-746-45; closed Tuesdays).

The best known of these hill towns remains **Sulmona**, right off route 17, just south of A 25, ideally situated in a rich green basin ringed by mountains. It doesn't take long to discover who the favorite native son of Sulmona is. "Sulmo Mihi Patria Est," declared the Roman poet Ovid, and the Sulmonese have taken his word for it. The principal thoroughfare is the corso Ovidio, the town's coat of arms bears the letters SMPE, a statue of him graces the largest piazza, and there are plenty of indications as to where "Ovid's Villa" can be found. Whether or not it even belonged to his distant kin, its size reminds us, as Ovid himself was wont to do, that he was a knight and born into a wealthy family, in a land "cool and rich in water." (The mountains around Sulmona frame a valley laced with streams.) The poet himself, hardly elegiac, was by no means addicted to country life; highly urbane, he preferred metropolitan Rome. His elegant, completely amoral verses described nature of another sort—without, miraculously, ever using an obscene word. Later, the natives of Sulmona became confused about his powers; it was said that Ovid was more literate than even Cicero because he could read with his feet (his statue in Sulmona has him standing on a book).

When Frederick II made Sulmona capital of its own province, it flourished as a center of learning and religion; today the town earns its prominence in a sweeter commerce—the production of *confetti* (colorful candy-coated almonds) and other nuts indispensable throughout Italy for conferring good wishes at weddings and christenings.

Along Corso Ovidio, you'll find the handsome **church of Santa Maria Annunziata** and its adjacent palazzo, a harmonious blend of three architectural styles—Medieval, Renaissance, and Baroque. Begun in 1320, the church is considered one of the finest in Abruzzi.

Sulmona was noted for its superior goldsmiths during the 14th and 15th centuries, and there is a magnificent collection of jewelry in the **Museo Civico**, on the first floor in the palazzo houses, as well as Medieval sculptures and archaeological remains. Throughout the city you'll find ghostly remnants of more vivid times.

Bounding the bustling **piazza Garibaldi**, from which the main street leads, are the fragments of a 13th-century aqueduct that supplied water to the town and its many mills. And across from this thriving marketplace, where stalls teem with everything from fruit to the latest duds, stands the remarkable Gothic portal of Santa Francesca della Scarpa, a Medieval prop covering the presbytery of a newer church behind it, in the piazza del Carmine. Across from here is the **Fontana del Vecchio**, so named because of the sweet old man who tops it.

The **Cathedral of San Panfilo**, at the north end of town, built on the remains of a Roman temple, has a fine Gothic portal, and inside a crypt containing a lovely 12th-century Byzantine-style relief of the enthroned Madonna, as well as a bust of Saint Panfilo and a 12th-century bishop's chair.

The **Europa Park Hotel**, roughly 3 km (2 miles) north of town on Strada Statale 17N, offers perhaps the most comfortable lodging, with tennis courts and a good restaurant on the premises. For dining, choose between **Da Nicola** (Tel: 0864-330-70), serving wonderful homemade pasta and grilled meats in a homey setting, and **Ristorante Cesidio** (via Sollimo 25; Tel: 0864-527-24), with simple furnishings that never detract from the dazzling antipasti and homemade soups and pasta with beans.

As you walk through the streets of Sulmona, you'll see shops festooned with the handicrafts of the region. Many are worth toting home—such as the gaily colored and handsome bedspreads and carpets that you are unlikely to find outside of Abruzzi.

As for ski resorts in this region, the town of **Campo di Giove**, 85 km (53 miles) southeast of L'Aquila and just 18 km (11 miles) east of Sulmona, stands in the shadow of Tavola Rotonda (6,703 feet), which is one of the peaks of the Maiella mountains. In the old village there are still some houses dating from the 15th century. The **Abruzzo**, a modest hotel popular with skiers, has 22 rooms and is very reasonably priced.

A mountain retreat on a grand scale at a very reasonable price is the **Castello di Balsorano**, a fine outpost on the western side of the national park from which to make forays into the park or nearby Lazio. This 13th-century fortress, miraculously spared by the barbarians and the earthquakes, is Medieval to the core. Inside coats of armor, shields, and daggers abound. Some bedrooms, though a bit frayed, are done up in baronial style, with silk wall hangings and ornately carved beds. Proprietor Mary Ricci is English, a help in this land where little *inglese* is spoken. The hotel is very small, however (five doubles, one suite, all with bath and central heating), so reserve well in advance. Meals are good and moderately priced; even so, you will pay more for them than for the room.

Elsewhere in the Abruzzi

The Abruzzi produced another poet, one of our century, and his birthplace is one of the few sights that the Adriatic port of **Pescara** has to offer. Gabriele D'Annunzio was to be as famous in his time as Ovid was in imperial Rome—and with some similarities: Both, in their youth, shocked the world with their poems of unbridled sensuality; both became the darlings of the aristocracy; and both treated their subject matter as masters of style. But there the resemblance ends. D'Annunzio was born into a humble family, and he was finally a very serious man who loved his country (he lost an eye for it in World War I, and soon after secured Fiume for Italy with his own army of companions). Ovid showed nothing but scorn for the rustic Abruzzese, whereas D'Annunzio, though born on the coast, was fascinated by the people of the mountainous interior, and in particular by their ventures into sorcery and witchcraft.

Witches and snake charmers descended upon the Abruzzi from the west in ancient times, when a people called the Marsi streamed over the mountains to settle around what is now Avezzano, leaving their name on many a village still there: *nei Marsi*. They brought their spells with them, and their ability with snakes, too. Every year at his festival at Cocullo, near Scanno, the image of San Domenico is carried forth covered with a writhing, hissing brood. Children here are taught to handle snakes without fear, and these reptiles even turn up on the coat of arms of the monastic order of San Celestino.

If you go to Pescara in July (and assuming the Adriatic has tidied up its present pollution), you can combine the pleasures of listening to the jazz festival with those of sunbathing on the city's long stretch of sandy beach, which is chock-a-block with hotels and families. The seaside terrace of the **Guerino** restaurant, viale della Riviera 4, is a delightful spot to feast on tasty Adriatic dishes, especially the house fish soup (closed Thursdays except in July and August; Tel: 085-421-2065). Be sure to try the *parrozzo*, a rich chocolate cake that is a specialty of the area. Particularly good value can be had at **La Cantina di Jozz**, via delle Caserme 61, which also serves regional specialties. Closed Sunday evening, Mondays, and June 24 to July 9. Tel: (085) 69-03-83.

Right outside the city, up in the hills, is one of Pescara's finest restaurants. **La Terrazza Verde** (largo Madonna dei Sette Dolori 6, reached by via Rigopiano) enjoys a panoramic setting and specializes in rich duck and goose dishes, such as *pappardelle* in a goose sauce, which it serves in its attractive garden. Closed Wednesdays and Christmas. Tel: (085) 41-32-39.

Roughly 8 km (5 miles) north of Avezzano are the remains of the ancient town of **Alba Fucens**, near the village of Albe. Founded as a Roman stronghold in 300 B.C., the ancient ruins sprawl over three hills, with ancient and Medieval ruins entwined. Excavations have yielded basilicas, baths, amphitheaters, and a long section of the original Via Valeria.

It was in the Abruzzi that the word *Italia* was born; and, whether Greek, Roman, or Italic, remains of Classical cultures litter the gentle slopes of Chieti and Molise as they descend toward the sea or toward Apulia to the south. **Chieti**, south of Pescara off A 25, has its own sterling repository of pre-Roman and Roman artworks; visit the **Museo Nazionale Archeologico di Antichità**, in the Villa Comunale, which itself is set amid spacious gardens. The star attraction is the eight-foot statue known as the *Warrior of Capestrano*, which dates from the sixth century B.C. and may be the best portrait of the ancient Italic tribe, the Picenes. From the belvedere of the villa you'll also have a good view of the Maiella mountains. If you head toward the cathedral from the museum you pass the **Tempietti Romani** (the remains of three temples dating from the first century), a Roman theater, and, at the edge of town, the ruins of baths. Eating establishments in Chieti are of a more recent vintage, and **Venturini**, via de Lollis 10, offers tasty regional cuisine on a spacious terrace (Tel: 0871-658-63; closed Tuesdays).

For more liberal interpretations of Abruzzi fare, try **D'Angiò e Ristorante La Regine**, a hotel/restaurant enterprise with comfortable, moderately priced rooms and moderate-to-expensive meals (via Solferino 20; Tel: 0871-34-73-56). This glass house perched on a hill just a few miles outside of Chieti is the venture of Nicola Ranieri, a charming host who once owned the renowned Taverna Ranieri in Lanciano. His welcome couldn't be warmer, with wine, fruit, and autographed copies of his recipe collection awaiting you. Though the quarters are undistinguished, the food is top-flight, with dishes such as shrimp over saffron risotto and tender boar atop polenta. Wines are superior here, and there's a good "tasting menu" for 45,000 lire. Try the unusual Picolit dessert wine from Lipari (75,000 lire per bottle).

Chieti makes a good base from which to explore the impressive **Abbey of San Clemente a Casauria**. Take scenic route 5 southwest in the direction of Tocco da Casauria. Founded in the ninth century near the ancient settlement of Interpromium, the abbey was restored in the 12th century and is one of the most beautiful examples of Abruzzi Romanesque-Gothic style, with distinct and individual interpretations of neighboring Apulian and Tuscan styles. The simple interior is a perfect backdrop for the ornate pulpit, a 13th-century Paschal candelabrum, and a stunning ciborium taken from an early Christian sarcophagus.

Molise

It is in the province of Molise, at the southern end of the Abruzzi, however, that you will come upon the most ancient towns, often Samnite in origin, with some ruins contemporary with the Golden Age of Greece. In the north of the province are the excavations at **Pietrabbondante**: a theater and scattered temples surrounded by the countryside and situated on a green tableland with views in every direction.

From here route 86, heading north, wraps around the

Selvapiana forest and leads to the pristine town of **Agnone**, which sits high above the beautiful Trigno valley. The "Athens of the Samnites," as Agnone is known, shapes bells for worshipers around the world. Visit the Marinelli Pontifical Foundry, the oldest in Italy and supplier to the Vatican. Agnone itself makes for a refreshing stay. Streets are lined with shops redolent of marzipan and display a rainbow of *confetti,* and there are many fine copper stores where you can find every sort of pot and utensil. Although there are no grand hotels here, the **Hotel/Ristorante Sammartino**, situated right in the city, is pleasant and serves excellent food (largo Pietro Micca 44; Tel: 0865-782-39).

Larger in scale than Pietrabbondante and not far south of Molise's capital, Campobasso (off route 87), is the city of **Saepinum**, set in the lovely Matese valley. Mysterious and strongly evocative of Roman vigor, its forums, temples, and monuments are in a miraculous state of preservation, and still set amid bucolic surroundings that recall its role as the stopover for the massive movement of herds twice a year between the heights of the Abruzzi and the Apulian plain. Here, at this important crossroads, shepherds met with farmers to trade their wool. Saepinum began as a Samnite village, founded by the Petri, a Samnite tribe. *Saipins* was the Oscan word for Saepinum (the Oscan language was spoken until the second century B.C.). During the frequent wars with Rome, the Samnites retreated to the surrounding hills to protect themselves. After they were defeated by Roman consul L. Cursor Papirius, they returned to Saepinum, which was later built up during the reign of Augustus (27 B.C. to A.D. 14). After Rome fell in the fifth century, the city was given by the Lombard Duke of Benevento to the Duke of Bulgari, but by this time its buildings had been abandoned and the surrounding farmland left fallow.

The outer wall of the theater has been converted into modest homes; otherwise, you can wander through a stone Pompeii reminiscent of those untouched towns we see in paintings from the 17th century. For the many travellers who will pass through here on their way south to the wonders of Magna Graecia, the museums of Bari and Taranto, and the temples of Calabria and Basilicata, it is a perfect preparation for things to come.

GETTING AROUND

Service between Rome and Pescara and L'Aquila is at present better by bus (ARPA line) than by train, which is direct but a longer ride by more than an hour. L'Aquila and Pescara are linked by rail and bus to Sulmona. The Parco Nazionale can be visited by taking the bus (ARPA) from Sulmona to Pescasseroli, the park's administrative center, or the train to Avezzano, on the Rome–Pescara line. Other connections can be made by bus within the region.

ACCOMMODATIONS REFERENCE

The rates given below are projections for 1992; always check for up-to-date information before making reservations. Wide ranges may reflect the differences between low- and high-season rates. Unless otherwise indicated, the figures indicate the cost of a double room (per room, not per person). However, half-board (mezza pensione) rates, which include breakfast and one other meal per day, are per person. Most hotels will add a service charge of 10 to 15%.

▶ **Abruzzo.** 67030 **Campo di Giove.** Tel: (0864) 401-05. Ŀ50,000; half board Ŀ50,000.

▶ **Le Cannelle.** Via Tancredi da Pentina 2, 67100 **L'Aquila.** Tel: (0862) 41-11-94; Fax: (0862) 41-24-53. Ŀ75,000–Ŀ100,000; half board Ŀ110,000.

▶ **Castello.** Piazza Battaglione Alpini, 67100 **L'Aquila.** Tel: (0862) 291-47; Fax: (0862) 291-40. Ŀ88,000.

▶ **Castello di Balsorano.** 67025 **Balsorano.** Tel: (0863) 952-36. Closed in November. Ŀ82,500; suite Ŀ110,000.

▶ **Duca degli Abruzzi.** Viale Govanni XXIII 10, 67100 **L'Aquila.** Tel: (0862) 283-41; Fax: (0862) 615-88. Ŀ74,000–Ŀ108,000; half board Ŀ84,000–Ŀ104,000.

▶ **Europa Park Hotel.** Strada Statale N, 67039 **Sulmona.** Tel: (0864) 346-41. Ŀ90,000; half board Ŀ80,000.

▶ **Grand Hotel del Parco.** Corso Federico II 74, 67100 **L'Aquila.** Tel: (0862) 41-32-48; Fax: (0862) 659-38. Ŀ90,000–Ŀ140,000; half board Ŀ120,000.

▶ **Grand Hotel del Parco.** Via S. Lucia 3, 67032 **Pescasseroli.** Tel: (0863) 91-27-45; Fax: (0863) 91-27-49. Ŀ145,000; half board Ŀ95,000–Ŀ160,000.

▶ **Hotel del Lago.** 67083 **Scanno.** Tel: (0864) 74-74-27 or 743-43. Ŀ75,000.

▶ **Hotel/Ristorante Sammartino.** Largo Pietro Micca 44, 86061 **Agnone.** Tel: (0865) 782-39 or 775-77. Ŀ35,000–Ŀ48,000; half board Ŀ42,000.

▶ **Mille Pini.** 67038 **Scanno.** Tel: (0864) 743-87. Ŀ70,000–Ŀ100,000; half board Ŀ90,000.

▶ **Sporting.** Via de Gasperi 41, 64100 **Teramo.** Tel: (0861) 41-47-23. Ŀ75,000–Ŀ120,000; half board Ŀ85,000–Ŀ95,000.

NAPLES, CAMPANIA, AND THE AMALFI COAST

By Barbara Coeyman Hults

C ampania, nature decreed, would be a balm to body and soul, a luxurious coastline of sheltered bays curving past Naples, down to the ancient Roman cities of Pompeii and Herculaneum, and beyond to the beautiful Amalfi coast and the ancient Greek city of Paestum. Running in back of the coastline are the Apennine mountains, and offshore lie Capri and the volcanic mysteries of Ischia. Even Vesuvius, the volcano that once covered Pompeii with ash, is lovely to look at, with its famous double curve completing the symmetry of the Bay of Naples. (Summer weekends here, however, are far from soothing, with Romans fleeing down the coast in their exhaust-spewing cars much as their ancestors did in their horse-drawn versions, dust billowing. Today's traffic jams, complete with noise and air pollution, make it imperative that off season be the time to visit. At the least, the month of August and summer weekends are to be avoided—or take the train from Rome to Salerno, and a taxi up the coast to the Amalfi Drive.)

Pompeii and Herculaneum are frozen moments, their life stopped suddenly in A.D. 79, when Vesuvius erupted. Pae-

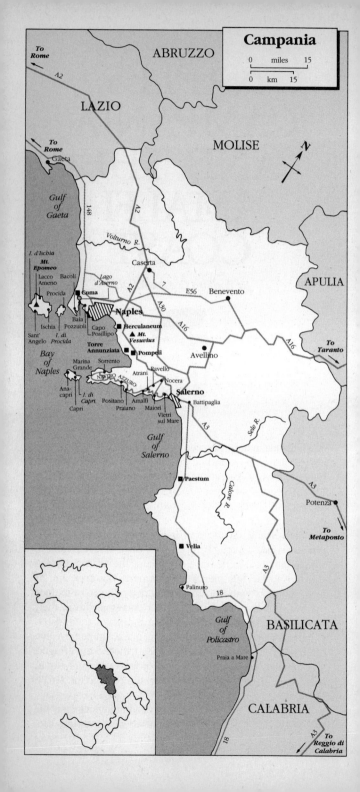

stum's Doric temples have kept their youth as a result of the
site being abandoned when malaria swept the South; Tiberius's beautiful villa on Capri fared less well, but the site is so
magnificent that ruins are secondary when visiting the island.
At Amalfi the cathedral recalls an Arab-Norman past, and the
churches and palaces of Baroque Naples are getting a long-
overdue face-lift. Naples and Campania combine the influences of, in succession, ancient Greeks, Romans, Byzantines,
Normans, Hohenstaufens, French Angevins, Spanish Bourbons, the Bonapartes, and Garibaldi's movement toward the
Risorgimento.

While the past is preserved here, the present is also
celebrated, at resorts as chic as the San Pietro in Positano or
as happily untouristed as Palinuro farther south. As a place to
relax in the shadow of antiquity, Campania still draws dream-
ers from throughout the world, rewarding them with days of
endless beauty, relaxation, and good food—seafood, macaroni (in a thousand shapes, it seems), pizza, fine wines, and
fruits and vegetables from the rich volcanic soil.

MAJOR INTEREST

Natural beauty along the coast
Unique mix of cultural influences

Naples
The Neapolitans
The Old City of Spaccanapoli (Gothic and Baroque
    churches)
Castel Nuovo
Teatro San Carlo
Castel dell'Ovo
The museums (Archeologico, Capodimonte, San Mar-
    tino)
The bay, from Naples to Capo Posillipo

Antro della Sibilla (Cave of the Sibyl) at Cuma
Pompeii, Herculaneum, and Paestum
Capri, Ischia, and Procida
The Amalfi coast

Campania is one of the easiest regions of Italy to visit
because the most sought-after destinations lie along the
coast, accessible by car, train, bus, and boat. The mountainous interior is rich with towns and valleys that recall the past,
but these are overshadowed by the formidable line of attractions along the seacoast extending southward from Naples.

NAPLES

Naples (Napoli) is not kind to the day visitor, who must combat traffic and noise in a city that offers no gracious piazzas in which to relax. The city bestows its favors only on those who take the time to know it; those who do often remain loyal friends of the city for life. The ancient city of hills follows the Bay of Naples, still a fine sight to behold. Unfortunately the port area itself is not a place to stroll. From the Castel dell'Ovo west to Mergellina is the nicest bayside area, and by night Mergellina can be enchanting. The bay, with the famous curves of Vesuvius dramatically visible on clear days, is an integral part of the drama of Naples. At the top of the residential Vomero hill, or higher up at the royal palace museum of Capodimonte, the bay is still the star, with promenades and balconies theatrically arranged to view it in its best light.

The urban sprawl outside the city is perhaps the ugliest in Italy, but this is not necessarily the view of the inhabitants, who often left damp, dark, small apartments in the city for what is to them a far better place. Naples, like the rest of the South, suffers from high unemployment. This is caused partly by the long-held policy of the industrial North of keeping the South a source of cheap labor, and also by the Camorra, Naples' Mafia, whose history of extortion and forcing employers to hire their cronies has made moving to the South less than tempting.

Watching a street scene in Naples is like watching a hundred television sets at once, each tuned to a different channel. The variety of expressions one eyebrow can engineer is amazing, not to mention the full repertoire of mime, both more subtle and more obvious than most actors use in a lifetime.

Naples is known for having given Italy—and the world— some of its greatest thinkers: Saint Thomas Aquinas and Benedetto Croce (1866–1952), among others.

Both Saint Thomas and Benedetto Croce lived in **Spacca-napoli**, an area that is the best introduction to a city that has no beginning and no end, only movement. Spaccanapoli was laid out along the precise grid plan of ancient Rome, but don't let that fool you. Nothing else seems planned once you enter these streets.

To get there, take the number 140 bus from Mergellina or the Santa Lucia section, and get off at the end of the line, piazza del Gesù Nuovo, the heart of old Naples (the bus starts at Capo Posillipo). Remember to catch the bus here on its rebound, or you'll have neither sitting nor standing room; sit near the door. At piazza del Gesù Nuovo a tourist office offers color-coded maps of Spaccanapoli, one of the most colorful parts of town. The main tourist office in the Palazzo Reale can also provide these maps, which are worth looking for: Ask for *The Old City: A Stratified Multiple Itinerary Map*.

In the piazza del Gesù Nuovo stands the **Church of the Gesù Nuovo**, and in front of it a *guglia*—a curious dethroned, steeplelike monument that seems to be waiting to be lifted back on top of the church. This one is especially Baroque in feeling—festooned with flowers, saints, and angels, with the Madonna on top, like a country processional captured in stone.

The rusticated façade of the Gesù itself is created of diamond-pointed *piperno,* a lava stone obviously easy to come by here in the shadow of the volcano. Inside is one of the typical surprises Naples has to offer: a joyous profusion of colored marble and frescoes. Neapolitans love to marry here in May (the month of the Madonna), with pomp and enthusiasm worthy of the setting. Despite earthquakes and bombs, the church has endured and kept its charm through restoration. The Jesuit architect Valeriani built this structure over an older palace between 1584 and 1601, when the Spanish viceroys ruled Naples. Above the door is *Heliodorus Driven from the Temple* by Solimena, which shows why he was unequaled as a fresco painter until Tiepolo appeared in the North.

Spaccanapoli District

After seeing the Gesù, enter the Spaccanapoli district, a sort of Baroque souk of flower stalls, street-corner transistor hawkers, dark cathedrals named after mysterious saints, and grand palace courtyards hung with flapping sheets and towels that signal the owners' presence.

Just left of the Gesù is via Benedetto Croce. He lived in the 14th-century palace at number 12, where he founded the Istituto Italiano per gli Studi Storici (Italian Institute for Historical Research) in 1947. This section of town has a certain cachet that is not always evident. Gray walls and unclean streets often hide some of the most interesting, artful apartments in the city. Croce was born in Abruzzo in 1866, but he is considered Neapolitan because he was educated in Naples and lived here until his death in 1952. Although his life was spent in practical politics—as a mem-

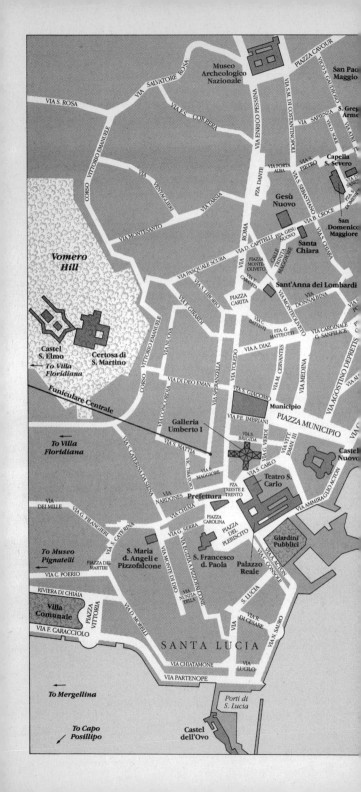

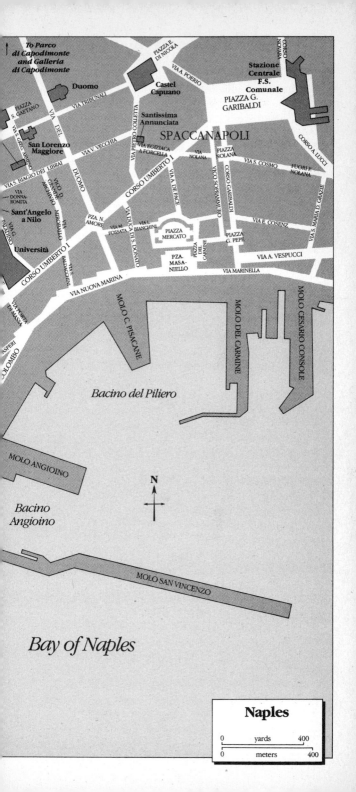

To Parco
di Capodimonte
and Galleria
di Capodimonte

PIAZZA E.
DI NICOLA

VIA A. POERIO

CORSO NOVARA

Stazione
Centrale
F.S.
Comunale

PIAZZA G.
GARIBALDI

Duomo

Castel
Capuano

PIAZZA
S. GAETANO

VIA DEL...

VIA TRIBUNALI

VIA S. GREG. ARMENO

Santissima
Annunciata

VIA PIETRO COLLETTA

SPACCANAPOLI

CORSO A. LUCCI

San Lorenzo
Maggiore

VIA V. VECCHIA

VIA EGIZIACA
A FORCELLA

VIA
NOLANA

PIAZZA
NOLANA

VIA S. COSMO

FUORI P.
NOLANA

VIA S. BIAGIO DEI LIBRAI

DUOMO

VICO D.
GIGANTE

CORSO UMBERTO I

VIA DE PACE

CORSO GARIBALDI

VICO SOPRAMURO

VIA S. MARIA D. GRAZIE

VIA
DONNA-
ROMITA

VIA G.
PALADINO

MEZZOCANNONE

Sant'Angelo
a Nilo

PZA. N.
AMORE

VIA M.
FOSSATA

VIA DUCA D. S. DONATO

VIA L.
BIANCHINI

PIAZZA
MERCATO

PIAZZA
G. PEPE

VIA E. COSENZ

Università

CORSO UMBERTO I

VIA S.
PIETR...

PZA.
MASA-
NIELLO

PIAZZA
DEL
CARMINE

VIA MARINELLA

VIA A. VESPUCCI

VIA PORTA
DI MASSA

VIA COLOMBO

ASPERI

VIA NUOVA MARINA

MOLO C. PISACANE

MOLO DEL CARMINE

MOLO CESARIO CONSOLE

Bacino del Piliero

MOLO ANGIOINO

N

Bacino
Angioino

MOLO SAN VINCENZO

Bay of Naples

Naples

0   yards   400

0   meters   400

ber of the Liberal Party in Parliament and a strong anti-Fascist—in his philosophical system the spirit is the only reality.

But first there is the lovely **Church of Santa Chiara**, now restored to its Gothic-Provençal charm, where Robert the Wise (who died in the 14th century) is buried. King Robert's court was as close as Naples ever came to Camelot—a time that Boccaccio described in the *Decameron,* though he changed the setting to Florence. Robert's wife, Sancia de Mallorca, had wanted to enter a convent, often a favored alternative to an arranged marriage, but fate or her father decided on Robert. As an act of secular devotion she had Santa Chiara and the cloisters built, giving Naples one of its most beloved churches.

Robert's regal tomb at the altar shows the king lying in the Franciscan robes he wore when he entered that order late in life. The section under the king's body, showing the Virtues, divided by six pilasters, is the only remaining part of the original monument. To Petrarch, of whom Robert was a patron, he was the "consummate king and philosopher, equally illustrious in letters and in dominion." His reign contrasted sharply with the Angevin rule in Sicily, which had ended in the bloody revolt of the Vespers in 1283.

The adjoining **Cloisters** is a peaceable kingdom hidden from the noisy streets. The columns and garden walls, brightly decorated with majolica scenes of life beyond the convent walls, kept the nuns from being homesick. Italian convents often attracted the aristocracy, who added the good life to good works by enjoying the world's beauty and developing a high level of cuisine, still found in some convent bakeries that sell to the public. (Not here, unfortunately, though there is a wonderful baker up the street at piazza San Domenico.)

Past Croce's palazzo is another *guglia*—this one a votive offering against the plague. It marks the **Church of San Domenico Maggiore** (1308), the church of the Aragonese nobility. During the late 1500s, when Naples was ruled by a Spanish viceroy, powerful religious landowners built hundreds of convents, monasteries, and churches here, creating a small ecclesiastical city for themselves, which is why churches seem to pop up on every block, though many are now closed or abandoned.

San Domenico is very much alive inside, with its elaborate Renaissance altars. In the candlelit Cappellone del Crocifisso, the painting of a crucifix is regarded as sacred because it spoke to Thomas Aquinas, one of the most prominent Neapolitan saints, who lived and taught in the adjoining monastery. Although Aquinas's rooms were destroyed by an earthquake and the bombs of World War II, a few relics remain: the bell he used, a portrait bust, the papal bull that proclaimed him Doctor of the Church. Stop in the sacristy to see the wonderful frescoes by Solimena and the unusual Aragonese tombs set into the walls. (Stop also at **Scaturchio**, across from the church, for coffee and *sfogliatelle,* light triangle-shaped layers of pastry with a soft ricotta center flavored with lemon or candied fruit bits.)

Off the right side of San Domenico is via De Sanctis, where the **Cappella San Severo** serves as a crypt/museum for the family of the alchemist prince Raimondo di Sangro (1711–1771). The bizarre statues *Modesty* (veiled) and *Disillusion* (netted) stand at the altar, flanking Sammartino's extraordinary *Veiled Christ,* a virtuoso work in marble that even shows Christ's wounds under a marble veil. Downstairs is something else again: two mummies, apparently a mass of veins and arteries, preserved by an ancient Egyptian formula. Gossip says that the woman, obviously pregnant, was Sangro's mistress and was caught with her lover. A likeness of the prince appears on the medallion on his tomb upstairs.

On via Nilo the **Church of Sant'Angelo a Nilo** contains the burial monument of Cardinal Brancaccio. Donatello carved the bas-relief of the Assumption of Mary, noted for its perspective, on the front of the sarcophagus, as well as the cardinal's head and the right-hand figure raising the curtain. (The church is open mornings.) The word *Nilo* here comes from the reclining figure lolling in the largo Corpo di Nilo, supposedly the river Nile, sculpted in Nero's time. For some reason the statue was beheaded, buried, and then resurrected, and a new head added. Perhaps it was his mischievous ways—he whispers to women who pass at night, say local residents. An espresso break at the **Bar Nilo** will let you observe wily Nilo and the passing throng.

A few blocks to the east is **via San Gregorio Armeno**, the street of Christmas past and present, where the makers of *presepi* fill their workshops with every object imaginable for their miniature Christmas villages. The village is Bethlehem, Neapolitan style of course: Tiny kitchens are filled with wee pizzas and the utensils used to make them, as well as all manner of fruit and vegetables (young family members roll out the pea-size tomatoes and apples); cows and camels; wise men and townspeople; and, of course, the Nativity scene and walls of angels, who also swing from the ceiling on wires. Although December is the street's prime time, you can shop for inexpensive *presepi* at **Esposito's** (number 46), and for fine reproductions of classical *presepi* at **Ferrigno** (number 10, at the top of the street), all year round.

The **Church of San Gregorio Armeno** has charming cloisters and Luca Giordano's frescoes of the life of Saint Gregory the Armenian. Giordano painted so many murals in Italy and at the European courts that he was called Luca *fa presto* ("Luca works fast").

At the top of the hilly, arched street stands the **Church of San Lorenzo Maggiore**, built over the ancient pagan basilica of Neapolis (currently being excavated). In about 555 a church was built here to honor Saint Lawrence, but it was replaced with this grander Gothic church in the 13th century by Charles of Anjou. In this mystical setting Boccaccio first saw his Fiammetta—supposedly Maria, natural child of Robert the Wise—during Mass one Easter Eve when the Pascal candle was lit from a brazier and incense permeated the very French setting of pointed arches and parapets. "As San Lorenzo was favored by the Angevin kings and therefore fashionable, there were present besides the devout folk many young men with curled and frizzed hair and many young women more luring than lenten in their dark dresses, who loitered beneath the Gothic arches and perhaps lipped a prayer or two between glances and signals and ogles; for even sinners do sometimes pray. . . . Among them was young Messer Giovanni Boccaccio," writes biographer Francis McManus.

Petrarch, too, came to mass at San Lorenzo, and in 1345 prayed with the monks throughout the night during an earthquake and tidal wave. Another drama is remembered in the left transept, where Joanna I, Queen of Naples and granddaughter of Robert the Wise, is buried. Her adopted son Charles poisoned her when she supported Louis of Anjou against him. Her body was first displayed in the cloisters of Santa Chiara, though she was not yet dead, according to some observers. Flanking the church is a fine museum related to its history. The enormous refectory, which can be visited, was once used for the parliament of the Kingdom of Naples.

Across the street, the figure of San Gaetano gestures to the sky in front of the **Church of San Paolo Maggiore**, built on the site of the pagan temple of the Dioscuri. The columns on the façade come from the early temple, as does the torso under the statues of Saints Peter and Paul. Nero also had his singing debut in this temple, despite an earthquake that shook the building.

Since body and soul are intimately related in Spaccanapoli, the *pizzaiolo,* or pizza maker, is also venerated. At the **Trattoria Lombardi**, via Benedetto Croce 59, *pizzaiolo* Mazza produces the adored Margherita pizza—made with fresh mozzarella, tomatoes, and fresh basil—kept simple so that the delicious crust can be fully appreciated. Drowning pizza or pasta with sauce is not a native tradition; Italians like the taste of the crust as much as the topping. The best pizza makers use a brick oven, sometimes throwing a sprinkle of wood chips in at the last minute to singe the cheese and crust perfectly. The simple Margherita was named for Queen Margherita of Savoy, who in 1889 first tasted this version as prepared by *pizzaiolo* Raffaele Esposito. Another pizzeria (also serving a full menu), the **Bellini**, also in Spaccanapoli (via Santa Maria di Costantinopoli 80), wins approval from finicky Neapolitans. Hearty, even rough, wines accompany pizza; more subtle flavors would be lost. Near piazza Dante, the **Porta Alba** is another venerated, and inexpensive, pizza spot (via Porta Alba, 18; Tel: 081-45-97-13; closed Sundays). It's always crowded, so go early.

From San Lorenzo it's easy to find the **Duomo**, off via Tribunali on via del Duomo. There the patron saint of Naples, San Gennaro, performs a miracle twice yearly (September 19 and December 16) by liquefying his congealed blood, which is kept in vials in a dazzling chapel here that has paintings by Domenichino. Multitudes gather for the occasion, waiting to judge the rapidity of the transformation—the quicker the blood liquefies, the better the outlook for the city. Gennaro, called Januarius by the Romans, was beheaded in nearby Pozzuoli in 305, after which he walked to Naples carrying his head (or so the story goes). The chapel where all this occurs is much admired in its own right. In the cupola is the fresco of *Paradise* by Lanfranco (1643). The other frescoes are the work of Domenichino, recently restored thanks to the Napoli '99 Foundation, a group of private and business patrons who choose individual artworks as projects for restoration. The entrance gate of gilded bronze was designed by Fanzago, as was the intarsia of marble on the floor.

In the crypt, or Cappella Carafa, a brilliant altar in Renaissance style contains San Gennaro's tomb. Among the other occupants of the Duomo are Charles Martel and Charles I of Anjou, entombed at the entrance door and surrounded by an elaborate Luca Giordano fresco. Opposite San Gennaro's chapel is the much-restored basilica of Santa Restituta, the oldest part of the Duomo, built during the fourth century on the site of a temple to Apollo, and with 27 columns that are probably relics of that early temple.

If you retrace your steps to piazza del Gesù Nuovo, detour briefly from the piazza down the calle Trinità Maggiore to piazza Monte Oliveto, where the **Church of Sant'Anna dei Lombardi** is full of wonders, including a life-size pietà of eight figures by Guido Mazzoni (1492). The chapel to the right of the entrance contains an *Annunciation* by Benedetto da Maiano (1498), who also finished the tomb of Mary of Aragon in the opposite chapel, where there is a fine *presepio* by Antonio Rosellino.

On nearby via Maddaloni (4/b), musicians will savor the instruments displayed at **Panharmonikon**, Dottore Mario Ascione's wonderful store. Tel: (081) 522-04-37.

The Museums of Naples

Antiquity was once considered the province of the king, but Garibaldi relieved the royals of that responsibility in 1860, and now museums are open to all. At the **Museo Archeologico Nazionale**, north of piazza del Gesù Nuovo at the far end of via Santa Maria di Còstantinopoli, the collection is one of the best in the world, especially the paintings from Pompeii and the small bronzes. The equestrian statue of Emperor Domitian and the Farnese Bull are among the treasures. Visit this museum before travelling to Pompeii and Herculaneum to get a clearer idea of those cities' original grandeur.

North of the archaeological museum is the **Palazzo e Galleria Nazionale di Capodimonte** (bus number 324 from piazza Vittoria), which occupies a hillside palace that enjoys a panoramic view of the bay. Charles III used the palace as a hunting lodge instead of a castle because it had no water. The art gallery has an important collection of works by Caravaggio, Rubens, Bellini, Titian, and Filippo Lippi. Napoli '99 has restored the brilliant portrait of *Antea* by Parmigianino and the *Assunzione della Vergine* by Pinturicchio. Also represented here is the lesser-known Artemisia Gentileschi. Influenced by Caravaggio, she favored gruesome scenes painted in bright, translucent tones with a strict attention to detail. Her paintings of Judith here and in the Uffizi are especially dramatic. Stop also at the Royal Apartments to see the Salottino di Porcellano, an all-porcelain room delicately decorated in Chinese motifs—peacocks and flowers and other objects. (A museum devoted to porcelain is located in the Villa Floridiana on Vomero hill; see below for Vomero.)

The De Ciccio collection in Capodimonte includes porcelain, tapestry, and small bronzes. Charles of Anjou was entranced by the *presepio* tradition and started making his own figures from clay while the queen and princesses sewed and embroidered the costumes. As the king did, so did society, and this once-simple tradition of keeping Christmas all year became a new way for the nobles to outdo one another in grandiosity.

On top of Vomero hill, to the north of the Santa Lucia area, is the **Certosa di San Martino**, a 14th-century monastery that is now home to examples of Naples' *presepio* art, including entire *presepi* as well as individual figures—not well presented but interesting nonetheless. Topographical maps, ship models, and the like evoke the city's cultural past, from the Bourbons to Garibaldi. In addition, the sweeping view of the bay and Vesuvius from the belvedere is one of the city's most dramatic. (Take the funicular from Piazza Duca d'Aosta near via Toledo.)

Fanzago's lovely white cloisters here contrast with the elaborately beautiful marble intarsia of the church, also his creation. The monks' chancel is the most remarkable section, with a superb marble communion table, a *Nativity* by Guido Reni, and *Christ Washing the Disciples' Feet* by Caracciolo, founder of the Neapolitan school, which opposed Mannerism in favor of Caravaggio's more emotional path. His young rival, the Spaniard Giuseppe Ribera (1591–1652), known in Italy as Spagnoletto, became the court painter because of his sensuous approach. In the treasury is his *Deposition* and Giordano's last work, *The Triumph of Judith.* Caracciolo's frescoes of *The Life of Mary* (1631) decorate the third chapel on the left. On the entryway arches are Ribera's *Twelve Prophets;* the *Deposition* (1638) at the door is the work of Massimo Stanzioni, the leader of the Neapolitan school at mid-century, known for his subtle chromatic values, melodious lines, and lyrical expressions.

The **Vomero** is a beautiful respite from the benevolent madness below. A short walk from San Martino will take you to the **Villa Floridiana**, a lovely park, scented with camellias in season, that has the added charm of a splendid view of the bay as far as Capri.

Dining up here is a pleasure: **Daniele**, via Scarlatti 104 (Domenico Scarlatti was born in Naples), is excellent and not expensive. Homey **Dona Teresa**, at via Kerbaker 58, serves a full dinner for about 20,000 lire—very reasonable.

From Castel Nuovo to the Villa Comunale

The enormous **Castel Nuovo**, a brick castle on the harbor northeast of Santa Lucia, was built (1279–1282) by Charles of Anjou and presents such a tough-looking, macho aura that it's called the *Maschio Angioino*. Naples, however, is ever the great deceiver, and the castle housed more than just artillery. In fact, the court of Robert the Wise enjoyed a style of life behind its walls that inspired much of the *Decameron*. Boccaccio and Petrarch were there, and Giotto painted frescoes, though they were subsequently destroyed when the Aragonese redecorated and did away with the Angevin decor. Two magnificent features remain: the Renaissance arch and the Cappella Palatina. The Arco di Trionfo that welcomed Alphonse of Aragón to Naples has been restored, thanks again to Napoli '99. In the Cappella Palatina (also known as the church of Santa Barbara) is a Madonna by Laurana—one of the most sensitive sculptors of Madonna and Child themes—and a fine rose window. The Sala dei Baroni, though damaged by fire, gives an idea of the castle's finest hours.

Farther east, near the bleak central railroad station, **Mimi alla Ferrovia** is a boisterous trattoria that has long been enjoyed by Neapolitans not seeking a quiet lunch. The food is very good, and the people-watching at its peak. It's not for the timid, however (via Alfonso d'Aragona 21; Tel: 081-553-85-25; closed Sundays).

To relive the postwar years that de Sica portrayed, go to the **Forcella** flea market, near the station and the **Church of the Santissima Annunciata**. The market is a warren of dubious salespeople selling even more ersatz products. (If they're real, they're contraband. Try not to be obviously a tourist, and don't carry anything you don't want to lose.) The church is a gem architecturally, but that's difficult to see beneath the rubble within and without. The 14th-century original was destroyed by an earthquake, but the building was restructured from 1760 to 1782 by the illustrious Luigi Vanvitelli and his son Carlo.

To the west of the castle, in the piazza del Plebiscito, stands the **Teatro San Carlo**, where a 250-year anniversary gala in 1987 brought music celebrities from around the world. The frayed red velvet and gilt interior has seen many of opera's most tearful moments. Although the season begins in December, musical productions are staged during much of the year. Take the tour if you can't see a performance.

Across the street is the **Galleria Umberto I**, usually less than sparkling clean and too drab to evoke its glamorous sister in Milan, and more interesting for its basic glass-and-steel form than for the shops inside. Finding a table for a coffee in one of the cafés affords you the pleasure of watching Neapolitans discuss politics. Nearby is the **Ristorante Ciro**, where most of San Carlo's musical stars have gained sustenance from the grilled meat and fine vegetable dishes (via Santa Brigida 74; Tel: 081-552-40-72; closed Sundays).

Next to San Carlo is the enormous **Palazzo Reale**, facing a piazza that is probably beautiful at dawn but for the rest of the day is a traffic cop's nightmare. The only effective preparation for crossing the street would be running with the bulls at Pamplona. Inside the 17th-century palace are a museum of paintings and the Bourbons' court theater, both at the top of a wonderfully dramatic staircase.

The piazza to the northwest of the palace, piazza Trieste e Trento, leads to via Toledo/via Roma, the main shopping street and the boundary imposed by the Spanish viceroy Don Pedro of Toledo in 1537 to separate royal Naples from the overpopulated streets beyond. The **Caffè Gambrinus** on the piazza still gives a hint of the Belle Epoque. The via Chiaia also starts at the piazza and leads to the most fashionable shopping areas in Santa Lucia and Mergellina. The via Chiaia is one of the nicest parts of Naples, a pleasure to explore (and the place to at least window-shop at Fendi and Armani).

From the Palazzo Reale you can also walk down the via Cesare Console to via Santa Lucia and straight on to the **Castel dell'Ovo** and its harbor, where you can have dinner at one of the seafood restaurants; none is particularly good but all are entertaining for the views of fishermen and contraband runners plying their catches.

The sandcastle form of the Castel dell'Ovo is said to have been built over an egg that the Roman poet-magician Virgil placed inside a glass container and secured in the foundation. If the egg breaks, the castle will fall and take all of Naples with it. A castle of Lucullus stood here, too, and then the castle-building Normans erected a structure, which was enlarged by the Hohenstaufen monarch Frederick II, who kept his treasury and held parliament here before embarking on his crusade. Thirty years later his grandchildren, the sons of Manfred, died while imprisoned at the castle. In 1379 Joanna I received the antipope Clement VII here, and later she was imprisoned in the castle until being poisoned. The situation now is happier: The castle has been restored, and you can wander through its dungeons and parapets. At night it's brilliantly floodlit, and the tourist office sponsors folk-dance performances here.

Turning away from the city and along the harbor to the west, you'll soon reach the **Villa Comunale**, an attractive area refreshed by a park full of tropical trees and plants. A flea market operates here the third week of each month. At its far side is **Mergellina**, one of the prettiest parts of Naples and the place for a seaside walk after dinner. (Remember the 140 bus that plies this route.) You might want to stay here, a less frenetic environment than center city—but then what isn't?

The **Museo Pignatelli**, opposite the middle of the park, is lodged in a splendid 19th-century Neoclassical villa. The carriage museum in the garden is charming; inside the villa there is a major collection of European porcelain. Evening chamber music concerts are frequently scheduled at the museum, and good trattorias are plentiful in the adjoining Mergellina district. A favorite with Neapolitans is **Palummella**, where the antipasto table is worth the trip and the amusing owner adds to the fun. Another small and charming place, **Al Poeta**, on piazza Salvatore di Giacomo, serves a wonderful *rigatoni alla montanara* made with artichokes, chopped meat, prosciutto, and mozzarella. At **Lo Scoglio di Frisio**, a bit fancier, a variety of sea creatures pass through the kitchen to be transformed into imaginative combinations—squid and artichokes, for instance—and even the fritters have a taste of the sea.

One of Naples' most fashionable restaurants, **La Sacrestia**, is located in a charming villa at via Orazio 116 in the Mergellina area, with a grand view of the bay. Sacrestia features traditional Neapolitan recipes and interesting culinary experiments in a sophisticated atmosphere. Reservations suggested; Tel: (081) 761-10-51; closed Mondays and August.

Neapolitan cuisine has touches of the Greek, Arab, French, and Spanish, yet the result is pure Parthenopean. Along the bay, *maccaruni* (the word used for all kinds of pasta in Naples) is prepared in as many ways as fish, meat, vegetables, and cheese require. A classic Neapolitan dish is *spaghetti alle vongole veraci,* made with tiny clams from the Naples area, the tastiest in existence. The sauce is white with garlic and parsley or red with small tomatoes. Vermicelli is sometimes served with a sauce of *polpetielli affogati* (tiny octopus in tomato sauce). *Lasagna alla napoletana, penne all' arrabbiata* (with hot peppers), *linguine alla puttanesca* ("whore's style"—spicy with black olives and capers), and the hearty *pasta e fagioli* all make eating here a joy. Vegetables, too, are given special attention. Eggplant is always a star, especially in *parmigiana di melanzane,* baked with cheese, tomato, and basil. *Peperoni* (large peppers) with cheese and *friarielli* (a kind of broccoli) cooked with a sauce of sausage can be eaten unadorned or in a pasta sauce. Meals often begin with *caprese*—fresh buffalo mozzarella from nearby Caserta's buffalo farms—and tomatoes with fresh basil.

Campania's volcanic soil is kind to grapes. Good whites include Fiano di Avellino, Vesuvio, Ischia, Falerno (of which Pliny spoke), Ravello, and Greco di Tufo. Lacryma Christi, best known because of its name (Christ's tear), can be quite good. Taurasi is a great red for hearty meals. Falerno's red is excellent, as is Gragnano, which can be *frizzante* (sparkling). Ravello also produces a very good red as well as a *rosato* (rosé) with which to finish the meal.

Continuing in Mergellina, near the church of Santa Maria di Piedigrotta and the Galleria Quattro Gironate, steps lead to the Parco Virgiliano and the so-called tomb of Virgil—which it probably is not but was so recorded by Seneca and Petronius.

If you continue on to the western limit of the curve of the Bay of Naples you'll reach **Posillipo** (po-SILL-ipo), a fashionable residential area that extends out along a cape—known to us from Clams Posillipo, found on many a menu. From the park near the cape's end a belvedere offers views of Naples, Vesuvius, and out to Capri. Under a wisteria-shaded terrace four generations of the Concetta family have served seafood and home-grown vegetables at their trattoria **Rosiello**. It's one of the most charming of the bay-view trattorias in Naples (via Santo Strato 10, Posillipo; Tel: 081-769-12-88; closed Wednesdays). At the busy fishing harbor at Capo Posillipo, **Giuseppone a Mare** (Tel: 081-76-96-002; closed Sundays) has long served fine seafood to Neapolitans. Though lately it hasn't lived up to its old standards, it's still amusing, informal, and a good place to enjoy the harbor sights. You may want to take a taxi to Capo Posillipo because the number 140 bus stops inland of the cape itself. The trip from Naples is expensive, however.

Naples' most famous hotels, such as the **Excelsior** and the **Vesuvio**, line the waterfront of the Santa Lucia area opposite the Castel dell'Ovo. The **Royal**, their less attractive sister, is alongside, with dramatic views of the Castel dell Ovo's majestic form against the bay. On a stormy night this is the place to be. (The Vesuvio and the Royal have bay-viewing restaurants.) The **Santa Lucia** has its devoted clientele because of its very individual, flamboyant style in private and public rooms. All these hotels are expensive. The **Belvedere** is a far more economical version, on the Vomero, with fine panoramas of city and bay.

An alternative is to stay in the western section called Mergellina, which has the advantage over all of them in being a place where it's possible and desirable to go walking at night. Mergellina evenings have a summer resort atmosphere, with fish restaurants and amusements along the sea promenade. The **Canada** is attractive and well maintained, with fine sea views. The **Muller** and the **Pinto-Storey** are two popular pensiones in the area, and the Muller has several rooms with harbor-view balconies, as well as a hotel bus that meets the trains. On the cliffs above the Mergellina dock, the **Hotel Paradiso** is a delight—small and well run, with splendid but pricey views.

To see Naples economically, you would do well to take the short hydrofoil or ferry ride from the Mergellina dock out to **Procida**, a charming and usually tranquil island that has maintained its fishing-village look. Boat service to Naples and Capri is frequent from Procida, and the **Arcate** and the **l'Oasi**, both pleasant hotels near beaches and greenery—are currently remarkably inexpensive.

WEST AND NORTH OF NAPLES

Campania's northern region still steams with volcanic activity; here and there fumaroles (jets of steam and mud) escape the earth. The steamy land seemed magical to the ancients, who were both repelled and fascinated by the dance of gases over the earth, which they called the Campi Flegrei, or "burning fields."

To continue the mood, go on to **Lake Averno** (take the SEPSA bus from Pozzuoli). It was here that Virgil located the mouth of the underworld, the Gate of Hell: "And here the unnavigable lake extends, o'er whose unhappy waters, void of light, no bird presumes to steer his airy flight. Such deadly stenches from the depth arise, and steaming sulfur that infects the skies. From hence the Grecian bards their legends make, and give the name Avernus to the lake." That no bird could fly over it and survive, as the legend has it, is not hard to believe—they may not have wanted to, after seeing this eerie place. Actually their deaths were caused by gaseous vapors that rose from the lake, then blocked from the sun by tall trees. But it must have been merrier when the Romans came to the Temple of Apollo; the remains of this vast spa can be seen on the other side of the lake.

Lago d'Averno today is not exactly paradise, but the infernal fumes are gone and the birds have returned. If it's Saturday and you want to hear more of the legend and to experience the true Neapolitan underworld, follow the path on the lake's south side (sign: **Grotta della Sibilla**). At the entrance to a vast underground grotto you'll find Carlo Sintillo, who guides (in his own English) people through the gallery and pools where a very mystical Sibyl bathed. His phone (at home) is (081) 86-73-256. The better-known Sibyl's Cave at Cuma may be an anticlimax after this.

The Greeks created myths around their fumaroles, but the Romans created spas and used the volcanic activity to heat the water and their villas. All the accoutrements of the good life (or bad life) followed quickly, especially around Baia, which became famous for its uninhibited lifestyle.

At Baia the **Scavi di Baia** (excavations) are reached by a steep path that begins near the station. The excavations are extensive and hard to decipher without a guide. Baia was a thermal spa and summer resort with nightlife suited to every taste, catering to wealthy Romans, whose extensive villas were built along this peninsula. The terraces at the site are splendid, and if most of the grandeur has been lost to earthquakes, this spot can sometimes evoke a touch of it. (Baia is also on the railroad line.)

The Ferrovia Cumana leads, of course, to **Cuma**. From the train station a bus leaves for the site. There is a long, pleasant walk from the bus stop to the entrance. Plan to be in this area, as in the others, only when other people are around. The lunch hours, when custodians are away, are prime time for thieves on Vespas.

Cuma's history began before the Greeks arrived, but it was they who made Cuma the most important city of its time along the coast, with an area that stretched as far as Pozzuoli. At Cuma there stands a marvelous acropolis where the temples of Apollo and Jupiter, and a Roman crypt, are interesting sites, but by far the most-visited attraction is that of the famous Sibyl of Cuma, **l'Antro della Sibilla Cumana**, dating from the sixth and fifth centuries B.C. This was one of the most sacred places of Classical Greece. Aeneas came to consult the Sibyl in these long arched corridors, and she scattered leaves and read his fate. Virgil speaks of the "frenzied prophetess, deep in the cave of rock she charts the fates, consigning to the leaves her words and symbols. . . ." When the wind rushes through, it's easy to imagine the leaves flying about while the questor awaited life-or-death answers.

Though sibyls can't be found, a local *mago* often has fliers distributed here, listing the hours he'll be available to tell your fortune, sometimes with a drop of oil in water. Near the entrance to the site, the **Taverna Giulia** conjures up exquisite dishes.

Pozzuoli is multi-leveled, not by design but by bradyseism, a condition in which the earth shakes, rises, and falls. This condition has given the coast a bizarre appearance. An ancient dock can be seen below the waterline, and water covers the floor of the **Serapeum**, part of the archaeological zone near the harbor. Although the area is the site of one of the oldest Greek settlements in Italy (530 B.C.), most of the ruins on view are Roman or Samnite. The Romans came in 194 B.C. and established the now half-sunken port for trade with the East. The Serapeum, which was a market hall, is often called the Temple of Serapis, although it was never a temple. A statue of the god Serapis was found there, which gave the structure its name.

Inland and across the railroad tracks stands the **amphitheater**, in its time (A.D. 67–79) one of the largest in Italy, and used for gladiatorial combat. The underground area where the wild beasts were kept is well preserved. It was in these cells that San Gennaro, Naples' patron, was kept before he was martyred by beheading—the legend has it that he walked from here to Naples, carrying his head. In the Duomo in Naples a vial of his dried blood is preserved and is said to liquify twice a year. The amphitheater was originally decorated with statues and marble pillars, appropriate for the wealthy Roman weekenders, down here for the hot springs at nearby **Solfatara**.

Pozzuoli, known more today as Sophia Loren's birthplace, has been the site of frequent natural disasters. Attempts to remove the citizens to more secure foundations have largely run aground; as soon as new housing is built, squatters move in, and evicting an Italian in Italy is rarer than sangfroid in Naples in August.

The port area here is about as salty as a port can get. But many of the dubious-looking trattorias attract a lunch and dinner crowd of bankers and lawyers—all lovers of good food—as well as the more colorful locals. Among the favorites are inexpensive **Da Giggetta** at the port (via Roma 4/4; Tel: 081-526-15-63) and **Don Antonio** (via Magazzino 20; Tel: 080-867-39-41). If the earth moves, just exchange "this may be it" glances with your fellow diners and then go back to the *frutti di mare*.

When visiting this area, and particularly the more remote sites, stay near other people. Vespa-riding thieves are plentiful. Leave any valuables in your hotel. If you can take a small camera, do so. Camcorders and expensive SLRs will make you very interesting.

To reach Pozzuoli, take the Ferrovia Cumana, which you can pick up in Naples at piazza Montsanto, to Stazione Cumana. To reach Solfatara, walk (or bus) along via Solfatara near the amphitheater for about ten minutes to see the steaming mud on the still-active crater, which is about a mile and a half wide. At the Bocca Grande (Big Mouth), vapors shoot up violently, reaching a temperature of 320 degrees F.

Caserta

Inland from Naples to the north (45 minutes by train), the **Palazzo Reale** at Caserta is not maintained royally but is still worth seeing for its evocation of the regal splendor of Versailles. Charles III had the palace built in 1752 from the plans of Vanvitelli. Inside, the grand staircase and apartments, the chapel and theater, are lavish in their use of marble; outside, the gardens are stunning—vast fountains, groves, statues, and cascades. The English gardens are the most beautiful of all. All of this leads inexorably to a desire for wild boar, which you can enjoy in an amazing number of ways—from fillet to sausage—at **Ritrovo dei Patriarchi**, where venison and rabbit also star on the menu (località Sommana; Tel: 0823-371-510; closed Thursdays).

SOUTH OF NAPLES

Ideally, you should allow three days to see Pompeii, Herculaneum, Vesuvius, and Paestum—after spending some time at the Museo Archeologico in Naples seeing its collection from the Roman sites. (Paestum has a fine museum of its own.) Since the site at Pompeii is extensive, it requires the better part of a day. You can easily see Herculaneum and Mount Vesuvius in a day, since a bus for Vesuvius leaves from the town of Herculaneum, which is only about 6 km (4 miles) from Naples (closer than Pompeii). Paestum, farther south, can be reached by train from Naples or Salerno. We discuss Pompeii first because, although Herculaneum is closer to Naples, Pompeii is the premier site in this area. Be aware that this very touristed area is popular with thieves.

Pompeii

Pliny the Younger tells us what happened on August 24, A.D. 79, from notes his uncle (the Elder) took while watching Vesuvius's eruption from the sea before the fumes killed him. Ashes were falling, hotter and thicker, as his ship drew nearer, followed by bits of pumice and blackened stone. It all seemed a great adventure to him at first. He went home and took a nap and awoke to find his house filling with pumice stone and ash. "Elsewhere," he wrote, "there was daylight by this time, but they were still in darkness, blacker, and denser than any ordinary night, which they relieved by lighting torches and various kinds of lamp."

The city of Pompeii itself tells the story clearly after that, especially in the tragic casts of figures caught under the ash, crouching under tables, struggling up stairs, a mother holding up her baby, a horribly contorted dog on a leash. The molten ash made sculptor's molds of them, which have been used to re-create the bodies displayed in the museum (Antiquarium) at the entrance to the excavations or returned to their original locations.

At both Pompeii and Herculaneum the fascination lies in the glimpses of everyday life frozen in time. Although Pompeii has a forum, major theaters, and all the trappings of a large Roman city, the private homes and small businesses are what intrigue archaeologists and social historians. The houses were often built in the classic Samnite style (the Samnites were settlers before the Romans arrived), with an atrium at the entrance; then a peristyle, or colonnaded courtyard, surrounded by the family bedrooms; then a dining area, or triclinium, where chaise longues were used for family and guests. The Samnites were the most influential architects in creating the city we see today, although the Romans, who had rebuilt it after an earthquake in A.D. 62, added grandiose touches and created a more luxurious lifestyle for themselves. (The famous Pompeiian red cinnabar dates from this period.)

Before starting the tour, which will take a few hours at least, buy the book (sold here) that has transparent sheets re-creating the look of the original buildings to aid the imagination. Guides and guards are also useful because they have the keys to everything—much of interest is locked away for security reasons. It's worth the tips.

A great deal of the artwork from Pompeii is in the archaeological museum in Naples, but the **Casa dei Vettii** has been allowed to keep its treasures and has been partly restored. Researchers have studied friezes and dead roots to re-create the garden's original look. The brothers Vettii, Aulus and Restituti, bought this gracious villa during the first century A.D. Thanks to the beams and roofs that covered it when it fell, it remained in good condition through the centuries. The house, also Samnite style, faces inward and encloses both atrium and impluvium (rainwater opening) as it unfolds toward the colonnaded garden. In the vestibule a phallic symbol—a familiar charm that, along with coiled snakes, was thought to bring good luck—wards off the evil eye. The sight and sound of water was used to refresh the garden, as in the Arab houses that Romans had seen in Egypt and the East. The dining room is also exquisite, thanks to its black borders—bright with *putti* going about their daily chores—and the frescoes of gods and goddesses, which are almost Baroque in feeling.

A few other villas worth visiting are the Casa del Menandro, the Casa di Loreius Tiburtinus, the Casa del Fauno, and the Villa di Diomede. The Villa dei Misteri was the scene of Dionysian cult rituals, some of which are dramatically portrayed on the walls.

There are four identifiable periods in Pompeii's painting: the first, Samnite, used stucco to imitate marble, as in the **Casa del Fauno**; the second introduced architecture with a skewed perspective, as in the **Casa di Sallustio**; in the third, imaginative architectural scenes abound—whole cities and harbors—as in the **Casa di Frontone**; and the last, as in the Casa dei Vettii, featured fuller perspective and dramatic scenes.

The excavation of Pompeii began during the mid-18th century, after a farmer discovered an enormous stone phallus while he was cultivating his garden. (At least that's the story told.) In any case, digging began and still continues. The Bourbon King Charles III, who had already inaugurated the Accademia Ercolanese in 1755, initiated the resurrection of Pompeii. As Goethe summed it up, "Many disasters have happened in the world, but few have brought such joy to posterity."

New this year at Pompeii are 15 **gardens** that re-create

their Roman originals, thanks to exhaustive research on burned pollen and seeds found during excavations (near the site on via Castriccio).

Dining in the town of Pompeii can be an elegant affair at the much-praised Il Principe (piazza Bartolo Longo, 8; Tel: 081-863-33-42; closed Mondays). At about half the price, Zì Caterina, at via Roma 16-22 (Tel: 081-863-12-63; closed Tuesdays), is a comfortable place to collapse after a day in the ruins. The Villa dei Misteri, near the excavation, is an inexpensive hotel if you want to spend the night.

Pompeii is about 40 minutes from Naples on the Circumvesuviana railroad, a pleasant ride that begins in Naples' Stazione Centrale, which is less pleasant. A new major music festival, the Panatenee Pompeiane, will present concerts each August at Pompeii's theaters.

Herculaneum

Herculaneum (Ercolano), named for its legendary founder, Hercules (Ercole), is much smaller and more intimate than Pompeii. Because the inhabited section of town above the site looks very similar to Pompeii, if you have seen Pompeii first it may seem as if Herculaneum were Pompeii come to life. When Pompeii, inland, was drowned in ashes, Herculaneum, on the coast, was flooded with mud churned up by the roiling sea. Consequently, even the wood survived in its mud and lava casing. Furnishings and foodstuffs, statues and mosaics, still decorate the houses and villas.

Although Herculaneum's past is detailed in this manner, its full history—whether the lovely villas belonged to Pompeii's merchants or to Romans using it as another holiday resort—is not known. According to Seneca, Caligula was among the social set in Herculaneum.

The early history of eighth-century B.C. Oscan and later Samnite civilization is similar to Pompeii's; in fact, graffiti in Oscan can be seen on Herculaneum walls. Herculaneum remained packed in mud until 1709, when an Austrian prince who was having a well dug found a theater where the water table should have been. King Charles III got into the picture in 1738, and in 1755 he established the Royal Herculaneum Academy. *The Antiquities of Herculaneum,* a book of engravings published by the academy, influenced European taste for the next half century, from jewelry and clothes to interior design and painting.

As at Pompeii, guides or guards have keys, making them

indispensable, and some of them are quite knowledgeable as well. Be sure to see the **Casa del Tramezzo di Legno** (House of the Wooden Screen), a patrician residence with a garden, and the new museum at the site, containing recently excavated material.

The **Terme**, for men and women, are also fascinating, with mosaics of Neptune and dolphins, seats for the bathers, and ledges for their clothing. In the **Casa del Mobilio Carbonizzato** (House of the Carbonized Furniture), the bedroom, painted in the warm red associated with Pompeii, has a bed and table from the original house. The **Casa di Nettuno** has a lovely nymphaeum in mosaic, and adjoining it is a shop with food staples still packed in storage jars. Be sure to visit the Palaestra and serpent fountain, the Casa dei Cervi (House of the Stags) and its fine sculpture, and the Terme Suburbane (Suburban Baths), with their marble rooms and windows opening on to the sea.

For lunch, try **La Piadina**, via Cozzolino 10 (Tel: 081-771-71-41; closed Tuesdays).

The Circumvesuviana train goes to Herculaneum, as does a trolley (*filovia*) from the piazza Municipio (but never take the trolley on Sunday or during rush hour; at any other time, it provides a nice way to see the neighborhoods around Naples). From Herculaneum buses go to Mount Vesuvius.

If you have extra time, visit the **Villa di Oplontis** at Torre Annunziata, also on the Circumvesuviana route, between Herculaneum and Pompeii, where brilliant murals have been uncovered in a splendid villa currently being excavated.

Mount Vesuvius

Vesuvius has come through history with very good press, given the horror it inflicted on Pompeii. Nowadays Neapolitans look fondly at Il Cratere, as they call it, a dear sight on the horizon that means home, not to mention good wines like Lacryma Christi from its slopes and succulent fruits and vegetables. The plume of smoke is no more; only an occasional fumarole escapes to let us know it's down but not out. The famous truncated cone, Mount Somma, rises 3,714 feet above sea level; and the smaller cone, Mount Vesuvius, rises to 4,190 feet. Probably the best way to see it is to take the bus from Herculaneum. From the bus stop it's about an hour's climb to the top, and you'll need a guide. The views from the summit, however, are spectacular.

Paestum

At the ancient Greek city of Paestum, south of the Amalfi coast and Salerno, wonderfully preserved Doric temples are set in a grassy field surrounded by gardens and hills. Although the site is small, it's so charming that you may want to spend time just relaxing here. The museum is also exceptional, especially since the Tomb of the Diver was discovered in 1968.

Greek Poseidonia (called Paestum by the Romans) was founded around 600 B.C. and dedicated to Poseidon, or Neptune, in 400. The founding Greeks came from Sybaris (itself an Achaean colony in Magna Graecia near the modern city of Taranto), whose lifestyle made the word *sybarite* synonymous with luxurious comfort. Their influence on the region was considerable, and the city they built impressive. The magnificent **Tempio di Nettuno** (actually dedicated to Hera and misnamed), set in lovely countryside, re-creates the Hellenic spirit with its symmetry, serenity, and grandeur. The sacred interior area was originally covered with white stucco. The **basilica** is the oldest structure here (mid-sixth century B.C.). Its columns are curved (entasis), an unusual feature, but Greek Italy was more cavalier in its approach to temple art than was Athens, where the rules of symmetry, variety, number of columns, and such were strictly adhered to.

Paestum is rich in detail. Exceptionally graceful figures, carved on the metopes that stretched across the top of the columns of the **Tempio Italico**, are still on the site and can be admired at close range. In the museum itself, metopes from the Sanctuary of Hera, 13 km (8 miles) north of Paestum, are exhibited on an impressive model. Hercules' feats, centaur battles, and the *Oresteia* are the themes. The museum's star attraction, however, is the **Tomb of the Diver**, considered the find of the century. Outwardly the tomb resembles others in this vicinity, but when opened it was found to be covered with intriguing frescoes, some subtly erotic. The diver is delightful, diving through frescoed space into eternity.

For lunch at Paestum go to **Nettuno**, near the site (Tel: 0828-81-10-28; closed Mondays). Paestum can be reached by train from Naples or Salerno; the excursion can also include a relaxing stop at a beach about a mile from the temples or at the little cove resort of **Palinuro** farther south along the coast, where simple accommodations are inexpensive and the coast is beautifully unspoiled. (Stay at the **Gabbiano**, with pool and beach.) Also, driving in this area is not the problem it is in Naples.

Palinuro was named for Ulysses' helmsman Palinurus, the inspiration for Cyril Connelly's *The Unquiet Grave*. Condemned "to lie naked on an unknown shore," he was finally buried at a place that "will always be called Palinurus," as Virgil tells the story in the *Aeneid*.

Just below Palinuro on the coast is the resort of Praia a Mare, where Calabria begins (see that chapter).

Velia, between Palinuro and Paestum, has a similar history, much that we know of it having been provided by Strabo. Founded in 535 B.C. by Greeks fleeing the Persians in Asia Minor, the town (whose ruins are not as well preserved as Paestum's, which were situated in the middle of a malarial swamp) is of great interest to archaeologists. However, since the remains are fragmentary, there is today little of interest to most visitors. Elea, which later became Velia, was the center of the Eleatic school of philosophy, which flourished during the fifth century B.C. and numbered Parmenides and Zeno among its leading lights. Parmenides, most important of the pre-Socratics, represents the appearance of metaphysics in philosophical thought, and with him philosophy became a strict discipline. Parmenides applied his talents to daily life as well and drew up Elea's constitution.

The Phoenician Zeno, Parmenides' most important pupil and his successor in the Eleatic school, is considered the founder of stoic philosophy. Zeno developed the dialectic method of argument, in which the adversary's thesis is examined and the consequences of the thesis are shown to contradict each other or the thesis itself. Zeno and Empedocles in Sicily developed systems that led to the art of rhetoric. Traditional customs and ethical principles were subjected to rational examination, raising the question—which would later cause the Cartesians sleepless nights—of how we know anything at all. (Zeno is well known even today for his various paradoxes.)

On a more worldly level, under later Roman domination Velia served as a base for Brutus when he was fighting Octavian. When Rome declined, trade routes moved to the Adriatic, depriving Velia of its prominent position and prosperity.

CAPRI

When Ulysses sailed past Sorrento, he looked westward and saw an island: "And lo, the Siren shores like mists arise. Sunk were at once the winds.... Some daemon calmed the air, and smoothed the deep. Hushed the loud winds, and charmed the waves to sleep."

Capri's siren still practices such seduction—even if in summer an hourly rush of tourists from the ferries clogs the narrow streets of its towns and creates a logjam of rowboats waiting to get into the Blue Grotto. Consider staying here and making day trips to other sites.

Go in the spring, when the island is pastel colored and fragrant with orange blossoms, jasmine, and roses, and the air seems to be filtered through a sparkling mist. In the fall the air becomes clearer, and the sea's emerald and sapphire tones are at their most intense. Some romantics even love the winter, when dark clouds shadow the steep cliffs and vineyards and the wind whips the waves about the harbor.

Your ferry or hydrofoil from Naples will land at Marina Grande. As you near the port, look to the far left on top of the cliff. This is where the villa of Tiberius stood, and is the destination of your first morning's walk—not just to see the villa but for the walk itself, one of the most dramatic on the island (although "dramatic" could be used to describe almost every natural sight on Capri). No cars can make the trip, and so the only way to get there is on foot. It takes about two leisurely hours to go and return, and much of the road is made up of gentle slopes, lovely and flower-scented.

The **Villa Iovis** (Tiberius's villa, dedicated to Jupiter and pronounced YO-vis) is reached by taking the funicular from the port of Marina Grande to the town of Capri. Near the funicular station is piazza Umberto I, and on the far side of the piazza is an archway that marks the beginning of the journey. Continue along the narrow streets (frequently marked with arrows to the villa) to a crossroads just outside of town. Just before the market and after the public phones, turn up the hill (the sign is visible after you turn) toward Villa Iovis. (Remember this turnoff, for you'll return here on your way to the Augustus Gardens and the Natural Arch, the Grotto di Matromania, and the Belvedere di Tragara, which overlooks the Faraglioni.)

As you approach the villa's entrance you'll see the **Torre del Faro**, the ancient lighthouse used by Tiberius from A.D. 26 to 37 to relay messages to other lighthouses and on to Rome. (The Faro collapsed just a few days before he died; some historians believe that this event may have killed him, fearful as he was of portents.) Beyond the Faro, signs point to the Salto di Tiberio, the cliff from which he is said to have thrown his enemies (almost 1,000 feet down). Just how evil the old emperor was is debatable, but his exploits have made good copy since Suetonius described his "exquisite" tortures and his seductions of young boys and girls. The Villa Iovis itself was the grandest of the 12 villas supposedly constructed during the Roman "occupation" of Capri. Although there were probably not 12 (for the 12 deities), there were enough buildings to obliterate almost every trace of the earlier Greek and Phoenician cultures.

At the villa the baths, imperial lodgings, kitchen, and the loggia with its spectacular views can be seen, though all are mostly in ruins, to be sure. This was a fortress as well as a home for Tiberius, built not just for the view but for the natural defense such a height provided.

Back at the crossroads (at the market) follow the signs to the **Giardini di Augusto**, designed to provide even more flowers for the island, which boasts some 850 species. Along with the flora you'll see statues of gods, nymphs—and Lenin, who enjoyed Capri's charms after the 1905 uprising. From here the **Faraglioni**, two huge vertical stones, are seen in their considerable splendor. (On clear days they are visible from Naples to Sorrento.)

Follow the signs down to the **Arco Naturale**, a fantastic upthrusted arch of limestone. On the way you might stop at the **Paradise Bar**, appropriately named given its location amid splendid scenery and the fragrant air and birdsong. If you decide to linger in this area you might like the **Hotel Bel Sito**, with pleasant, simple rooms, views of the town and the sea, and its own trattoria and garden. **La Tosca**, via Birago 5, is inexpensive, and some of the rooms have splendid views.

From the Arch you can walk down to the **Grotta di Matromania**, which may have been the site of ancient cult worship but was certainly used by the Romans as a nymphaeum, a place of art and beauty to relax in. From here you can walk around the base of Mount Tuoro to the Porto di Tragara and then make the steep climb to the town of Capri.

Before returning, you might seek out **Luigi's** restaurant (Tel: 081-837-0591) near the Faraglione on strada dei Faraglioni, with a beach nearby, the latter a rare item on the island. Open from Easter to September (lunch only), it's a half-hour walk or a boat trip from Marina Piccola. Next to Luigi's, separated by a cliff, lies a languid trattoria, **La Fontelina**, a perfect retreat from the tourist hordes if you care to climb the cliff or have a boat. At nearby Marina Piccola, the perennial sun-and-seafood luncheon spot is the **Canzone del Mare** (Tel: 081-837-0104), where the food competes with the views and year-round tans for attention (open from Easter to October). The best beach is here, with lockers and showers. In the town of Capri, **La Capannina** (Tel: 081-837-0732; open from March to October; closed Wednesdays except in August), on via Le Botteghe, is popular. The inexpensive **La Cantina del Marchese** (via Tiberio 7e; Tel: 081-837-08-57) is worth the uphill walk from piazza Umberto for its excellent fresh pasta dishes and homemade cheeses and cured ham. Open daily in summer; closed Thursdays off-season.

From the town of Capri you can reach **Anacapri** by bus or taxi—a convertible if you can find one. These are a pleasant way to get around for a group of three or four, and cost about $10 each for a ride of over an hour.

Anacapri is known for the brilliantly beautiful **Villa San Michele**, which was built on the ruins of a Roman villa (some of which is preserved inside) by the Swedish writer and physician Axel Munthe. Munthe lived on Capri for 40 years (arriving in 1910) and wrote *The Story of San Michele* here. The 17th-century furnishings, Roman statues, and garden are among the treasures to enjoy. The villa also is frequently the setting for concerts, so watch for notices. The Church of San Michele nearby dazzles with its majolica floor depicting Adam and Eve in a Medieval bestiary of an Eden.

Anacapri has several comfortable, reasonably priced trattorias, including **Mama Giovanna** (via Boffe 1, Tel: 081-837-20-57; closed Mondays off-season) and **Il Cucciolo**, which has lovely views and fine fish (via La Fabbrica 52; Tel: 081-837-19-17; closed November to March 15). Among other restaurants, the **Villa Eva** (via La Fabbrica 8; Tel: 081-837-20-40) is moderately inexpensive and an excellent choice, partly because of its friendly owners. The **Caesar Augustus** still boasts the views of the Caesars and is moderately priced, but the interior is a bit stressed. They provide a bus from the port for a small charge.

While at Anacapri, take the chair lift to **Mt. Solaro** if possible. The chair lift is just that—you alone on a chair attached to a cable that rises to the top of the world—or so Mt. Solaro seems. (You are actually only about eight feet above the ground as you're lifted to the top.)

The **Grotta Azzura** (Blue Grotto) was, before the sea claimed it, a nymphaeum for Tiberius, filled with statues long lost or stolen. It gained international fame only in 1826, when a Slavic poet was enraptured by it and told his friends. It is the mysterious light, blue in one cavern, silver or pearl in another, that still draws tourists, and this light is best about midday. If there are many tourists about you will probably have to wait in a long line: the larger boat you leave in will transfer you to a little rowboat so that you can enter the low opening into the Grotta. Take a book, a hat, and suntan oil, and then wait; it's worth it. Or, if you prefer, you can walk down to the grotto's entrance from above, near the ruins of the Roman villa at Damecuta, on the northwest part of the island. A taxi will take you there and wait as part of the trip.

The tour of the island by boat (from Marina Grande) is delightful, for Capri is as lovely and full of natural enchantments from without as within.

If you have a few days to enjoy Capri, there are other Roman ruins such as the Palazzo a Mare and the Baths of Tiberius, the monastery called La Certosa (if open), and many other grottoes and natural wonders you can visit. From Capri you can also take day trips to Ischia, Procida, Naples, or Sorrento, or even farther south to Positano and Amalfi (in summer) if you decide to use the island as a base.

If a room with a view is of paramount importance to you, and you don't arrive in high season (when you'll usually need a reservation), you can leave your luggage at the Deposito Bagaglio at the top of the funicular in the town of Capri and set out to find the view that makes it all worthwhile. The best hotels are located far from the tourist throngs, which can be annoying even in spring. Below are some hotels that enjoy superb views and are easily accessible to shops and transportation. To live in the kind of luxury even ancient Greek Sybarites would envy, stay at the **Punta Tragara**, where the view, the gardens, the isolation, the private terraces, and the Corbusier-designed villa itself are perfect. **La Scalinatella** has similar amenities, and both hotels have private pools.

Just a ten-minute walk from the town of Capri is the less expensive but equally intimate and luxurious **Villa Brunella**, where 11 rooms share a pool and a flower-bedecked terrace with a grand view. The **Villa Sarah** is another charming place, small and well appointed, with a solarium as well. In Anacapri the family-run **Villa Patrizia** is simple and quiet, with lovely terraces and wonderful gardens.

In Capri **La Parisienne** on the piazzetta is the smartest shop. And for knitwear, two hours is enough for **Moda Caprese**, on via Camerelle, to finish your custom-made pants. It's **Chantecler** (via Vittorio Emanuele) and **Campanile** for hand-crafted jewelry, and **Massimo Goderecci** on via Valentino for ceramics.

ISCHIA

Beautifully green Ischia (ISS-kee-ah), a Greek trading station
in the eighth century B.C., is the quiet sister of chic Capri,
with comfortable beaches, friendly people, and bizarre
troglodytic dwellings high in its volcanic mountains. **Lacco
Ameno** is the smart resort, where the luxury sister hotels
Regina Isabella e Royal Sporting sheltered Liz and Dick from
the paparazzi when love was new and *Cleopatra* was a wrap.
Their spa is one of the best for mud (*fango*) baths; those of
the **Jolly** at Porto d'Ischia are also excellent, and one-day
treatments are available. Whatever the volcanic mud from
Monte Epomeo does for the body, it introduces an entirely
new world of relaxation. The process begins in a darkened
room, when a bell signals the approach of a scuttle of hot
mud from somewhere below the floor, presumably Vulcan's
forge. Then someone appears to spread *fango* on your
sheeted bed; you sink in, are wrapped like a mummy, and
are covered with the rest. Primeval ecstasy ensues, followed
by a firehose-like shower, herbal wraps, almond rubs—
whatever the new creature wishes. All cares are banished.

Elsewhere on the island, little towns like picturesque
Sant'Angelo are interspersed with white beaches and gentle
seascapes; less gentle but more mystical are the mountain
roads that seem to go back in time as you climb. The
restaurant **Girasole** can be reached by water taxi from
Sant'Angelo, and you can precede your luncheon with a
relaxing immersion in the hot volcanic sand followed by
sauna and swimming. Tel: (9081) 99-92-97. At Sant'Angelo
have seafood (of course) at salty **Dal Pescatore** (Tel: 081-99-
92-06; closed January 15 to March 15). Near Lacco Ameno the
Negombo has a great view of the bay. The Regina Isabella
has an excellent dining room and a barman who remembers
Liz's favorite drinks from the wild days. At **Forio**, on the
western coast, stay at the **Residence Villa Tina** if you'd like
an apartment sleeping four to six, with terrace and kitchen.

THE AMALFI COAST

Beyond Pompeii, where the Salentine peninsula curves seaward, the Amalfi coast begins. (The town of Amalfi itself is on
the southern shore of the long coastline.) From the coast's
northernmost town, Sorrento, to Positano, the road called

the Nastro Azzuro (Blue Ribbon) rises over the magnificent crest of land at the top of the peninsula, stretching north toward Naples and south toward Positano.

One of the most beautiful roads in the world, the **Amalfi Drive** curves along majestic cliffs terraced with vineyards and lemon groves, and is bordered by a rocky shore far below, dotted with fortress towers that once defended the towns from sea raiders. The sea views are as fresh as watercolors, splashed with pine and cactus and brightened by wild roses and bougainvillaea.

Since relaxing is the point of being there, a few days' stay is in order; don't try racing along the hairpin turns—a diversion best left to the locals. Though August is impossibly crowded, July is often surprisingly less so. Weekends bring bumper-to-bumper traffic to the narrow coast road.

Sorrento

Sorrento, hugging the top of cliffs that reach 150 feet in height, is a big city when compared with Positano and Amalfi. Its grand hotels in the Belle Epoque style, luxuriant gardens, and splendid views recall Sorrento's former glorious days as a regal summer spot. The rocky shore has bathing pavilions built out like cruise-ship decks. Torquato Tasso, the 16th-century author of *Jerusalem Delivered,* was born in Sorrento, and is fêted with a statue and a piazza named for him. The hotels **Excelsior Vittoria** and **Parco dei Principi**, although near the town center, are surrounded by dazzling gardens and panoramic views, their grand appearance seeming to suggest that guests play croquet on the lawn all summer in white suits or starched dresses.

Sorrento has a wide variety of accommodations at all prices. Although it lacks Positano's glamor, it has a faded charm that many find seductive. The **Hotel Elios** is a good choice for dazzling tiles and views of the bay, and the **Loreley et Londres** has similar charms. Dinner at **La Favorita—o'Parrucchiano** will give you a taste of the cooking that people come back to Sorrento for (corso Italia 71; Tel: 081-878-13-21).

Furniture is now a main industry here, particularly intarsia work, in which paper-thin wood stencils of varying patterns are laid one on top of the other and lacquered. Sorrento is also a terminal for trains and buses and has frequent boat service to the islands of Capri and Ischia as well as the other towns of the Amalfi coast.

Positano

Pastel sweet by day and as magic as a Christmas village by night, Positano is set into the cliffs. The streets are steep or stepped, so espadrilles or rubber soles are necessary, especially after a rain. For a quick view of the town, take a ride on the orange bus marked *"Interno Positano,"* which runs about every hour.

Some of Italy's best and most expensive hotels are located here, including the splendidly hidden **San Pietro**, dazzling with its azaleas and hand-painted tiles, thanks to the inventive whimsy of the late Carlino Cinque, who created this delightful place. However, its once international tone is now decidely American. The San Pietro also has a lively restaurant. Reservations are suggested for non-guests; Tel: (089) 87-54-55. The hotel, just beyond town, has a private bus to provide transport. In the town proper, the **Sirenuse** is a posh, sparkling hotel with antiques, huge terraces, and a pretty pool. High above the town sits the **Poseidon**, a fine villa with a sweeping view of the coast as well as a pool and restaurant. Less pricey is the charming **Palazzo Murat**, in an 18th-century palazzo where Murat, once king of Naples, spent some time.

Among the reasonably priced are the **Hotel California**, a comfortable spot with spacious rooms and terraces, tiles and greenery; and the **Marincato**, which also has comfortable rooms, many with terraces. Down on the beach the **Buca di Bacco** restaurant has created a hotel in a 19th-century villa; balconies face the sea. This tends to be a lively spot, and may be best in the off-season unless you like the late-night life. Both the **Casa Albertina** and the **Casa Maresca** are family run and offer perfect views, and both are less expensive than most of the other hotels in Positano.

In addition to its flower-laden hotels and villas, Positano has a tiny harbor, a cathedral, and lots of boutiques—and not much else (aside, of course, from the marvelous scenery). The **Cambusa** (Tel: 089-87-54-32), **Buca di Bacco**, **Covo dei Saraceni**, and **O'Caporale** are good places to eat fish while enjoying the harbor sights.

Pretty **Praiano**, the next town along the coast, is quieter than Positano, and has a lovely harbor and beach. The **Grand Hotel Tritone** sits high on the cliffs and looks out at a dazzling panorama; each room has a terrace, and the swimming pool and restaurant are each nestled on their own terrace levels. A late-night disco down at sea level welcomes guests coming by boat or down the cliff steps.

Also at Praiano is the delightful **Villaggio Tranquillità**, an economical luxury run by the handsome Maresca brothers: private cottages with flowery sea-viewing terraces, outdoor dining, and a comfortable bar.

Amalfi

The town of Amalfi, across the Furore Fjord bridge, has an imposing history for a little place that's nestled beneath ponderous cliffs and wanders up into the mountains. During Amalfi's days in the sun, the city was an important maritime republic, like Pisa and Venice, with trade routes extending as far as Constantinople, where the bronze doors of its cathedral were forged in 1066. The **Cathedral of St. Andrew** is among the most beautiful in southern Italy, intricate in its Arab-Norman design and detail, with a cloisters even more Eastern in its intertwining arches and palm trees. Dedicated to Andrew, patron saint of sailors, it was begun during the ninth century and remodeled three centuries later.

The interior, jubilant even on the darkest day, has been restored in Baroque style, with a ceiling of intaglia woodwork. Even the crypt is radiant, and the altar, the work of Fontana, as well as the statues of Saints Peter and Paul by Pietro Bernini, are magnificent. Under the altar lie Saint Andrew's bones, but not quietly. The bones exude a fragrant oil called the manna of Saint Andrew, and when it miraculously appears, it portends good fortune if it flows quickly, like San Gennaro's blood. Slow manna is less auspicious.

The 11th-century art of papermaking is still practiced here. At the top of the central street (number 92) is a mill where fine paper with Amalfi watermarks is made. If you ring and the time is right, you may get to see the production process, from pulp to sheets. Watercolor paper sold here is excellent, as is the stationery.

In the piazza near the harbor stands a statue of Flavio Gioia, inventor, they say, of the compass he is consulting. In back of him the Municipio, or Town Hall, houses the Tabula Amalfitana—long accepted as the law of the sea—and the costumes for the Regatta of the Four Maritime Republics (Venice, Pisa, Genoa, and Amalfi), celebrated each year in alternating cities. Unfortunately, Amalfi's harbor area is largely used as a bus park, which takes away from its charm but is apparently necessary, given the rocky terrain the town has to cope with.

Christmas and New Year's bring feasting and fireworks over the sea, making it a nice time to be here—it's never cold, just a little rain now and then. The **Santa Caterina**, Amalfi's deluxe hotel, serves wild boar along with turkey, *baccalà,* and Champagne; at midnight the coast lights up with pyrotechnics from Positano to Amalfi and Atrani. The hotel curves along the coast, and many of its rooms open onto terraces above lush gardens and lemon groves, with only the sea beyond. The lemons are used by the chef in a sauce for pasta that can be made successfully only with Amalfi's lemons. In summer, the hotel opens one long seaside terrace under a pergola of grapevines as an informal trattoria, complete with excellent pizza and a new favorite, pesto made with arugula.

High above Amalfi, the hotel **Cappuccini Convento**, reached by cliff elevator, evokes the Medieval monastery it once was, set as it is amid a terraced garden with a grape arbor. The **Hotel Amalfi** is in town on the hill, amid terraces and lemon groves. It's one of the least expensive. Nearer to sea level, the **Luna Convento** hotel recalls its cloistered past, with vaulted rooms and antiques, and, of course, cloisters. Ibsen, a sign says, wrote *The Doll's House* here, and the hotel is still run by the same family. Near the harbor the **Residence** is inexpensive and atmospheric. The Santa Caterina and the Luna also have fine restaurants. The **Baracca** on piazza Ferrari (Tel: 089-87-12-85) is the town's oldest trattoria— friendly and family-run. Near the cathedral are the **Taverna degli Apostoli**, at via Sant' Anna 6 (Tel: 089-87-29-91), which has a traditional atmosphere and good pasta sauces such as *frutti di mare* (seafood), and the simple, family-run **Gemma** (Tel: 089-87-13-45; closed Wednesdays).

The white town of **Atrani**, just up the coast from Amalfi, is easily missed because the highway overpass obscures part of it. Walk down into the piazza, from which you will see a maze of houses rising up the hill. These can be reached only by staircases, as private and elusive as a North African village. A few alfresco restaurants on high are worth the climb; the cathedral bears a bronze door like Amalfi's, made in Constantinople during the 11th century.

Ravello

High above Amalfi, Ravello rises serene and aloof, embodying a rare combination of spaciousness, grace, and mood. Even the light at Ravello is rarefied, and is most beautiful during the afternoon when the air is clear. Have lunch near the Duomo at the **Hotel Palumbo**, still owned by the distinguished Pasquale

Vuillemier, who is often in attendance. The Palumbo and the **Caruso Belvedere** are Ravello's most charming hotels, each furnished with antiques and graced with superb views of the coast; the Caruso also counts spacious grounds among its attractions.

Just a few minutes' walk from the central piazza, the **Villa Rufolo** is so romantic and atmospheric that Wagner, on seeing it, exclaimed, "The magic garden of Klingsor has been found." He was then (1880) living in southern Italy and orchestrating *Parsifal*. Today, each July a Wagner festival is held on the grounds. During the 12th century the noble Rufolo family had the Villa Rufolo built in front of the boundless sea; Boccaccio was one of their guests, and he mentioned it in *The Decameron*. No ruins are more evocative of the period, and the effect is heightened by the gardens, with their palms, Judas trees, papyrus, and flowers—all serving as a counterpoint to the arabesques of the arches and the rugged old tower, now tastefully crumbling.

The **Villa Cimbrone**, a short walk away, evokes another mood entirely, without the romanticism of its neighbor but with its own humor and panoramas to satisfy even the wide-angle weary. Over the central arch of the entryway are two boars' heads representing the coat of arms of Lord Grimthorpe, the eccentric gentleman who was behind the villa's creation.

The first unusual sight is in the cloisters: the seven deadly sins, represented by seven little unrepentant heads. Then, across wide lawns, through rose gardens, past Greek statues, and into a nymph's grotto, a belvedere seems to unfold above the whole Mediterranean. Grimthorpe is buried nearby. His epitaph (1917) is as bizarre as his villa: "Glad I came, not sorry to depart."

Before leaving Ravello, stop at the cathedral (built in 1086) named for the doctor/saint Pantaleone. The cathedral façade is obviously restored, but the great door, made by Barisano of Trani in 1179, is divided into 54 panels featuring beautifully executed lives of Christ and the saints. Inside is a superb pulpit by Niccolo di Foggia, commissioned by the Rufolo family in 1272. Topped with a majestic eagle, it glitters with mosaics, while its columns rest on sculpted lions. In front of it the smaller pulpit, a rare piece built in 1130, shows Jonah and the whale, a metaphor of Christ's resurrection, delightfully documented in mosaics.

The museum downstairs is singular. The bust of the Signora da Ravello is thought to be of a Rufolo family member, and the elegant silver head is that of Saint Barbara, perhaps with her real skull still inside. (During the Middle Ages trade in saints' relics was frantic. For all of them to have been authentic, saints would have had to have had myriad necks and thighbones and hundreds of extra fingers.)

Ravello's wines are quite good—and even better on the Palumbo dining terrace, with the coast spread out below. The restaurant **Cumpa' Cosimo**, via Roma 48, is cozy and serves exquisite pasta at moderate prices (Tel: 089-85-71-56; closed Mondays). The **Garden**, at about the same price, is beautifully situated at the cliff and serves crêpes and seafood (via Chiunzi; Tel: 089-85-72-26; closed Tuesdays). Staying in Ravello can be enchanting if getting away from it all is your desire. During the summer months a bus makes frequent connections between the piazza del Duomo and Amalfi's central piazza.

Vietri sul Mare

On a very different kind of day, when you are in the mood to shop for ceramics, head east along the coast from Ravello to Vietri, a town completely devoted, it seems, to ceramics, with its colorful wares displayed on every street. The **Solimena factory** is the one to see first; it's in an imaginative building designed by Solari on via Madonna degli Angeli. The little tourist office on the central piazza will guide you to the latest exhibits and other ceramicists.

Salerno, the next town to Vietri sul Mare, has an excellent restaurant: **Maria Grazia** (località Nerano Marina del Cantone; Tel: 081-808-10-35; closed Wednesdays). After lunch, visit the **cathedral**, built by the Norman Robert Guiscard in 1086, but much restored of course. Many of its original details can be seen in the museum (adjacent; open mornings and 4:00 to 6:00 P.M.)

GETTING AROUND

A sea express (hydrofoil) is available during the summer, connecting Rome's Fiumicino airport with Capri and Naples. For information contact Medmar, in Rome at via Ofanto 18; Tel: (06) 844-05-78. In Naples the address is via Caracciolo 11; Tel: (081) 66-73-27.

Campania is so well interconnected by boat, train, and bus that it is possible to stay almost anywhere and still be able to get to its main attractions. It's not necessary to stay in Naples, and in summer probably not desirable, given the heat and traffic. Stay on one of the nearby islands—Capri, Ischia, or Procida—and hydrofoil into Naples (less than an hour's trip) to take the train north to Cuma or south to Pompeii and Herculaneum. Then move south to Positano, Amalfi, or Ravello to enjoy the beauty of this popular resort area. Do not go in August, when all of Italy and Europe descends, and again, avoid weekend travel. (Get a copy of *Qui Napoli,* a bilingual booklet that features special events and tours, found at hotels with concierges and sometimes at the tourist offices.)

If you are travelling to Naples by train from Rome, get off at the first stop, Mergellina, a nicer introduction to the city and a better place than the central station to find taxis, especially at night. (Ask when reserving—not all trains stop there.)

Money belts are advised in the Naples area, and if possible do not drive in or near the city. Park at your hotel unless you know the territory.

From Naples there are good train connections to western and northern Campania as well as to Pompeii, Herculaneum, and Paestum. For the Amalfi coast you can take the train to Sorrento and the bus (all year) or the ferry or hydrofoil (in summer) to Positano or Amalfi. For Amalfi it's sometimes easier to take the train to Salerno and the bus or a taxi back up the coast.

Ferries and hydrofoils (*aliscafi*) leave Naples frequently for Capri and Ischia. In summer the Amalfi Drive can be reached from Naples by hydrofoil to Amalfi or Positano. For the hydrofoil from Naples to Capri, Ischia, or Procida, go to the pier at Mergellina (ten minutes from the Royal or Excelsior hotel by taxi; a half hour, at least, by the 130 bus); the buses are usually crowded to the point of immobility, so you might consider walking, allowing a half hour or more. For the ferries, which take longer but cost less, go to the port in back of the Castel Nuovo in central Naples.

Cars are not needed on Capri, but one might be handy on Ischia. All three islands have good bus service, or you can hire a taxi for a few hours, which comes to about $15 per person for a group of four.

In Naples a car is a hindrance; traffic and parking problems make walking or getting about by bus or taxi a much more practical means of transit. Buses can be entered only by pushing and being pushed, unless you enter at the beginning of the route and leave at its termination. The Amalfi Drive should be approached with caution—it is an extremely tortuous, narrow, cliff-hugging road. If you want to drive, rent a car before leaving Naples and take an inland route to Vietri, near Salerno; then double back up the drive to Amalfi and Positano, a much easier approach, at least until you know the territory.

Many hotels in Positano and Amalfi will send a car to the Rome or Naples airport for clients if requested—for a healthy fee, of course. A taxi from Naples to Positano costs about $70. To reach Amalfi or Positano from Rome, take the train to Salerno or Sorrento, and then a taxi, hydrofoil, or local bus to your destination. Local buses do not regularly transport luggage, however, so a taxi makes better sense.

If you stay in Positano, Pompeii is conveniently reached by car; there are also regular bus excursions. Bus and train connections are less convenient but possible. A bus from Amalfi's central piazza climbs the high, winding road to Ravello at frequent intervals.

The Naples daily paper, *Il Mattino,* lists train and boat departures. Vietri adjoins Salerno, and from there the train leaves for Naples or Rome—a last-minute swim or a plate of *spaghetti con vongole veraci,* and you're on your way.

ACCOMMODATIONS REFERENCE

The rates given below are projections for 1992; always check for up-to-date information before making reservations. Wide ranges may reflect the differences between low- and high-season rates. Unless otherwise indicated, the figures indicate the cost of a double room (per room, not per person). However, half-board (mezza pensione) rates, which include breakfast and one other meal per day, are per person. Most hotels will add a service charge of 10 to 15 percent.

▶ **Hotel Amalfi.** Via dei Pastai 3, 84011 **Amalfi.** Tel: (089) 87-24-40. Ł60,000.

▶ **Arcate.** Via Marcello Scotti 10, 80079 **Procida.** Tel: (081) 986-71-20. Ł85,000.

▶ **Hotel Bel Sito.** Via Matromania 11, 80073 **Capri.** Tel: (081) 837-09-69; Fax: (081) 837-66-22. Ł120,000.

▶ **Belvedere.** Via Tito Angelini 51, 80129 **Naples.** Tel: (081) 578-81-69. Ł150,000.

▶ **Buca di Bacco.** Porto, 84012 **Positano.** Tel: (089) 87-56-99; Fax: (089) 87-57-31. Open mid-March to mid-October. Ł100,000–Ł162,000.

▶ **Caesar Augustus.** 80071 **Anacapri.** Tel: (081) 837-14-21. Ł90,000.

▶ **Hotel California.** Via Cristoforo Colombo, 84017 **Positano.** Tel: (089) 87-53-82. Ł50,000.

▶ **Canada**. Via Mergellina 43, 80142 **Naples**. Tel: (081) 68-09-52. Ł90,000.

▶ **Cappuccini Convento**. Via Annunziatella 46, 84011 **Amalfi**. Tel: (089) 87-10-08. Ł170,000.

▶ **Caruso Belvedere**. Via San Giovanni del Toro 52, 84010 **Ravello**. Tel: (089) 85-71-11; Fax: (089) 85-73-72. Ł125,000–Ł160,000.

▶ **Casa Albertina**. Via della Tavolozza 4, 84017 **Positano**. Tel: (089) 87-51-43; Fax: (089) 81-15-40. Ł80,000–Ł130,000.

▶ **Casa Maresca**. Viale Pasitea, 84017 **Positano**. Tel: (089) 87-51-40. Open Easter–October. Ł90,000.

▶ **Hotel Elios**. Via Capo 33, 80066 **Sorrento**. Tel: (081) 878-18-12. Ł55,000.

▶ **Excelsior**. Via Partenope 48, 80121 **Naples**. Tel: (081) 41-71-11; Fax: (081) 41-17-43. In U.S., Tel: (800) 221-2340 or (212) 935-9540; Fax: (212) 421-5929. In U.K., Tel: (071) 930-4147 or (0800) 28-92-34; Fax: (071) 839-1566. Ł286,000–Ł429,000.

▶ **Excelsior Vittoria**. Piazza Tasso 34, 80067 **Sorrento**. Tel: (081) 807-10-44; Fax: (081) 877-12-06. Ł280,000–Ł305,000.

▶ **Gabbiano**. 84064 **Palinuro**. Tel: (0974) 93-11-55. Ł90,000.

▶ **Grand Hotel Tritone**. 84010 **Praiano**. Tel: (089) 87-43-33; Fax: (089) 87-43-74. Ł210,000.

▶ **Jolly Hotel delle Terme**. Via de Luca 42, 80077 **Porto d'Ischia**. Tel: (081) 99-17-44; Fax: (081) 99-31-56. In U.S., Tel: (212) 213-1468 or (800) 221-2626; Fax: (212) 213-2369. In U.K., Tel: (923) 89-62-72 or (0800) 28-27-29; Fax: (923) 89-60-71. Open mid-March–mid-November. Ł175,000–Ł320,000.

▶ **Loreley et Londres**. Via A. Califano 2, 80066 **Sorrento**. Tel: (081) 878-15-08. Ł65,000.

▶ **Luna Convento**. 84011 **Amalfi**. Tel: (089) 87-10-02; Fax: (089) 87-13-33. Ł140,000.

▶ **Marincato**. Via Cristoforo Colombo 36, 84017 **Positano**. Tel: (089) 87-51-30. Ł100,000.

▶ **Muller**. Piazza Mergellina 7, 80122 **Naples**. Tel: (081) 66-90-56. Ł90,000.

▶ **L'Oasi**. 80079 **Procida**. Tel: (081) 896-74-99. Ł75,000.

▶ **Palazzo Murat**. Via dei Mulini 23, 84017 **Positano**. Tel: (089) 87-51-77. Ł135,000–Ł160,000.

▶ **Hotel Palumbo**. Via San Giovanni del Toro 28, 84010 **Ravello**. Tel: (089) 85-72-44; Fax: (089) 85-73-47. In U.S., Tel: (212) 599-8280 or (800) 223-9832; Fax: (212) 599-1755. Ł275,000–Ł360,000.

▶ **Hotel Paradiso**. Via Catullo 11, 80122 **Naples**. Tel: (081) 761-41-61; Fax: (081) 761-34-49. Ł150,000–Ł240,000.

▶ **Parco dei Principi**. Via Rota 1, 80067 **Sorrento**. Tel: (081)

878-46-44; Fax: (081) 878-37-86. Open April–October. ₤200,000–₤300,000.

▶ **Pinto-Storey**. Via Martucci 72, 80121 **Naples**. Tel: (081) 68-12-60. ₤90,000.

▶ **Poseidon**. Viale Pasitea, 84017 **Positano**. Tel: (089) 87-50-14; Fax: (089) 87-58-33. In U.S., Tel: (212) 599-8280 or (800) 223-9832; Fax: (212) 599-1755. Open April–mid-October. ₤190,000–₤280,000.

▶ **Punta Tragara**. Via Tragara 57, 80073 **Capri**. Tel: (081) 837-08-44; Fax: (081) 837-77-90. Open mid-March–mid-October. ₤530,000.

▶ **Regina Isabella e Royal Sporting**. Piazza Santa Restituta, 80076 **Lacco Ameno**. Tel: (081) 99-43-22; Fax: (081) 98-60-43. In U.S., Tel: (212) 599-8280 or (800) 223-9832; Fax: (212) 599-1755. Open mid-April–mid-October. ₤220,000–₤392,000.

▶ **Residence**. Via Repubbliche Marinare 9, 84011 **Amalfi**. Tel: (089) 87-11-83; Fax: (089) 83-03-03. Open April–October. ₤95,000.

▶ **Residence Villa Tina**. Via delle Vigne 6, 80077 **Porto d'Ischia**. Tel: (081) 99-19-03. ₤80,000.

▶ **Royal**. Via Partenope 38, 80121 **Naples**. Tel: (081) 764-48-00; Fax: (081) 764-57-07. ₤196,000–₤293,000.

▶ **San Pietro**. Via Laurito 2, Località San Pietro, 84017 **Positano**. Tel: (089) 87-54-55; Fax: (809) 81-14-49. In U.S., Tel: (212) 599-8280 or (800) 223-9832; Fax: (212) 599-1755. Open April–November 4. ₤475,000–₤550,000.

▶ **Santa Caterina**. 84011 **Amalfi**. Tel: (089) 87-10-12; Fax: (089) 87-13-51. In U.S., Tel: (212) 599-8280 or (800) 223-9832; Fax: (212) 599-1755. ₤220,000–₤380,000.

▶ **La Santa Lucia**. Via Partenope 46, 80121 **Naples**. Tel: (081) 41-65-66. ₤180,000–₤240,000.

▶ **La Scalinatella**. Via Tragara 8, 80073 **Capri**. Tel: (081) 837-06-33; Fax: (081) 837-82-91. Open March 15–November 5. ₤220,000–₤420,000.

▶ **Le Sirenuse**. Via Colombo 30, 84017 **Positano**. Tel: (089) 87-50-66; Fax: (089) 81-17-98. In U.S., Tel: (212) 838-3110 or (800) 223-6800; Fax: (212) 758-7367. In U.K., Tel: (0800) 18-11-23; Fax: (071) 353-1904. ₤470,000.

▶ **La Tosca**. Via Dalmazio Birago 5, 80073 **Capri**. Tel: (081) 837-09-89. ₤75,000.

▶ **Vesuvio**. Via Partenope 45, 80121 **Naples**. Tel: (081) 41-70-44; Fax: same. ₤200,000–₤290,000.

▶ **Villa La Brunella**. Via Tragara 24, 80073 **Capri**. Tel: (081) 837-01-22; Fax: (081) 837-04-30. Open mid-March–November. ₤250,000.

▶ **Villa Eva.** Via la Fabbrica 8, 80073 **Capri.** Tel: (081) 837-20-40. ₤40,000.

▶ **Villa dei Misteri.** Via Villa dei Misteri, 80045 **Pompeii.** Tel: (081) 861-35-93. ₤60,000.

▶ **Villa Patrizia.** Via Pagliaro 55, 80071 **Anacapri.** Tel: (081) 837-10-14. ₤150,000.

▶ **Villa Sarah.** Via Tiberio 3/a, 80073 **Capri.** Tel: (081) 837-78-17. Open Easter–October. ₤90,000–₤150,000.

▶ **Villaggio La Tranquillità.** Via Roma 10, 84010 **Praiano.** Tel: (089) 87-40-84. ₤50,000.

APULIA

By Dwight V. Gast

Often described as "the heel of the Italian boot," Apulia (Puglia in Italian—pronounced POOL-ya) has from prehistoric times had the heels of various peoples planted onto its flat and vulnerable topography. It has been occupied to a greater or lesser extent by the ancient Apuli tribes (from which it takes its name), Greeks, and Romans; it was at various times subjugated by Byzantines, Lombards, Franks, and Saracens; heavily built up by Normans and Hohenstaufens; and was then ruled at a distance by Angevins, Aragonese, and Bourbons. Every town seems to have its ruined castle or musty museum to attest to some aspect of that past.

In short, Apulia has a history that would drive the brightest schoolboy mad. The region's most distinctive architectural style, for example, is a complex blend of French and northern Italian architectural forms with Byzantine ornamentation of Saracen inspiration, all of it brought together under the Normans. Whatever its confusing origins, the Apulian Romanesque resulted in some of Italy's most significant cathedrals stretching heavenward above the coastal plain. Yet the region draws visitors not just because of its peculiar artistic heritage but also for the natural wonders of its spectacular coastline, caves, and forests; for its own distinct cuisine; and for the chance to venture off the well-beaten tracks in Italy.

MAJOR INTEREST

Multicultural artistic heritage
Less visited and more intact
Coastal drive of the Gargano massif
Romanesque cathedrals in and near Bari
Frederick II's hunting lodge at Castel del Monte

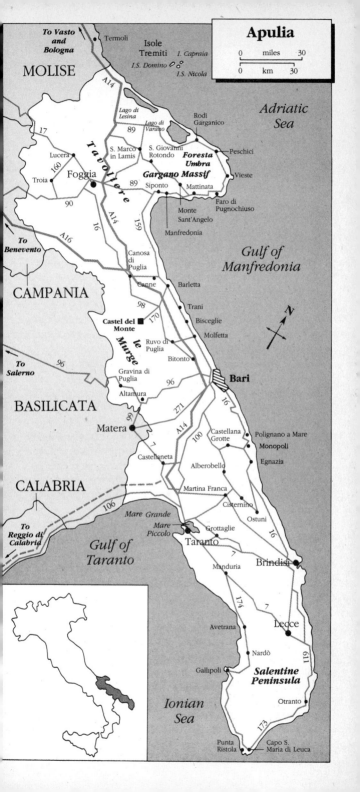

Cave city of Matera in neighboring Basilicata
Limestone alabaster caves of Castellana Grotte
Trulli structures in and around Alberobello
Archaeological excavations at Egnatia
Baroque architecture of Lecce
Treasures of Magna Graecia in the Museo Nazionale
    in Taranto

Most of Apulia's overlords were either passing through on their way to more strategically protected destinations or occupying territory that formed part of a greater empire. The overwhelming exception—and the dominant figure of Apulia to this day—was Frederick II of Hohenstaufen, *stupor mundi et immutator mirabilis,* a progressive 13th-century leader and man of letters whom Dante called "the father of Italian poetry." With his son Manfred, Frederick was responsible for much of what Apulia still looks like. He not only filled it with castles but stayed on to make use of them. Later, the demise of the Hohenstaufen family dragged Apulia's prosperity down with it.

Most modern invaders were as negligent toward Apulia as the rulers who preceded and succeeded Frederick. Apulia was seen as a place to pass through on the way to and from the port cities of the Adriatic. Today, however, the region is on the rebound. Witness Bari's thriving Fiera del Levante, a trade fair, or the bounty of the region's extensive fields, vineyards, and olive groves. The tourist trade has also begun to flourish—mostly on the beaches of the longest coastline of any Italian region—and those who come here find more and more in the way of hospitable hotels and, especially, restaurants.

Luckily, none of Apulia's magic has been sacrificed so far, and an almost fairy-tale atmosphere persists throughout. The shadowy Foresta Umbra on the Gargano massif is the closest thing Italy has to an enchanted forest; and the burial markers of the Daunian people, who inhabited northern Apulia in ancient times—thin, flat stones with helmet-headed tops—are reminiscent of Alice's pack of cards. The Rubian drinking vessels shaped like animal heads in the Museo Jatta in Ruvo would put Walt Disney to shame, as would the beast motifs on Apulian Romanesque cathedrals. Animals figure prominently in folklore to this day in rural Apulia, where farmers won't slice milk-soaked bread for fear their cows will go dry, and horses wear beads to ward off the evil eye. In the caves of Castellana Grotte, unusual rock formations have prompted imaginative names. And the already exuberant Baroque found especially fertile ground in Lecce, far down the heel of Italy's boot, where the soft tufa stone, as Osbert Sitwell wrote, "allows the rich imagination of the south an unparalleled outlet."

All this provides a fitting backdrop to the traditional spirituality of many of the region's people, some of whom lived and worshipped until recently in the caves of Matera in the neighboring region of Basilicata. (Other unusual dwellings are the beehive-shaped structures known as *trulli* in the Murgia of the Trulli, including practically the entire town of Alberobello.)

When, according to legend, the Archangel Michael appeared in a grotto on the Gargano in the fifth century and left behind his great red cloak (part of which is now at Le Mont-St-Michel in France), the cult that arose around him merely replaced that of a local oracle on the same sacred spot, mentioned by Strabo in antiquity. And so it goes down the long coast: Saint Nicholas is celebrated in Bari, and an important Holy Week procession takes place in Taranto. Apulia's latest religious cult figure is Padre Pio, a Capuchin monk who died in 1968 and is buried at San Giovanni Rotondo, just a few miles from where Saint Michael made his original appearance. Born in Benevento, Pio, too, was an outsider, but his remains seem to be right at home in this magic and mystical land.

CAPITANATA

The northernmost section of Apulia (and therefore its most frequent point of entry from the rest of Italy), Capitanata is a union of topographical opposites. Jutting out into the Adriatic to form the spur of the Italian boot is the mountainous and forested Gargano massif; below it is the flat and treeless Tavoliere (Italian for chessboard, from the grid pattern of roads traced there by the ancient Romans), the largest plain in southern Italy, undulating with waves of wheat and barley. Nature and sea lovers might want to stay (with large numbers of northern Europeans) on the Gargano at the quiet and—like virtually all accommodations in Apulia—modern **Hotel del Faro**, on its own promontory on the rocky shore near Faro di Pugnochiuso to the east, or at the more moderately priced **Apeneste** in Mattinata on the south coast. However, the **Hotel Cicolella** in Foggia, the bustling provincial capital, is a more convenient base for exploring the immediate area and, because it is primarily a businessperson's hotel, has the advan-

tage of housing the town's best restaurant, also called
Cicolella (Tel: 0881-321-66; closed weekends), which provides a superb introduction to most Apulian specialties.

Predictably, Apulia has a lot of food prepared especially
for religious holidays, but dishes to be savored year-round
include *orecchiette con cime di rapa,* the ear-shaped pasta
ubiquitous in Apulia, here cooked with turnip greens;
troccoli con sugo di seppie, flat noodles prepared with a
sauce made from squid; *capriata,* pureed beans served with
chicory or other vegetables; *tiella di funghi,* a mushroom
casserole; lamb, kid, or game; and local versions of such
cheeses as pecorino, ricotta, scamorza, and the local
provolone. Usually it is all accompanied by the ring-shaped,
fennel-flavored bread called *scaldatelli.* Much rosé wine is
drunk in Apulia, but the robust food is best accompanied by
the mellow reds Cacc' e Mitte or Rosso di Cerignola; lighter
foods go well with a refreshing San Severo white. There are
plenty of grapes in the region, including some of Italy's best
table varieties. Liqueur lovers might try the local Amarella,
made with black cherry leaves.

Foggia, Lucera, and Troia

Despite Frederick II's frequent stays in Foggia, nothing remains of his palace there, as a result of an 18th-century
earthquake and heavy bombing during World War II. In fact,
except for a moderately interesting Baroque cathedral and
an archaeological museum, Foggia serves best as a place to
gather your energies for exploring the rest of Capitanata
(Foggia is just off Autostrada A 14 and a main train line, and
has a small airport), perhaps invigorated by a walk on the
extensive grounds of the **Villa Comunale** or through the five
little outdoor chapels leading to the **Chiesa delle Croci.**

From Foggia it is a short, straight hop by car or bus west
across the Tavoliere to **Lucera.** Just outside the city is its
magnificent castle, the **Fortezza Angioina,** begun by Frederick II. Norman Douglas begins his *Old Calabria* ("Calabria"
once referred to more of southern Italy than it does at
present) with a description of the castle's position, looking
toward the Apennines and the Gargano, as the "key of
Apulia." The castle itself is equally impressive, with dozens
of towers and almost half a mile of encircling walls. Also on
the outskirts of town is a Roman amphitheater, currently
being restored and used for performances during the summer. In the Arabian-looking town proper (Frederick II
stocked it with Saracens from Sicily) we get our first glimpse

of Saint Michael on the **Duomo**, one of the few intact
examples of Angevin architecture in Italy: The archangel is
in the center portal, flanked by two lesser angels.

Troia, directly south of Lucera by car or bus, has another
fine view of the surrounding countryside. Though Frederick II destroyed much of the evidence of its noble past,
Troia's **Duomo** remains the happiest marriage of Romanesque architectural forms with Eastern sculptural ornamentation in Apulia. The intricate latticework of its huge rose
window shows Saracen sources, while beneath it the bronze
doors teem with Byzantine dragons, animals, saints, and a
portrait of the sculptor of the doors, Oderisio da Benevento,
less than humbly placed next to Christ.

The Gargano Massif

The Gargano, served by trains and buses from Foggia, gets
two types of tourists: nature lovers from Italy and northern
Europe during the summer and tour buses full of religious
pilgrims from all over the world year-round. From Foggia,
pilgrims generally head north across the Tavoliere to the
town of San Marco in Lamis to see the convent of San Matteo;
then they go east to San Giovanni Rotondo to pay homage to
a statue of the Madonna in the 16th-century convent of Santa
Maria delle Grazie, to Padre Pio's tomb in the modern
church of the same name, and to see the American-funded
Fiorello La Guardia Hospital. The final stop on the route is
Monte Sant'Angelo, the windswept and rather desolate town
perched on a rock still farther east near the Gulf of Manfredonia, where the Archangel Michael made his appearance
to San Lorenzo, Bishop of Siponto, on May 8, 490. Subsequently, the **Santuario di San Michele** became one of the
most important religious sanctuaries in the Christian world.
Its miraculous grotto was consecrated in the fifth century,
and works of art followed over the years. The bronze door at
the entrance to the inner vestibule comes from Constantinople and is the oldest in Apulia; also significant is the stone
bishop's throne in the grotto, where a marble statue of the
saint, attributed to Andrea Sansovino, presides. Devotees
often make the steep descent to the inner sanctum in their
bare feet, and some continue their penance by licking the
floor of the grotto. Those who would like to stay at the site
may arrange to do so (Tel: 0882-623-96); other monasteries
in the area are the **Convento di San Matteo** (Tel: 0882-83-11-
01) and the **Convento della Madonna di Stignano** (Tel: 0882-

83-10-90) in San Marco in Lamis, and the **Convento dei Cappuccini** in San Giovanni Rotondo.

The **Gargano coast route**—route 89—from Foggia begins with a stop at **Santa Maria di Siponto**, a recently restored 12th-century cathedral; it is a survivor of the earthquake that leveled the important port town of **Siponto**, east of Foggia, in the 13th century. From there, it is a short distance to industrial **Manfredonia**, founded by Frederick II's bastard son Manfred. Its massive castle houses the **Museo Nazionale Archeologico del Gargano**, which contains the enchanting Daunian stelae, or grave slabs, covered with cartoonlike representations of nature. For those interested in art but not in making the entire religious pilgrimage route, it is a short distance from Manfredonia to **Monte Sant'Angelo**, where in addition to the sanctuary there is an interesting 12th-century structure called the Tomba di Rotari, which originally may have been a baptistery or a mausoleum, and the **Museo delle Arte e Tradizioni Popolari del Gargano**, a museum devoted to daily life in former times. (The folk tradition is still evident in the town's production of wood carving.) Driving back down to the coast you pass through **Mattinata**, where a curious private collection of local art from Daunian stelae to alabaster statues of Saint Michael is on display in the **Farmacia Sansone**. Mattinata also boasts the **Trattoria dalla Nonna** (Mattinata Mare; Tel: 0884-492-05), where *zuppa di pesce* (a fish stew) and other delights from the sea may be enjoyed *in situ* overlooking the Adriatic.

The coast road around the promontory is spectacular. Odd rock formations and intriguing grottoes rise above a series of beautiful coves and beaches. Medieval **Vieste** (where the elegant **Pizzomunno** hotel houses the restaurant **Il Trabucco**), whitewashed **Peschici** (where **Solemar**, a peaceful, modern hotel with beach and private pool, is located), and hillside **Rodi Garganico** are pleasant towns, if not of overwhelming historical significance. Equally pleasant is the **Foresta Umbra**, an extensive forest of old beech, oak, pine, and chestnut trees. It is surprisingly clean and peaceful—almost spookily so, but companionship may be found at the Centro Visitatori, a visitors' center with exhibits explaining the human and natural history of the forest.

The Isole Tremiti

The Isole Tremiti require a full day's trip from the mainland no matter how you get to them—by ferry during the summer from Termoli, Manfredonia, Vieste, Peschici, Rodi Garganico, or Vasto; by hydrofoil from Peschici, Rodi Garganico, or Termoli; or even by helicopter from Foggia. The large number of hotels on **San Domino**, the largest of the islands, allows visitors to stay overnight as well, provided they have reservations. The *Insulae Diomediae* of Greek mythology, these were the isles inhabited by Diomedes' Illyrian companions, who were transformed by a vengeful Aphrodite into herons and are still said to be heard crying for their hero at night. The islands have been a place of exile, self-imposed or otherwise, from the days when Augustus's granddaughter Julia was banished to them for adultery through to the Fascist years, when they held political prisoners. These days, the preference is to escape *to* them, and pine-covered San Domino becomes especially overrun each summer. Its **Kyrie** hotel, with beach, pool, tennis court, and private garden, gets the cream of the local agriculture-magnate crop; the less expensive **Gabbiano**, also in a garden but with lovely views of the sea, gets a more diverse crowd. Of the other two main islands, **Capraia** (rarely visitable) is known for its rock formations, while **San Nicola** has the most cultural pursuits, with a Medieval fortress offering lovely views of the archipelago, and the **Abbey Church of Santa Maria a Mare**, which contains a well-preserved mosaic pavement, a Byzantine crucifix, and a Venetian polyptych.

THE ROAD TO BARI

Apulia's most famous Romanesque cathedrals and more may be taken in during a day's drive from Foggia southeast to Bari, weaving in and out to towns and other places along the Adriatic coast. It is an ambitious drive, but since there is little of interest here outside of the architecture, a necessary one. If you're interested in a more leisurely approach, break it up with a night at **La Vecchia Masseria**, a tiny and inexpensive hotel housed in an ancient farmhouse at Castel del Monte (described below). Most of the towns are also served by trains and buses, but allow ample time to make connections. The first stop is **Canosa di Puglia**, which was founded by Diomedes according to legend. Its cathedral contains the oldest bishop's throne in Apulia as well as the tomb of Bohemond, son of the crusader Robert Guiscard. Continuing toward the coast, you pass the site where Hannibal won the battle of Cannae (Canne in Italian) in 216 B.C., only to lose the war later. It takes a lot of imagination to make this archaeological site come alive, however; it's best, instead, to move on to **Barletta** on the coast. Its Romanesque cathedral, now in rather sad repair, houses a sensuous Madonna commemorating the "Disfida di Barletta," a 16th-century battle reenacted with much pageantry each July. Outside the basilica of San Sepolcro stands Barletta's major monument, a 16½-foot-high **Colossus**. An ancient Roman bronze washed ashore in the 14th century, it was almost immediately dismembered by Dominican monks, and the arms and legs melted down to make bells for their church in Manfredonia; new limbs were later added to the original head and torso. The best dining in town is at **Ristorante Bacco** (via Sipontina 10; Tel: 0883-383-98).

Heading inland again, drive due south to Apulia's most famous single piece of architecture, **Castel del Monte**. Built by Frederick II, it was his favorite hunting lodge and retreat, as well as where he composed *De arte venendi cum avibus,* to this day the standard text on falconry. The golden octagonal stone castle, sitting like a crown on an isolated hill, still conveys a sense of majesty and peace. The nearby restaurant **Ostello di Federico** (Tel: 0883-830-43) offers a relaxing spot for lunch and an excellent opportunity to sample Castel del Monte wines (which come in red, white, and the ever-popular rosé); if you're staying at La Vecchia Masseria you'll want to try its equally fine regional restaurant.

Returning to the coast southeast of Barletta: In the white town of **Trani** is one of Apulia's most impressive Romanesque cathedrals, situated dramatically at the edge of the Adriatic. Farther along the coast past Bisceglie (its Romanesque cathedral was much altered during the Baroque period and can be skipped in good conscience) is **Molfetta**, a commercial town whose old cathedral (ask directions to the Duomo Vecchio, since there is also a less interesting Baroque Duomo Nuovo) is also on the sea. The town also has one of the area's nicest restaurants, **Alga Marina** (Strada Statale 16; Tel: 080-94-80-91; closed Mondays and November), which serves regional pasta and fish specialties. Back inland, **Ruvo di Puglia** has another lovely Romanesque cathedral as well as the **Museo Jatta**, an extensive private collection of terra-cotta vases, and especially noted for its rhytons (drinking vessels in the shape of animal heads) from the city's ancient incarnation as Rubi. From there it is a short drive to see the cathedral at **Bitonto**, considered the culmination of the Apulian Romanesque, and then on to Bari.

BARI AND ENVIRONS

La gente di Bari o vende o muore (the people of Bari sell or die) is a saying that aptly describes the city, whose September Fiera del Levante is the most important trade fair in Italy after Milan's. Apulia's largest and busiest city, Bari is primarily a port and commercial and administrative center (it is the regional capital of Apulia), but it does have some sights worth seeing. These are found mainly in the **Città Vecchia** (Old City), which boasts the prototypical Apulian Romanesque church of **San Nicola di Bari**, housing an important bishop's throne as well as Saint Nicholas's tomb in the crypt below. (He *is* the same as Santa Claus. Saint Nick is also the patron saint of sailors, and the anniversary of the arrival of his remains in Bari, brought by local sailors from Asia Minor, is elaborately celebrated each May.)

Another Frederick II castle stands in the Città Vecchia, and is most comfortably explored if you leave your valuables elsewhere. Points of interest outside the Old City are the **Museo Archeologico**, an important archaeological museum; the **Pinacoteca Provinciale**, an art museum housing an extensive collection of artifacts from the 11th to the 19th century; and the **Teatro Petruzzelli**, Italy's third-ranking opera house. Apulia's most prestigious publisher, Laterza, operates an excellent Italian-language bookstore in Bari, and at the other end of the spectrum, a lively flea market takes place Monday mornings on via Calfati.

Bari is also proud of its contemporary aspect, best exemplified by its soccer stadium, which was designed by internationally renowned architect Renzo Piano for the 1990 World Cup soccer finals. Most major Italian designers are well represented in the shops at prices competitive with the rest of the country. Though modern Bari's efficient-looking grid plan belies a horrendous traffic problem, the city is nonetheless a relatively reliable base for trips throughout central Apulia. Virtually all the city's accommodations are geared to businesspeople and thus are of the practical and pricey persuasion. The best hotel for the visitor in the city is the **Villa Romanazzi-Carducci**, a modernized mansion set in its own private garden. Expect crowds during the September Fiera del Levante, when reservations are a must. A luxurious alternative to the Bari hotels is **Il Melograno** in nearby Monopoli. The hotel itself is a converted *masseria,* or farmhouse, and boasts one of the area's best regional restaurants (closed Tuesdays). A less expensive alternative is the equally rustic

Villa Meo-Evoli, a few miles outside of Bari in the Apulian countryside.

Bari also has excellent restaurants. **Ai 2 Ghiottoni** (via Putignani 11; Tel: 080-523-22-40; closed Sundays), **La Pignata** (via Melo 9; Tel: 080-23-24-81), and **Vecchia Bari** (via Dante Alighieri 47; Tel: 080-521-64-96; closed Wednesdays and August) are all good places to try Apulian classics along with such local specialties as seafood and lamb dishes (make sure the latter is local—a lot of lamb from New Zealand and Australia passes through the busy port). Recommended regional wines are Rosso di Barletta, a tart red, and dry whites from Castel del Monte and Locorotondo. The local liqueur, flavored with walnuts, is the potent Padre Peppe.

Inland from Bari

Some odd spots in the rocky, rolling inland plateaus known as **le Murge** make a pleasant day trip from Bari by car; again, trains and buses service the area (including a special vintage train for tourists; see "Getting Around," below), but such a trip requires precise schedule-juggling. You begin innocently enough in the hilltop town of **Altamura,** southwest of Bari, admiring the delicate rose window and richly carved door of its cathedral, which was begun by Frederick II when he reestablished the Saracen-sacked city on its ancient, privileged site and stocked it with neighboring Latins, Greeks, and Jews, who were given further privileges. In **Gravina di Puglia,** built into the side of a ravine to the west of Altamura, you will notice strange stone skeletons reclining above the door of the Purgatorio church. On a narrow street farther down the ravine is the **Church of San Michele dei Grotti,** completely carved out of the rock, where more bones—this time real—left over from the Saracen attack are on display.

The neighboring province of Matera (once part of Apulia but since redesignated to the otherwise largely undistinguished region of Basilicata) is the site of another ravine city, **Matera.** Inhabited since Paleolithic times, it is famous for its **sassi,** the extensive area of dwellings carved into the side of the ravine whose inhabitants' poverty was so poignantly described by Carlo Levi in *Christ Stopped at Eboli.* By now most of the residents have been relocated to proper housing projects in the modern upper town, but urchins still prowl the rocks and will divulge the secrets of the caves' chapels and cubbyholes for a fee, though they're not needed to explore the town's Apulian Romanesque cathedral and the macabre façade of its Purgatorio church. For those who want to try Basilicata's cuisine, stop in at the **Terrazzino Bocconcino II** restaurant on vico San Giuseppe 7 (Tel: 0835-22-20-16). It serves pasta, lamb, and kid dishes adorned with the region's spicy sausages, all to be respectfully downed with the extremely robust red wine Aglianico del Vulture and an appreciative toast to Horace (he was born in the Basilicatan city of Venosa). (*Aglianico* means Hellenic, another example of the mix of history here.) On the way back to Bari, movie buffs may want to loop over to **Castellaneta**, perilously perched over yet another ravine. This town was the birthplace of Rudolph Valentino, and the ceramic monument erected there in his honor stands as silent as the screen star, at once as odd and devout as any piece of Apulian religious sculpture.

Southeast of Bari

Some of Apulia's most primitive and most sophisticated sights can be seen as a day trip by car in the area southeast of Bari; more time is necessary to see it using public transportation. This area makes for one of the region's most pleasant drives, filled as it is with gnarled gray-green olive trees, often planted side by side with almond trees, on red earth sectioned off with dry-laid walls made of weathered gray stone. This same stone is used for the area's most singular architectural feature, the conical dwellings known as **trulli**, most of which are less than 300 years old (although the construction method is prehistoric). In this part of Apulia you also begin to notice another type of structure characteristic of Apulian architecture: *masserie,* or fortified farmhouses, some of which date from Roman times.

Castellana Grotte, southeast of Bari, is the site of the largest and most spectacular caverns in Italy. Though people have left their imprint on nature through litter and the inevitable coins tossed into any body of water that can be loosely construed as a fountain, the names of the beautiful colored alabaster rock formations—such as the Madonna, the altar, and the Leaning Tower of Pisa—attest to Italians' devotion to the caverns; the in-depth two-hour tour is recommended over the hour-long one.

Alberobello, southeast of Castellana, is a town with a central area of more than 1,000 *trulli* that, despite concerted panderings to the tourist trade such as the omnipresent billboards advertising a liqueur called Amaro dei Trulli, is still something out of a fairly tale. You may stay in one of the *trulli* cottages at the **Hotel dei Trulli**—which has clean and surprisingly spacious accommodations, complete with garden and pool—and have lunch in another *trulli* at the **Trullo d'Oro** at via Cavallotti 29 (Tel: 080-72-18-20; closed Mondays and January), which offers a number of lamb specialties along with local wines. Even more acclaimed is **Il Poeta Contadino**, at via Indipendenza 21 (Tel: 080-72-19-17; closed Fridays and August), serving many of the same local specialties with a much larger wine list.

An alternative for lunch is located farther southeast, in elegant **Martina Franca**, a Baroque town whose Palazzo Ducale is the appropriate setting for a festival of 17th- and 18th-century music each summer. The town is famous for its sausages, spit-roasted meats, and strong white wine, some of which is sent north to make vermouth and spumanti. Just out of town is *its* restaurant in a *trullo,* the **Trattoria delle Ruote**, on via Ceglie E (reservations needed; Tel: 080-70-54-29; closed Mondays). Closer to the Baroque churches and palazzi (the town hall is attributed to Gianlorenzo Bernini) is an excellent and inexpensive restaurant: **La Rotonda**, at the Villa Comunale.

On the way to Ostuni near the coast you may pass through **Cisternino**, a whitewashed hill town that gives a tiny taste of the splendor to come in Ostuni. Built on three hills, with a Gothic cathedral and some Renaissance and Baroque buildings, **Ostuni** itself is most remarkable for the immaculate appearance of its whitewashed houses, which give the city its nickname, *la città bianca* (the white city). Ostuni offers two relaxing accommodations (also white): the modest and modern **Incanto** in town (a restful spot with spectacular views of the city, plains, and the Adriatic), and the huge **Grand Hotel Rosa Marina** resort on the coast, with private beach, tennis facilities, and restaurants much frequented by the more prosperous local gentry.

Alternatively, the coastal road back to Bari makes for a lovely drive. Along the way is **Egnatia** (Egnazia in Italian, from the Greek Gnathia), a town written about by Horace and inhabited until early Christian times. Today it is a vast, flat archaeological site with a recently opened museum housing examples of Gnathian ware, the delicate black pottery that takes its name from the town. Closer to Bari, at **Polignano a Mare**, is the hotel/restaurant **Grotta Palazzese**, at via Narciso 59 (Tel: 080-74-06-77). Its seafood, regional cheeses, desserts, and wines are all quite good, but the location—in a cave overlooking the Adriatic—is what makes it so spectacular.

THE SALENTINE PENINSULA

The southernmost part of Apulia is the true "heel" of Italy's boot. Called the Salentine peninsula (Salento in Italian), it is easily explored from Lecce, which has two comfortable hotels, the modern and efficient **President** and the more centrally located **Risorgimento**, which has seen better days and is all the more charming for it. Both have good regional restaurants.

Brindisi

From Bari southeast to Lecce by car or train, the routes hug the coast to Brindisi, a city worth a quick visit—if only as a passing nod to history, since its present aspect is rather horrendous—even if you are not passing through its port to Greece, the city's raison d'être since ancient times. Strabo praised its wines (*fare un brindisi* means to make a toast), Horace mentions it in his first *Satire,* Virgil died here, and many other ancients saw Brindisi because it was the end of the Appian Way. One of the two columns that marked this terminus may be seen near the harbor (Lecce took the other one). The **Museo Archeologico**, the **Cathedral of San Benedetto** (where Frederick II married his second wife), and the churches of **San Giovanni al Sepolcro** and **Santa Maria del Casale** (just north of town) also merit seeing, but expect tumultuous traffic during the summer. If you can brave the cars, have a meal at **La Lanterna** restaurant near the Duomo (via Tarantini 14; Tel: 0831-56-40-26; closed Sundays and August). Its menu is one of the most refined you'll find in the region.

Lecce

Lecce's 16th- and 17th-century literary academies gave it the nickname "The Athens of Apulia," and its architecture from the same period earned it the epithet "The Florence of the Baroque." The soft and golden local tufa sandstone is easily carved and was handled with such vigor that it gave rise to an indigenous style called *Barocco Leccese,* a religious and secular architecture known more for its lavish decorative elements than its formal innovation. (The decorative tradition continues with a flourishing production of papier-mâché and terra-cotta figurines available in many shops. The most extensive display of these and other crafts is at **Mostra**

Permanente dell'Artigianato, via F. Rubichi 21.) You can easily spend a day in Lecce, a bustling provincial capital. In addition to seeing the **Duomo**, the churches of **Santa Croce**, **Rosario**, and **Santi Nicola e Cataldo**, and the **Palazzo Vescovile** and **Palazzo del Governo**, you'll also want to wander the streets and look for the rich Baroque decorative details on the humblest of buildings. Among the Baroque splendors of Lecce is the Franciscan monastery called the **Convento di Sant'Antonio** (Tel: 0832-94-70-11), which in rare cases admits overnight guests. The town's long history is further evidenced by a half-excavated Roman amphitheater and the **Museo Provinciale**, which is noted for its collection of Italian archaeological artifacts dating from Paleolithic times.

Some of the Salento's regional food specialties include *ciceri e tria,* tagliatelle pasta cooked in chick-pea broth; *cappello da gendarme,* a pastry shell stuffed with veal, eggplant, and zucchini; and *mercia,* a hard-to-find sheep's-milk mozzarella cheese. The full-bodied Salice Salentino is the area's best-known red wine; the mellow Malvasia is the popular choice for white. Gran Liquore San Domenico, made in Lecce's convent of San Domenico, is the local liqueur. These specialties can all be well sampled at the **Risorgimento** restaurant in the hotel of that name at via Imperatore Augusto 19, where the slightly formal surroundings contrast with the robust food and local clientele.

The Salentine Coast

The Greek influence in Apulia becomes most apparent toward the end of the peninsula, where cultural ties with Greece are still evident in the local dialects. The coastal drive is the most pleasant way to see it, since train and bus routes generally take you inland.

Otranto, the easternmost city in Italy, was founded by the Greeks and became an important center of the Byzantine Empire. Until recently, residents practiced the Greek Orthodox religious rite, and they still call themselves *Idruntini,* a reference to the town's ancient name of Hydruntum. In 1480 Otranto was the site of a vicious Turkish attack, and its castle, made famous by Horace Walpole's Gothic novel *The Castle of Otranto,* was built soon afterward for defensive purposes; these days it is more likely to serve as a backdrop to a lazy game of bocce played by the elderly men of the town. ("I did not even know there was a castle of Otranto," Walpole later wrote. "When the story was finished, I looked to the map of the kingdom of Naples for a well-sounding name, and that of Otranto was very sonorous.") The extensive mosaic floor of Otranto's cathedral is currently being restored, but still visible are its rose window and the chapel containing the bones of the martyrs slain by the Turks—a gruesome sight, and one that explains why the townspeople continue to speak of the tragic event.

Apulia's natural drama has its denouement at **Capo Santa Maria di Leuca**, a lonely white limestone cliff at the very tip of the peninsula. On this site is the church of Santa Maria Finibus Terrae, usually visited by romantic types who thrill at the idea of being at the ends of the earth. (The southernmost point of Apulia, however, is actually at Punta Ristola, a nondescript beach a short distance farther on.)

Up the western coast of the Salento is **Gallipoli**, a fishing town and agricultural center founded by the Greeks, who gave it the name Kallipolis (beautiful city). The name is still an accurate description of the town, as evidenced by the lavish, almost Spanish Baroque interiors of its **Duomo** and the **Church of San Francesco**, which contrast with the simple whitewashed façades of the **Old City**. There is also the inevitable imposing castle and museum, but Gallipoli's setting will put you in the mood instead for lunch at its fine seafood restaurant, **Marechiaro**, which overlooks the Ionian Sea on lungomare Marconi (Tel: 0833-47-61-43; closed Sundays and October to May). An excellent, if expensive, place to linger in the area is the modern resort of **Costa Brada**, on its own private beach just outside of town. Inland to the north, the noble Baroque churches and palaces of **Nardo**, reminiscent of Lecce, are worth inspecting, as is the town's oddly Oriental-looking pavilion, the Osanna.

From Lecce to Taranto

The highway and railroad from Lecce west to Taranto pass through **Manduria**, another dignified-looking town with interesting Renaissance and Baroque buildings but known mostly for the nearby ruins of the Messapian civilization that ruled the Salentine peninsula before the Greeks arrived. The archaeological site contains ancient walls (where the Messapians battled the Tarantines), numerous tombs, and the Well of Pliny, so called because the phenomenon of its constant level is thought to be the one mentioned in Pliny's *Natural History.*

Most of the colonies of Magna Graecia were in what is now Calabria. But the port of **Taranto** (the ancient Spartan colony of Taras, or Tarentum), situated between two bays called Mare Piccolo and Mare Grande, was its greatest city, with a population exceeding the present one. Then, as now, it was famous for the oysters plumped in the Mare Piccolo, but the city's current role as Italy's second largest naval dockyard and headquarters of the country's largest steel corporation, Italsider, should make you wary of finding more than pearls when biting into them. Taranto's seafood is safely sampled at its best restaurant, **Al Gambero**, which overlooks the harbor at vico del Ponte 4 (Tel: 099-41-11-90; closed Mondays and November). Whatever is fresh goes well with Verdea Bianca, a local white wine; the local vanilla-and-chocolate–flavored liqueur is called Amaro San Marzano.

Under the Spartans, Taranto became a center of Pythagorean philosophy, though Pythagoras himself lived in Croton, in what is now Calabria. Taranto was also the birthplace of the mathematician Archytas, whom Plato visited, and Aristoxenes, who wrote the first known treatise on music. Crafts flourished in the ancient colony, as well. The city produced its own pottery and was famous for a purple dye extracted from the murex, a type of shellfish. (The nearby town of **Grottaglie** has become noted for its ceramics in more recent times, and the colorful wares produced there in blue floral patterns on beige backgrounds may also be found in many shops in Taranto.)

Taranto's Città Vecchia occupies an island. Like Bari's Old City, it has a magnificent if somewhat rundown castle and cathedral and is the scene of important religious processions during Holy Week. Also like Bari's Città Vecchia, it is poverty-stricken and reputedly dangerous. The remains of a Doric temple dedicated to Neptune, which is the only outdoor remnant of Taranto's Greek past, are also located there. The city's real Greek treasures lie in the **Museo Nazionale**, just over the ponte Girevole, a swinging bridge connecting the old city with the newer part of town. The collections of sculpture, jewelry, and pottery make this the world's most important museum devoted to Magna Graecia; at least half a day should be spent seeing it.

Hotels, again as in Bari, are generally pleasant but impersonal in appearance; try the expensive waterfront **Grand Hotel Delfino** or the more moderate **Plaza**. Both are modern and centrally located. Otherwise, a half-hour's drive away at Avetrana is the **Castello di Mudonato**, which offers excellent accommodations in the peaceful country setting of a refurbished *masseria*.

To further the study of Magna Graecia, each year in

October Taranto hosts the *Convegno di Studi sulla Magna Grecia,* an important meeting on various aspects of that ancient civilization.

GETTING AROUND

Foggia, Bari, and Brindisi all have airports served by Aliblu Airways or Aerea Trasporti Italiani out of Rome and Milan. Trains connect the major cities with Rome, Naples, and Milan; the smaller towns can be reached by local train and bus. Since connections can require some time, a car (rented at the airports or in the larger cities) offers the most freedom, although it should be closely watched when parked, especially in Bari and Taranto.

A guided tour of Apulia is organized by Central Holiday Tours (Tel: 800-526-6045).

One unusual way of seeing part of Apulia is the Murge Express train. The turn-of-the-century carriages leave Bari each morning for a day-long excursion (combined with coach connection) to the Murge sites. For information, contact Italsud Tours, 101 Ridge Avenue, Passaic, NJ 07055; Tel: (201) 779-2495; Fax: (201) 779-4538. Butterfield & Robinson (70 Bond Street, Toronto, Ontaria, Canada M5B 1X3; Tel: 800-387-1147) runs week-long bicycle tours of the *trulli* country between Brindisi and Bari.

Monte Sant'Angelo celebrates Saint Michael on May 8 and September 29. Barletta's Disfida (a reenactment of the battle of 1503) takes place on the third Sunday in July. In Bari Saint Nicholas's feast takes place from May 7 through May 10, and the opera season at Teatro Petruzzelli runs from January to March. In Martina Franca, the music festival takes place in July and August. In Taranto the processions of Our Lady of the Sorrows (L'Addolorata) and the Mysteries (Misteri) take place on Maundy Thursday and Good Friday, respectively.

ACCOMMODATIONS REFERENCE

The rates given below are projections for 1992; always check for up-to-date information before making reservations. Wide ranges may reflect the differences between low- and high-season rates. Unless otherwise indicated, the figures indicate the cost of a double room (per room, not per person). However, half-board (mezza pensione) rates, which include breakfast and one other meal per day, are per person. Most hotels will add a service charge of 10 to 15 percent.

Unusual accommodations in the beehive-shaped structures called trulli *may be rented by the week or month*

*through Agenzia Fittatrulli, via Duchessa Acquaviva 5,
70011 Alberobello; Tel: (080) 72-27-17.*

► **Hotel Apeneste**. Piazza Turati 3, 71030 **Mattinata**. Tel:
(0884) 47-43; Fax: (0884) 43-41. Ł66,000–Ł80,000; half board
Ł58,000–Ł85,000.
► **Castello di Mudonato**. 74020 **Avetrana**. Tel: (099) 870-
4597. Ł95,000–Ł105,000.
► **Hotel Cicolella**. Viale 24 Maggio 60, 71100 **Foggia**. Tel:
(0881) 38-90; Fax: (0881) 789-84. Ł115,000–Ł184,000; half
board Ł180,000.
► **Costa Brada**. Lungomare Costa Brada, 73014 Gallipoli.
Tel: (0833) 225-51; Fax: (0833) 225-55. Ł119,600–Ł127,500.
► **Gabbiano**. San Domino, 71040 **San Nicola di Tremiti**.
Tel: (0882) 66-30-44; Fax: (0882) 66-30-90. Ł78,000–Ł96,000;
half board Ł71,000–Ł80,000.
► **Grand Hotel Delfino**. Viale Virgilio 66, 74100 **Taranto**.
Tel: (099) 32-05; Fax: same. Ł110,000–Ł160,000; half board
Ł130,000.
► **Grand Hotel Rosa Marina**. 72017 **Ostuni**. Tel: (0831) 97-
00-61. Ł85,000–Ł99,000.
► **Hotel dei Trulli**. 70011 Alberobello. Tel: (080) 72-11-30;
Fax: (080) 72-10-44. Ł77,000–Ł132,000.
► **Hotel del Faro**. 71019 **Faro di Pugnochiuso**. Tel: (0884)
70-90-11; Fax: (0884) 70-90-17. Open April 20–October 20.
Ł129,000; full board Ł234,000.
► **Incanto**. Via dei Colli, 72017 **Ostuni**. Tel: (0831) 30-17-
81; Fax: (0831) 33-83-02. Ł80,000–Ł120,000; half board
Ł80,000–Ł100,000.
► **Kyrie**. San Domino, 71040 **San Nicola di Tremiti**. Tel:
(0882) 66-32-32; Fax: (0882) 66-30-55. Open May 15–
September. Ł135,000–Ł210,000; half board Ł155,000–
Ł180,000.
► **Il Melograno**. Contrada Torricella 345, 70043 **Monopoli**.
Tel: (080) 80-86-56; Fax: (080) 74-79-08. Ł320,000; half board
Ł200,000.
► **Pizzomunno Vieste Palace Hotel**. Via Spiaggia di
Pizzomunno, 71019 **Vieste**. Tel: (0884) 70-87-41; Fax: (0884)
70-73-25. Open March 25–October 27. Ł192,000–Ł204,000;
half board Ł170,000–Ł340,000.
► **Plaza**. Via d'Aquino 46, 74100 **Taranto**. Tel: (099) 919-25;
Fax: (099) 947-71. Ł100,000.
► **President**. Via Salandra 6, 73100 **Lecce**. Tel: (0832) 31-
18-81; Fax: 59-43-21. Ł100,000–Ł172,000; half board
Ł120,000.

► **Risorgimento.** Via Imperatore Augusto 19, 73100 **Lecce.** Tel: (0832) 421-25; Fax; (0832) 455-71. £59,000–£103,000.

► **Solemar.** Località San Nicola E, 71010 **Peschici.** Tel: (0884) 96-41-86; Fax: (0884) 96-41-88. Open May 12–September 20. £105,000; half board £56,000–£104,000.

► **La Vecchia Masseria.** 70031 **Castel del Monte.** Tel: (0883) 240-08. Closed December–February. £46,000–£76,000.

► **Villa Meo-Evoli.** Via Provinciale per Conversano, Contrade Cozzana, 70100 **Bari.** Tel: (080) 80-30-52. £110,000.

► **Villa Romanazzi-Carducci.** Via Capruzzi 326, 70124 **Bari.** Tel: (080) 522-74-00; Fax: (080) 36-02-97. £318,000.

CALABRIA

By Dwight V. Gast

Having been extensively colonized by the Greeks from the eighth century B.C. as part of Magna Graecia, subsequently inhabited by Byzantines, and finally overrun in turn by the Saracens, Normans, Hohenstaufens, Angevins, Aragonese, and Bourbons, Calabria should be used to outsiders. But as recently as 1911, when Norman Douglas, the author of *Old Calabria,* visited San Demetrio Corone, he discovered that "within the memory of living man no Englishman has ever entered the town. This is quite possible; I have not yet encountered a single English traveller during my frequent wanderings over South Italy."

Douglas travelled on foot throughout the "toe" of Italy, but even with the improved highways built during recent years Calabria attracts fewer visitors than practically any other region in the country. Most of those who do go are drawn not by its rich history or ethnic diversity but by invitations from distant relatives or by the beauties of some of Italy's most unspoiled beaches and panoramic mountain scenery, which only now is beginning to be developed for skiing in winter and spas year-round. A half-century ago Walter Starkey wrote that "one of the charms of a journey through Calabria is that it sets in continual antithesis the coast and the mountain," a phenomenon that is still true; Calabrians trying to impress their American friends have characterized the region as "Calabrifornia."

Calabria is slow to reveal its historical and cultural secrets. Many artistic treasures still remain buried beneath the earth. The exact location of the ancient colony of Sybaris, for example, has never been determined, let alone excavated. Furthermore, much of what is above ground lies hidden in small seaside and mountain towns that retain the attitudes, customs, and occasionally even the dress of centuries past.

Such places are more common in Calabria than in any other region, and for the imaginative visitor, happening upon them presents a picture of what life must have been like in much of preindustrialized Italy, when cows grazed in the Forum, women turned themselves out in full skirts and peasant blouses, and mustachioed men dashed about in capes and hats.

MAJOR INTEREST

Italy as it used to be

Ethnic diversity

Medieval charms of the old city of Cosenza

Natural Alpine beauty of the Sila massif

Picturesque fishing villages and fabulous views along the southern Tyrrhenian coast

Art of Magna Graecia at the Museo Nazionale in Reggio di Calabria, especially the Riace Bronzes

Windswept Medieval town of Gerace

Byzantine monuments of Rossano

Extensive archaeological ruins of the ancient Greek colony of Metapontum in neighboring Basilicata

Calabria's scenic terrain is the most seismic in Italy, a fact that, coupled with centuries of feudal and baronial rule, accounts for the region's alienation, isolation, and poverty. These aspects of modern Calabria are especially ironic considering the area's magnificence as Magna Graecia as late as the fifth century B.C.: Rhegion (modern-day Reggio di Calabria) was a prosperous trading center; Locri Epizephyrii (Locri), lauded by Pindar for its good government, was the first Greek city to write a code of laws; Croton (Crotone) was where Pythagoras developed the ideas of freedom and self-reliance that eventually became permanent themes in Hellenic thought; and the very name of Sybaris (Sibari) was a synonym for luxury. Spiritually and materially, however, there is little present-day evidence of the Greeks in Calabria outside of the museums, although the dark and diminutive population bespeaks Hellenic origins.

The centuries of alienation eventually gave rise to romantic brigands, male and female, who roamed the mountains of the Sila and Aspromonte (still favorite hiding places for fugitives from the law) until the last century. Now the local version of organized crime, the 'ndrangheta, has dispelled, with its sporadic bloody outbursts, most of the romance of the outlaw.

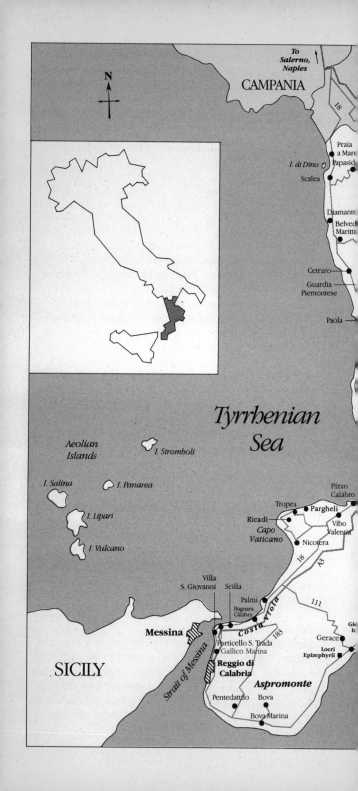

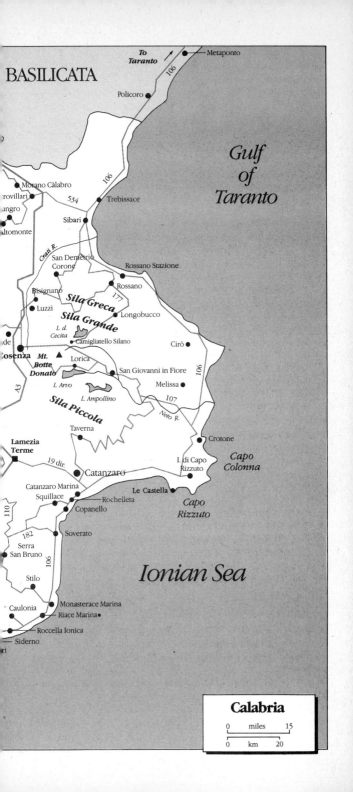

BASILICATA

To Taranto

Metaponto

106

Policoro

Gulf
of
Taranto

Morano Càlabro

rovillari

534

Trebissace

ngro

ltomonte

Sibari

106

Crati R.

San Demetrio
Corone

Rossano Stazione

Bisignano

Sila Greca

Rossano

Luzzi

Sila Grande

177

Longobucco

L. d.
Cecita

de

Camigliatello Silano

Cirò

osenza

Mt.
Botte
Donato

Lorica

San Giovanni in Fiore

106

A3

L. Arvo

Melissa

L. Ampollino

107

Sila Piccola

Neto R.

Taverna

Lamezia
Terme

Crotone

19 dir.

Catanzaro

I. di Capo
Rizzuto

Capo
Colonna

Catanzaro Marina

Le Castella

Squillace

Rochelleta

Capo
Rizzuto

110

Copanello

182

Soverato

Serra
San Bruno

106

Ionian Sea

Stilo

Caulonia

Monasterace Marina

Riace Marina

Roccella Ionica

Siderno

ri

Calabria

0   miles   15

0   km   20

Isolation brought about a spiritual side to the superstitious nature of the Calabrians, however. Gazing at the stars in the deep night skies of the mountains, it is easy to imagine how the Pythagoreans conceived the notion of celestial music. That same mystical terrain has attracted monks—from Byzantines to Carthusians—the last of whom even now are busy praying for the sins of the world at their far-removed monastery in Serra San Bruno, in the mountains of south-central Calabria.

Though the government's special fund for the South, Cassa Agenzia per il Sud, is gradually improving economic conditions, much of Calabria's historical poverty remains. The traveller, however, need no longer be wary of brigands or expect to have to share a hotel bed with a stranger, as Douglas did. A number of comfortable and efficient, if not altogether luxurious, hotels have been built in recent years in the larger cities and resort towns. Even in remote rural areas the grimness and suspicion that have traditionally greeted strangers are giving way to increasing invitations to share homemade *paisanella* brandy or *vino greco* in a toast to the memory of some relative who long ago left Calabria for the outside world.

THE NORTHERN TYRRHENIAN COAST

The entry point to Calabria by car or train from the north is the Tyrrhenian coast below Naples and Salerno. The short stretch of beaches here is so spectacular that this is the final destination of many travellers attracted to the civilized amenities offered by the **Grand Hotel De Rose**, located near a gray pebble beach in Scalea, a peaceful modern resort hotel with pool and full family facilities such as a playground, as well as an excellent regional restaurant, or to the lavish cliffside **Grand Hotel San Michele** at Cetraro, a converted villa with similar facilities and its own private beach. The area is an appropriate beginning for an exploration of Calabria, since it was one of the first parts of the region to be inhabited. **Isola di Dino**, reached by boat from Praia a Mare, is a tiny island where prehistoric relics have been unearthed in grottoes, and where Ulysses allegedly landed on his journeys. (One of its grottoes is also the home of the statue of the ancient Madonna della Grotta, celebrated in an annual religious procession.) More prehistoric relics may be seen at Scalea and at the inland town of Papasidero.

The resort town of **Diamante**, between Praia a Mare and Cetraro, is a good place to stop for a meal. Its moderately priced **La Pagoda** restaurant (Tel: 0985-814-28) in the beachfront Ferretti hotel gently eases the palate from the cuisine of Campania, just to the north, to the cuisine of Calabria, serving equally excellent seafood and eggplant dishes. Farther down the coast, past the citron groves of Belvedere and Cetraro and up a winding mountain road, is one of southern Italy's most ethnically important communities, **Guardia Piemontese**. Founded by Waldensian refugees, the town has retained its Provençal dialect and distinctive folk costumes to this day, and a walk among its stone houses and along the promenade overlooking the Mediterranean gives a preview of the ethnic diversity and visual splendor of the Calabria to come. The final stop in this stretch of Calabria is **Paola**, birthplace of Saint Francis of Paola, where an important Minim monastic complex attracts religious pilgrims, especially during this saint's feast on May 5, when his miraculous passage to Sicily—he was blown over in his own robes—is celebrated by rowing his statue out to sea. Travellers, especially groups, may avail themselves of the facilities (Tel: 0982-25-29).

COSENZA AND ENVIRONS

Cosenza, reached by train or car from Naples and just inland from Paola, is a busy modern city with an extensive Medieval quarter. Located in a mountain valley near some of the region's most interesting sights, it also makes a good base for side trips to the northern Tyrrhenian coast just described, to the unusual Medieval and Albanian towns in the highlands to the north, or to the Sila massif, each of which can be seen in a day's drive from here. The contemporary **Hotel Centrale**, true to its name, *is* central, and convenient to both the modern and the Medieval city on foot, which accounts for its popularity with everyone from businesspeople to the occasional visiting artists in town for theatrical and musical activities (ask for a room with a balcony). The Centrale also has a good, reasonably priced regional restaurant and a garage, but travellers with cars might prefer the even more up-to-date conveniences and swimming pools of the clean-lined **Europa** and

San Francesco hotels in suburban Rende, which are spare on charm but away from the bustle of the provincial capital and still convenient to Cosenza and environs. **La Calavrisella** restaurant at via Gerolamo De Rada 11/a in Cosenza provides the best local introduction to Calabrian cuisine (closed Saturday and Sunday evenings; Tel: 0984-280-12). The region is known for antipasti such as *rosa marina* or *mustica*—a spicy spread made with fish fry, referred to as "the caviar of the south"—and the pungent *soppressata* and *capocollo* sausages; pasta dishes served with eggplant or artichokes, or *con lumache,* with a snail sauce, as well as *schiaffettoni* stuffed with meat and cheese; spicy main courses of roast lamb, kid, or eggplant; and buttery *caciocavallo* cheese or luscious prickly pears for dessert. La Calavrisella also has ample stocks of Calabrian wine. Ciro, which comes in red, rosé, and white varieties, is the best-known wine of the region; its supporters say its origins in Magna Graecia make it the oldest wine in the world. Other robust reds—Donnici Savuto and Pollino—produced even closer to Cosenza, are descendants of the wines praised by Pliny. Desserts such as *mostaccioli* (animal-shaped cookies made with honey and white wine), *chinulille* (dough fried with ricotta cheese), and *crucette* (figs stuffed with nuts and citron) are typical of the region. The local liqueur is called Amaro Silano.

Cosenza

Cosenza is Calabria's most culturally lively city, home to the Teatro Rendano, where operas, concerts, and classic and contemporary theater are performed; the Accademia Cosentina, a literary academy that has been active for centuries; and Italy's newest university. Of its Medieval quarter, which comprised the entire city until World War II, George Gissing wrote in his *By the Ionian Sea* at the turn of the century, "Cosenza has wonders and delights which tempt to day-long rambling." In fact, the area, relatively untouched by the disasters that have ravaged much of Calabria, is still lined with narrow streets that wind up the side of a hill. It makes, if not a day-long rambling, a pleasant half-day's stroll. Of particular interest are the **Church of San Domenico**, which has a beautiful rose window, and the **Duomo**, allegedly consecrated in the presence of Frederick II (its Byzantine reliquary cross, donated by the emperor, is usually kept in the adjacent Palazzo Vescovile but is currently in Florence for restoration). The **Museo Civico** houses a collection of prehistoric bronzes, and at the church of San Francesco di

Assisi exhibitions are often held in the former monastery next door. Dominating the city is a **Norman castle** housing a restored baronial hall. Though the castle is often closed, it affords great views of the old city, and the adjacent olive grove is an ideal spot for a picnic. Provisions can be picked up in the modern part of town before starting out. The **Ente Sviluppo Agricolo Calabria** (viale degli Alimena 72–74), which sells Calabrian wines, olive oil, dried mushrooms, stuffed figs, cheeses, and other regional produce, is the local branch of a chain of stores found throughout the region.

North of Cosenza

The inland towns north of Cosenza are difficult to see conveniently without a car, but for those not dependent on public transportation or with more than a day at their disposal they provide a glimpse of unexpected artistic riches and an ethnic diversity unlike anywhere else in Italy. Farthest north, almost on the border of Basilicata (and east of Praia a Mare), is **Morano Calabro**, a lovely hill town spilling down a slope beneath its Norman castle. Its church of San Pietro contains statuary by Pietro Bernini, and two other churches, the Maddalena and San Bernardino, are also worth your attention. Back in the direction of Cosenza is **Castrovillari**, a bustling regional seat where the local women occasionally still wear red, white, and blue folk costumes. The Old Town has a castle, an abandoned synagogue, and the church of Santa Maria del Castello, with Byzantine beginnings oddly elaborated by Baroque additions. Just outside the town is the **Alìa Restaurant**, via Jetticelle 71, considered by many to be the best in Calabria. In an incongruously upscale setting, two brothers have set out to initiate the locals to the ways of the contemporary table. However didactic the means may be, the moderately priced results are delicious renditions of regional dishes; be sure to ask for the *menu regionale*. Reserve; Tel: (0981) 463-70; closed Sundays.

The next town worth visiting is **Lungro** (southwest of Castrovillari), location of the oldest salt mine in Italy, where the ancient Romans extracted the *salarium* they paid their soldiers. Today, Lungro's cathedral of San Nicola di Mira is the seat of the bishop of the largest expatriate Albanian community in Italy, descendants of refugees who settled throughout southern Italy hundreds of years ago to escape the Ottoman Turks. Called *Arbereshi* in local dialect, they continue to practice Greek Orthodox rites and maintain Albanian dialect, dress, and customs. Except for the town's

TV antennas, beat-up Alfa Sud cars, and other modern in-
fringements, its caped and costumed citizenry, which puts
on its finery to celebrate many Albanian festivals throughout
the year, could have stepped out of the 15th century.

Up a narrow mountain road from Lungro is **Altomonte**, a
peaceful, well-kept hamlet seemingly constructed by artists
and craftsmen who got lost on their way to Siena. Its **Church
of Santa Maria della Consolazione** is a gem of Gothic architecture, and the adjacent museum houses a number of
minor masterpieces, including a tiny painting of Saint
Ladislas attributed to Simone Martini. A stroll through the
town leads to the Municipio (municipal building), housed in
a lovingly restored former convent of the Minim order. If
you find yourself caught by Altomonte's bucolic charms, you
can ask at the Municipio's Agriturismo office (piazza Santa
Maria della Consolazione; Tel: 0981-94-81-85) about taking
one of the comfortable rustic rooms offered in the nearby
countryside. Almost as tranquil, and located on a hill opposite the town, is the **Hotel Barbieri**, a modern hotel providing great photo opportunities of Altomonte. The hotel also
houses an unassuming, moderately priced regional
restaurant—an excellent spot for a meal overlooking
Altomonte—as well as a shop selling the simple local produce in elegant packages that make wonderful gifts.

On the way back to Cosenza are two other Albanian
communities, less important politically if more attractive
visually than Lungro. **San Demetrio Corone** (east of the A 3),
Douglas's discovery, was originally settled by emigrants from
Corone, Albania, and is the site of an Albanian festival each
spring. Its church of Sant'Adriano, with its Roman, Byzantine,
Basilian, and Norman elements, even predates this 15th-
century Albanian settlement. Another worthwhile detour is
to the little town of **Bisignano**, a well-preserved hamlet
dating from the 16th century and famous for its *maestri
liutai,* or master lute-makers, who work in the town's
Giudecca quarter. Bisignano's **Il Puccio** restaurant is noted
for its *maccheroni fusilli con capretto e patate,* macaroni
and fusilli pasta with kid and potatoes. Just south of
Bisignano is **Luzzi**, where Medieval churches and the nearby
Cistercian abbey of La Sambucina are the main attractions.

The Sila

Rising in the middle of Calabria is the Sila, a massif known to
Strabo. Considered "the great woods of Italy," its name
derives from the Latin word for woods, *silva;* its pinewood,

pino laricio calabro, was used by the ancients to build ships
and by early Christians for churches in Rome. Its northern
third is called the Sila Greca (Greek Sila) and is home to
most of Calabria's Albanian communities; the central part,
Sila Grande (Great Sila), has other ancient settlements as
well as modern facilities for skiing; Sila Piccola (Little Sila),
as its name implies, is the small southern section. Panoramic
views and pine-scented air make a drive in the Sila refreshing, especially during weekdays, when it is completely free
of crowds. Its forests are home to wolves and all types of
game, its streams and lakes filled with trout (freshwater
fishing licenses can be obtained at the Ufficio Caccia e Pesca
in any town hall for a small fee), and wild strawberries and
rosito mushrooms ripen for gathering during the summer
and fall, respectively.

A large part of the Sila's villages, lakes, forests, and mead-
ows may be seen in a day trip from Cosenza, to which the
massif is connected by train and bus service, but those who
want a maximum dose of mountain air can stay at one of the
Sila's modest hotels. The rustic lakeside **Grand Hotel Lorica**
in the town of the same name is perhaps the most pleasant,
especially for its views of Lago Arvo. Closest to Cosenza to
the east is the town of **Camigliatello Silano**, of little interest
except for its modest ski facilities, and even those are frequented mostly by locals during the long winter season.
(One such lodge is the plain but efficient hotel **Aquila-
Edelweiss**.) Farther on to the northeast, past the placid
shores of Lago di Cecita, is **Longobucco**, a town of Medieval
origin known for its weavers, who display their wares (carpets and bed covers with Oriental motifs) each August in a
crafts fair.

To the south is **San Giovanni in Fiore** (east of Cosenza on
107), another town with Medieval roots, where the women
wear black-and-white costumes said to have been designed
by the town's founder, Gioacchino Da Fiore, a 12th-century
abbott. The town is the Sila's largest, and is also home to a
thriving community of weavers (this time Armenian inspired), whose work is on sale year-round at the Santa Lucia
hotel. An inexpensive restaurant in San Giovanni is **Florens**,
which serves such specialties of the Sila as trout and wild
boar, as well as *butirro,* a dollop of creamery butter encased
in *caciocavallo* cheese (Tel: 0984-99-27-57). A few hours at
one of its simple tables enjoying the local delicacies—
perhaps over a bottle of Savuto or Pollino—is one way of
paying homage to Pliny or any one of the ancients who
praised the bounty of the Sila. The lazy drive west back to

Cosenza may be interrupted with a stop for a digestive stroll in the quiet town of **Lorica** (perhaps taken literally with a glass of Amaro Silano), on the slopes of Monte Botte Donato, the latter easily scaled in the comfort of an automobile for a last look at the great woods of Italy as they spread out beyond the shores of Lago Arvo.

THE SOUTHERN
TYRRHENIAN COAST

Most people explore the southern Tyrrhenian coast as a day trip by car from their hotel in Cosenza, or from one of the nearby coastal towns, south to Reggio di Calabria. Seen from train or car, the coast offers spectacular views of the Tyrrhenian Sea and, at its southern end, the Aeolian Islands and Sicily. Some 59 km (35 miles) south of Cosenza on the autostrada is **Pizzo Calabro**, known for its castle and its small church, Piedigrotta, which is carved out of the stone cliffs. Just ahead is **Vibo Valentia**, admired by Cicero for its good government when it was the ancient colony of Hipponium, and today an active little town whose modern and moderately priced **Hotel 501** makes it an appealing place from which to base excursions along the coast. (Another option is the luxurious resort complex **Baia Paraelios** in the village of Fornaci, near Parghelia.) Hotel 501 also houses two fine restaurants, both of which serve superb meat and seafood dishes along with the local specialty of *pecorino* cheese, creamier and more flavorful than other Italian varities. The city has a surprising range of monuments, including a recently restored Norman castle, the Renaissance church of San Michele, and the Baroque cathedral of Leoluca and church of the Rosario. Artifacts from the excavations at Hipponium may be seen at the Museo Civico in Palazzo Cordopardi, and in the private collection housed in Palazzo Capialbi.

Travelling down the coastal route, what you see next are the tile roofs of the town of **Tropea**, almost as red as the onions for which the town is famous, not to mention the sunburns acquired on Calabria's best-known beaches. An earlier visitor, Hercules (Pliny called the town Portus Herculis), supposedly first glimpsed its cliffs from the sea. The cliffs have since been graced with a lovely castle and cathedral, the latter containing a painting of the Madonna allegedly by Saint Luke. Visitors should also stroll through the Old Town and out to the abandoned Benedictine sanctuary of Santa Maria dell'Isola.

Farther down the coast, around Capo Vaticano, is **Nicotera**, another picturesque town with a minor castle and an archaeological museum. It is best appreciated, however, for its *tonnetto all'aceto,* a tuna dish garnished with mint leaves, and the dry red Limbadi wine produced nearby. **Palmi**, a short distance onward, is where the so-called **Costa Viola** (Violet Coast) begins. Outwardly modern (its namesake palms are very old, though), the town has an important ethnographic museum, the **Museo Calabrese di Etnografia e Folklore,** which has an extensive collection of antique crafts, useful for honing your eye before you consider purchasing any of their contemporary counterparts, readily available in local pottery shops. The town was also the birthplace of one of Calabria's most famous personages, Francesco Cilea, composer of *Adriana Lecouvreur,* and though Palmi has no official memorial to him, the mere mention of his name inspires snippets of his operas from the locals.

Down the coast is **Bagnara Calabra**, a hardworking community with a long-standing tradition of division of labor. Its men, using age-old methods, catch swordfish in late spring and summer, and spend much of the rest of the year working on their wooden boats, while the women of the town prepare the catch *alla bagnarese* (with oil, lemon, capers, garlic, parsley, and oregano) and make a hard-nougat candy called *torrone,* which is prized throughout Italy. People from all over the country come to take part in the town's swordfish festival as soon as the season has ended, in July. A good place to sample swordfish year-round is the **Taverna Kerkyra**, at corso Vittorio Emanuele 217 (Tel: 0966-37-22-60; closed Mondays, Tuesdays, and June, October, and November).

Just ahead along the coast is **Scilla**. This fishing village and its castle are Medieval in appearance, but the rock crowned by the castle is none other than the one mentioned in the *Odyssey* as the dwelling place of the six-headed monster Scylla. (The whirlpool of the monster Charybdis is across the Strait of Messina.) The treacherous seas that gave rise to the myth have calmed over the centuries, but the action continues in a youth hostel and discotheque in the castle. The Costa Viola ends with a bang at **Porticello Santa Trada**, a tourist center full of even more discotheques, and temptingly close to Sicily. This is the point at which the mainland and the island come closest—2 km (just over a mile)—and will be the site of a bridge if the government ever decides to go through with its long-discussed plans for one. The next town, **Villa San Giovanni**, however, is where the car and train traffic is actually ferried across to the island.

REGGIO DI CALABRIA
AND VICINITY

The ancient Greek colony of Rhegion has had quite an extraordinary series of misfortunes since its founding: It has been sacked by invaders, racked by earthquakes, and was heavily bombed during World War II. Virtually nothing remains of its glorious past. Its current incarnation has a pleasant but uninspiring appearance, yet offers some otherworldly elements. Looking into the Strait of Messina under the right conditions, for example, you may see what appears to be a sunken city, a phenomenon named after a sprite called the Fata Morgana and described in meteorological detail by Swinburne in his *Travels in the Two Sicilies*. (It is actually an optical illusion, a reflection of Reggio di Calabria and the city of Messina on the other side.)

Most visitors come to Reggio, as it is commonly called, for the **Museo Nazionale della Magna Grecia**, but the indoor treasures of the museum can be complemented by the outdoor pleasures of a stroll in the nearby **Lido Comunale**, a panoramic promenade designed by Pier Luigi Nervi. The museum is the most important such institution in Calabria, and the single most significant in the world for its rich archaeological remnants of Calabrian Magna Graecia. A half day is recommended to take in the entire collection, which extends from prehistoric artifacts through two Renaissance paintings by Antonello da Messina. The museum's main attraction, however, is its Classical section. As the numerous replicas on sale near the museum entrance and throughout the city attest, the undisputed stars of the Museo Nazionale are two fifth-century B.C. statues of warriors, dubbed the **Riace Bronzes** after the Calabrian town near which they were discovered underwater in 1972. In the same downstairs room is another rare Greek bronze dating from the same period, a bust called the *Head of a Philosopher*.

Traditionally considered Reggio's best regional restaurant, the moderately priced **Conti**, at via Giulia 2 (Tel: 0965-290-43; closed Mondays), is located near the museum and is as good a place as any to sample Calabrian cuisine and the spicy local seafood influenced by nearby Sicily, perhaps finishing up with sweeter Sicilian specialties that have made their way across the strait—marzipan or *granita,* an ice usually flavored with almond, coffee, or lemon. Also nearby is **Rodrigo**, via XXIV Maggio 25 (Tel: 0965-201-70), whose regional cuisine is ever so slightly more refined.

Hotel options in Reggio include the **Grand Hotel Excelsior**, a modern building conveniently located behind the museum, and the modern **Grande Albergo Miramare** near the Conti restaurant. For a more relaxing stay head a few miles north to Gallico Marina, where the **Fata Morgana** hotel offers modern accommodations, including a pool and disco, right on the beach. More tranquil respite may be taken at the modern monastic facilities called the **Eremo della Madonna della Consolazione** (Tel: 0965-214-97), run by Capuchin Franciscan monks.

Around the Toe
of Italy

There is much to be seen in a half-day's drive from Reggio rounding the toe of the Italian boot along the coast of the Aspromonte, the usually dry massif, which, like much of mountainous Calabria, becomes riddled with violent torrents called *fiumare* during the spring thaw. The land is planted with almonds, citrus, jasmine, and other fragrant trees, and is the only place in the world where the bergamot orange, used in eau de cologne, is cultivated. Driving along the Costa dei Gelsomini (Jasmine Coast), you pass **Pentedattilo**, a tiny village set beneath the breathtaking five-fingered rock formation that gives the town its name. Farther along the coast is **Bova Marina**, site of Italy's oldest synagogue (it dates from the fourth century B.C.), which was uncovered during the construction of the highway. Inland is the town of **Bova**, the center of Calabria's Greek community, where the inhabitants speak a dialect of Greek and hold an annual summer festival for the region's Greek communities. The somewhat severe-looking Renaissance architecture of the town frames beautiful views of the Ionian Sea at the southernmost point of continental Europe. Up the coast, just before the modern town of Locri, are the excavations of the ancient Greek colony of **Locri Epizephyrii**. The extensive site also houses a modern museum of the finds, though most of the major works are in Reggio. Locri itself boasts the **Hotel Demaco**, a small and modern structure right on the beach, as well as **La Fontanella** (piazza Contrada

Moschetta; Tel: 0964-203-84), a family-run restaurant serving
the best regional offerings. From Locri, a scenic road leads
inland to **Gerace**, dramatically perched on a small mountain
plateau overlooking the surrounding plain. Calabria's largest
cathedral (with interior columns possibly taken from the temples of Locri) is here, as are other Byzantine and Medieval
churches. The town also has a thriving crafts industry, notable
for its weavers as well as its potters, who reproduce the ancient vases and tablets of Locri Epizephyrii. A sampling (in
one of the many cantinas) of Gerace's strong, sweet, amber-
colored *vino greco* is also recommended.

THE SOUTHERN IONIAN COAST

Continuing north along the Ionian, the peaceful coastal
route alternates with awe-inspiring excursions to the *serre,*
inland villages dramatically set overlooking gorges. From
Locri, modern resort towns (Siderno and Roccella Ionica are
among many such crowded, family-oriented places along the
Calabrian coast; excellent beaches stretch from Soverato all
the way up to Crotone) are interwoven with ghosts of
ancient ones such as Gioiosa Ionica. Inland from Roccella
Ionica is **Caulonia**, the site of another excavation of artifacts
on display in the museum in Reggio, though some impressive foundations of a Doric temple may be seen *in situ.*

Stilo and Serra San Bruno

The road inland from Monasterace, up the coast from
Roccella, leads to Stilo, birthplace of the philosopher
Tommaso Campanella, and where tiny **La Cattolica**, a restored and highly important Byzantine church, heads a list of
monuments that includes a Gothic cathedral and a Norman
castle. A series of sharp, spectacular curves then leads to
Serra San Bruno, a town founded in the 11th century as an
adjunct to the **Monastery of Santo Stefano del Bosco**, begun
by Bruno of Cologne, founder of the Carthusian order. The
monastery, on the outskirts of town, offers tours twice daily,
at 11:00 A.M. and 4:00 P.M. However, only men are permitted
to visit, and they are accompanied by one of the monks (who
make a refreshingly delicious cheese for sale at the entrance). Men only, too, may stay at the monastery (provided
they participate in the rigid monastic life), but both sexes

may glimpse the monks on Mondays, when they take their weekly walk in the woods of the abbey. Near the abbey is the church of Santa Maria del Bosco, where Bruno of Cologne resided and died, as well as a pool of clear, pure water that Bruno allegedly made miraculous. In the town proper are the Baroque churches of San Biago and L'Addolorata, and shops selling wood, stone, and wrought-iron crafts as well as the local sweet, *inzudda,* made with almonds and honey. The invigorating drive on 182 down to Soverato back on the coast will put you in the mood for lunch in the restaurant of the seaside **San Domenico Hotel** (via della Galleria; Tel: 0967-231-21).

Catanzaro and Taverna

Pass the resort town of Copanello and make a quick detour inland to **Squillace**, birthplace of Cassiodorus (the great minister of the Ostrogoth Theodoric, the conqueror of Italy who is also remembered for having executed the Roman philosopher Boethius). This ancient town is also noted for its early Christian cathedral and its Norman castle, as well as its own sweet white wine and the production of pottery. Its restaurant, **La Cripta**, on via Porta Giudaica (Tel: 0961-91-25-00), serves traditional Calabrian cuisine in the intimate setting of a former Dominican sacristy. Return to the coast, then head inland again at Catanzaro Marina. Drive through the plains that were once considered the Garden of the Hesperides, past (for now) golden Catanzaro, and up the mountain road to **Taverna**, in the foothills of the Sila Piccola. This town should be on the itinerary of every art lover, for it is famous as the birthplace of Calabria's most famous painter, Mattia Preti, known in the art world as Il Cavaliere Calabrese. Though he painted extensively throughout Italy and in Malta during the 17th century, the churches of San Domenico, Santa Barbara, and San Martino in Taverna contain several of his early works.

From Taverna return to **Catanzaro**, famous in Medieval times as *la città dei tre V: venti, velluti, e San Vitaliano.* Of the three Vs referred to—wind, velvets, and the protector San Vitaliano—little remains except the first, but Catanzaro's role as the regional capital of Calabria has endowed it with agreeable accommodations and restaurants. The few sights to be seen include the Baroque church and oratory of the Rosario, the Museo Provinciale (a museum with a *Madonna and Child* signed by Antonello da Messina), and a promenade in the adjoining Villa Margherita, which offers a lovely view of the sea across a plain once held to be the Garden of the Hesperides of ancient mythology. Modern Catanzaro offers such amenities as the basic comforts of the **Hotel Guglielmo**, and **Uno più Uno**, a moderately priced restaurant in galleria Mancuso, good for sampling *rosito* mushrooms from the Sila, the local dish *murseddu* (veal and pork innards seasoned with a peppery tomato sauce), and the local *pecorino* cheese (Tel: 0961-265-32). The dry Lamezia red wine makes a nice accompaniment to the hearty fare. If the view of the sea is too tempting, try staying at **Stillhotel e Ristorante** at Catanzaro Marina, a modern hotel with panoramic views of the Ionian. Its restaurant also serves a sophisticated version of many regional specialties. A quieter option is to head down to the inexpensive **Hotel Residence Gavius**, a family-style hotel near the beach community of Roccelletta.

THE NORTHERN IONIAN COAST

The main points of interest on Italy's instep spark the imagination; most of the glories here are ghosts of their former greatness. Rounding Capo Rizzuto from the south, you reach the ruined **Le Castella**; it's worth wading through the water to inspect the ancient stone structure supposedly built by Hannibal but actually erected by the Aragons. (Le Castella is also the site of the nicest family-style resort in Calabria, **Hotel Club Le Castella**, an elaborate, landscaped complex with pool, beach, and disco.) You can bypass Isola di Capo Rizzuto (actually a tiny Medieval town, not an island, though set apart by its sinister air of organized crime) farther on and head directly to **Capo Colonna** to see the single column left (there were once 48) from a Doric temple dedicated to Hera and erected earlier than the Parthenon. Isolated on a rocky shore above the crashing surf, the spot is one of the most conducive in all of Italy to Byronic fantasies and is still the location, each spring, of an important religious procession of a Byzantine Madonna from Crotone to the tiny church next to the temple site.

Just ahead is **Crotone**, the ancient Greek colony of Croton, home to Pythagoras and his school. Unfortunately, little geometry or any other trace of the pre-Socratic Greeks is left in this modern commercial city. Its cathedral houses the Byzantine Madonna of Capo Colonna, and there is also an Aragonese castle and an archaeological museum nearby, but as is the case throughout the region the most significant finds from local excavations have been sent to Reggio. **Bella Romagna** (via Poggioreale 87; Tel: 0962-219-43; closed Mondays) is a good restaurant in which to sample the local specialty, *zuppa di pesce* (a spicy fish stew), taste Crotone's version of *pecorino,* and drink the wines from Ciro and Melissa, which lie just to the north.

Pass through both these wine-producing areas on the long coastal route from Crotone to Rossano Stazione, where you take a steep road—with wonderful views of the Gulf of Taranto—to **Rossano**, another of Calabria's inexplicably untouristed (except perhaps because of its lack of good hotels and restaurants) hill towns. Rossano's church of San Marco ranks with La Cattolica as the most important example of Byzantine architecture in Calabria, and the town was once one of the most monumental cities in the Byzantine Empire; the churches of Panaghia, Santa Maria del Pilere, Santa Anna, and Ospedale are also Byzantine constructions. The town's **Museo Diocesano** houses another Byzantine masterpiece, the Codex Purpureus, an extremely rare illuminated manuscript of the Gospels made in ancient Antioch on purple vellum and brought by monks to Rossano sometime during the seventh or eighth century. Outside Rossano the Byzantine Santa Maria del Patire, a former monastery, is important for its mosaic pavement but equally rewarding simply as a restful spot in the woods for a picnic on provisions picked up in town. Back at Rossano Stazione the modern, modest **Europa Lido Palace** provides the best accommodations for the night.

Beyond Rossano

Continuing north along the lovely Gulf of Taranto, archaeology aficionados will find the trip to neighboring Basilicata worth the distance involved. The town of **Policoro**, halfway between Rossano and Taranto, houses the **Museo Nazionale della Siritide**, a modern museum displaying artifacts from excavations at the nearby colony of Heracleia. Farther north is the vast and important archaeological site of the former Greek colony of **Metapontum** (today's Metaponto), founded by the Sybarites, and where Pythagoras transferred his school after being exiled from Crotone. Its modern **Antiquarium** provides elaborate documentation of the excavations as well as an impressive collection of coins, vases, and statuary unearthed at the site. The grounds are extensive enough for an hour or two of pleasant ruminating in the

250   CALABRIA

ruins, which contain the remains of a Greek theater and the Doric temple of Apollo Lycius.

(Beyond Metaponto on the coast road to the northeast is the city of Taranto, the end point of the chapter on Apulia, above.)

Otherwise, you can settle for **Sibari**, a small site just a short distance northeast up the coast from Rossano, and named after ancient Sybaris. The exact location of the corrupt and luxurious Greek colony (according to legend, destroyed in 510 B.C. by the men of Croton, who flooded it with the waters of the river Crati) still has not been determined, but it probably lies somewhere on the vast flood plain surrounding the train station of Sibari. Near the station is a small museum, the Museo della Sibartide, which displays objects unearthed during local attempts to uncover Sybaris. The most comfortable accommodations for the Rossano–Sibari area are to be had up the Ionian coast at Trebisacce, where **Torre di Albidonia** offers upscale rustic accommodations in converted farmhouses surrounded by some 200 acres of coastal property.

GETTING AROUND

Calabria has airports in both Reggio di Calabria and Lamezia Terme. The latter is halfway down the region's Tyrrhenian coast and an hour away from Catanzaro and Cosenza by car or by the airport bus called ADABUSSING, better alternatives than the unsavory taxi drivers who linger at the airport exit waiting to take tourists for a ride. Each airport is served by Aerea Trasporti Italia from Rome and Milan. Trains run frequently along the coast, which, with its mild climate, is visitable year-round, and they also go inland. Be forewarned, however, that some of the train routes are operated by the small-gauge Ferrovia Calabro-Lucane, for which separate tickets must be purchased locally, and that many stations in Calabria are named after communities miles from where the trains actually stop. Bus service also connects many coastal points with the inland cities. The Sila, still snowbound at times during the winter but usually kept passable for the ski resorts, is reached by regular train and bus service from Cosenza.

However, because public transportation in Calabria is not geared to the tourist, a car (rented at either airport or in the larger cities) is more highly recommended here than in practically any other Italian region. Over the past few years roads have been improved, government subsidies (some say guilt) have kept the Autostrada in Calabria free of tolls, and driving—whether along the coast or in the mountains—is almost always scenic.

In Praia, the feast of the Madonna della Grotta al Santuario takes place August 15; in Paola, the feast of Saint Francis of Paola is held May 5; in Cosenza, opera season at the Teatro Rendano runs from December through February; in Lungro, the largest Albanian festival takes place December 6; in San Demetrio Corone, the week-long Albanian festival, Primavera Albanese, takes place each spring; in Bova, the Graecanic Festival is held in either June or July; and at Capo Colonne the procession of the Madonna di Capo Colonne takes place the second Sunday in May.

ACCOMMODATIONS REFERENCE

The rates given below are projections for 1992; always check for up-to-date information before making reservations. Wide ranges may reflect the differences between low- and high-season rates. Unless otherwise indicated, the figures indicate the cost of a double room (per room, not per person). However, half-board (mezza pensione) rates, which include breakfast and one other meal per day, are per person. Most hotels will add a service charge of 10 to 15 percent.

▶ **Aquila-Edelweiss.** Viale Stazione 11, 87052 **Camigliatello Silano.** Tel: (0984) 57-80-44; Fax: (0984) 57-87-53. Ł75,000–Ł101,650.

▶ **Baia Paraelios.** Località Fornaci, 88035 **Parghelia.** Tel: (0963) 60-30-00; Fax: (0963) 60-00-74. Open June–September. Full board Ł205,000–Ł255,000.

▶ **Hotel Barbieri.** Via San Nicolà 30, 87042 **Altomonte** (Cosenza). Tel: (0981) 94-80-72; Fax: (0981) 94-80-73. Ł70,000–Ł80,000.

▶ **Hotel Centrale.** Via del Tigrai 3, 87100 **Cosenza.** Tel: (0984) 736-81; Fax: (0984) 757-50. Ł68,000–Ł101,650.

▶ **Hotel Club Le Castella.** Località Le Castella, 80076 **Isola di Capo Rizzuto.** Tel: (0962) 79-50-54; Fax: (0962) 79-51-50. Ł70,000–Ł160,000.

▶ **Hotel Demaco.** Via Lungomare 28, 89044 **Locri.** Tel: (0964) 202-47. Ł68,000–Ł85,000.

▶ **Europa.** Via Kennedy, Contrada Roges, 87036 **Rende.** Tel: (0984) 46-50-64; Fax: (0984) 46-46-03. Ł103,000–Ł133,750.

▶ **Europa Lido Palace.** Strada Statale 106, 87068 **Rossano Stazione.** Tel: (0983) 220-95; Fax: (0983) 220-96. Ł68,000– Ł101,650.

▶ **Hotel Fata Morgana.** Lungomare, Località Gallico Marina, 89055 **Reggio di Calabria**. Tel: (0965) 37-00-09. Ł109,000.

► **Hotel 501**. Via Madonnella, 88018 **Vibo Valentia**. Tel: (0963) 439-51; Fax: (0963) 434-00. Ł148,000.

► **Grande Albergo Miramare**. Via Fata Morgana 1, 89100 **Reggio di Calabria**. Tel: (0965) 81-24-44; Fax: (0985) 81-24-50. Ł90,000–Ł155,000.

► **Grand Hotel De Rose**. Viale Mediterraneo, 87029 **Scalea**. Tel: (0985) 202-73. Fax: (0985) 92-01-94. Ł99,000–Ł131,000.

► **Grand Hotel Excelsior**. Via Vittorio Veneto 66, 89121 **Reggio di Calabria**. Tel: (0965) 258-01; Fax: (0965) 930-84. Ł131,000–Ł176,000.

► **Grand Hotel Lorica**. Viale Libertà 57, 87050 **Lorica**. Tel: (0984) 53-70-39. Open May 15–October 15. Ł80,000.

► **Grand Hotel San Michele**. Strada Statale 18, 87022 **Cetraro**. Tel: (0982) 910-12; Fax: (0982) 914-30. Closed November. Ł140,000–Ł260,000.

► **Hotel Guglielmo**. Via Tedeschi 1, 88100 **Catanzaro**. Tel: (0961) 265-32; Fax: (0961) 419-00. Ł120,000–Ł175,000.

► **Hotel Residence Gavius**. Località Roccellatta, 88021 **Borgia**. Tel: (0961) 39-12-54. Ł45,000–Ł71,000.

► **San Francesco**. Contrada Commenda, 87036 **Rende**. Tel: (0984) 86-17-21. Ł102,000–Ł133,750.

► **Stillhotel**. Via Melito Porto Salvo 102A, 88063 **Catanzaro Marina**. Tel: (0961) 328-51. Ł80,000–Ł100,000.

► **Torre di Albidonia**. Lungomare, 87075 **Trebisacce**. Tel: (0981) 512-90. Ł80,000.

SICILY

By Barbara Coeyman Hults

Sicily is mysterious. Even though the island lies in full view of mainland Italy, across the Strait of Messina from Calabria, Italians from other regions still regard Sicily as a region apart, a seductive puzzle. Sicilians, for their part, still talk of "going to Italy" when they travel 20 minutes across the strait by hydrofoil.

In many ways Sicily *is* a world apart. Life is lived more intensely here, even today, when the highway system has connected the island's cities and television has entered almost every home, for better or worse. Colors, too, are more brilliant: The sea is bluer on the southern coast, the contrasts of light and dark greater in the almost tropical sun; the pottery has taken on the hues of the natural world and explodes in reds, yellows, and greens. Jasmine and orange blossoms, mint and wild fennel, produce strong scents here, and the perfumed air of a cloister garden or private patio recalls *The Arabian Nights.* Food is tinged with sweet and sour blends from the East and North Africa, and desserts— sweet mulberry ices or super-rich cassata—could have been served by Scheherazade. The architecture, too, recalls other times and places—especially Agrigento's Vallata dei Templi, a line of Greek temples overlooking the sea and softened by pink and white almond blossoms each spring; and Palermo's massive Norman walls lightened by interlacing arches that open onto cloisters of lemon and orange trees, bamboo and papyrus. Sicilians themselves are intense: Glances become penetrating stares—not hostile, just fascinated; each moment seems savored as emotions run their course.

The Sicilian writer Tomasi di Lampedusa and the director Luchino Visconti captured some of this spirit in *The Leopard*—the colors of the plains, the love of show inher-

253

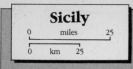

Sicily

0   miles   25

0   km   25

Tyrrhenian Sea

Egadi Islands

I. Marettimo

I. di Levanzo

I. Favignana

I. Mozia

S. Vito lo Capo

Erice

Scopello

Trapani

Gulf of Castellammare

Mondello

▲ *Mt. Pellegrino*

Monreale

Contrada Lenzitti

Palermo

Solunto

Bagheri

■ **Segesta**

Calatafimi

Marsala

115

A29

Salemi

Gibellina

Sambuca di Sicilia

Menfi

Caltabellotta

▲ *Mt. San Calogero*

■ **Selinunte**

Porto Palo

Sciacca

Agrigento

■

Mediterranean Sea

Porto Empedocle

11

Caos

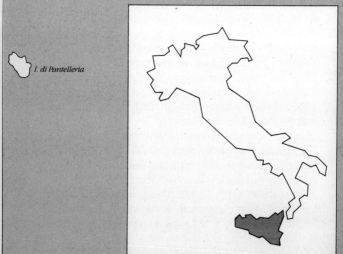

I. di Pantelleria

ited from the Spanish Bourbons, the feasts, feuds, and passions. Francis Coppola and Mario Puzo revealed a less savory aspect in *The Godfather,* which is still accurate to some extent, although today the Mafia is less secret—the daily papers chronicle its increasing number of murders and bombings, and extortion is common in Palermo and Catania. Unfortunately, the success of U.S.–Sicilian police forces in jailing Mafiosi has broken up many of the old families only to let loose new, totally uncontrolled gangs whose greed for drug money and power has led to countless deaths. Younger and younger recruits are involved, and the result is closer to *Goodfellas* than to *The Godfather,* but without the humor of the former.

Tourists, fortunately, encounter them only as street criminals looking for wallets and gold chains, like their counterparts throughout the world. Avoidance is the key: don't take anything of value with you, and be aware of your surroundings in Palermo or Catania. Smaller towns have fewer problems of this nature. (The "old families" don't need to be mourned, by the way. They're alive and well and infiltrating business, from banking to roulette.)

Although it takes time to see beneath surface impressions in Sicily, spending a week or two there will open some doors to this fascinating conundrum that remains a mystery even to Sicilians. For a look at today's Sicily, read *On Persephone's Island,* a year's journal by Mary Taylor Simeti, an American expatriate who divides her time between the archaic rhythms of a Sicilian farm and the corroded and corrupt beauty of Palermo.

Sicily (Sicilia) has been inhabited for more than 20,000 years. Cave drawings dating back to the Ice Age have been found on Monte Pellegrino near Palermo as well as on the island of Levanzo. In fact, the early tribes, Sicani and Siculi, along with the Elymi, were already established residents when globe-sailing Phoenicians dropped anchor here during the eighth century B.C.

Greek settlement began along the east and north coasts and soon spread throughout most of the island. By the fifth century B.C. Sicily as a group of Greek colonies was more powerful than Greece itself. Its sophisticated cities attracted Plato and Pindar; Empedocles and Archimedes were native sons. Legend-loving Greeks found a natural home on an island that worshiped the Mediterranean fertility goddess Astarte in a mystical temple high on Erice's peak, and where Sicilian myth had Persephone kidnapped near Lago di Pergusa. Carthage had a foothold here, too, contesting control of the island first with the Greeks and then with the Romans. Not until Garibaldi and the Thousand landed at Marsala about 2,500 years later would Sicily be rid of foreign domination.

This intricate web of historical roots has created an emotional tug-of-war in the Sicilian of today. Contemporary novelist Leonardo Sciascia writes: "They love their island, but they constantly escape or dream of escaping from it. And when they are away from it, they love it even more and dream of returning." Young Sicilians, surrounded by TV, rock music, and video tapes, often think of themselves as Italians or even Europeans, rather than just Sicilians as their grandparents did. The modern world here, as everywhere, is a mixed blessing: greater conveniences but conflicting values and less direction.

To see Sicily in all its variety, start at Palermo and travel counterclockwise around the coast (first making a short detour east to Cefalù), with occasional forays into the interior. Before Messina and a return to the mainland, make your last stop Taormina—so extravagantly beautiful that it's difficult to leave. But avoid the summer months, especially August, when heat everywhere in Sicily is extreme and Taormina is packed with vacationing Europeans and movie festival–goers. Spring is best: April through June, when the wild flowers bloom. March can be lovely, too, but showers are likely in early spring (almond trees flower in early February, celebrated in Agrigento with a folk-dance festival).

MAJOR INTEREST

Unique mix of Greek, Roman, Arab, Norman, Spanish, and Italian cultures

Lush Mediterranean vegetation

Sophisticated Sicilian cuisine

Palermo for Norman sites and for dining

Segesta, Agrigento, Syracuse, Selinunte, and Taormina for Greek temples and amphitheaters

Erice and Taormina for Medieval mountaintop villages with unparalleled views

Piazza Armerina for a Roman villa and mosaics

Caltagirone for ancient and contemporary ceramics

Syracuse, Noto, and other towns of the southeast for Baroque splendor

Mountain villages of the Madonie near Cefalù

The Aeolian and Egadi islands

PALERMO

This chaotic capital of Norman kings and Spanish viceroys has both panache and poverty. An interesting and sometimes beautiful city, it's intriguing to explore on foot for its street sounds, its savory street snacks (many found only in Sicily), and for conversations with Palermitani, who often speak some English and, like most Sicilians, usually have a relative in America, England, or Australia. When walking about, take big-city precautions (a money belt and an eye on the camera).

The Arab-Norman buildings are incomparable. Next in interest come the Baroque oratories, the museums, and the Vucceria—an outdoor market stretching through a raucous, riveting old neighborhood that is lined with carts of olives of every tint, pyramids of blood oranges, mounds of purple cauliflower, and burgeoning banks of sea creatures that would astonish even Jacques Cousteau.

Palermo's grand days, when the Arabs made it their capital from the 9th through 11th centuries, rivaled the splendor depicted in *The Arabian Nights*—a world of jasmine and roses, mosques and fountains, harems and the good life as only Oriental potentates knew how to live it. The Normans and then the great Hohenstaufen Frederick II continued this tradition, even after control of Sicily had been wrested from the Arabs. While their brother Crusaders were attacking Islam in the east, the Normans found coexistence a rewarding system in Sicily.

This exuberant mix is best and most beautifully seen in the **Cappella Palatina** (Palatine Chapel), part of the **Palazzo dei Normanni**, which today is the seat of the Sicilian Parliament. King Roger's chapel (constructed between 1132 and 1140) is a rhythmic fusion of the best of Latin, Byzantine, and Islamic architecture. Guy de Maupassant found it the "most amazing jewel ever imagined by human thought." Not only the fine mosaics but even the wooden stalactite-style ceiling is extraordinary, and the Persian-influenced Arab paintings rival anything in Cairo. These paintings are the earliest known of their kind: a magic world of camels and lions, dragons and monsters, scenes of hunting and picnicking with the harem, and Kufic inscriptions praising the Norman King Roger.

Upstairs in the **royal apartments** (which, for security reasons, are not always open, especially when Parliament is in session) court life was as exotic as any ever lived. Frederick II's court rivaled the Normans' as one of the most sophisticated in Europe, a center of arts and sciences where Arab mathematicians and astronomers had their theories translated and propagated, Greek philosophy and poetry influenced European literature, and Italian poetry and music flourished. The extravagance of those days—and his childhood in Palermo—remained with Frederick, the future head of the Holy Roman Empire, as he travelled about Europe with an entourage—his harem and his elephants—in tow.

Not far from the palace is the **Church of San Giovanni degli Eremiti**, bursting with vermilion domes from the outside, and just as charming from within thanks to its courtyard and cloisters of lush palm trees and papyrus.

Palermo's **Cathedral** is a short walk down corso Vittorio Emanuele. Though it suffers from too much redoing, the façade is a record of the city's history, as each new ruler had his era included. The best part is the back, still Norman despite some embellishment. Roger II is buried in a simple tomb near the entrance, next to his daughter Constance and directly behind Frederick II. (Roger wanted to be interred in the cathedral of Cefalù, east of Palermo, but city politics kept the king here.) The Cappella Novella features the *Madonna della Scala* (1503) by Antonello Gagini, a fine sculptor who, with his family, is responsible for hundreds of little-heralded works throughout Sicily. Francesco Laurana, the great master who was Gagini's teacher, is known for his exquisite Madonna and Child statuary. The *Madonna* in the chapel before the left transept is his work, with student participation.

In back of the Duomo, along Corso Alberto Amedeo, you can find antiques shops and the **Flea Market** (Mercato delle Pulci), where unique items are often discovered. Treat yourself to a very figgy pastry, the *buccellato,* as made superbly at the **Pasticceria Scimone** at via Imera 8 (closed Tuesdays). Ahead on the corso is the famous **Quattro Canti**, at the intersection of via Maqueda. Four palaces face one another on their concave corners, producing a circular effect that recalls the Quattro Fontane in Rome. On each façade, figures and symbols represent a season, a king, and a saint who protects the region of Palermo stretching out behind her.

At the next major street, via Roma, a left turn leads to piazza San Domenico, where the **Vucceria** begins. Turn right into the piazza and then right down the hill. The Vucceria is not just a market; it's an introduction to the basics of Sicilian cooking. Traditional Mediterranean blends of eggplant, tomato, olives, onions, and garlic are combined with capers, wild fennel, and other bitters—cheese and pine nuts are added to soften the edge—to produce hundreds of sophisti-

Palermo

| 0 | yards | 300 |
| 0 | meters | 300 |

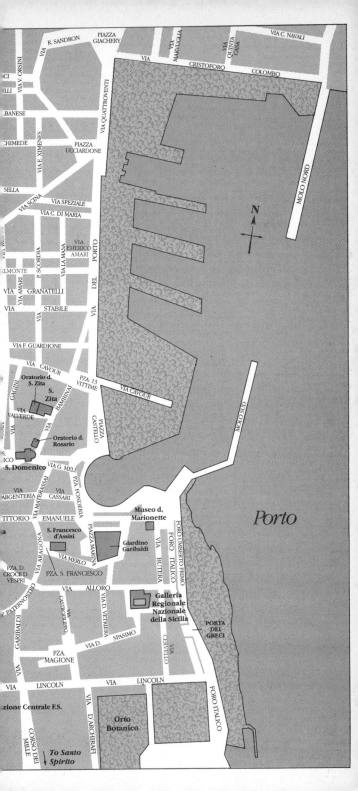

cated sweet-and-sour tastes. *Pasta con sarde,* a tradition in Palermo, is the perfect paradigm: a blend of sea and forest derived from fresh (no kin to canned) sardines, fresh wild fennel, sultanas, pine nuts, tomato paste, and saffron. The taste is exotic, and the following devoted. Like many such dishes, a bit more of this or that or a change in flavor because of regional soil differences will create a wholly new taste; as a result, each dish is orchestrated differently in each kitchen.

The seafood in the Vucceria—sea urchins and lamprey, oysters and swordfish, crabs, and even that blob of gray called *neonata,* the newborn fish that are a delicacy in Palermo—raw or frittered, is difficult to resist, though the cacophony of the hawkers is rarely directed at non-buying tourists, except to amuse. Two restaurants, the **Shangai**—which you'll see just above the piazza on a first-floor terrace—and tiny **Da Totò**, a very simple spot on the side street to the left, will sometimes even cook what you buy or what you point to—if the restaurant isn't crowded and if you can explain to the owner that you want to choose a fish yourself. Fish is often stuffed (*a beccafico*) with bread crumbs, sultanas, pine nuts, and lemon juice, and then rolled. Swordfish and tuna are staples: broiled, stuffed, *alla marinara,* with lemon and olives, or some home-devised variant. (Fish couscous, another touch of North Africa, is found mainly near Trapani on the western shore of Sicily.) Try the local wines, too. Sicily is now a major exporter of very good wine; among the most frequently encountered products are Corvo and Regaleali.

Since Sicilian lunches are never rushed (the owners at Shangai and Totò sing to the guests when the mood hits), and nothing reopens until 4:00 P.M. anyway, retrace your steps to the **Oratorio del Rosario** in back of San Domenico on via Bambinai. Beyond the Oratorio at via Bambinai 16 is, appropriately, a bizarre shop of tiny, delicate wax *bambini,* elegantly dressed and mounted on velvet cushions as ex-votos. If the Oratorio is closed, they will know where the key is. Palermo's oratories are amazing fantasies of Baroque cum Rococo. At the Rosario, in 1720, Giacomo Serpotta created a world of stucco that climbs the walls like ivy and is dotted with tiny figures. Serpotta was not only a master of the *putti,* those cherubs so characteristic of the Baroque, but also a fine sculptor of refined, almost Neoclassical figures such as *Courage,* on view here in the form of a woman with a plumed hat. At the altar is Van Dyck's *Virgin of the Rosary with St. Dominic and the Four Saints of Quattro Canti,* created by the artist after a visit to Palermo. If this oratory interests you, visit **Santa Zita** (next to the church of that name), where extraordinary reliefs of the New Testament and the battle of Lepanto reveal more of the Serpotta genius.

Piazza Pretoria, just off Quattro Canti on via Roma, looks awkward by day but intriguing by night. The vast **Fontana Pretoria** (intended for a Tuscan villa) is called the "Fountain of Shame," either because of the nudity on display or because "Venus is in love with a horse." When fighting was at a brutal pitch in adjoining streets during the 1870 Garibaldi campaign, the Great One showed his powers of leadership by calmly sitting on the fountain steps day after day while local residents brought him flowers and fruit. Though much of the square was destroyed, he was not touched, and his heroism gave the citizens fresh courage.

On the same piazza, the **Church of Santa Caterina** is amazing inside, every inch of it busily Baroque. Yet even here Sicilian restraint in linear boundaries can be seen. At the right transept is a statue of Santa Caterina (1534) by Antonello Gagini.

In the adjoining piazza Bellini, the red domes bulging beneath a graceful campanile announce the **Churches of the Martorana** and **San Cataldo**, which together make up a charming Arab-Norman complex, complete with palm trees and cloister. George of Antioch, Roger's admiral, founded the Martorana (also known as Santa Maria dell' Ammiraglio) in 1143, and its lovely campanile survived the church's Baroque renovation. Inside, historian John Julius Norwich says you must run the gauntlet "of simpering cupids and marzipan Madonnas" to get to the Norman original. But it's worth the run. The interior, created with marbles and mosaics, has the intimacy of the Cappella Palatina. Services in the Greek rite are still conducted here—most dramatically at Easter. At the west end are original mosaics of Christ crowning Roger (thought to be a true likeness of the Norman king) and of George of Antioch at the Madonna's feet. Across from the Martorana, the church of San Cataldo (1161) has been restored to its original Norman simplicity.

A morning's walk might begin at the Kalsa, an old section of Palermo where the buildings are literally falling down. To the left of the Kalsa Gate, just off via Lincoln, are botanical gardens (Orto Botanico) with a renowned collection of tropical vegetation. Enter from the harbor side through the Porta dei Greci and turn into the via Alloro, where the **Galleria Regionale della Sicilia**, housed in the Catalan-Gothic Palazzo Abatellis, exhibits such masterpieces as Antonello da Messina's *Annunciata*. Portraying a transcendent moment, the artist catches the Virgin between two worlds, physically resisting with her hand while spiritually accepting what she is being told. The bust of Eleanora of Aragon by Laurana and the *Triumph of Death* by an unknown painter are among the great works of the gallery, which is beautifully housed in a restored palace setting.

At piazza San Francesco stop for a Palermo favorite, *guasteddu,* a sesame roll with slices of tasty spleen and *cacciacavallo* cheese. Even if the notion of innards makes you recoil, stop at the **Foccacceria San Francesco** anyway, a wood-and-mirrors place where Garibaldi probably enjoyed his *meusa* (Sicilian for *spleen*). Delicious *arancini*—rice balls with a bit of prosciutto and cheese inside—and *panelle*—light chick-pea fritters found everywhere in Palermo—are best here or from street vendors. *Sfincioni,* high, light pizzas with tomato and onion, are another street specialty.

Across the piazza, the Gothic doors of the **Church of San Francesco d'Assisi** date from 1302, a period when devotion to the saint was most fervent. Serpotta's statues and Laurana's Mastrantonio chapel (1468) are distinguished. Just left of the church a gate leads to another of Serpotta's joyful marvels, the **Oratorio di San Lorenzo**, diminished by the loss of a large Caravaggio painting, stolen from the altar some years ago. Ring the bell for entry.

Several other museums merit attention, certainly the **Museo Archeologico** in piazza dell'Olivella, where a fine collection of antiquities includes some lovely metopes from temple friezes at Selinunte, a Greek city on Sicily's south coast, and a model of the cave drawings at Addaura on nearby Monte Pellegrino. (To visit the actual cave site, apply at the museum. If you go, stop at the shrine to Santa Rosalia, a chaste noblewoman whose bones, an angel revealed, would stop the plague in Palermo. The patron saint of Palermo, she is celebrated with processions and feasting from July 12 to 15 and on September 3 and 4.)

Puppet shows based on the Carolingian cycle of Roland (Orlando) battling the Saracens (instead of the Basques, in this version) are a charming form of entertainment in Palermo. You can probably see one at the **Museo delle Marionette** (Marionette Museum) on via Butera near the port or at the **Pitrè**, an ethnographic museum in the outlying Parco della Favorita; check the schedules at the tourist office. These puppets, even originals, are sold in all tourist areas of Sicily, competing with that other superstar, Pinocchio. Originals are also sometimes sold at Palermo's flea market and in antiques shops (see the section on shopping, below).

The Pitrè also exhibits carts, ceramics, ex-votos, and other aspects of 19th-century Sicilian life. Not far from it in the park is the curious **Palazzo Cinese**, built in 1799 for Ferdinand III, Bourbon king of the Two Sicilies—as the realm whose capital was Naples was called. This bit of chinoiserie entranced his queen, Maria Carolina, and their guests Lord Nelson and Lady (and Lord) Hamilton at a time when Nelson and Lady Hamilton were the talk of the royals. Harold Acton described a nocturnal *fête champêtre* thrown by Ferdinand at the Palazzo Cinese to thank his English guests for saving his life: life-size wax figures of the three "were enshrined in a classical Temple of Fame, topped by a goddess blowing a trumpet. Fireworks represented the explosion of *L'Orient* at the Battle of the Nile. Paeans of praise were sung to the deliverer, and the nine-year-old Prince Leonard, his mother's darling, dressed as a midshipman, raised the laurel wreath from the waxen admiral's brow and planted it on that of the living one."

Santo Spirito, the church that was the setting for the "Sicilian Vespers," the 1282 uprising against the detested French Angevin occupiers, almost all of whom were massacred, stands in the cemetery of Santa Orsola, south of the city near the railroad station. It was built in 1173 by Palermo bishop Walter of the Mill, an Englishman known in Italian as Gualtiero Offamiglio, who also had the Duomo erected in Palermo.

La Ziza, in the dismal western reaches of the city, was King William I's earthly paradise, once surrounded by luxuriant greenery. The palace's interior has now been restored to its original grandeur. In Norwich's words, "Nowhere else on the island is that specifically Islamic talent for creating quiet havens of shade and coolness in the summer heat so dazzlingly displayed." At the **Catacombe dei Cappuccini**, near La Ziza, about 8,000 corpses, sitting on the floor or hanging fully clothed from the walls in oddly vivacious poses, provide memento mori for all viewers. Males and females have separate rooms of course; Sicilians are very proper about death.

Staying in Palermo

The important decision is whether to stay in the city or at a nearby resort—Mondello or Cefalù (see those sections below)—and take the train or bus back into Palermo to sightsee. (Don't drive in; chaos and auto theft make that prospect unattractive in the city.) If you choose not to stay in

Palermo, you'll have to rise early: Cefalù is almost an hour away by train, though Mondello is closer, by bus.

The **Villa Igiea** is the grande dame of Palermo hotels, with its own tropical garden, swimming pool, and outdoor dining terrace and bar. The Art Nouveau (Liberty-style, in Italian) rooms are stunningly decorated by Basile. The best rooms face the pool (and the sea beyond); the other part—the main building, which includes the bar and disco—is often noisy and is favored by affluent young Palermo. The management has changed frequently, and staff enthusiasm is not always high. A taxi will be necessary to get into central Palermo. Salita Belmonte 43, 90142; Tel: (091) 54-37-44; Fax: (091) 54-76-54. In U.S., Tel: (212) 599-8280 or (800) 223-9832; Fax: (212) 559-1755. Ł260,000–Ł400,000; half board Ł260,000.

Perhaps the best choice in Palermo is the **Excelsior Palace**, located outside the city center in an attractive residential area, but just off a main artery, the via Libertà. Via Marchese Ugo 3, 90141; Tel: (091) 625-61-76; Fax: (091) 34-21-39. Ł120,000–Ł210,000; half board Ł140,000.

The **Grand Hotel delle Palme**, the stately palace where Wagner wrote parts of *Parsifal,* has been renovated. Service, once less than cordial, has recently improved—or at least long enough to pamper the cast of *The Godfather III.* Suites are particularly lovely, but back rooms are dark and crowded. The hotel cannot be beaten for its convenience to Palermo's sights, however, and the restaurant, under separate management, is delightful (see below). Via Roma 398, 90139; Tel: (091) 58-39-33; Fax: (091) 33-15-45. In U.S., Tel: (212) 599-8280 or (800) 223-9832; Fax: (212) 599-1755. Ł120,000; half board Ł140,000.

The **Jolly Hotel** is not grand but is well equipped to satisfy clients, with good service and simple, comfortable rooms. Garden dining is romantic, thanks to a vine-covered crumbling palazzo adjoining the hotel. The quietest rooms face the swimming pool. In front of the hotel lies a stretch of beach that Fellini fans will love—a tired Ferris wheel and other dubious amusements line an enervated, unswimmable sea. Foro Italico 22, 90133; Tel: (091) 616-50-90; Fax: (091) 616-14-41. In U.S., Tel: (800) 221-2626 or (212) 213-1468; Fax: (212) 213-2369. In U.K., Tel: (923) 89-62-72 or (0800) 28-27-29; Fax: (923) 89-60-71. Ł145,000–Ł190,000.

Among the less expensive hotels, the **Albergo Sole** is located in the heart of the city, just off the famous Quattro Canti corner. It offers simple rooms with fine views of

Palermo from the roof. Corso Vittorio Emanuele 291, 90139; Tel: (091) 58-18-11. ₤90,000.

The **Europa** is simple, convenient, and favored by businesspeople. Via Agrigento 3, 90141; Tel: (091) 625-63-23; Fax: same. ₤75,000–₤110,000; half board ₤90,000–₤110,000. On a budget, try the **Albergo Orientale**, located on one side of a Renaissance palazzo and run with care. Via Maqueda 26, 90100; Tel: (091) 616-57-27. ₤40,000.

Dining in Palermo

At **L'Approdo da Renato**'s, a little outside the center of town to the northeast—and well worth the 15-minute taxi ride—Gian Rodolfo and Francesca Botto have created one of Palermo's best restaurants, where *zuppa di pesce,* crêpes stuffed with *frutta di mare,* wonderful raw fish marinated in oil and herbs, and swordfish in almond sauce are happily devoured before the cannoli, which are specially made at Piana degli Albanesi (a town to the south that has an Albanian population). The attractive seaside setting is enhanced by antique furnishings and the relaxing though fashionable atmosphere. Let the owner choose the wine. Sicily takes olive oil seriously; an olive-oil list is often available. Via Messina Marine 224. Reserve; Tel: (091) 630-28-81. Closed Wednesdays.

For a good comfortable trattoria with traditional and innovative Palermo fare, go to **Papoff**, where you can taste *u maccu,* a puree of favas with herbs. Via La Lumia 28/b.

The **Charleston** is still very good and quite fashionable, despite its ups and downs. It's decorated with Art Nouveau charm, and the chef has made eggplant a vegetable of Dionysian aspects. Piazzale Ungheria 30; Tel: (091) 32-13-66; closed Sundays and June 16–September 25.

The **Hotel Patria**—not a hotel, but a restaurant—has a charming outdoor court where veal and lamb are braised over a grill on cool summer nights. At via Aragona 6, the Patria has caught on with Sicilians (Tel: 091-616-1136).

La Scuderia, near the Parco della Favorita, is a favorite with well-to-do Palermo—a sizable population. Its stuffed perch served with charcoal-grilled vegetables and *cacciacavallo* cheese is pointless to resist, as is its roast lamb with fresh mint. The super-rich dessert *sole* (sun) *di Sicilia* is a *semifreddo* (half-frozen) luxury spiked with Moscato wine from Pantelleria (Sicily's island down near Africa; see "Trapani," below), and the outdoor terrace is a joy in summer. Via del Fante 9; Tel: (091) 52-03-23.

Another favorite in the center of town is the informal **Bellini's** on piazza Bellini, where a full Sicilian menu includes such innovations as the red-leaf lettuce *radicchio* stuffed with meats, cheeses, onions, and eggs. Wonderful pizza can also be enjoyed here, most of the year at tables set outside.

La Trattoria Primavera, where basics are inexpensive and nicely presented, is found at piazza Bologna 4 (closed Fridays). Try the *sarde a beccafico* (stuffed sardines).

Al Ficodindia is a popular trattoria, bright with Sicilian decor. Tournedos are a specialty. Via Emerico Amari 64; Tel: (091) 32-42-14.

La Palmetta, whether you have a table inside the Grand Hotel delle Palme or on its airy roof terrace with mountain views, is one of Palermo's finest restaurants, with a menu of Sicilian and Continental dishes and an attentive staff. Grande Hotel delle Palme, via Roma 396; Tel: (091) 58-39-33.

For picnics, **Mangia** will see that you *mangia* well. Via Principe Belmonte 17. Then for bread it's **Spinnato**'s bakery across the street.

PASTRY SHOPS AND ICE-CREAM PARLORS

Palermo's pastry shops are not hard to come by, and the quality is generally high, given the collective Sicilian sweet tooth. An unusual spot is the **Convent of St. Benedict**, piazza Venezia 38A, which is famous for its *minne di Vergini* (virgin's breasts), cannoli, and *trionfo della golla* (the triumph of greed)—the last word on the deadly sin: layers of sponge cake, marzipan, and pistachio with cream fillings. Their *grappola d'uva* is a bunch of grapes made with almond and pistachio paste. Orders are placed and received through a convent wheel by a lay worker or novitiate with the silent order. The more elaborate pastries can be bought only in about four-pound quantities.

For secular sweets, try **La Martorana**, corso Vittorio Emanuele 196; or **La Rosa Nero**, via Lincoln at via Cervello, near the Botanic Gardens. Sicilian ice cream is an art form in which all sorts of fruits, nuts, and creams are utilized. Even *tiramisù* and *zabaglione* are *semifreddo,* and the jasmine-petal ice is a delicate treat. The **Gelateria Ilardo**, Foro Umberto Primo 6, near the Porta dei Greci, is a popular summer place. (Also see "Mondello," below.)

Shopping in Palermo

Antiques shops, elegant boutiques, and jumbled flea markets offer some interesting items, but bargains are rare. Go to the **Mercato di Pulci** (flea market) behind the cathedral on corso Alberto Amedeo, where a variety of stores present their wares—often interesting antiques.

Art Nouveau (Liberty) collectibles can be found at **Cravosio** at via Ventidue Gennaio 1 and at **Il Mercato**, via Garzilli 73, a couple of blocks west of viale della Libertà.

Sicilian ceramics vary with the region: strong patterns of vivid color in Palermo; blue and white in the south and Caltagirone, the ceramics center; and intricate earth-tone patterns at Erice. The **Artigianato Siciliano**, via Amari 13, is the largest center, with ceramics from all over Sicily. Contemporary artisans are naturally more experimental. **De Simone** has stores throughout Sicily featuring bright, bold patterns and interesting shapes, some for dinnerware, some for decoration. In Palermo, De Simone shops are located at piazza Leone 2 and via Stabile 133.

Mondello

A popular getaway for ice cream on a summer's night is Mondello, up the coast northwest of Palermo, where the **Antico Chiosco** will sell you fresh flavors of everything from fruit ice to *tartufo* cream. During the day the beaches here are noisy and crowded, but the town is pretty and certainly animated. At night its streets are lined with fish vendors, and you can eat oysters as you stroll. More likely you'll go to the trattoria **Sympathy**—the origin of its name is a mystery—or to the **Gambero Rosso** for a sit-down meal of one of the sea fantasies you saw at the Vucceria. *Ricci,* or sea urchins, are a great delicacy here. Along the shore near the Mondello Palace (see below), the **Charleston Le Terrazze** shimmers white against the sea—a splendid restaurant, almost offshore at viale Regina Elena. Call for reservations. Tel: (091) 45-01-71. You can get to Mondello easily by bus from Palermo.

Staying in Mondello is a quiet alternative to a hotel in Palermo if you don't want to be in the city's center. The **Mondello Palace** is set in lush palm gardens and has its own swimming pool, tennis courts, and private beach. Ask for a sea-view room with terrace (rates are reasonable). The **Villa Esperia**, with its own beach, is relatively inexpensive.

EXCURSIONS FROM PALERMO

A morning bus trip to Monreale and an afternoon train excursion to Cefalù can be easily arranged. Each town has a majestic Norman cathedral, and Cefalù adds the pleasures of a beach resort.

Monreale

William II (a.k.a. the Good), Roger II's grandson, was the guiding light behind the Monreale cathedral, which he had built in 1174. According to legend, William was resting in his deer park when the Madonna appeared to him, promising to show him where his grandfather had hidden treasure if he would use it for a holy purpose, and so we have Monreale.

Though William was a man of spiritual depth, his detractors claimed the story was a ruse to justify the vast sums he spent on construction of the cathedral. As heir to the creator of the Cappella Palatina and the cathedral at Cefalù, he could hardly build a simple shrine. However, politics entered in as well. Walter of the Mill, the bishop of Palermo, was busy creating a political constituency of his own, attracting barons and prelates. By building a new bishopric near and equal to Palermo's, William would be ensured of a direct link to the pope, a pipeline the pontiff supported. When Walter heard this he decided to build a new cathedral in Palermo (the present structure), whose grandeur, it turned out, never threatened Monreale's.

"If the Palatine chapel is a Medieval carol, then Monreale is the *Canterbury Tales*," wrote Vincent Cronin in *The Golden Honeycomb*. Against a gold background, cycles of the Old and New Testament unfold, played out in 130 large panels inscribed in Greek and Latin. A curious presence is Thomas à Becket (middle lower right at the altar), since William the Good, the cathedral's creator, had Henry II of England for a father-in-law, and Becket had been martyred only a few years earlier by Henry. It's the earliest portrait of Becket yet identified.

The dominating mosaic is of the Pantocrator, brilliantly executed for so vast a work (his hand alone is six feet long). The mosaics themselves represent the beginning of a change from the formal style of Byzantium: draperies swirl, gestures relax, and rhythms are smoother.

Above the royal throne, at left, William receives the crown from Christ, and above the bishop's altar he offers the crown to the Madonna. In a chapel south of the choir the two Williams, the Bad and the Good, are buried, and an inscription marks the place where the body of Saint Louis, brother of the later Sicilian king Charles of Anjou, lay on its way back to France from his fateful Tunisian crusade. Some say his heart is buried here, for the Sicilians couldn't bear to part with him entirely. Charles himself was parted with easily, however, during the Vespers revolt, when he and those Angevins who weren't slaughtered were thrown out.

The treasury and the view of Palermo from the roof are good diversions. So, too, are the cloisters, which are extraordinarily impressive and peaceful, a joy for those who want to read a book in a sunny corner. Intricacy is everywhere in the patterns of the 104 arches suspended by slender columns and enhanced with mosaics and carved inlays. Taken together, the capitals are a tour de force of Romanesque stone carving, with themes varying from daily life to the Bible to pagan Mithraic sacrifice. A belvedere, reached from outside the cloisters, opens onto a panorama of the Conca d'Oro valley—now a victim of urban sprawl. (Monreale is located on Monte Pelligrino, about 45 minutes southwest of Palermo by city bus.) A prettier scene unfolds a couple of miles south of Monreale in Contrada Lenzitti (on route 186), where **La Botte** is a good place to lunch, with an open terrace (Tel: 091-41-40-51; taxis are available).

The Vespers revolt not only ended the Angevin era in Sicily, it brought the house of Aragón into the European spotlight and ended the papal authority's hold on international politics. Sponsoring the Anjou regime had been a disastrous idea for the papacy. According to Steven Runciman, author of *The Sicilian Vespers,* "Their choice of Charles of Anjou is easy to understand; but it was fatal. When Charles's power was broken by the Vespers at Palermo they were too inextricably involved. The story led on to the . . . Babylonian captivity of Avignon, and through schism and disillusion to the troubles of the Reformation."

Cefalù

Cefalù, revealed gradually as the train approaches from Palermo, is unforgettable. An enormous cliff rises like a tidal wave; the town huddles below, dominated by the twin campanile of the Cathedral of Cefalù.

Now a lively summer resort, Cefalù (on the coast, some 50 km/30 miles east of Palermo) has been inhabited probably as long as Sicily has, as witnessed by the prehistoric relics found in outlying grottoes. Carthage established a colony here, and Greeks, Byzantines, and Arabs followed. In 1063 Count Roger relieved the Arabs of command. It is to his son, King Roger, that we owe the extraordinary honey-colored **Cathedral**. One night when he was caught in a storm at sea, he vowed to build a cathedral—a regal ex-voto—at whatever safe harbor he found. The harmonious Romanesque façade that unfolds as you approach from below is lovely, the church even more so as you see it in the round. But it is the interior, being restored to its original simplicity after Baroque errors, that elicits the greatest admiration. The Christ who follows you with his mosaic eyes is unlike any other Pantocrator, and many observers consider it an unsurpassed representation, one where mercy is mingled with justice. The wisp of hair that has fallen over his forehead, the softened eyes, and the casual robes combine to create a portrait of power and majesty. The Bible he holds is open to "I am the light of the world," in Latin and Greek. The Madonna, too, is a rare creation and would be admired more if the Christ were not of such beauty. The strong-winged angels are transitional in Christian iconography—between the winged bull of Jewish art and the delicate winged messengers who would come later. In the left transept stands a *Madonna and Child* by Antonello Gagini, and in the narthex is a curious cat on the coat of arms of Monsignor Chat, who consecrated the cathedral.

Directly in front of the Duomo is the **Osteria del Duomo**, probably the best place to dine in Cefalù (Tel: 0921-218-38). Pastry and ice cream are the tours de force of the bakery across the piazza at the corso Ruggero.

Via Mandralisca, in front of the cathedral's piazza, leads down to the **Museo Comunale Mandralisca**, which contains one of the world's greatest portraits, *Unknown Man* (1465–1470) by Antonello da Messina. His smile, sensuous and sly, has been called quintessentially Sicilian, as mysterious as that of the *Mona Lisa*. Among the archaeological relics here is a rare krater (Greek vase) from the Aeolian island of Lipari showing a tuna merchant arguing with a customer (fourth century B.C.).

On the corso Ruggero is a fragment of the **Osterio Magno**, Roger II's palace, with its graceful Norman touches still visible despite the weeds. In front is the **Osterio Piccolo**, the residence of the powerful Ventimiglia counts, who dominated the Madonie mountains to the south.

If you decide to stay here—and it's an excellent choice, since the city is among Sicily's prettiest and cleanest—the best hotels are about a mile from Cefalù. The **Kalura** and **Le Calette** are pretty little harbor-side resort hotels with swimming pools. Driving is easier, although you can go by bus or taxi. The **Carlton Riviera** is a modern, fully equipped hotel with a miraculous view of Cefalù and the surrounding sea; there are bus connections to town. The **Baia del Capitano**, located in an olive grove, has a private beach, pool, sauna, tennis court, and such. The price is right too.

In Cefalù, the **Riva del Sole** is pleasantly located across from the beach and very reasonably priced. In the summer the road here is a long snarl of traffic, however.

From Cefalù, trips to Solunto, Bagheria, and some of the small towns in the Madonie mountains are convenient by car. **Solunto**, a seaside town (about 40 km/25 miles back toward Palermo) dating from the fourth century B.C.—with Phoenician, Greek, and Roman relics on a site above the sea and mountains—is one of the most evocative of these ancient settings. Much of the island, even Mt. Etna, can be seen by taking bus excursions organized by Cefalù travel agencies.

Bagheria

Bagheria, near Solunto, is something else entirely, a bizarre blend of decaying 18th-century Baroque villas, the most famous of which is the **Villa Palagonia**, the creation of a deformed prince who decorated his garden wall with 62 grotesques. Goethe catalogs the eccentricities carefully in his *Italian Journey*. The interior, though in sad ruins, can be appreciated still; it is easy to imagine what the room of cracked mirrors (to make everyone appear to be deformed?) looked like in its original state. In the prince's day, entire rooms were decorated with fragments of picture frames and broken glass, pyramids of porcelain teacups, and marble reptiles, and in the chapel there was a huge crucifix from which Saint Francis hung by his neck. The town, known as a Mafia stronghold, is surprisingly like the South Bronx (Hollywood's version) for so monied an environment. Like much of the South, the town hides its treasures behind dilapidated façades; an odd cachet is attached to a trashy outside hiding a chic interior.

Enjoyable—and less bizarre—is the **Villa Cattolica**, a contemporary-art museum where the works of the late Sicilian painter Renato Guttuso are exhibited. An entirely delightful setting in Bagheria is the little town house restaurant **I Vespri**, especially pleasant when the roof terrace is open. The exceptional cuisine is a mix of Sicilian and French (as are the owners), with seafood crêpes and linguine Wellington. Since it has now been discovered by chic Palermo, reservations are advised (corso Butera 423; Tel: 091-93-40-40). A simple trattoria, **Don Ciccio**, at via Stazione 8, is known throughout the island as one of the fine family-run places that serves the traditional Sicilian menu without pretense or elevated prices (Tel: 091-93-43-66).

Though the days of the Leopard are but a memory, Sicily's noble traditions are lovingly maintained at nearby **Regaleali**, a family estate and vineyard (producing one of Sicily's finest wines). Countess Franca and Count Giuseppe Tasca d'Almeira have arranged several weeks a year for cooking enthusiasts to live within the castle keep and learn the artistry of their cook, Mario lo Menzo, considered the last Monzù. *Monzù* (from Monsieur) was a term given to French master chefs who became fashionable with southern Italian noble families during a brief French reign in 19th-century Naples. A rare and expensive week. For information, write Ann Yonkers, 3802 Jocelyn Street NW, Washington DC, 20015; Tel: (202) 362-8228; or Anna Tasca Lanza, viale Principessa Giovanna 9, 90139 Palermo; Tel: (091) 45-07-27; Fax: (0921) 54-27-83.

The Madonie Towns

It takes a bit of driving along tortuous but scenic roads to reach the Madonie towns south of Cefalù. Castles and churches here are the legacy of Norman and feudal times, but the region owes its charm to its people and atmosphere, its food and way of life—in other words, the things that are the essence of a Sicily that is fast disappearing. From **Castelbuono**, continue to **Petralia Sottana** and **Petralia Soprana** (this mountaintop town is one of the most beautiful in Sicily, with its winding streets of sand-colored palazzi and churches), then west to **Polizzi Generosa**, where you might want to stop at the tiny **Itria** for fresh pasta with asparagus in spring, or hearty mixed grills or pizza (via Itria 3; Tel: 0921-885-43). If the mayor (*sindaco*) is dining there, he may be able to find someone to show you the town. The cost is modest, probably about Ł25,000. Or head east to **Gangi** and **Nicosia**. Stop and enjoy what you see at will.

Accommodations are few in the mountains, and fewer are very good. An exception is the **Milocca** in Castelbuono, which is beautifully situated and has a pool and riding horses. For a simple chalet with outstanding meals, go to

Isnello's **Club Alpino Siciliano**, near Polizzi Generosa, an ideal mountain retreat (but with camplike rooms).

If you prefer to stay in Cefalù, you'll find that travel agencies arrange trips to the mountains as far as Gangi, which is the best way to go for those uncomfortable driving the hairpin turns of mountain roads, If you go in spring, the vast splashes of purple *sulla* and yellow mustard plants along with frothy almond trees will highlight the drama even further.

SEGESTA

Southwest of Palermo, more than halfway to Trapani, Segesta's lonely ruins evoke the romantic spirit. A **Doric temple** sits on a flower-dotted hillside, the Classical ideal of order amid wild nature. Along with nearby Erice, Segesta was settled by the Elymi about the 12th century B.C. Although little is known of them, it seems they were of Greek and Trojan ancestry and certainly got along better with the new Greek colonizers than the native Sicani and Siculi did, sharing many aspects of the former's religious and cultural life. The temple's singular charm lies partly in its roughness. Never finished, the columns were left smooth in preparation for fluting; bosses that held the columns' hoist ropes can be seen along the steps. The foundation for the *cella,* the shrine inside, was laid but never built upon. Why it was never completed is the subject of speculation; some think the temple itself was begun only to attract Greek backing for the Elymi's interminable struggles with Selinunte to the south. Down the hill toward the amphitheater, the two defense towers and a fortified gate were used in frequent battles with Selinunte and Syracuse.

The **Amphitheater**, still used for performances, is well preserved. Situated with the Greek genius for capturing the best possible view from the *cavea,* or seating area, it looks out on sea and mountains.

Segesta can be reached by train from Palermo; day trips organized by CIT tour operators in Palermo visit Segesta and Erice.

An important detour southward for "Garibaldini" is **Calatafimi**, scene of a famous 1870 battle; red shirts and scarves are sold as souvenirs. The **Mille Pini Hotel and Restaurant**, at piazza Fosco Vivona 2 here, is a good road stop (Tel: 0924-95-12-60).

ERICE

Northwest of Segesta, along the coast above Trapani, Monte Erice (pronounced AY-ree-chay) rises abruptly from the surrounding plains of salt fields and windmills. From its peak the coast of Africa can be seen to the southwest beyond puffs of clouds that drift past the nearly 2,300-foot summit. Once a beacon for Phoenician sailors, Erice has enchanted mythmakers and travellers throughout recorded history.

Atop Monte Eryx, as it was called by the Phoenicians, a temple was built to pay tribute to Astarte, a Mediterranean fertility goddess. "A different goddess, this Eryx Astarte," wrote D. H. Lawrence, "in her prehistoric dark smiling, watching the fearful sunsets beyond the Egades." The temple stood on the rim of land where Roman, Greek, and Norman ruins now lie. The Pozzo di Venere (Venus's Well) was the fate of maidens cast down as a sacrifice to the goddess after a ritual orgy. (That version is from guides who tell stories with drama; its real use is unknown.) The historian Jacob Burckhardt described the festivities as practiced in the eastern Mediterranean to honor this goddess-mother of all living things: "Joyous shouts and mourning wails, orgiastic dances and lugubrious flute music, prostitution of women and self-castration of men had always accompanied this cult of the sensual life of nature."

When spring came, a flock of doves would be released from Erice to fly to Africa. In nine days they would return, preceded by a red dove, who was Astarte, ensuring a bountiful harvest after the summer to come.

The Medieval maze of steep streets and alleys (rubber soles are needed) that run up and down the town is lined with gateways that look in on courtyards flowering with tubs of plants, giving the town a domestic, contented air. Pottery of dark earth tones and almond pastries are Erice's specialties. Lots of pretty cafés here serve madeleine-light sweets to enjoy with your coffee. Before leaving, stop at the main piazza to see the *Annunciation* by Gagini in the museum there.

Couscous, the North African grain, is the thing to eat now that you're in the west; also sample some new wines, Feudo di Fiori, Donnafugata, Steri, and Etna. Honey-sweet desserts as well as almond concoctions are found widely in this part of Sicily, where ties with North Africa are strongest. For dining in Erice, go to the **Ciclope**, with an outdoor garden, or to the **Taverna di Re Alceste** on viale Conte Pepoli (Tel: 0923-86-91-39; closed Wednesdays and November. Or you may want to go down to nearby Trapani for dinner along the harbor—see below. To enjoy the town's night magic, stay at the **Ermione**, with a swimming pool and views of the Egadi Islands. The **Elimo** is at the center of town, converted from a 17th-century palazzo. If you prefer a beach setting, ask for a sea-view room at the **Astoria Park**, also with a pool and good restaurant.

If you are driving, which will be easier now that you're away from Palermo, the resort area of **San Vito lo Capo**— north of Erice, where the pretty cape's white beaches are relatively unspoiled by tourism—also makes for a fine base from which to explore the area. The **Hotel Capo San Vito** here is a comfortable retreat.

The lovely town of **Scopello**, on the same peninsula but closer to Palermo, is a perfect spot to overnight while visiting the **Zingaro Natural Reserve**, a spectacular combination of mountain and sea views. The place to stay is the comfortable and friendly **Pensione Trantino**, whose owners take pleasure in helping their guests enjoy the peninsula.

TRAPANI

Trapani, which stretches along the west coast below Erice, is a port city that looks so North African it almost seems like a set out of *Casablanca*. The dockside trattorias here make good fish couscous. Go also to **P & G**, an excellent and popular restaurant on via Spalti, more elegant than the dockside places. There you'll feast on shrimp in Cognac, grilled meats, *palombo* ("dogfish") *alla marinara,* and a sugary *cassata.* A wonderful fish trattoria is **Peppe's**; like P & G it is near the railroad station. The catch of the day is the specialty.

Coral-work was a local art form during the 17th century, and some notable examples, even a *presepio* (Christmas village), are found in the **Museo Pepoli**, which also has a good collection of paintings. The **Church of Santa Maria del Gesù** contains a Della Robbia *Madonna* under a marble *baldacchino* by Antonello Gagini.

The Egadi Islands

From Trapani ferries leave for the **Egadi Islands**—Favignana, Levanzo, and Marettimo. On **Levanzo**, which is sparsely populated, the Grotto del Genovese contains Paleolithic drawings of great beauty and a Neolithic group of paintings, both sets discovered in 1949. Getting to the cave is an adventure, however. You can rent a mule from Giuseppe Castiglione, the cave's owner (Tel: 0923-92-40-32; 10,000 lire; 6 miles round trip). Or you can take a boat from the port of Cala Dogana (arrange a price with the boatman), which is a good way to see the grottoes and white sand beaches that dot the shoreline. To stay the night, reserve at the **Paradiso**, where all eight rooms in the pensione have sea views and the little restaurant serves good home cooking. **Marettimo**, the most distant of the islands, remains very much in its natural state, thanks to the lack of roads and cars on the island. Good walking shoes will come in handy for its cliffs and valleys, fishing villages and caves. Small seafood restaurants are open on the island during the summer months, and rooms are also available in private homes. If seclusion is your goal, this would be the place. **Favignana**, the large island, is better equipped for tourism, though its undeveloped western side is the more attractive.

Isola di Pantelleria

From Trapani you can also take a ferry to the volcanic island of Pantelleria, which can be reached from Trapani and Palermo by air as well.

Pantelleria, way off by itself, is so close to the African continent it could easily belong to Tunisia. Stark and fascinating, it is famous for its raisin wine, Tanit. Made from the *zibibbo* grape, this sweet and sometimes sparkling wine is usually called Moscato di Pantelleria. The dark earth is dotted with vines of capers as well, which contribute sizably to the economy.

Dammuso houses are tomblike cells used by early inhabitants, somewhat similar to the *nuraghi* of Sardinia. Tourist villages are built in this style to try to keep the island from becoming just another hotel-strewn resort. The **Cossyra Club** is a full-service hotel with pool and a restaurant that conjures up delightful island combinations such as salads of capers, meat, and potato, or sea bass seasoned with parsley, oil, and capers. For dessert ask for sweet ravioli or *budino de zibibbo*—a pudding made from grape sugar. Accommodations in private homes are the least expensive option. The **Zzú Natale** is a fine seafood spot. Stay at the pretty **Del Porto** if you're a scuba diver.

Mozia

The mysterious island of Mozia was an eighth-century B.C. Phoenician base; today, you can visit the Whitaker villa museum of ceramics and other objects from that period as well as a house decorated with fourth-century B.C. mosaics. At Tophet, on the opposite side of the island, is a Punic (Phoenician) burial ground dedicated to their goddess Tanit, to whom children were sacrificed, a practice discontinued during the fifth century B.C.

To get to Mozia, turn off the highway south of the Trapani airport. Signs say Mozia, Stagnone, or Ragattis. The custodian will row you across the narrow waterway. Tel: (0923) 95-95-98.

MARSALA

Marsala was founded at the westernmost tip of Sicily by Phoenicians during the eighth century B.C. as a trading port and resettled 400 years later by those latter-day Phoenicians, the Carthaginians. Then called Lilibeum, Marsala continued to have strategic importance under the Arabs, who gave it its present name, a derivation of *Marsa Allah*, the harbor of Allah. In 1773 the Englishman John Woodhouse began a profitable business by shipping the local wine—with alcohol added as a preservative—to England. Marsala, so-called, soon became a popular drink, rivaling sherry. In 1806 Benjamin Ingham and his nephew Whitaker founded another prosperous Marsala-exporting company, which eventually was taken over by the Sicilian entrepreneur Vincenzo Florio. The house of Florio, with new owners, still flourishes, and you can visit the premises at via Florio 1, south of the town on the Lungomare Mediterraneo. The Rallo family produces Donnafugata as well, a good wine now exported.

During World War II, Marsala was almost leveled by bombing, and the city has been substantially rebuilt. In the **Cathedral** (a war survivor) you can see a fine assemblage of Gagini statuary. The new **Museo degli Arazzi**, behind the cathedral, houses a fine collection of 16th-century Flemish tapestries illustrating the life of the emperor Vaspasian, the gift of King Philip II of Spain. One of the most important Punic discoveries occurred off Marsala in 1971, when a warship nearly 114 feet long was found offshore. Once powered by 48 rowers, the ship is now on view at the **Archaeological Museum**, at the far southern end of the city. At nearby **Lilybaeum** a third-century B.C. Roman villa can be seen, especially for its mosaics.

Marsala's big day in modern times was May 11, 1860, when Garibaldi and the Thousand landed, the first footfall of the revolution.

A harbor-side dinner at **Zio Ciccio** may be in order before heading south.

SELINUNTE

Moving southeast along the coast about 40 km (25 miles), you'll come to the extensive remains of the seventh-century B.C. Greek city of Selinunte, which is spread over three hills. Much of the marble (travertine) would still be here if the Spanish hadn't carted it off to build their palaces and churches. Segesta and Selinunte were always at odds over territory, but Segesta had the edge because Carthage was an ally; Hannibal destroyed much of Selinunte in 409 B.C. An earthquake during the seventh century A.D. delivered the coup de grace.

At the center of the area is the **Acropolis**, and to the west is the sanctuary of Demeter, where more than 12,000 votive objects have been found around the graves, which stretch for miles along the coast. The three temples to the east are in the process of being restored; the one called Temple E is now recognizable, with its righted columns. (It is missing the lovely metopes from the frieze that ran across the top of the columns, however, because they are in the archaeological museum in Palermo.) Temple G was one of the largest in Greek Sicily, left unfinished when the slaves saw Hannibal's ships heading toward them in 409 B.C. Some of the huge unworked column blocks lie on the ground nearby; other half-cut ones can be seen at the nearby Cusa quarries, with the chisel marks of the laborers still visible. On the Acropolis itself the familiar grid plan is evident; to the north of it are remains of the residential section.

Another attraction in this corner of Sicily is **Il Vigneto**, housed in a hacienda-like building with a wide veranda overlooking fields of grain and fruit trees. Il Vigneto is the realization of a dream long held by proprietor Marco Bursi, who left his legal practice to prepare dishes using the best of the local products. Couscous, with fish in summer and meat in winter, is a specialty, but you might want to try the *tre assagi*—three ample tastes of pasta sauces, perhaps with salmon *seppia,* or just tomatoes and herbs. The fish is apt to have been caught that morning at Porto Palo, which was once the port for Selinunte (now a resort town). To find Il Vigneto, take the shore road from Selinunte east to Porto Palo. Turn left at the hotel Miramare and continue until you see the sign (about 1 mile) for Il Vigneto. The address is officially Bivio (crossroads) Porto Palo–Menfi (Tel: 0925-717-32); they're closed Sunday evening and Mondays except in summer. You might want to return to **Porto Palo** later for a swim or to stay at the **Miramare**, a simple, fresh hotel with fine views of the gentle surf a few yards from the windows.

If you could drive blindfolded from Selinunte to Agrigento, you would miss nothing except Sciacca (below), for the rest of the coast is a long line of unattractive cement-block construction.

SCIACCA AND AREA

This part of Sicily is a little out of the way. If time is no problem for you, it's a pleasant place to explore. Especially tempting are the spa town of **Sciacca**, the white village of Caltabellotta, and the Baroque town of Sambuca in the interior. Sciacca, on two levels above the sea, is a pleasant surprise: quaint enough to draw tourists but not enough to be overrun. It's a thermal spa, as a stop at the newly reno-vated **Grande Albergo delle Terme**, sparkling white on a long promenade above the sea, will reveal. **Monte San Calogero**, about 8 km (5 miles) to the northeast, is the spa's origin, a thermal station hollowed out by Daedalus (legend has it). Before him the Copper Age residents of the area made human, animal, and grain sacrifices to placate the steaming gods below the ground.

High above Sciacca in the Sicani mountains to the north-east is **Caltabellotta**, a sun-bleached Medieval town where hermits and monks sought solitude in the rock caves that dot the surrounding woods. The **Chiesa Madre** here was created in 1090 by Count Roger, who must have enjoyed the view across the "African Sea," as Pirandello called it, and eastward as far as Etna. But the city's most important date is 1299, when Charles of Valois, the Angevin, and King Frederick of Aragon signed the Treaty of Caltabellotta, ending the war of the Sicilian Vespers.

Sambuca di Sicilia, to the west, is delightfully floodlit by night, turning its Baroque palaces gold. Until 1921 the little town was called Sambuca Zabut, for the Emir Zabut's castle, now in ruins. Adjoining it is the tiny Arab quarter of seven

streets and a merlon tower with an ancient clock. Sambuca
has its own wax museum, complete with Chopin, George
Sand, Garibaldi, and other notables, in the **Palazzo Panitteri**.
Have dinner at the **Barone di Salinas**, part of a baronial estate
that is now the property of Tommaso di Prima, a local farmer
who bought the estate—his lifelong fantasy—and who enjoys showing visitors about the premises.

AGRIGENTO

"Fairest of all mortal cities" was Pindar's tribute to Akragas,
now Agrigento. Its location in a rolling valley and the grandeur of the long line of Doric temples drew high praise
from visiting Greeks, who found life here much as it was in
Athens, a worldly blend of philosophy, science, and art.

To enjoy the temples fully, stay at the **Villa Athena**, located
just across a tropical garden from the fifth-century B.C.
Tempio della Concordia. Seen from the hotel's terrace,
dawn's brilliant pink light, the gold-red sunset, and the
floodlit night view of the site rival one another in beauty. In
Sicily's early spring the fields are covered with pink and
white almond blossoms, heralding the festival in early February that brings folk dancers from around the world to dance
at the temple. (The hotel is a bit run-down; you're there for
the view.)

The city was established when residents of Gela moved
west along the coast in 582 B.C. to take advantage of the area's
fine harbor (now the overbuilt Porto Empedocle) and im-
mensely rich grain fields (which would feed the Roman
legions a few hundred years later). The first ruler was
Phalaris, whose tyrannical acts included roasting his enemies
in a huge bronze bull, perhaps harking back to a Rhodian bull
cult. That he was assassinated is hardly a surprise, even if not
all the tales of his treachery are true. Carthage, by then grown
from Phoenician outpost to major power, was not happy to
see another important city expanding across the sea and
launched an invasion in 480 B.C. With the aid of Gelon, tyrant
of Gela and Syracuse, Akragas triumphed, winning 70 years of
peace for Sicily—her Grecian golden age—until the final
defeat by the Carthaginians in 406 B.C.

In a time when Greek philosophers were examining the
very basis of prescientific understanding, Empedocles of
Akragas developed the theory of the four elements: that all
things are compounded of earth, air, fire, and water, with love
and strife acting as alternating currents. Unlike the Eleatics (at

Velia, across the Strait of Messina), Empedocles insisted that the senses, not just the mind, if properly used, were routes to knowledge. His *On Nature* covers subjects from astronomy to zoology, and his work in physics is basic to the field today. In later years he apparently believed himself a god, having already been a bush, a bird, and a fish. To die a death worthy of a god he is supposed to have leaped into the crater at Etna. (Some contend he died in Greece.) Of his native city he said, "The Agrigentines enjoy luxury as if they would die tomorrow, but they build palaces as if to live forever."

Agrigento's wealth was so enormous as to be eccentric: Young girls even had tombs built for their birds. Although a dictatorship, the city did not maintain an army of highly disciplined warriors (one military directive limited soldiers to using only two pillows per bed). During the Punic wars Rome attacked Carthage at Agrigento, which Carthage controlled by that time. Victorious in 241 B.C., Rome sold the people into slavery and used the grain to feed its armies, while the corrupt Roman governor Verres collected a crippling corn tax. The city subsequently fell to the Saracens, who were routed by the Norman Count Roger in 1087.

From the northern entrance to the **Valley of the Temples**, the road leads up to the temples of Heracles, Concord, and Hera, and then on up to the Rupe Athena, the most ancient part of the settlement. The warm-ocher temples were originally painted with white stucco and are Doric in construction, simple and sturdy, yet elegant in this setting of fields and, in the spring, wild flowers. The **Temple of Heracles**, reached through a lovely garden, is the oldest. Built about 520 B.C., it is still scarred by the fires set by Carthaginian invaders. Once richly decorated and considered the most beautiful of the temples, it housed a splendid statue of Heracles whose chin and lips, according to Cicero, were worn smooth by adoration of the faithful.

On high is the **Temple of Concord**, focus of a dramatic approach along a road bordered with tropical plants and ancient tombs, a route that's even more theatrical by night, when it's floodlit. Up close the tawny tones of the temple vary from pale yellows to rich ochers. One of the best-preserved Doric temples in the world, it exudes solidity and self-confidence. During the sixth century A.D. the Tempio della Concordia was converted into a church, thereby escaping the vengeance of Christian iconoclasts. When the church was created the columns were walled in and the walls of the central Greek shrine, the *cella,* were removed. Beyond the temple to the east is the sacrificial altar. A sacred enclosure containing shrines and niches for ex-votos originally surrounded each temple.

If you continue to the top of the ridge, you'll see the **Temple of Hera Lacinia** (called Giunone) (470 B.C.), which overlooks the valley. Still higher is the Norman **Church of San Biagio**, in which the temple of Demeter is incorporated, at the top of a road worn with ancient cart tracks.

You'll need a guide to climb to the Rupe Athena. At the top, down rickety steps, is a shrine to Demeter and Persephone around which hundreds of votive objects have been excavated. Beneath the shrine is an elaborate system of terra-cotta pipes used during the underground rituals of a water cult.

In the section down the hill, on the far side of the road, stand the ruins of part of the enormous **Temple of Olympian Zeus** (Giove Olimpico), the largest of Doric temples. The enormous stone sunbather on the ground, called the Sleeping Giant, is a copy of one of 38 *telamones*—figures used as columns—that once decorated the temple. The original of this figure as well as a scale model of the temple are in the Museo Archeologico (see below).

Chthonic rituals took place on the round altars and around the three-column remnant of the **Tempio di Castore e Polluce**, which is a pastiche of several buildings. Some of the earth-goddess shrines were built during the seventh century B.C., when such cults were popular.

Agrigento today, apart from the temples, is a hideous example of urban sprawl—hideous to us, that is, not to the Agrigentines, whose former homes were damp, poorly heated, and inadequately lighted. Whole blocks of older, quainter homes collapsed some years ago when the substructure of the town—a maze of Roman pipes and whatnot—caved in. This tragedy made the brutal cement-block apartment houses look like palaces to many of the relocated.

Although the modern urban sprawl in the distance is uninviting, Agrigento's small, attractive Medieval center is partially preserved, despite the presence of such modern stores as Fendi. The **Museo Archeologico** is well organized, well lit, and a pleasure to visit. It houses an impressive collection of antiquities that includes a child's sarcophagus depicting his birth, death, and journey to the next world; and Phaedra's sarcophagus, Greek in design but probably Roman in workmanship, decorated with scenes of her tragic love affair.

Nearby in the section of Agrigento called Caos is the **Casa di**

Pirandello and a museum by the tree where his ashes are buried. Of Caos, his birthplace, Pirandello said: "One night in June I dropped down like a firefly beneath a huge pine tree standing all on its own in an olive grove on the edge of a blue clay plateau overlooking the African sea." He would scarcely recognize his Caos today, full as it is of condominiums and second homes. A beautiful new addition to Caos, however, is the hotel **Kaos**, owned by Francesco d'Alessandro, proprietor of the Villa Athena. The villa in Caos has been remodeled with great attention to form and color, and the swimming pool is exceptionally lovely, a white oval of blue water surrounded by bougainvillaea, with olive trees and the deep blue sea beyond. From each room, Pirandello's tree on the adjoining property is poetically framed. There is also a **Hotel Pirandello** in Agrigento; it is quite comfortable.

Apart from the Villa Athena, which has a good restaurant that serves pumpkin sauces with pasta in the fall, try the **Taverna Mosé** for dinner, where the beefsteak is seasoned with fresh herbs and the *falsomagro* is delicious (*falsomagro* is a roast stuffed with meats, cheese, vegetables, and bread crumbs, thus "falsely thin," as the name says). **Del Vigneto** and **Le Caprice**, both near the temples, serve good grilled meats. Try the wonderful red Regaleali wine called Rosso del Conto.

Because of the highway system, Syracuse is reached most quickly from Agrigento by taking the dismal highway to Catania on the eastern coast and then heading south past the industrial zone into Syracuse. However, a nicer route would be to meander through the southern and eastern coastal towns (see "The Baroque Southeast," below).

SYRACUSE

Once greater than even Athens, and briefly capital of Byzantium when Muslims threatened the Eastern Empire, Syracuse (Siracusa in Italian) now shows off its Classical past in an archaeological zone just outside the modern city. But its greatest beauty today is Ortygia, an island of Baroque fantasy connected to the modern city by a bridge.

Before the Corinthian Greeks arrived in 734 B.C. and moved them out, Siculi inhabited this part of the island. The Greeks valued Syracuse's natural harbors for their beauty and defensibility, and so the harbors often saw violent battles, as Thucydides chronicles faithfully in *The Peloponnesian War*. Though tyrants dominated Greek Sicily, the court

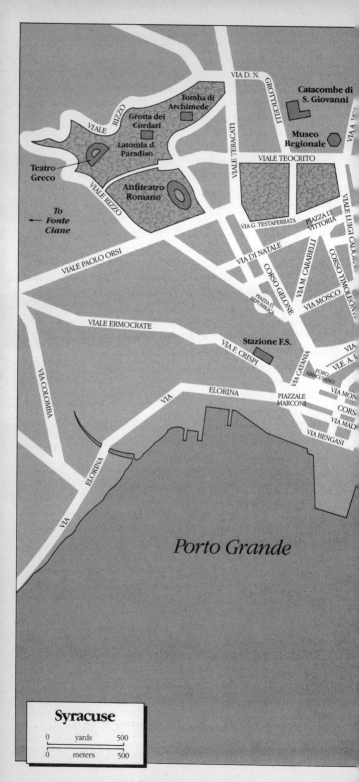

VIA D. N.

GROTTICELLI

Catacombe di
S. Giovanni

Tomba di
Archimede

Grotta dei
Cordari

Museo
Regionale

VIA V. G.

VIALE RIZZO

Latomia d.
Paradiso

VIALE TERACATI

VIALE TEOCRITO

Teatro
Greco

VIALE RIZZO

Anfiteatro
Romano

To
Fonte
Ciane

VIALE LUIGI CAD...

VIA G. TESTAFERRATA

PIAZZA D'
VITTORIA

VIALE PAOLO ORSI

VIA DI NATALE

CORSO GELONE

VIA M. CARABELLI

CORSO TIMOLEON...

VIA MOSCO

PIAZZA D.
REPUBBLICA

VIALE ERMOCRATE

Stazione F.S.

VIA F. CRISPI

VIA

VLE. A. D...

VIA COLOMBA

VIA CATANIA

FORO
SIRACUSANO

VIA MON...

VIA

ELORINA

PIAZZALE
MARCONI

CORS...

VIA MALT...

VIA BENGASI

VIA

ELORINA

VIA

Porto Grande

Syracuse

| 0 | yards | 500 |
| 0 | meters | 500 |

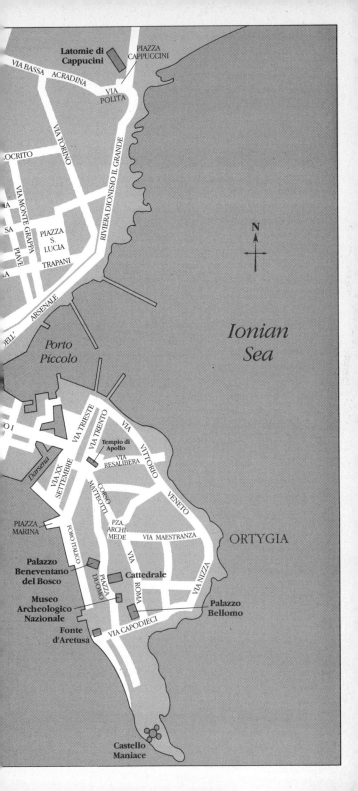

Latomie di Cappucini

PIAZZA CAPPUCCINI

VIA BASSA

ACRADINA

VIA POLITA

VIA TORINO

LOCRITO

RIVIERA DIONISIO IL GRANDE

VIA MONTE GRAPPA

SA

PIAVE

PIAZZA S. LUCIA

TRAPANI

A

ARSENALE

DELL'

Porto Piccolo

N

Ionian Sea

O I

Darsena

VIA TRIESTE

VIA TRENTO

Tempio di Apollo

VIA RESALIBERA

VIA VITTORIO

VIA XX SETTEMBRE

CORSO MATTEOTTI

VENETO

PIAZZA MARINA

FORO ITALICO

PZA. ARCHI MEDE

VIA MAESTRANZA

ORTYGIA

Palazzo Beneventano del Bosco

PIAZZA DUOMO

Cattedrale

VIA ROMA

VIA NIZZA

Museo Archeologico Nazionale

Palazzo Bellomo

Fonte d'Aretusa

VIA CAPODIECI

Castello Maniace

of Hieron attracted Pindar and Aeschylus, who probably wrote *Prometheus Bound* for its theater. The tyrant Dionysius, who defeated the Carthaginians in 397 B.C., was a military genius and poet manqué. After years of hissing at him whenever he read his poetry in competitions, Athenians finally awarded him a medal, but the honor prompted Dionysius to treat himself to an orgy so intense that he died as a result. His son Dionysius II was once admired by Plato, who was always on the lookout for a philosopher king, but Plato left in dismay at his tyranny. Timoleon (343–337 B.C.) gave Syracuse the closest thing to good government it would ever have, rebuilding and concluding a treaty with its perennial enemy, Carthage. He died quietly, a rarity for the time.

When the Romans invaded Syracuse, they "failed to reckon with the ability of Archimedes," as Polybius put it, for Archimedes' genius had helped create the brilliantly strategic fort of Euryalus as well as ingenious war machines. When the Greek forces were finally beaten, however, Rome sent Verres to govern Sicily. His habit of taking every Greek statue or frieze—no matter how large—was reported by Cicero in the *Verrine Orations*.

Syracuse would not flower again until the Spanish made it a Baroque fantasy, especially the city's island of Ortygia, where women still carry decorated lacy fans in summer and cover their shoulders with embroidered shawls.

Ortygia

Ortygia's charm is seductive, especially when night brings out the Baroque shadows. By day, the delightful museum at the **Palazzo Bellomo** is open, and has another version of the *Annunciata* by Antonello da Messina—a damaged masterpiece; Caravaggio's *Burial of St. Lucy,* moved from the church of Santa Lucia; and a section devoted to folklore, with charming *presepi.*

At the nearby spacious, windswept promenade, a freshwater fountain flows into the sea—although the **Fonte d'Aretusa** may be salted by now, owing to the earthquakes that have split the land around it. The last recorded taste was when Nelson took on freshwater provisions on his way to the Battle of the Nile. The fountain, legend says, is actually the nymph Arethusa, who, fleeing the river god Alpheus, jumped into the sea in Greece. Artemis changed her into a fountain, and she travelled undersea across the Mediterranean and emerged here, with Alpheus in pursuit. The Delphic Oracle confirmed the story: "An isle, Ortygia, lies on the misty ocean, over against Trinacria [as Greece called three-cornered Sicily], where the mouth of Alpheus bubbles mingling with the bubbles of broad Arethusa." Strabo also reported that a cup thrown into the river at Olympia in Greece reappears here.

Ortygia's most popular square by night is **piazza Duomo**, the most beautiful piazza in Sicily, bounded by the splendid cathedral and grand palaces. The Duomo's site was sacred to the Siculi, who built a temple here, which was to have been followed by another one dedicated to Athena, some columns of which appear in the present church. Because the fleet-fingered Verres stripped the temple, however, we have a record of it only in Cicero's indictment: "More splendid doors, exquisitely wrought in ivory and gold, have never existed." On the roof stood a triumphant Athena whose gold shield flashed like a beacon for sailors at sea.

The façade of the present **Duomo** was designed by the Sicilian Andrea Palma (1728–1751) to replace a Norman one that was the victim of an earthquake. The Duomo is praised for the brilliant execution of broken masses that create chiaroscuro. In front are statues of Saints Peter and Paul, the work of the Palermitan Marabitti. Inside, the centuries are harmoniously joined: Greek columns project from walls and chapels; fine wrought-iron work adds intricacy; a Norman font stands in the baptistery. At the end of the right aisle is the chapel of the Crucified Christ, with a painting of *Saint Zosimus* attributed to Antonello da Messina. Antonello Gagini's *Madonna of the Snow* graces the north aisle.

At the far end of the piazza Duomo stands the church of Santa Lucia alla Badia, dedicated to the Sicilian-born patron saint fêted on December 13. In the other direction the splendid **Palazzo Beneventano del Bosco**, with its grand courtyard, retains its dignity despite the restaurant and disco on the ground floor. The palace is the work of Luciano Ali (1775) and is still inhabited by the descendants of the noble family that commissioned it.

Like much of the Baroque southeast, Ortygia's pleasing mix of Baroque façades, staircases, balconies, and details is the indirect product of a devastating earthquake in 1693. Baroque in Syracuse is more restrained than in Catania, more conscious of Classical order and simple elegance—perhaps because of the city's strong Hellenic past.

Before returning to the mainland, stop at the **Temple of Apollo**, just before the bridge. Here excavations continue around the oldest Doric temple in Sicily, built about 565 B.C. It had six columns in front and 17 along its sides, placed unusually close together. The name of Apollo derives from an inscription chiseled on the front of the temple, although Cicero attributed the temple to Artemis—an affirmation of the existence of the two cults here.

Mainland Syracuse

The **Catacombe di San Giovanni**, entered from the church of San Giovanni (St. John) on viale Teocrito back on the mainland, evokes the paleo-Christian past, a time when Saint Paul delivered a sermon at the altar of San Mariano in the catacombs on his way back from Malta. Frescoes, graffiti, and other remnants of the early Church lend the site a mystic aura (unless a school class arrives). The nearby archaeological museum, the **Museo Regionale**, newly reopened and expanded near the catacombs, is an invaluable resource featuring objects taken from the city's Zona Archeologica: metopes, statues, and such—a stone diary of Sicily from prehistory to the days of Greek and Roman occupation.

Near the museum, at viale Teocrito 80, the **Galleria del Papiro** tells the story of papyrus—apparently introduced to Sicily by the Ptolemaic kings. The gallery owners demonstrate the Egyptian technique from stalk to finished painting.

The **Zona Archeologica** contains the major Classical sites that remain. The Roman amphitheater, off the corso Gelone's far (northwestern) end, is surpassed in size only by the arena in Verona, but much of its stone was carried away by the Spanish—a familiar story in Sicily. The *cavea* (audience section) built into the hillside is topped by a parapet engraved with the names of box holders. To the west is the largest sacrificial altar known to the Greek world, with ramps that could hold 450 oxen on their way to sacrifice. Once monumental in aspect, today it demands imagination. The structure called Archimedes' tomb is not, though Cicero did see the Greek mathematician's now-lost tomb somewhere in Syracuse.

The **Latomie** are deep limestone quarries where hapless slaves (often prisoners of war) cut stone for the city's buildings. The earlobe-shaped cave in Latomia del Paradiso was dubbed by Caravaggio the Ear of Dionysius; legend has it that the acoustics are so good that the tyrannical one listened at the opening on top to hear what the slaves were saying. In the **Grotta dei Cordari** (Cave of the Rope Makers) the work is clearly evident, almost as if the site were recently abandoned. Contrasting with the stone is luxuriant vegetation: lemon and orange trees, capers, palm, prickly pear, and particularly oleander—which lines the streets of Syracuse with dark rose and white flowers.

The **Greek theater**, among the most beautiful of its kind, originally enjoyed a view of the harbor and hills, but the Romans added a backdrop to facilitate their more elaborate productions—simplicity not being a Roman attribute. Syracuse was famous throughout the world for its dramatic productions, and Aeschylus and Euripides were performed regularly. When Hieron I founded a colony at nearby Mount Etna, Aeschylus wrote *Women of Etna* (lost) to be performed here; his Prometheus plays were also produced at Syracuse. All was not tragedy, however, for Epicharmus raised ancient comedy to artistic heights, and mime was popular as well. Above the theater are the remains of a nymphaeum to which Hieron's guests could run during a downpour.

Syracuse has inspired more than just great theater. Lentini, near Syracuse, was the birthplace of the philosopher Gorgias (483 B.C.), whose Sophist views led Cicero to say that doubt was born in Sicily. According to Gorgias nothing exists, for if it did it would have to come from something, and something can't come from nothing. And if something did exist, it could not be known, given the difference between thought and thing. Objective truth being thus impossible, there remained only the art of the Sophists: persuasion. Gorgias's challenge to speculative thought stimulated a more sophisticated approach to the problems of philosophy (see the eponymous dialogue by Plato), and he became known as the philosopher who introduced rhetoric, the art of persuasion that yields belief about things just and unjust, to Greece.

Follow viale Teocrito east from the Zona Archeologica toward the sea and stop at the **Villa Politi** (where you may want to stay—if it's open). The gardens here, part of the adjoining catacombs of the Cappuccini, are an organized jungle of palms and oaks, flowers and statues, and limestone quarries. Views from the front rooms are enchanting at night, when garden lights turn the outdoors into a Gothic mystery.

The adjoining Cappuccini catacombs are closed now, but they once held Athenian prisoners captive until they died—or could recite Euripides, a feat that would free them. The hilltop **Castello Eurialo**, a fortress 8 km (5 miles) northwest of town that you can get to by bus, is a fascinating war machine engineered by Dionysius and Archimedes. Underground trench networks allowed soldiers on the deck of a boat-shaped structure to drag bodies away, along with whatever objects of warfare the enemy propelled in.

If the Villa Politi's somewhat faded charms (Churchill was entranced) and antiquated cooling system aren't enticing (though there is a lovely pool), stay at the **MotelAgip**, well liked by Sicilian businesspeople for its comforts and very good food, even if it is a chain. It is not Romantic Sicily, but Syracuse is poorly endowed with hotels. (It's also close to the Zona Archeologica.) The **Gran Bretagna** has faded charms but a certain odd appeal—and sea views.

Everyone who visits Syracuse has a favorite restaurant. A common choice is **Ionico**, set on a beautiful quarry by the sea, just north of the center (near the Villa Politi) in a little garden filled with antiquity and kitsch. Fish is, of course, on center stage here—swordfish, bass, tuna, mackerel—seasoned with capers, fresh anchovies, wild fennel, black olives, and rich olive oil. Spaghetti may come topped with tuna eggs and herring. The menu is in Sicilian, but the staff speaks English (even Italians look at the menu in bemusement). When owner Pasqualino is there the food is exquisite, but alas, he too often travels, like many chefs of Italy.

Arlecchino's proprietor, Baldassare Ponza, comes from Palermo and serves his native dishes, as well as local ones, in a pretty trattoria decorated with masks of the commedia dell'arte. Bass *in cartoccio* (baked in a paper case) tastes of the sea, fresh and moist, and the vegetable pastas are excellent (via dei Tolomei 5; Tel: 0931-663-86).

Acting students crowd **Archimede** (via Gemmellaro 8, in Ortygia; Tel: 0931-697-01; closed Sundays), projecting over fresh fish and game and seductive desserts. Near piazza Archimede, **Don Camillo** (via Maestranza 96; Tel: 0931-671-33; closed Sunday evening and Mondays) has a distinguished reputation. Also in Ortygia, the little **Minosse** (via Mirabella 6; Tel: 0931-663-66) is known for its wonderful fish stew (*zuppa di pesce*), breaded swordfish, and tender calamari steamed in white wine. (King Minos, the restaurant's namesake, came to Sicily to find Daedalus, the master sculptor, and take him back to Greece; but Minos was murdered in his bath by the daughters of Cocalus, the Siculi king.)

The pastries and ice cream in Syracuse are too good to ignore: almond pastry; super-rich *cassata* filled with pistachio cream and chocolate and candied fruit bits; the richest, lightest cannoli. Stop at **Marciante** in via Maestranza or at the **Bar Viola** in corso Matteotti (both in Ortygia) for ice cream.

THE BAROQUE SOUTHEAST

Almost every town in the Sicilian southeast, no matter how humble, boasts a Baroque church of distinction, and often a palace as well.

Noto

Noto, about a half hour by bus southwest from Syracuse, is the rarest gem of all. Designed as a golden urban unit, it was used by Antonioni as a symbol of past architectural triumph in his film *L'Avventura*. Much of the town is the work of the architects Gagliardi and Landolina.

The central corso Vittorio Emanuele leads past three piazzas. The street to see, though, is **via Corrado Nicolaci,** so perfect as to seem trompe l'oeil (when cars aren't parked along it). Its balconies burst with griffins, mermaids, medusas, lions, and other oddities of decorative splendor.

Stop at the ultrasimple **Trattoria Carmine** on via Carmine for a pasta with vegetable sauce and grilled shrimp that cause even Nettini (as Noto residents are called) to flock to the popular spot. In back of the Municipio is the **Gelateria Costanzo**, where wonderful ice cream, sometimes even *gelsomino*—made from jasmine petals—is prepared. Noto has a music festival and an ice cream festival during the summer, caring for both body and soul.

Other Baroque Towns

Among the towns to include on a Baroque itinerary are Ragusa, Modica, Scicli, Grammichele, Canicattini Bagni, and Palazzolo Acreide. Archaeological excursions, carefully outlined in a booklet available from the tourist office in Ortygia, will take you to the vast Siculi necropolis at Pantalica (13th to 8th centuries B.C.) as well as to other ancient towns.

Ragusa, west on N115 from Noto, was designed by Gagliardi, Noto's genius. The old town, called **Ibla,** is exquisite, but was deserted after the earthquake and is now a ghost town. The **Church of San Giorgio** is a sandstone gem of the Sicilian Baroque.

To prepare yourself for the journey, have a meal at **Majore** (Tel: 0932-92-80-19; closed Mondays), a family restaurant at Chiaramonte Gulfi and the ultimate pork establishment (with wild rabbit and partridge, too). Pork—always with a special taste, for the Majore's pork is fed a special diet—is prepared in sausages, roasted, jellied, and thrown into pasta sauces. Ragusa (the province) is the center for *cacciacavallo* cheese, the taste of which changes noticeably from region to region.

Just outside the town of **Palazzolo Acreide** in the hills due west of Syracuse is the Templi Ferali, with 12 rough figures called the Santoni, representing aspects of the goddess Cybele, who was worshiped here. (Ask the custodian to open the shrine.) In Palazzolo Acreide itself, a "house-museum" has been delightfully assembled to re-create the spirit of country life at the turn of the century. Stop also at the church of the Immacolata to see a lovely Laurana *Madonna*.

Caltagirone

Caltagirone, northwest of Palazzolo Acreide, is a paradise for ceramics fanciers and worthy of a detour inland. Not only is there a museum devoted to pottery and tiles through the ages, but the town's walls, railings, even the 142-step staircase—each step differently tiled—glow with multicolored ceramic designs. Small artisan shops continue the tradition, most of their tiles more modern than the age-old simple blue and white with an orange dab. This sophisticated town also has a charming Art Nouveau park designed by Basile. Stay at the modern **Villa San Mauro**, with its lovely view and friendly bar for the travel weary.

Piazza Armerina

Northwest of Caltagirone, picturesque Piazza Armerina is visited mainly by travellers en route to the Roman villa at nearby **Casale**. (You may have to taxi from Piazza Armerina to Casale if you're not driving your own car.) The luxurious **Roman villa** at Casale was an imperial retreat during the third century B.C. Mosaics depicting chariot races, hunts, picnics, and bikini bathers cover a multiroomed villa. The children's section shows imperial *bambini* at play.

CATANIA

The Baroque architecture of Catania, up the coast from Syracuse, is impressive—and impressively in need of renovation. Palermo-born Giovanni Battista Vaccarini settled here in 1730, after the catastrophic earthquake, and brought about what Rudolph Wittkower calls "a Sicilian Rococo, by blending Borrominesque with the local tradition," admirably demonstrated by the cathedral façade. In the piazza del Duomo is another of his designs, an elephant fountain similar to Bernini's in Rome.

Catania composer Vincenzo Bellini is buried inside the church (his house-museum on piazza San Francesco is filled with memorabilia from *Norma* and *I Puritani*). To the right of the altar is the chapel of Saint Agatha, where the city's patron saint, whose veil stopped a lava flow from nearby Etna, is buried. Her martyrdom included having her breasts cut off, and they now reappear as pastries (*seni di vergine*) all over Sicily, an odd symbol of devotion. Catania frequently wins pastry design awards; Baroque didn't stop at stucco *putti* after all. The pastry shop to the left of the Duomo displays some amazing marzipan.

The Municipio in the same piazza demonstrates Vaccarini's flair, and the nearby market adds Baroque drama to fish selling. One of Frederick II's many castles, the **Castello Ursino**, also can be visited, thanks to the eclectic **Museo Comunale** housed there (from pre-Roman terra-cottas to *Saint Luke* by Mattia Preti; embroidery; weaponry). It's worth going in, if only to see Frederick's interiors.

Catania Barocca is at its best on via dei Crociferi, whose scenographic allure derives partly from such lovely façades as that of the **Church of San Benedetto**, and at night from the merry *putti* streetlamps. Via Etnea—looking north toward its namesake—is home to a university with a fine school of vulcanology, and for good reason. At the end is **Giardino Bellini**, a pleasant place to relax in an otherwise chaotic city as you enjoy the flower clock-calendar and busts of Bellini and other musicians. For an overview of Catania and some exercise, climb to the cupola of the church of San Nicolà on via Gesuiti, in the southwestern part of town.

A choice restaurant in Catania is **La Siciliana**, in a former villa at viale Marco Polo 52 (Tel: 095-37-64-00), where *rigatoni alla Norma,* made with eggplant sometimes seared for added flavor, is a delicious tribute to Bellini. Stuffed fresh sardines, roast lamb, *involtini,* and such can be accompanied by wines from Mount Etna or selections from the La Rosa family's extensive cellars. A specialty you might try is *ripiddu nivicatu* (lava of snowy Etna), a plate of rice blackened with cuttlefish ink, covered by snowy white cooked ricotta, and flaming with red pepper sauce. *Tiramisù* and *cassata* are sweet finishes.

The **Costa Azzurra**, a bit out of town at the port, Ognina, is worth the trip for the sea urchins (*ricci*) and similar treats.

Località Ognina, via De Cristofaro 4, Tel: (095) 49-49-20; closed Mondays.

For tranquility, the best place to stay is the **Catania Sheraton**, outside of town and connected by bus. It's ultra-modern—a shock after the Baroque forms of the island. But the saltwater pool and adjacent bar, restaurant, tennis court, and parking garage are up to Sheraton standards and are welcomed by business travellers. Ask for a sea-view room.

In town, the **Villa Dina**, a centrally located converted palazzo, is a good choice. The **MotelAgip** is convenient and predictable (if anything is in Sicily).

MOUNT ETNA

"Etna, that wicked witch, resting her thick white snow under heaven, and slowly, slowly, rolling her orange-colored smoke," was D. H. Lawrence's response to the still-active volcano. Pindar and Plato spoke of it, and Homer's Cyclops hurled rocks from its sides at Odysseus—rocks that now can be seen where they fell along the coast at Aci Castello (*I Ciclopi*).

To climb the volcano or drive up near the top is to pass through botanical zones of great beauty. Rare plants such as the Etna violet grow in the volcano's fertile soil, as do citrus, olives, and vineyards that produce very good wines. Chestnut trees from ancient forests turn golden in autumn, while in winter broom, lichen, and wild flowers are dazzling against the dark slopes higher up. Pistachio—probably planted by Arabs—is cultivated under the volcano, and the white birches are as noble as Robert Frost's. Daily excursions to Mount Etna are arranged through CIT tours in Catania and Taormina. If you have the time, take the Circumetnea railway around the volcano, stopping at some of the picturesque towns, such as **Randazzo**, that line the slopes. From **Sapienza**, reached by train or bus, a four-hour hike will take you to the crater—or as close as you can get. You can also rent a Jeep there. Skiing on the slopes is also permitted when the volcano has been quiet.

TAORMINA

North of Catania along the east coast, Taormina is at its most magical when approached gradually from the resort-flanked sea road. As you climb the steep, tortuous hill toward the summit, the sea, the castle-topped cliff, and Mount Etna take their places in an incomparable panorama.

The lure that has drawn the titled and the famous through the years is still strong, despite the hotels and shops that threaten to overwhelm the Medieval charm of its steep streets, flower-bedecked balconies, Renaissance palaces, and tropical gardens. Avoid visiting in July and August, of course; but come in spring or fall, or even at Christmas and New Year's, when the feasting board groans and fireworks light up the sea.

Taormina is perched high above the water; you can reach the beaches at **Mazzarò**, directly below, or at **Naxos**, visible from the heights, by car or funicular. Naxos was the first Greek colony in Sicily (735 B.C.), though its ruins are few compared with the treasures of Agrigento. Those that remain are found in the **Parco Archeologico**. Otherwise Naxos is a long line of hotels.

Taormina was established by Dionysius I in 403 B.C. after he destroyed Naxos (they were Chalcideans and Ionians; he was Corinthian). The Arabs subsequently destroyed and re-built the city, and Count Roger rousted them in turn, as was his wont, in 1078. Its well-preserved Medieval look is due in part to the care of the House of Aragon and in part to the Allied bombers' unwillingness to do much damage when they attacked Marshal Kesselring's fine quarters here.

The view from the central seats of the **Teatro Greco**—of Etna, the sea, the coast, and the sky framed by the theater's open walls—is one of the most beautiful sights in the world. Coming here in early morning or late afternoon to see the light change makes the experience even more rewarding.

The theater is carved out of the rock and was so exten-sively made over by the Romans that most of the present structure dates from the Empire. But the site itself is Greek—a location only they could choose. Its acoustics are still excellent, and the theater is used frequently for a variety of artistic productions.

Most churches here are attractively simple in construction, and palaces such as the **Corvaia** on the piazza Vittorio Eman-uele are typical in their ornamentation of black lava and pumice inlaid in the limestone foundation. Its attractive court-yard, with panels depicting Adam and Eve, and with an out-side stairway as well as a grand hall and salons, is interesting to visit—a nice stop as you wander the maze of streets and alleys. Stop at the **Interpress Bookshop**, piazza Umberto 37, if you're hungering for books and newspapers in English.

If you've watched your calories, you may fit up the **Vicolo Stretto** (Narrow Alley) to the restaurant of that name at number 6—perhaps the best in Taormina and moderately priced (Tel: 0942-238-49).

The best hotels in Taormina are the **San Domenico Palace**, a converted 16th-century convent that counts among its expensive charms spectacular panoramas from its many terraces, a pool, and a dining room; the less expensive **Jolly Diodoro**—where you should try to take an end suite with views of Etna, pool, and garden; the **Villa Belvedere**, still less expensive, and with the same panorama and its own flowery gardens and pool; and the small **Villa Fiorita**, with outdoor terraces, pool, and, of course, spectacular views. The most charming of the small hotels, however, is the **Villa Paradiso**, stylishly redesigned with Sicilian antiques and serving very good Sicilian food in its restaurant. Nearby, at via Bagnoli Croci 50, is one of the best trattorias in the area—U **Bossu**. Grilled fish is the specialty (Tel: 0942-233-11; closed Mondays).

Budget travellers will enjoy the **Villa Pompeii**, across from the public gardens, and the **Pensione Svizzera**, with gorgeous coastal views.

At Mazzarò, on the beach just below Taormina, is the luxurious **Mazzarò Sea Palace** hotel and the charming **Villa Sant'Andrea**, which is merry with fabric prints and resembles an English seashore villa. The front rooms with terraces facing the sea are the best, but the back faces Taormina's semitropical lushness. And the price is right. One of its two restaurants is on the beach. Both hotels are reached by cable car from Taormina, but if you're athletically inclined you can make the ascent to town via the stairs, and if you are stuck in town late at night you can take a taxi back to the hotel.

For lunch go to the terrace of the sweet family-run **Il Faro**, high in the Taormina hills, which are terraced with vineyards above lush valleys and have views of the sea beyond (via Rotabile Castelmola; Tel: 0942-281-93; closed Wednesdays). After lunch, explore Castelmola's ancient streets and sample its almond cake drenched with almond wine.

For a day's excursion from Taormina you can easily explore Mount Etna and the surrounding towns by train or tour. For a glimpse of Medieval Sicily, go to **Forza d'Agrò**, a clifftop town reached by car only (bus service requires spending hours there between buses). In the town's piazza only the click of embroidery needles breaks the silence, except for an occasional blast of Michael Jackson from a passing tape deck.

MESSINA

North of Taormina, Messina is the ferry entrance to Sicily from Reggio di Calabria, worthy of a visit if only for its museum's two Caravaggios and a magnificent fragment of a polyptych by the town's famous native son, Antonello da Messina. The city has known destruction from its beginning—first by war, then by earthquake, tidal wave, cholera, and recently by Allied bombs; but it is now cheerful-looking and energetic, a busy port and university town. In the central piazza a noontime performance by the amazing clock tower features a crowing cock, a roaring lion, and Christ arising. Thus awakened, head for fashionable **Alberto** (via Ghibellina 95; Tel: 090-71-07-11), considered one of Sicily's best restaurants, and have fish *carpaccio* with herb sauce, scampi in crab sauce, and one of their superb lemon sorbets. Unfashionable, except in a radical chic way, is the **Trattoria del Porto**, a mariner hangout— and who knows fish better? (Via Vittorio Emanuele 71; Tel: 090-548-73.)

If you spend the night in Messina, try the **Jolly dello Stretto**, which has a fine view of the harbor. While in Messina you can cross the strait by hydrofoil in a few minutes to see *I Bronzi,* the bronze warriors the sea gave up to a Calabrese fisherman, and now exhibited in Reggio di Calabria's Museo Nazionale. You can see Messina on a day trip from Taormina or visit it en route while circling the island.

THE AEOLIAN ISLANDS

The Aeolians (also known as the Lipari Islands), off Sicily's northeast coast, were once ruled by the god of the winds, Aeolus, if we are to believe Homer—and we should, given the wildly sculpted shapes the wind has carved in the soft volcanic rock. The rich volcanic soil is excellent for growing grapes and vegetables, prickly pears, capers, carobs, and palms. During the Punic wars, Carthage used the islands as a base, until Rome conquered all in 252 B.C. The Aeolians were inhabited well before that, however—traces of Stentinello culture, especially pottery dating from the Neolithic period, have been found on Lipari. The Greeks were there later, but as early as 600 B.C. The Phoenicians and Greeks prized Lipari's obsidian, which proved ideal for making tools and weapons (since it is both strong and malleable), thereby putting the island on the map.

Lipari is the largest of the islands and the one most adapted to tourism, with relics of its ancient past to marvel at in the **Museo Eoliano**—one of Europe's most important museums of prehistoric artifacts. Terra-cotta Greek theater masks and figures are attractively presented on an upper floor. It's situated within the confines of the **Castello**, where extensive excavations into Lipari's multilayered history can be observed.

The views from Lipari, and from all the islands, are striking in color and sculpturesque rock carvings. A friendly island home away from home is the **Villa Diana**, where terraces and private gardens overlook Lipari from on high; the local dishes and wines are wholesome. More hotel-like are the **Meligunis**, with beach and garden, and the **Carasco**, with fine sea views and a pool. The **Poseidon**, by the sea, is reasonably priced and well equipped. It's worth the trip to Lipari if only to dine at **Filippino's**. Signor Bernardi's restaurant is one of the finest in Italy, and surely the friendliest to have ever won the Michelin star—rarely awarded in Italy (Tel: 090-981-10-02). The house specialty is a pasta with a splendid eggplant sauce and flavored with local *pecorino* cheese. Seafood is king of course, but all the grilled meat dishes are inviting. If you happen to be there when *cassata* is on the dessert menu, do indulge, for it's among the lightest and most subtly flavored in Sicily.

Panarea is perhaps the most dramatically beautiful of the Aeolians, with its bizarre formations of volcanic rock and its clear water. In addition, prehistoric villages dating from the 14th and 13th centuries B.C. can be seen on its volcanic slopes. Panarea is also a chic resort, attracting Italian celebrities who want to be alone—and without outdoor electricity. (Stargazing here is an extraordinary experience.) **Il Raya** is the place where they are found; no children, please. The **Residence** and **La Piazza**, with many amenities, are also charming. Scuba diving is the sport of choice.

Stromboli (STROM-boli) must be seen from the sea. Take the boat from Naples at night to see its volcanic triangle rising out of the dawn mists. Nighttime trips are organized from Stromboli or Lipari to see the brilliant spectacle of fiery coals shooting into the air. On terra firma, if such can be said of Stromboli, the scene is surprisingly cheerful—white houses, bougainvillaea, almond blossoms, grape and caper vines, and even orange and lemon trees enliven the dark earth. Hotels are plentiful (usually open spring to fall); **La**

Sciara Residence and La Sirenetta–Park Hotel even have swimming pools. The Villaggio Stromboli is somewhat less expensive, as is the Pensione Scari. If you arrive at night, be sure to have the hotel meet you: There are *no* streetlights. At La Sciara, look for Teresa Trusnach's boutique. If you're staying a while, she'll make you an exquisite outfit (she also carries ready-to-wear). This is the same Teresa who has a shop in Rome.

Climb the volcano only with a guide. The volcano is active, and approaching the summit can be dangerous. Smoke and rumbling will be apparent as you climb, as stones are constantly tossed about at the base of the cone. (Only those that shoot higher than 350 feet can be seen, however.) Allow about six hours to get to the top and back, assuming that you'll stop often to enjoy the view. Take a jacket, snack, and a bottle of water, as there is no place to stop for a drink. The tourist office near the boat dock, or your hotel, can arrange for a guide.

Vulcano is the island for mud baths; white steam and sulfur rise from the fumaroles, and you can walk along the rim of the dormant crater, which hasn't been heard from since 1890. Dine at Al Cratere (Porto Levante; Tel: 090-985-20-45) to know what "under the volcano" means. It's a good fish place with a cheerful terrace.

Elegantly alone and remote are Filicudi and Alicudi, where prehistoric dwellings are to be found. Filicudi is extraordinary. The island swells upward from a small port toward a high tableland. Beyond the tableland, steep cliffs rush down to valleys of vineyards and caper plants, and, in the spring, white almond blossoms. Nature lovers, artists, and lovers find the extravagant beauty and privacy of Filicudi ideal. The hotel at the port, the Phenicusa, has good views of the sea and a restaurant. Rooms can also be found with local people, and houses may be rented for longer periods. (The tourist office at the port has information.) While here, be sure to take an excursion by boat to Filicudi's Bue Marino cave, which is preferred by many to Capri's Grotta Azzurra, so dramatic are the displays of reflected light.

If you really want solitude, then Alicudi, farther west, is your island. Its *total* lack of electricity keeps all but those most devoted to moonlight away. The Ericusa, its tiny hotel, will supply you with lamps, but don't plan on nighttime reading.

To visit the islands, leave your car at the car park at the pier in Milazzo, west of Messina. Cars are permitted only on Lipari and Vulcano. Daily sailings are available from Milazzo (and sometimes Messina and Palermo) for Lipari and Vulcano, less often (usually three times a week) to the others. During the summer there is daily hydrofoil service to all the islands, as well as among them. Palermo also is connected to the islands in summer by hydrofoil. An overnight ferry from Naples links them all, year-round (see "Getting Around," below). Small motor vehicles take care of luggage and local transport. Walking is the best means of touring, however, with the exception of frequent boat trips.

If you travel back to Palermo along the scenic north coast, stop at **Tindari** to see the fourth-century B.C. Greek amphitheater, situated with the infallible Greek eye for spectacular natural sites. This theater opens onto wondrous views of the Aeolian Islands ahead and Mount Etna in back—a fitting end to this island journey.

GETTING AROUND

You can reach Sicily by plane, arriving in Palermo or Catania, or by train across the Strait of Messina from Reggio di Calabria. If you reserve this flight with Alitalia when making your reservations to Italy, the price will usually be considerably reduced. The most beautiful approach, however, is from Naples on the overnight car ferry, which arrives in Palermo in time for the deep pink African dawn over the city. First-class cabins are reasonably comfortable (reserve ahead) and there is a cafeteria on board. (A business-class ferry began service recently also.) The Naples–Aeolian Islands ferry lands at Stromboli, Salina, Lipari, Vulcano, and, on the Sicilian mainland, at Milazzo or Messina. Hydrofoil service from Naples also is available in summer.

Car ferries (*traghetti*) run all year from Naples to Palermo. First-class cabins (small, two beds, double-decker) and second-class (small, four beds, double-decker) can be reserved—and should be, for a soccer game will sell out second class easily. In the U.S., bookings for the Tirrenia line can be made through Extra Value Travel: 683 S. Collier Boulevard, Marco Island, FL 33937; Tel: (813) 394-3384; Fax: (813) 394-4848. In Naples Tirrenia is located at the Stazione Marittima at the port (Tel: 081-551-21-81).

The Siremar line runs car ferries all year from Naples to Milazzo, and hydrofoils (in summer) that serve the Aeolian Islands as well. In Naples the address is via Depretis 78; Tel: (081) 551-21-12.

The Aeolians are also linked all year by SNAV (via Caracciolo 10, 80100 Naples; Tel: 081-66-04-44; Fax: 081-66-03-65. In Milazzo, Sicily, Tel: 090-928-45-09).

A car is the thing if you want to see the smaller towns, because bus service is infrequent. Train and bus connections to all major cities, however, are quite good. Taxi drivers frequently agree to reasonable rates for long trips. Cars are not recommended in Palermo and Catania, where traffic and auto theft make them a headache. (Nothing should ever be left in a car, even if it is locked.) Outside these two cities you'll encounter fewer problems, and the local people will be happy to tell you where to park.

Tour operators such as Italiatour and CIT offer independent packages, including hotel and car rental, or sometimes a rail pass, which can be booked ahead through a travel agent.

ACCOMMODATIONS REFERENCE
The rates given below are projections for 1992; always check for up-to-date information before making reservations. Wide ranges may reflect the differences between low- and high-season rates. Unless otherwise indicated, the figures indicate the cost of a double room (per room, not per person). However, half-board (mezza pensione) rates, which include breakfast and one other meal per day, are per person. Most hotels will add a service charge of 10 to 15 percent.

(See also the separate accommodations listings for Palermo, above in the chapter.)

▶ **Astoria Park Hotel.** Lungomare Dante Alighieri, 91016 **Trapani.** Tel: (0923) 56-24-00. Ł60,000.

▶ **Baia del Capitano.** Contrada Mezzoforno, 90015 **Cefalù.** Tel: (0921) 200-03; Fax: (0921) 201-63. Ł42,000–Ł80,000; half board Ł84,000–Ł126,000.

▶ **Le Calette.** Località Caldura, 90015 **Cefalù.** Tel: (0921) 241-44. Ł80,000.

▶ **Hotel Capo San Vito.** 91010 **San Vito lo Capo.** Tel: (0923) 97-22-84; Fax: (0923) 97-21-22. Ł95,000.

▶ **Carasco.** Porto delle Genti, 98055 **Lipari.** Tel: (090) 981-16-05; Fax: (090) 981-18-28. Open April–late September. Ł110,000; half board Ł100,000–Ł160,000.

▶ **Carlton Riviera.** Località Capo Plaia, 90015 **Cefalù.** Tel: (0921) 203-04; Fax: (0921) 203-04. Open March–October. Ł78,000–Ł158,000; half board Ł83,000–Ł145,000.

▶ **Catania Sheraton.** Via Antonello da Messina 45, 95020 **Cannizzaro.** Tel: (095) 27-15-57; Fax: (095) 27-13-80. In U.S., Tel: (800) 325-3535. Ł155,000–Ł200,000; half board Ł149,000–Ł189,000.

▶ **Club Alpino Siciliano.** Isnello, 90010 **Palermo.** Tel: (0921) 499-95. ₤40,000.

▶ **Cossyra Club.** Località Mursia, 91017 **Pantelleria.** Tel: (0923) 91-11-54; Fax: (0923) 91-25-46. ₤85,000.

▶ **Elimo.** Via Vittorio Emanuele 23, 91016 **Erice.** Tel: (0923) 86-93-77; Fax: (0923) 86-92-52. ₤80,000; half board ₤90,000–₤100,000.

▶ **Ericusa.** Via Regina Elena, 98055 **Alicudi.** Tel: (090) 988-99-10. ₤50,000.

▶ **Ermione.** Via Pineta Communale 43, 91016 **Erice.** Tel: (0923) 86-91-38. ₤85,000.

▶ **Gran Bretagna.** Via Savoia 21, 96100 **Siracusa.** Tel: (0931) 687-65. ₤75,000.

▶ **Grande Albergo delle Terme.** Lungomare Nuove Terme, 92019 **Sciacca.** Tel: (0925) 231-33; Fax: (0925) 217-46. Closed December–January. ₤52,000–₤80,000; half board ₤68,000.

▶ **Jolly dello Stretto.** Corso Garibaldi 126, 98126 **Messina.** Tel: (090) 434-01; Fax: (090) 590-25-26. In U.S., Tel: (212) 213-1468 or (800) 221-2626; Fax: (212) 213-2369. In U.K., Tel: (923) 89-62-72 or (0800) 28-27-29; Fax: (923) 89-60-71. ₤150,000–₤190,000; half board ₤140,000–₤185,000.

▶ **Jolly Diodoro.** Via Bagnoli Croce 75, 98039 **Taormina.** Tel: (0942) 223-12; Fax: (0942) 233-91. In U.S., Tel: (212) 213-1468 or (800) 221-2626; Fax: (212) 213-2369. In U.K., Tel: (923) 89-62-72 or (0800) 28-27-29; Fax: (923) 89-60-71. ₤150,000–₤210,000.

▶ **Kalura.** Località Caldura, 90015 **Cefalù.** Tel: (0921) 213-54; Fax: (0921) 225-01. ₤80,000.

▶ **Kaos.** Frazione Caos, 92100 **Agrigento.** Tel: (0922) 59-86-22; Fax: (0922) 59-87-70. ₤105,000–₤155,000; half board ₤125,000.

▶ **Mazzarò Sea Palace.** Via Nazionale 147, 98030 **Mazzarò.** Tel: (0942) 240-04; Fax: same. In U.S., Tel: (212) 838-3110 or (800) 223-6800; Fax: (212) 758-7367. In U.K., Tel: (0800) 18-11-23; Fax: (071) 353-1904. Open April–October. ₤220,000–₤380,000; half board ₤205,000–₤265,000.

▶ **Meligunis.** Via Marte, 98055 **Lipari.** Tel: (090) 981-24-26; Fax: (090) 988-0149. ₤240,000; half board ₤150,000–₤177,000.

▶ **Milocca.** 90013 **Castelbuono.** Tel: (0921) 719-44. ₤80,000.

▶ **Miramare.** Via Piemonte 34, 92013 **Porto Palo di Menfi.** Tel: (0925) 712-78. ₤85,000.

▶ **Mondello Palace.** Viale Principe di Scalea 2, 90151 **Mondello.** Tel: (091) 45-00-01; Fax: (091) 45-06-57. ₤135,000–₤210,000; half board ₤145,000–₤165,000.

▶ **MotelAgip**. Via Messina 626, 95126 **Catania**. Tel: (095) 71-22-300; Fax: (095) 71-21-856. ₤80,000–₤130,000.

▶ **MotelAgip**. Via Teracati 30, 96100 **Siracusa**. Tel: (0931) 669-44; Fax: (0931) 671-15. ₤110,000–₤140,000; half board ₤106,000–₤135,000.

▶ **Paradiso**. Via Calvario 133, 91010 **Levanzo**. Tel: (0923) 92-40-80. ₤40,000.

▶ **Pensione Scari**. Contrada Scari, 98050 **Stromboli**. Tel: (090) 98-60-06. ₤60,000.

▶ **Pensione Svizzera**. Via Pirandello 26, 98039 **Taormina**. Tel: (0942) 237-90. ₤60,000.

▶ **Pensione Trantino**. Via A. Diaz 7, **Scopello**, 91014 Trapani. Tel: (0924) 59-60-63. ₤50,000.

▶ **Phenicusa**. Filicudi Porto, 98050 **Filicudi**. Tel: (090) 984-4134. ₤60,000–₤70,000.

▶ **La Piazza**. Contrada San Pietro, 98050 **Panarea**. Tel: (090) 98-30-03; Fax: (090) 98-31-76. Open April–September. ₤190,000; half board ₤90,000–₤140,000.

▶ **Pirandello**. Via Giovanni XXIII, 92010 **Agrigento**. Tel: (0922) 556-66. ₤80,000.

▶ **Del Porto**. Via Borgo Italia, 91017 **Pantelleria**. Tel: (0923) 91-12-57; Fax: (0923) 91-15-16. ₤65,000–₤76,000.

▶ **Poseidon**. Via Ausonia 7, 98055 **Lipari**. Tel: (090) 981-28-76. ₤60,000.

▶ **Il Raya**. Costa Galletta, 98050 **Panarea**. Tel: (090) 98-30-13. Open May–October. ₤60,000.

▶ **Residence**. Contrada San Pietro, 98050 **Panarea**. Tel: (090) 98-30-29. ₤50,000.

▶ **Riva del Sole**. Via Lungomare Colombo 25, 90015 **Cefalù**. Tel: (0921) 212-30; Fax: (0921) 219-84. ₤60,000; half board ₤65,000.

▶ **San Domenico Palace**. Piazza San Domenico 5, 98039 **Taormina**. Tel: (0942) 237-01; Fax: (0942) 62-55-06. In U.S., Tel: (212) 599-8280 or (800) 223-9832; Fax: (212) 599-1755. ₤320,000–₤580,000; half board ₤315,000–₤400,000.

▶ **La Sciara Residence**. Via Cincotta, Piscita, 98050 **Stromboli**. Tel: (090) 98-61-21; Fax: (090) 98-60-04. Open May–October. ₤133,000–₤186,000; half board ₤110,000–₤168,000.

▶ **La Sirenetta–Park Hotel**. Via Marina 33, 98050 **Stromboli**. Tel: (090) 98-60-25; Fax: (090) 98-61-24. Open March 26–October 29. ₤70,000–₤130,000; half board ₤80,000–₤140,000.

▶ **Villa Athena**. Via Passeggiate 33, 92100 **Agrigento**. Tel: (0922) 562-88. ₤107,000–₤140,000.

▶ **Villa Belvedere**. Via Bagnoli Croce 79, 98039 **Taormina**.

Tel: (0942) 237-91. Open March 16–October. ₺73,000–
₺136,000.

▶ **Villa Diana**. Località Diana-Tufo, 98055 **Lipari**. Tel: (090)
981-14-03. Open March–October. ₺90,000.

▶ **Villa Dina**. Via Caronda 129, 95100 **Catania**. Tel: (095)
44-71-03; Fax: (095) 43-69-35. ₺69,000–₺180,000.

▶ **Villa Esperia**. Viale Margherita di Savoia, 90151
Mondello. Tel: (091) 45-00-04. ₺65,000.

▶ **Villa Fiorita**. Via Pirandello 39, 98039 **Taormina**. Tel:
(0942) 241-22. ₺80,000.

▶ **Villa Paradiso**. Via Roma 2, 98039 **Taormina**. Tel: (0942)
239-22; Fax: (0942) 62-58-00. Closed November–mid-December. ₺120,000–175,000.

▶ **Villa Politi**. Via Politi 2, 96100 **Siracusa**. Tel: (0931) 321-
00. ₺80,000.

▶ **Villa Pompeii**. Via Bagnoli Croci 88, 98039 **Taormina**.
Tel: (0942) 238-12. ₺40,000.

▶ **Villa San Mauro**. Via Portosalvo 18, 95041 **Caltagirone**.
Tel: (0933) 265-00; Fax: (0933) 316-61. ₺100,000–₺120,000.

▶ **Villa Sant'Andrea**. Via Nazionale 137, 98030 **Mazzarò**.
Tel: (0942) 231-25; Fax: (0942) 248-38. ₺180,000–₺214,000;
half board ₺160,000–₺192,000.

▶ **Villaggio Stromboli**. Via Regina Elena, 98050 **Stromboli**.
Tel: (090) 98-60-18; Fax: (090) 988-01-70. Open March 15–
October. ₺45,000–₺90,000; half board ₺75,000–₺85,000.

SARDINIA

By Barbara Coeyman Hults

Sardinia (Sardegna), a name that conjures up images of the Emerald Coast, pleasure dome of the Aga Khan, is often ignored by those in search of less extravagant pleasures. Relatively few travellers, Italians included, take the island seriously on a cultural level. Perhaps because mainland Italy is so famous for the glories of Rome and the Renaissance, the natural beauty of the island seems less impressive. However, as congested cities and polluted water awake both Italians and visitors to more basic treasures, the island is coming into its own. The rough energy of the thousands of stone structures that were built in ancient Sardinia is similar to that of much modern sculpture, an ironic twist of artistic fate. And although Sardinia has no cities of great beauty, Cagliari has its charms, and some of the towns, such as Castelsardo, are enchanting.

While it's true that the Aga Khan's lovely and expensive resort has brought fame and considerable fortune to that part of the northeast called the Costa Smeralda (Emerald Coast), Sardinia is much more than just another pretty beach.

Not that the coastline is to be ignored, for spectacular it is, and not only in the north. Long white beaches stretch out near Cagliari, the capital and commercial port on the island's southern coast, and brighten the coastline at frequent intervals around the rest of island. Clear water of emerald and cerulean hues surrounds headlands of oak and pine, and rocks thick with macchia, a heatherlike shrub that provides ground cover and splashes of color, from green to bright orange, are scattered everywhere. (Plan to go in June or September, definitely not in August, when Europe heads seaward en masse.)

Sardinia's interior is mountainous, but cut through with

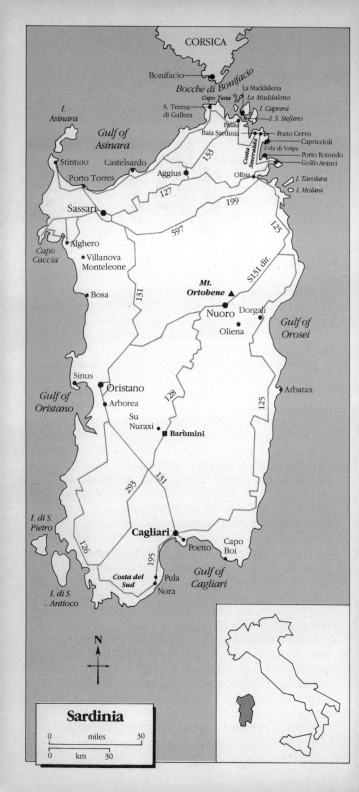

dramatic gorges and rivers. From Cagliari northwest to Oristano on the west coast extends the Campidano, a fertile plain that ends on the Sinis peninsula, where lagoons shelter flamingoes and salt mines have created mountain deserts.

On the north coast the wet mistral, blowing down from Provence in France—as if envious of the Emerald Coast's reputation—has sculpted amazing rock formations.

Not only naturalists, but anyone interested in art or the early history of man will find Sardinia an exhilarating adventure. Although Sardinia arose from the depths of the Mediterranean long before most of prehistoric Italy, the island's rugged coastline discouraged settlement. But traces of Neanderthal man have been discovered at Dorgali on the east coast, revealing an ancient presence as early as the Paleolithic period. The earliest identified culture, the Protosards, left considerable traces: intriguing dolmens—huts made of massive stone slabs in square post and lintel forms (one of the best preserved is at Mores near Alghero); megalithic stone circles that generally held tombs (like the *tomba di gigante,* wonderfully restored on a hilltop near Nuoro); and a variety of fertility figures, such as the large-breasted earth mother and the ram, which can be seen in the museums of Cagliari and Sassari. The greatest civilization of the island (the nuraghic) existed between the Bronze and Iron Ages (1600 to 111 B.C.), which seems only yesterday in Sardinia, given the 8,000 examples of ancient houses, altars, fortresses, and even towns (especially at Barùmini) that can be seen throughout the island. Their sculpture, called *bronzetti* (little bronzes), are works of art that provide invaluable records of early human society, its gods and its warriors, and even the boats used to cross to Etruscan Italy. Early contact with Phoenicians, Greeks, and Etruscans is evident in ceramics and sculpture from these areas.

The Phoenicians, the Mediterranean's ubiquitous traders, established colonies here about 800 B.C.; Sardinia offered a convenient way station on their commercial routes. The Carthaginians (actually latter-day Phoenicians) overcame the island's nuraghic colonies in about 600 B.C. in order to control the obsidian and other minerals to be found there. With Carthage came a social split in Sardinian culture, between the conquering Carthaginians and the earlier tribes, and slavery was introduced. Rome soon discovered the advantages of an island strategically located in the Mediterranean. With Rome came a further division of the culture, with the earlier societies retreating inland, creating a mountain people who today still prefer the interior to modern coastal settlements. At Nora, south of Cagliari on the southern coast, a fine Roman town is preserved, with its decorative mosaic-tiled baths—an essential to Roman well-being—and amphitheater nearly intact.

During this Roman period Sardinia became an island of deportation, a handy Siberia for discordant elements. Tiberius sent 4,000 Jews into exile here (A.D. 19), and Nero sent a few of his many enemies; Marcus Aurelius deported Christians to Sardinia, among whom was Callistus, who would become pope. Some of the early Christian churches in Sardinia, such as San Giovanni on the Sinis peninsula, are splendidly evocative of the simple faith of early Christianity.

The Roman legions left a lasting record here in the form of Vulgate Latin, which has been closely preserved in the Sardinian language.

The Vandals, after laying seige to Rome, did not neglect Sardinia, and remained here until the Byzantines arrived in 534. With Byzantium came the Greek language and churches in the Greek cross and round cupola form, such as Santa Sabina near Nuoro and the enchanting San Giovannini at Sinus, near Oristano. After Arab invasions from 711 to 1015, during the spread of Islam in the Mediterranean, Sardinia became tied to the Italian mainland more closely; expelling the Saracen had brought Pisa and Genoa, nearby seaports, into the fray, and they stayed on to enjoy the view. (The Doria family of Genoa made its mark on the island in many a castle and palace, notably at Castelsardo on the north coast.)

Now began a period that saw a flourishing of fine Romanesque architecture in Sardinia. This northern Italian style of the 12th and 13th centuries can still be enjoyed in cathedrals such as San Michele di Salvenero near Sassari and a wealth of other churches. At this time, Sardinia was partitioned into four political entites, as it is today: Cagliari, Nuoro, Sassari, and Oristano. Castles and towers arose on the hilltops as a new propertied class emerged and sought protection for their land; the others, the *servi,* did as their name implied.

The House of Aragon (1323–1478) kept its strong hold on Sardinia for centuries; in 1479 Ferdinand of Aragon married Isabella of Castile, and the Spanish language was heard until at least 1714, when the Peace of Utrecht gave Sardinia to Austria. In Alghero today you'd think they never left, for Catalan is strong in the dialect, and street names appear in Catalan as well as Italian.

Apart from beautiful churches and a lilting language, Spain left Sardinia bankrupt, as it was when the House of Savoy gained control in 1720; but the Savoy nobility were the ancestors of the kings of the united Italy that was to come. Although many Sardinians participated in the battle for Italian independence in 1870, Sardinia remained somewhat aloof from the struggle, its own advantages and disadvantages in the conflict never clearly understood. However, Garibaldi chose Sardinia for his own self-imposed exile later in life, and died here on the island of Caprera, off the northeast coast, where his house and grave can be visited.

Before World War II, the Fascist government initiated large-scale land reclamation programs, such as the agricultural development at Arborea, on the west coast, then called Mussolinia. But interest in the island was short-lived as new foreign wars created economic and manpower needs. In 1948 the Italian government conferred upon Sardinia a special status, giving it a degree of regional autonomy, which it holds today.

Today the island is divided between the political agendas of the Green parties and the developers, a struggle similar to those taking part in most developed countries.

Because Sardinia's culture has been so well insulated in the interior regions, we know a good deal about ancient daily life. The simple, nutritious diet of the past also survives—meat roasted with herbs on an open fire or in a pit; breads festively sculpted or roasted and touched with olive oil (called *carta da musica,* or sheets of music); goat and sheep cheese, creamy or sharp; and sweets made with honey, nuts, and cheese. *Cucina povera,* or poor-person's cooking, is prized for its fresh and subtly delicious taste.

In many ways Sardinia is an island for the 1990s, a natural preserve for marine and wildlife, trees and flowers, as well as for natural foods, healthy lifestyles, and a connection with the ancient past. Unfortunately, ecological concerns have not yet been extended to transportation. Without a car, transit is difficult, for the most interesting parts of the island generally are not in the cities.

MAJOR INTEREST

The *nuraghi*
Nuraghic statues (*bronzetti*) in the museums of
  Cagliari and Sassari
Beaches and grottos such as the Grotte di Nettuno
The cities: Alghero, Sassari, Cagliari
Romanesque architecture
The folk museum at Nuoro
Festivals, especially the Cavalcata at Sassari in May

Elegantly simple food
Handicrafts, especially gold rings

Oliena

A visit to Sardinia might well begin where Sardinia began, in a cultural sense: in the interior. Take the overnight ferry from Genoa or Civitavecchia near Rome to Arbatax or Olbia (or fly to Olbia) on the eastern coast. From there it is a short drive to Oliena, a town of about 8,000, just southeast of Nuoro. Here, in the wild, forested heart of Sardinia, you'll find **Su Gologone**, which has grown from a local café to a splendid white hacienda with red tile roofs, set amid glorious mountain scenery. The name is derived from a spring that gushes from between nearby boulders.

The restaurant is not for dieters—vast sides of meat and dozens of lake fish are roasted on the open hearth. The **carta da musica**, waferlike unleavened bread filled with herbs and dripping with olive oil, and the dessert menu destroy any plans for moderation. Swimming, horseback riding, and trips through the interior by Land Rover are arranged by the management. The only drawback is that its popularity brings small conventions and weekend luncheon groups out in force. Luckily the restaurant is laid out in separate sections, and proprietor Signora Palomera makes sure that no one is left out.

Oliena itself is famous for its wines, sweets, lovely jewelry, and the wonderful costumes its women still wear occasionally (and always on the feast day of San Lussorio, August 21). Although it is not a charming town, its site is superb and its friendliness is legendary. The winding streets, painted courtyards, and external staircases are set off by the sharp incline of the Sopramonte. In driving around Oliena you may find yourself on corso Martin Luther King: King's significance is keenly understood in Sardinia and the south of Italy, where economic and social discrimination are still common.

Using Su Gologone as your base, head northwest to Nuoro. About 10 km (6 miles) from the hotel you can detour to **Monte Ortobene** (some of the roads are tortuous). From the statue of the Madonna at the top, the view of Nuoro and the surrounding countryside is spectacular. The hills are covered with oak trees, cork (a major export), and a medley of flowers.

Nuoro

At Nuoro, a rather bedraggled-looking but ingratiating town of about 40,000, stop at the house of the 1926 Nobel Prize–winning writer Grazia Deledda on the street bearing her name. The house is charming, with mementos of her career in an unassuming upper room. The folk museum, **Museo della Vita e delle Tradizioni Popolari Sarde**, houses a marvelous collection of lavish costumes worn by Sardinian women through the ages, and in which the glamour of Spanish lace, the opulence of Greek and Arab jewelry, and the talent of local artisans have been combined with stunning results. In the room devoted to the pre-Lenten Carnevale costumes, frightening masks and costumes that were once thought to placate the gods vividly represent the primeval fear of the unknown. If you can be there for Carnevale, on Shrove Tuesday, you'll see one of the most memorable festivals anywhere. (Nuoro's other important folk festival takes place on the last two Sundays of August.) Also in Nuoro is the **Civico Museo Speleo-Archeologico**, where ceramics and bronzes retrieved from nearby caves are exhibited.

From Nuoro, you can either drive southeast to the nuraghic city of Barùmini and then return to Oliena at night, or you can continue south and stay in Cagliari (see below) for a night or two, visiting Barùmini, about 48 km (30 miles) north of Cagliari, from there.

For splendid beaches, travel eastward to Cala Gonone. From here boat trips can be arranged to **Cala Luna** and **Cala Sistine**, small white-sand islands with clear pools and grottos. Boat trips also leave for the **Grotta del Bue Marino**, a spectacular site but best undertaken when the tourists are not boat-to-boat. (If they are, take a sunshade and a book, and relax on the beach.)

Barùmini

Barùmini, or Su Nuraxi, as the village itself is called, is a rare treasure, a well-preserved nuraghic city dramatically located on a hillside south of Nuoro. The town dates from about 1700 B.C.; its walls and towers and houses were built with basalt rock—so perfectly balanced without the benefit of mortar that the stones continue to withstand the ravages of time. In the "Parlamento" hut, the round seat and wall niches, as well as a number of objects found there, have led anthropologists to theorize that religious rituals were part of the governing process.

Cagliari

As buoyant and blowsy as most port cities, Cagliari (CA-lya-ree), on the south coast, has sights enough to detain anyone with an interest in art. Its **National Archaeological Museum** on piazza Indipendenza houses an exceptional collection of *bronzetti,* relics from the nuraghic period. Gold jewelry from the Punic days and Roman glass are also well represented. Stop at this museum early, since it is quite extensive, and then take a stroll through the public gardens to the **Citadella Museum,** where there are frequent exhibitions. From there you can head to the Roman amphitheater to the west or start down to the Duomo at the center of the Castello section, the old city. The **Duomo** (Cattedrale di Santa Maria) is a mix of styles, but the Pisan predominates. Inside, Maestro Guglielmo of Pisa sculpted two fine pulpits. The cathedral has a museum of some note, and members of the House of Savoy are buried in its sanctuary.

Have lunch at the elegant **Dal Corsaro**, considered Cagliari's best by many restaurant critics. If you want to try their Sardinian specialties, ask for *cucina tipica,* specifying *carne* (meat) or *pesce* (fish). (Viale Regina Margherita 28; Tel: 070-66-43-18. Closed Sundays and August.) Or try the charming **St. Remy**, at via Torino 16 (Tel: 070-65-73-77) in the herbalist's shop of a former monastery (Tel: 070-65-73-77; closed Saturday lunch, Sundays, and August). You can watch the busy Sardinian business folk enjoying the fare at **Italia**, via Sardegna 26 (Tel: 070-65-79-87; closed Sundays), in the busy shopping area near the port (watch your wallet). Down the street at via Sardegna 60, the **Trattoria Gennargentu** is a good choice for palate and wallet (Tel: 070-65-82-47; closed Sundays). And for a sweet finish, have coffee and ice cream at the traditional **Caffè Genovese**, piazza Costituzione 10-11 (closed Thursdays).

When you are in the port area, do stop at **Giesse**, a tiny shop at via Sardegna 32, where delicate gold filigree wedding rings are hand-crafted. They seem to be made of gold petit point. If a wedding is not imminent, you can do as the doge of Venice did and marry the sea. The rings are worth a bit of artifice.

Since the sea is part of the reason for coming here, stay on the coast, 3 km (2 miles) outside of Cagliari, at the **Hotel Calamosca**, where you should ask for a room with a view of the *pineta,* or little pine grove. The view of the cove, its beach, and the working lighthouse make this hotel well worth the few minutes' drive from Cagliari.

For a seaside lunch go to **Ottagono** on the gulf strip called La Poetto, on viale Poetto (Tel: 070-37-28-79; closed Tuesdays, January, and February), not far from Calamosca. Have *aragosta* (lobster), the local specialty. **Lo Scoglio**, nearby, also has a sea-view terrace (Tel: 070-37-19-27).

If, instead, you'd like to experience Sardinian country life, you can stay with a family in a bed-and-breakfast–like arrangement that includes supper as well. The ecology-minded **Terranostra** organization (via Sassari 3, Cagliari; Tel: 070-668-83-67) arranges such stays. This is a new, exciting, and very inexpensive way (about 26,000 lire per person, including dinner) to experience Sardinian life as it is lived by real families. You stay at the family's *azienda,* a small farm where they raise animals, fruits and vegetables, probably have a small vineyard, and make their own sheep's-milk cheeses. From this bounty you'll be fed, and not sparingly, using traditional family recipes. (Note: These are working farms and not on the main highways, so be sure you can drive on unpaved roads. Take a dictionary, for English won't be spoken; communication should be easy, however, because the families are well briefed about tourists and their needs. Such farms are located throughout the island.)

Travel down the coast about 45 km (28 miles) in the opposite direction from Poetto (southwest) and you'll reach the Punic-Roman city of **Nora**, with its columns brilliantly outlined against the sea (stop in **Pula** to shop for ceramics en route). A Roman amphitheater and baths (nicely mosaicked, as usual) are spread out amid earlier Punic remains, such as the temple to Tanit, a Mediterranean fertility goddess.

Su Gunventeddu is tranquil, whether you can pronounce its name or not. Here fresh fish and seafood are the specialty. (On the road between Nora and Pula; Tel: 070-920-90-92; closed Tuesdays and from mid-December to mid-January.)

Alghero

Leaving Cagliari, head northwest toward Alghero, stopping first at **Bosa** on the coast to see the **Castello di Malaspina**, whose dramatic walls and tower dominate a hilltop. Inside the walls is the **Church of Nostra Signora di Regnos Altos**, in which a cycle of frescoes depicts scenes from the life of Christ. Bosa produces a good Malvasia wine, and you might want to stop to see some of the lacemakers at work, often outdoors. Continue along the sea until, past the city of Villanova Monteleone, the rugged outline of the coast at Capo Caccia appears, signaling that you are nearing Alghero (al-GAYR-oh).

Though Alghero was apparently founded in the 11th century by the Genoese, today the city is Catalan in look and spirit. Street signs are written in both Catalan and Italian, and the panache of Moorish Spain—vividly evoked by the interlaced arches and arabesques that decorate windows and courtyards—is happily fused with the solemnity of tall Gothic windows and reliefs of leaves and lilies. The Old City is still bound with massive towers and walls, which protect it from the busy harbor and esplanade below. A walk around the town's sturdy sand-colored walls is an exhilarating way to begin the morning. Some cafés set up their tables on the walls near the port side for cappuccino and *cornetti* while the fishing fleet sets sail.

In 1353 the Catalan Aragonese—with the help of Genoa's rival, Venice—defeated the Genoese. Expelling Sard and Ligurian, Peter IV of Aragón repopulated the city with Catalans. Alghero remained a possession of the Aragón crown until 1714, when it was transferred to the House of Savoy. Since then the city has expanded well beyond its walls, and this part of Sardinia has become one of the most popular with tourists for its picturesqueness, its location near beaches and dramatic cliffs and grottos, and its proximity to important nuraghic sites and the museum at Sassari, with its fine collection of nuraghic art (see below).

A walk through Alghero might start at the piazza Porta a Terra, at the eastern edge of the Old City. (Just outside the walls are the extensive public gardens.) In the piazza is the 14th-century Jewish Tower, or **Torre degli Ebrei**, so called because it was built by the Jews of Alghero before they were expelled by the Inquisition.

From here follow via Roma a short way, turning left at the via Barcellonetta, to via Machin, where a right turn leads to the beautiful 14th-century **Church of San Francesco**. Here the marriage of two cultures is evident in soaring Gothic arches and dramatic Catalan sculpture. The statue by an unknown 17th-century Spaniard of Christ tied to the pillar, at the left of the central nave, is exceptionally fine. Along with the star vaulting at the altar, notice the fine cabinet (*paratore*) of intarsia in the sacristy, as well as the cloisters, where concerts are often held. From there, the view of the bell tower contributes a vertical accent to the horizontal harmony below. The Franciscans, who live in the adjacent monastery, provide simple rooms if you'd like to stay here overnight.

Turning right at the exit you'll reach via Roma, close to the **Cattedrale** (which closes at noon). Its late Renaissance portico of Doric columns lends it the solemnity appropriate to the burial place of members of the House of Savoy.

Close by is the piazza Civica, where you can stop for a coffee and sandwich at the delightful café on the ground floor of the palace. You might mistake it for an antiques shop, but inside there are tables and a handsome bar.

This is one of the busiest and prettiest sections of town. As in an Arab town, tiny streets head off in all directions. To buy some of the finest coral and gold (including the gold wedding rings), go to **Orafart**, nearby at via G. Ferret 53, where a model of the sea bottom illustrates how coral is formed. Today it is difficult to obtain coral because fishing boats scraping the bottom unintentionally have destroyed much of it. The largest pieces are found at such depths that divers can remain there only a short time. Since harmony of color is part of its beauty, a necklace must come from one piece of coral to be considered fine jewelry. There is much imitation and much Asian coral masquerading as Sardinian.

Right off the piazza Civica is the Bastione della Maddalena, and beneath it is the port from which boats leave for a three-hour excursion to **Neptune's Grotto**, considered Sardinia's most beautiful. The cliffs at **Capo Caccia** (24 km/15 miles from Alghero) above the grotto possess great dramatic beauty (also enjoyed by tour buses, especially in summer, so go early in the morning or off-season). You can rent a bungalow near this glorious sight at **Campeggio Porticciolo**, with facilities that include a restaurant and tennis courts.

Between Capo Caccia and Alghero, be sure to visit the nuraghic village of **Palmavera**, where 50 nuraghic huts and a fine tower can be explored. The tower's intricate vaulting—called a "false dome" because from the outside only the usual truncated cone is visible—is well developed, and you can climb the prehistoric stairs to enjoy the view.

Ask at the Alghero Tourist Office (Piazza Porta Terra 9) whether a trip to **Arca di Noë** (Noah's Ark) can be arranged. A guide is required to see this wild stretch of land where the rare white donkey (*asino bianco*), wild quarter horses, and the almost-extinct griffin vulture live in an Eden all their own.

In Alghero you may want to stay at the modern **Carlos V,**

just outside the city walls, with a pool and terraces on the sea, or at the refurbished home of Spanish royalty located on a little rocky peninsula across from the Carlos V, the **Villa Las Tronas**, which has restored some of its grandeur of days gone by. The most beautiful hotel in the area is **El Faro**, on a private promontory 13 km (8 miles) from the city. The spacious white building is warmed with antiques, and each room has a sea-facing terrace. Pool and courts, sauna, and private beach plus water sports such as underwater photography, windsurfing, and sailing are all at hand. Full summer is the best time here, unless you like a little Gatsby-type off-season melancholy.

Less expensive and far less glamorous is the **Bellavista**, near the lovely beach at Fertilia, just outside Alghero.

Have a lavish dinner at **La Lepanto** at via Carlo Alberto 135 (Tel: 079-97-91-16; closed Mondays), where lobster is served Alghero-style—the meat is marinated in a sauce of lemon and orange peel, with tomatoes and herbs. A glass of Vernaccia, a fine Sardinian dessert wine, writes a happy ending. At **Tuguri**, in a 15th-century palazzo at via Maiorca 57 (Tel: 079-97-67-72), try the risotto *con verdure* (with vegetables), or ask Carbonella to choose your meal for you. A fine wine with seafood is Tere Bianche (Torbato di Alghero). Less expensive is the Spanish-style **El Pultal**, at via Colombano 40 (Tel: 079-97-80-51).

When you leave Alghero, take the road toward Porto Torres, turning west a few miles before town when you see the sign for **Stintino**, which is located on a stretch of land that shoots up from Sardinia's extreme northwest coast. Stintino was strictly a fishing village until recently, but has made itself more attractive to tourists. Stay at the hotel **Roccaruja**, with a view of the island of Asinara, which has the dual distinction of being the only place where the white ass, *l'asino bianco,* is bred and also the home of a penal colony specializing in Mafiosi. No visitors.

To the southeast lies Sassari.

Sassari

Sassari is an attractive, vivacious city, thanks to its nicely preserved Medieval Old City (**Centro Storico**) and the presence of a major university; you would do well to include it in your itinerary. A visit to its Sanna Museum (see below) is a wonderful way to learn about nuraghic society, for the exhibits are carefully arranged with both enjoyment and education in mind.

As capital of the province of the same name, Sassari is a major commercial center, yet it retains the quaint charm characteristic of smaller towns. If you stay at the modern, comfortable hotel **Grazia Deledda**, you can walk to most sights of interest.

The **Duomo**, at the center of the Centro Storico, was begun during the 12th century and rebuilt during the 15th. In its museum, reached from inside the church, is the *Madonna and Child with Saint Veronica,* considered one of the most beautiful paintings in all of Sassari. A few blocks away and just outside the city walls is the **Church of Santa Maria di Betlem**, in which enormous painted candlesticks are kept until August 14 of each year, when (on the eve of the Feast of the Assumption of the Virgin Mary) they are carried in a procession through the city.

If possible come to Sassari on the next to last Sunday in May, when the Cavalcata Sarde with its galloping horses begins; look for the riders straddling two horses. The brilliant parade of Sardinians in lavish traditional dress lasts for hours.

Stroll from the cathedral along the viale Coppino past the city park (**Giardino Pubblico**), where the Folk Arts Pavilion (**Padiglione dell'Artigianato**) has exhibits of rugs, jewelry, and other folk crafts, as well as copies of *bronzetti,* earth goddesses—all made in the traditional way and thus somewhat expensive.

Nearby on via Roma is the **Museo Sanna**, the modern archaeological museum mentioned above. The museum is laid out spaciously, with minute attention paid to exhibits, which range from prehistoric finds and nuraghic-era relics to Punic and Roman collections and a sampling of folk art.

Sassari has several good restaurants. Among the best is the **Trattoria del Giamaranto** at via Alghero 69 (reserve; Tel: 079-27-45-98; closed July 22 to August 22, Saturday evenings, and Sundays in summer). Although the atmosphere is stylishly minimalist, the cooking is decidedly natural, offering such pleasures as homemade ravioli filled with porcini mushrooms or artichokes. If you haven't yet tasted Sardinia's caviar, called *bottarga* (mullet eggs), now is the time. The grilled fish is always the freshest possible and may be a welcome option if you've indulged in the meat dishes typical of Sardinia. **L'Assassino** is simple in style but interestingly complex in its offerings, which include game dishes such as wild boar and rabbit, and pizzas for the lighter appetite (via Ospizio Cappuccini 1/b; Tel: 079-23-50-41; closed Sundays and August).

The Fabled North Coast

From Sassari, head north toward **Castelsardo**, one of Sardinia's most dramatic coastal towns, founded, it's thought, in 1102 by the Doria family of Genoa, in part because of its strategic importance. In 1448 the Aragonese conquered the city, but with less lasting impact than at Alghero. Today this fishing town is known for its *aragosta,* and you really should indulge in one or two. Local women can also be seen weaving baskets, which they sell (you'd better buy if you want to take their picture).

Continue along the beautiful coastal drive north to **Santa Teresa di Gallura**. The coast from here to the Emerald Coast (the color is emerald here, too, and cerulean blue in broad expanses) on the eastern coast is composed of new settlements; the towers and churches of Aragonese days are rarely seen. Stay just outside town at **Shardana**, a pretty resort with private bungalows, swimming pool, private beach, and tennis courts.

The best place to try the local dishes is at **Canne al Vento** (named for a novel by Grazia Deledda). You need only ask for *cucina tipica* and a wealth of good food will appear (via Nazionale 23; Tel: 0789-75-42-19; closed October and November).

From town (or the Shardana, which is closer), you *must* take an excursion to **Capo Testa**, a promontory about 3 km (2 miles) to the west and one of Sardinia's most scenic places. Some of the mistral-sculpted rocks at Capo Testa are astonishingly beautiful; the odd animal shapes of others are amusing. At Tibula on Capo Testa you can walk along the cove of Santa Reparata to see the granite columns carved by the Romans for the Pantheon but left behind after their unexpected departure. If you'd like to stay in the area, try the **Bocche di Bonifacio**, where the owners do the fishing and the catch of the day is always fresh. Room and board, including dinner, costs about 80,000 lire. **Da Colomba**, on a rocky shore with a nearby marina, is another simply furnished and reasonably priced hotel. The hotel **Li Capanni** at Cannigione, near Porto Cervo, is away from it all on a tranquil macchia-covered bit of land near the sea. Meals are quite good.

Sardinia also has many comfortable campgrounds, an excellent choice for families. For detailed information on sites and facilities, ask the tourist office in any major Sardinian city for *Campeggi 1992*.

Another excursion from Santa Teresa is to **Bonifacio** in Corsica, named for Napoléon. Or sail to the lovely islands of **La Maddalena** archipelago and the island of **Caprera**, just to the east across a causeway, to see Garibaldi's last home and final resting place. On La Maddalena, dine at **La Grotta** (via Principe di Napoli 3; Tel: 0789-73-72-28; closed Sundays and October), a traditional place for good Sardinian-style seafood, including of course the classic *spaghetti alla bottarga* (Sardinian caviar) and *aragosta* (lobster) with onions and tomatoes, a combination that works well with this variety of crustacean, unlike its American cousin. Vernaccia is the wine of choice.

Continuing on to the **Costa Smeralda**, you may find Porto Cervo a bit disappointing, given its advance publicity. The town is a pretty, suburban-type shopping mall with Rodeo Drive labels—a Disneyland for the inveterate shopper where Mickey and Minnie are stylishly played by Armani and Krizia. Watch the helicopters land on the power yachts in the harbor; Aga Khan's yacht has space for two.

The hotels of the Costa Smeralda complex, of which the Aga Khan is principal stockholder, are indeed luxurious. The **Pitrizza** is the most exclusive, with private villas scattered picturesquely about, spacious terraces, and lots of space to moor your yacht. The **Balocco** is a good choice at about a quarter the price, with scenic terraces and a swimming pool.

Apart from sailing, tanning, hiking, enjoying nature, grotto exploring, scuba diving, swimming, water skiing, eating, and shopping, there simply isn't a thing to do here; and when you're ready to return to the mainland, the air- and seaports of Olbia are only a short drive to the south.

GETTING AROUND

Sardinia can be reached from all Italian airports via Alisarda Airlines (sometimes you must change planes in Rome). Incoming flights land at Alghero, Cagliari, and Olbia. Many European airports—Paris, Geneva, Nice, Frankfurt, and Düsseldorf, among them—have direct flights to the island. By sea there are frequent overnight ferries from Toulon, Genoa, and Civitavecchia (near Rome). State railway-ferryboats take you to Sardinia directly from Rome and other cities; ask for information at the Italian Railways Information Service or from CIT, the Italian tour company. The Tirrenia Line in Italy services the island; tickets can be bought from travel agents in Italy. In Great Britain, booking can be made through

Normandy Ferries, Arundel Towers, Portland Terrace, South-ampton; Tel: (703) 321-31 and 441-41.

In Sardinia, Roberto Salmon, a well-informed guide who also teaches English, arranges tours for individuals and small groups. He can be reached at via Perpignan 27, Alghero; Tel: (079) 97-69-98.

Driving is the best way to see the island, since many sights are far from the main roads and public transportation is a sometime thing.

ACCOMMODATIONS REFERENCE

The rates given below are projections for 1992; always check for up-to-date information before making reservations. Wide ranges may reflect the differences between low- and high-season rates. Unless otherwise indicated, the figures indicate the cost of a double room (per room, not per person). However, half-board (mezza pensione) rates, which include breakfast and one other meal per day, are per person. Most hotels will add a service charge of 10 to 15 percent.

▶ **Balocco**. Liscia di Vacca, 07020 **Porto Cervo**. Tel: (0789) 915-55. Open April–October 15. £260,000.

▶ **Bellavista**. Via Rovigno 13, 07041 **Fertilia** (Alghero). Tel: (079) 93-01-24; Fax: same. £41,000–£66,000; half board £61,000–£75,000.

▶ **Bocche di Bonifacio**. Capo Testa, 07028 **Santa Teresa di Gallura**. Tel: (0789) 75-42-02. Closed November 10–March 10. £50,000.

▶ **Hotel Calamosca**. Viale Calamosca 50, 09126 **Cagliari**. Tel: (070) 37-16-28 or 37-02-52. £90,000.

▶ **Campeggio Porticciolo**. Capo Caccia, 07041 **Alghero**. Tel: (079) 91-90-07. £60,000.

▶ **Li Capanni**. Golfo Saline, 07020 **Cannigione**. Tel: (0789) 860-41. £85,000–£120,000.

▶ **Carlos V**. Lungomare Valencia 24, 07041 **Alghero**. Tel: (079) 97-95-01; Fax: (079) 98-02-98. £140,000–£190,000; half board £133,000–£173,000.

▶ **Da Colomba**. Capo Testa, 07028 **Santa Teresa di Gallura**. Tel: (0789) 75-42-72. £45,000.

▶ **El Faro**. Porto Conte, 07041 **Alghero**. Tel: (079) 94-20-10; Fax: (079) 94-20-30. Closed September 20–May 15. £120,000–£200,000; half board £140,000–£180,000.

▶ **Grazia Deledda**. Viale Dante 47, 07100 **Sassari**. Tel: (079) 27-12-35; Fax: (079) 28-08-84. £91,000–£137,000; half board £99,000–£146,000.

► **Pitrizza**. Liscia di Vacca, 07020 **Porto Cervo**. Tel: (0789) 915-00; Fax: (0789) 916-29. In U.S., Tel: (800) 221-2340 or (212) 935-9540; Fax: (212) 421-5929. In U.K., Tel: (0800) 28-92-34 or (071) 930-4147; Fax: (071) 839-1566. Open May 15–September. Half board Ł557,000.

► **Roccaruja**. Località Capo Falcone, 07040 **Stintino**. Tel: (079) 52-70-38. Open May–October. Full board (3 meals) Ł130,000–Ł190,000.

► **Shardana**. Santa Reparata, 07028 **Santa Teresa di Gallura**. Tel: (0789) 75-43-91; Fax: (0789) 75-41-29. Ł88,000–Ł110,000.

► **Su Gologone**. Oliena, 08025 **Nuoro**. Tel: (0784) 28-75-12; Fax: (0784) 28-76-68. Ł60,000–Ł80,000; half board Ł80,000–Ł95,000.

► **Terranostra**. Via Sassari 3, 09100 **Cagliari**. Tel: (070) 66-83-67. Half board Ł30,000.

► **Villa Las Tronas**. Lungomare Valencia 1, 07041 **Alghero**. Tel: (079) 97-53-90; Fax: (079) 98-10-44. Ł150,000–Ł200,000; half board Ł120,000–Ł170,000.

CHRONOLOGY OF THE HISTORY OF ITALY

Prehistory

Italian prehistory extends at least as far back as 700,000 B.C., when the earliest known relics of humanoids were left in Molise in central Italy. On the rugged hillsides of Sardinia, Stone Age inhabitants built towers called *nuraghi,* and archaeologists in Apulia and Sicily have uncovered Paleolithic cave drawings. After 3000 B.C. the peninsula was settled by migrating Indo-Europeans.

From their base in Carthage, the sea-travelling Phoenicians established settlements in western Sicily and Sardinia during the eighth century B.C. Their influence eventually spread across the sea to the shores of Latium.

Between the eighth and fifth centuries B.C., Italy was colonized in the north and south by Etruscans and Greeks respectively. The Etruscans, an advanced people probably from Asia Minor, are believed to have absorbed the culture of Greece without relinquishing their own cultural identity. Little is known about their architecture, but wall paintings and decorated sarcophagi found at their burial grounds attest to a pronounced realism, a love for drama, and an attraction to the grotesque.

The Greeks

In the early eighth century B.C. Greeks from various centers founded more than 40 colonies on the coasts of Sicily and southern Italy, which in the aggregate were called Magna Graecia. A number of pre-Socratic philosophers, including Pythagoras and Parmenides, made important contributions here, and Plato himself lived in Magna Graecia for a time. The Greek Doric temples in Sicily are more numerous and better preserved than those in Greece.

The Foundations of the Roman Empire

Some of the most lasting expressions of Roman artistic creativity are in the areas of architecture, engineering, and urban planning. Highly successful open spaces, such as the forum, continue to ensure the vitality of civic and commercial life today. As Jacob Burckhardt observed, the Romans set the seal of immortality on everything they did.

The major architectural contribution of Roman art was the refinement of vaulted construction (for the vast spatial advantages it allowed) and its use in the building of baths, amphitheaters, palaces, aqueducts, and triumphal arches. During the republican period (510–30 B.C.) portrait sculpture became more realistic, departing from the ideal.

- **753 B.C.:** According to legend, Rome is founded by Romulus on April 21.
- **800–500 B.C.:** Sardinia is occupied by Phoenicians from Carthage, who war with the Greeks and eventually take over large sections of Sicily.
- **600–501 B.C.:** Greeks bring olive trees to Italy.
- **700–500 B.C.:** Etruscan political and cultural power at its highest in Italy.
- **510 B.C.:** Rome is transformed from a kingdom into a republic.
- **500 B.C.:** The Greeks begin their intermittent war with the Carthaginians.
- **500–451 B.C.:** Viticulture begins.
- **494 B.C.:** Led by Rome, 30 Latium cities form the Latin League.
- **396 B.C.:** Rome captures the Etruscan city of Veii, which marks the decline of Etruscan rule.
- **390 B.C.:** Gauls invade Italy and occupy Rome.
- **348 B.C.:** League of Latin Cities dissolved.
- **312 B.C.:** Construction of Appian aqueduct and Appian Way begins.
- **264–241 B.C.:** First Punic War. Rome wars with Carthage and drives it out of Sicily.
- **220 B.C.:** Flaminian Way finished.
- **219–201 B.C.:** Second Punic War. Hannibal crosses Alps, invades Italy, and captures Turin; defeats Romans at Lake Trasimeno (217 B.C.). Romans, led by Scipio, carry war back to Spain and Carthage; Hannibal is defeated by Scipio at Zama (203–202 B.C.).
- **209 B.C.:** Taranto, the last Greek city-state in Italy, is subjugated by Rome.
- **149–146 B.C.:** Third Punic War—Carthage destroyed.
- **133–17 B.C.:** Sicily becomes the "granary of Rome." Numerous slave revolts, including one led by Spartacus, result in protracted, bitter wars; reform movement of the Gracchi.

- **60 B.C.:** The first Triumvirate is created by Pompey, Crassus, and Julius Caesar.
- **58–51 B.C.:** Julius Caesar conquers Gaul.
- **49–45 B.C.:** Caesar defeats Pompey; in 45 B.C. he is elected dictator for life.
- **44 B.C.:** At the height of the internal wars in Rome, Julius Caesar is assassinated. His great-nephew and ward Octavius ushers in a new form of government, the *principate*.
- **43 B.C.:** The second Triumvirate is formed by Mark Antony, Lepidus, and Octavius, Caesar's great-nephew.

The Early Empire

In the early Roman Empire the equestrian statue is perfected, as evidenced by the bronze statue of Marcus Aurelius (A.D. 165) on the Capitoline Hill in Rome. Painting reaches its highest achievement in the Roman cities of Pompeii and Herculaneum.

- **31 B.C.:** Battle of Actium; Mark Antony and Cleopatra defeated by Octavius, and commit suicide; Egypt becomes a Roman province.
- **30 B.C.–A.D. 14:** Octavius, given the name Augustus by the Senate in A.D. 27, establishes the Roman Empire and presides over a cultural awakening (Virgil, Horace, Livy, Seneca, and Ovid are among the writers and thinkers of the time); Pantheon in Rome is begun.
- **A.D.14:** Tiberius assumes *principate,* followed by Caligula in A.D. 37.
- **54–68:** Reign of Nero; has his mother, Agrippina, and wife, Octavia, killed; commits suicide.
- **79:** Pompeii and Herculaneum are demolished by the eruption of Mount Vesuvius.
- **98–117:** Under the emperor Trajan, the Roman Empire reaches its pinnacle.
- **161–180:** Reign of philosophical emperor Marcus Aurelius; writes his *Meditations;* beginning of barbarian attacks.
- **200:** Bishops of Rome gain predominant position.
- **212:** "Civis Romanus Sum"—every freeborn subject in Empire is granted Roman citizenship.
- **220:** Arabs, Germans, and Persians, among others, begin attacking the frontiers of the Roman Empire.

- **249–269**: Persecution of Christians increases.
- **284–305**: The Illyrian emperor Diocletian reforms government.

Constantine and the Later Empire

- **313**: Emperor Constantine (306–337) formally recognizes Christianity with the Edict of Milan. In 330 he moves the capital to Byzantium and renames the city Constantinople. Rome is in decline.
- **349–397**: Saint Ambrose becomes bishop of Milan (374); refuses surrender of church to Arians; converts and baptizes Saint Augustine of Hippo.
- **391**: Theodosius declares Christianity to be the state religion; becomes last ruler of a united Empire.
- **395**: The Roman Empire is divided into a western empire, with its capital at Ravenna, and an eastern empire (Constantinople).
- **410**: Alaric, king of the Visigoths, invades Rome; Saint Augustine writes *The City of God* (411).
- **425**: Valentinian III is western Roman emperor under guardianship of his mother, Galla Placidia. During fourth and fifth centuries, Latin begins to replace Greek as the formal language of the Church.
- **455**: The Vandals, led by Gaiseric, sack Rome.
- **476**: The German general Odoacer brings an end to the western Roman Empire, although a strip of coast around Ravenna remains under eastern Roman rule until 751.

The Founding of the Holy Roman Empire

From the fourth century, when Constantine moved the capital from Rome to Byzantium, until the 13th century, Byzantine art, mainly Christian in its themes, dominates the Italian peninsula. The most significant monuments of early Byzantine art are its catacombs and basilicas (Ravenna, Venice, and Rome).

- **480–543**: Saint Benedict of Nursia, patriarch of Western monasticism, devises his "rule."
- **493**: Odoacer is succeeded by Theodoric the Great.
- **500**: First plans for Vatican palace drawn up.
- **524**: Boethius, Roman scholar and adviser to Emperor

Theodoric, is accused of treason; while imprisoned, he writes his *De consolatione philosophiae.*

- **532–552:** Ostrogoth kingdom of Italy occupied by Byzantine general Belisarius; Totila ends Byzantine rule in Italy and becomes king; begins ravaging Italy.
- **553:** The Byzantine emperor Justinian succeeds in reimposing the rule of Constantinople on Italy.
- **568–572:** The Lombard king Alboin drives the Byzantines out of northern Italy, Tuscany, and Umbria. Lombards establish strong principalities in these areas. The rule of the eastern empire extends to Ravenna, Rome, parts of the Adriatic coast, and sections of southern Italy.
- **590–604:** Papacy of Gregory the Great, architect of Medieval papacy.
- **751:** Ravenna falls to the Lombards.
- **754–756:** The Carolingian king Pepin defeats the Lombards and forces them to recognize Frankish sovereignty.
- **773–774:** Charlemagne unites the Lombard kingdom with the Frankish kingdom.
- **800:** Charlemagne is crowned emperor in Rome by Pope Leo III. In southern Italy, the sea republics of Amalfi and Naples and the duchy of Gaeta seek protection from Byzantium. Sicily and Sardinia are conquered by the Arabs as Islam expands in the Mediterranean.
- **Ninth century:** Rival states are established and anarchy reigns with the demise of the Carolingian Empire.
- **828:** Founding of St. Mark's, Venice.
- **846:** Arabs sack Rome and damage Vatican; destroy Venetian fleets.
- **879:** The pope and patriarch of Constantinople excommunicate each other.
- **962:** The German king Otto I is crowned emperor and founds the Holy Roman Empire of the German Nation. His attempts to conquer southern Italy fail.

The Papacy and the Empire

The Romanesque style developed from Early Christian architecture in the 11th century and embraced numerous regional variations. In architecture, the Romanesque style is characterized by round arches and by large, simple geometric masses. The Duomo at Pisa is one of the finest examples. The figurative sculpture and the painting that began to appear in the Romanesque churches of the 11th century showed considerable Byzantine influence.

- **1000–1200**: The Normans combine southern Italy and Sicily into a new kingdom. Byzantine and Arab cultural influences continue. Independent city-states emerge. The sea republics of Genoa, Pisa, and Venice emerge.
- **1053**: Under the leadership of Robert Guiscard, the Normans conquer Pope Leo IX's forces in Apulia. In 1059 the pope invests him with southern Italy and Sicily.
- **1076–1122**: In the confrontation between the empire and the papacy, known as the Investiture Conflict, the pope distances himself from the emperor and focuses on the emerging states.
- **1077**: The excommunicated emperor Henry IV humbles himself before pope Gregory VII.
- **1095**: Pope Urban II declares the First Crusade.
- **1119**: Establishment of the first university in Europe at Bologna.
- **1130**: Roger II founds the Norman kingdom in Italy and is crowned king of Naples and Sicily.
- **1152–1190**: Frederick Barbarossa of Hohenstaufen wars with Lombard cities and destroys Milan; Saint Francis of Assisi is born (1182); communes arise and northern and central cities in Italy experiment with self-government.
- **1194–1268**: Southern Italy and Sicily come under Hohenstaufen rule. Emperor Frederick II moves the palace from Palermo to Naples.
- **1198–1216**: Papacy of Innocent III, great church reformer; Fourth Crusade; Venice leads in fighting Constantinople; introduction of Arabic numerals in Europe.
- **1224–1250**: Inquisition under Dominicans commences; Pope Gregory IX excommunicates Frederick II; Frederick II's court establishes first school of Italian poetry; crusades and commerce enlarge intellectual boundaries of Italy, and Arab scholars translate the Greek classics; commercial and industrial boom in northern and central Italy.
- **1256**: Hundred Years War between Venice and Genoa begins.
- **1265**: Pope Clement IV gives Sicily and southern Italy to Count Charles I of Anjou as a fief. The French put an end to the rule of the Hohenstaufen. In 1268 the last of the Hohenstaufen, Conradin, is beheaded in Naples.

The Renaissance and the Emergence of the City-States

From 1250 to 1600 a politically fragmented Italy saw its city-states grow in both cultural and economic importance. During this same period humanists (Dante, Petrarch, Boccaccio) rediscovered ancient (so-called Classical) literature.

The Gothic style, represented most notably in church architecture by pointed arches, was introduced into Italy by the mendicant orders. The earliest Gothic church in Italy was completed in Assisi in 1253. The Duomo in Milan maintains true northern Gothic style; large public buildings and palaces, among them the Palazzo Vecchio in Florence and the Doges' Palace in Venice, also exemplify its lofty principles. Gothic painting was advanced by Giotto (1266–1337), who, breaking away from Byzantine iconography, imbued biblical scenes with naturalism and humanism.

With the patronage of wealthy ruling princes, and a theologically less restrictive approach to architecture, painting, and sculpture, the Renaissance evolved. In 15th-century Florence it reached its zenith. The architects of the Quattrocento (1400s), as the early Renaissance is known, adopted a new style modeled on Classical architectural forms. The subject matter of sculpture, heavily influenced by Classical art, now included secular, mythological, and historical themes. Portrait sculpture emphasized greater realism.

- **Late 13th–early 14th century**: Thomas Aquinas (1225–1274) writes *Summa contra Gentiles* and *Summa theologica;* teaches at Orvieto; Cimabue begins to soften the Byzantine look in art; Marco Polo (1254–1324) journeys to China, and returns to Italy in 1295. Giotto (1266–1337) revolutionizes painting by cracking the Byzantine mold; frescoes painted in Assisi and Padua. Dante Alighieri (1265–1321) writes *La vita nuova* (1290) and the *Divina commedia* (1307). Pisano family of sculptors works in major cities. Boccaccio (1230–1313) writes the *Decameron*. Petrarch crowned poet on the Capitol (1304); Pisa University founded; plague devastates Italy and rest of Europe.
- **1282**: The rule of the House of Anjou over Sicily comes to an end with the massacre in Palermo of the French, an event known as the "Sicilian Vespers." Charles of Anjou retains only the kingdom of Naples.
- **14th century**: Italian cities divide their allegiance be-

tween pope (Guelphs) and emperor (Ghibellines). The sea republic of Venice is at the height of its power. Florence establishes its reign over a large section of northern and central Italy. In Milan the House of Visconti emerges as sole ruler (later replaced by the Sforzas).

- **Late 14th–early 15th century**: Flourishing artistic period—works of Botticelli, Titian, Bramante, Piero della Francesca, Perugino. Ascent of Medici in Italy; become bankers to papacy. Great Schism (1378–1417) begins after Pope Gregory XI dies; two popes elected. Papal exile in Avignon (1309–1377); Saint Catherine of Siena (1347–1380) helps bring back popes from Avignon. Brunelleschi (1377–1446) discovers perspective.
- **1442**: Alfonso IV, king of Aragon, conquers Naples and becomes "King of the Two Sicilies."
- **1451**: Christopher Columbus (Cristoforo Colombo) is born.
- **1453**: Fall of Constantinople.
- **1466**: Probable year of birth of Andrea Doria, admiral and statesman, who governed the republic of Genoa and was instrumental in defeating Barbarossa.
- **1493**: Lodovico "Il Moro" Sforza is invested with the duchy of Milan.
- **1463–1498**: Giovanni Pico della Mirandola (1463–1494), humanist and wandering scholar, writes *Oration on the Dignity of Man*. Aldine Press in Venice publishes comedies of Aristophanes.

The High Renaissance

From the first half of the 16th century onward the High Renaissance spread to the great cities and courts of Europe. It was during this period that Donato Bramante (1444–1514) designed the new St. Peter's in Rome, and Michelangelo Buonarotti (1475–1564) executed the plan. Michelangelo's works in Florence included the famous statue of *David* and the mausoleum of the Medici in San Lorenzo. In Rome he painted the magnificent ceiling frescoes in the Sistine Chapel. Leonardo da Vinci (1452–1519), sculptor, architect, painter, scientist, and builder, worked in Florence, Rome, France, and at the Sforza court in Milan. Major scientific discoveries, particularly the Copernican revolution, shook the foundations of the religious community. The Neoclassical architecture of Andrea Palladio (1508–1580) evoked the splendor of ancient Rome in San Giorgio in Venice and the Venetian villas, and provided a model for all of Europe. Titian's (1477–1576) paintings presaged the development of the Baroque style.

- **1492**: Columbus sails from Spain on the flagship *Santa Maria* with a crew of 70; discovers Watlings Island (San Salvador), Cuba, and Haiti.
- **1493**: Columbus returns to Spain and then leaves for a second voyage, during which he discovers Dominica, Jamaica, and Puerto Rico. Travels for three years.
- **1494**: Italy is invaded by Charles VIII of France, who deposes Piero de Medici and then captures Rome.
- **1494–1498**: Leonardo da Vinci paints *The Last Supper* and develops his scientific studies.
- **1496**: Michelangelo's first stay in Rome; begins to paint Sistine Chapel (1508).
- **1502**: Columbus sails to Honduras and Panama, marking his fourth and last voyage. Returns in 1504 and dies in 1506.
- **1512**: Copernicus produces his *Commentariolus,* in which he asserts that the Earth and other planets revolve around the Sun.
- **16th century**: The Austrian House of Hapsburg and the French kings begin their struggle for northern Italy, which is divided into numerous small states as a result. Subsequently, almost all ruling houses of Italy are subjugated by either the Austrian or the Spanish line of the House of Habsburg. Palladio works on villas, theaters, and churches in the Veneto.
- **1521**: Machiavelli writes *Dell'arte della guerra,* and *Il Principe* in 1532.
- **1527**: Castiglione writes *Il libro del cortegiano;* Rome sacked by Charles V's troops.
- **1545**: Council of Trent meets to discuss Reformation and establish principles of Counter-Reformation.

The 16th Century to the Napoleonic Era

The art of the Counter-Reformation (mid-16th century to mid-17th century) became known as Mannerism because it emphasized the study of attitudes and expression. The Baroque style developed out of Mannerism in the 17th century and the early part of the 18th century. Painters of the Baroque style included Caravaggio (1573–1610), who delighted in the theatrical and emphasized the effects of lighting, movement, perspective, and trompe l'oeil.

No form of music is more Italian by nature than opera, and no country is more passionate about opera than Italy. Claudio Monteverdi (1567–1643) was the first composer to make opera available to a wider audience. The operatic music of Alessandro Scarlatti (1660–1725) and Giovanni Battista Pergolesi (1710–1736) set the stage for the flowering of Italian opera in the next century.

- **1570**: The Turks declare war on Venice.
- **1573**: Peace of Constantinople establishes peace between the Turks and Venice.
- **1578**: The catacombs of Rome are discovered.
- **1598–1680**: Life and works of Bernini, master spirit of the Baroque, in architecture and sculpture; splendid colonnade of St. Peter's.
- **1600**: First opera, Florence.
- **1601**: The University of Parma is founded.
- **1608**: Galileo constructs an astronomical telescope, which he uses in 1610 to observe the planets and discovers Jupiter's satellites.
- **1615**: Galileo faces the Inquisition for the first time. The following year he is prohibited from further scientific study.
- **1626**: The pope inherits the duchy of Urbino from the last of the Della Rovere family.
- **1633**: Galileo is forced by the Roman Inquisition to recant his acceptance of the Copernican view of the universe. Dies in 1642.
- **1648**: Aria and recitative become two distinct expressions in opera.
- **17th century**: The popes join the French in the battle against the Spanish-Austrian rulers. Savoy becomes the strongest state in northern Italy.
- **1706**: As a result of the victory of Prince Eugene near Turin, Austria controls all of Lombardy.
- **1713**: Following the Spanish War of Succession, Austria receives the kingdom of Naples and the island of Sardinia, making Austria the major power in Italy.
- **1713–1714**: With the Treaty of Utrecht, Austria receives large sections of central Italy, but in return must yield Naples and Sicily to the Spanish Bourbons. With the demise of the Medici in Florence, the Grand Duchy of Tuscany also becomes part of Austria.

- **1725:** Casanova, author and adventurer, is born. Dies in 1798.
- **1796:** Napoléon Bonaparte begins his Italian campaign.
- **1797:** The French defeat the Austrians at Marengo. With the Peace of Campoformio, Italy is ruled by France. Austria retains Venice and land south of the Adige. Eventually, Napoléon dissolves the papal states and incorporates them into Italy.
- **1805:** Napoléon crowns himself king of Italy.
- **1806:** Joseph Bonaparte, Napoléon's brother, becomes king of Naples.
- **1809:** The papal states are annexed to the French empire. Pope Pius VII is imprisoned in France in 1812.
- **1814:** The demise of the Napoleonic regime. Pope Pius VII returns to Rome.

The 19th-Century Unification Movement

The ornate Baroque style of the 18th century gave way to the simpler lines of Classicism (or Neoclassicism), which was modeled after Greek and Roman art forms. The foremost Italian painter of the style was Antonio Canova (1757–1822). Verdi (1813–1901), whose works include *Rigoletto, Il Trovatore, Aida,* and *Otello,* escalated opera to an extraordinarily popular music form. Puccini (1858–1924) continued the development of the operatic form with *La Bohème, Tosca, Madama Butterfly, Gianni Schicchi,* and *Turandot.*

- **1814–1815:** The Congress of Vienna reestablishes the former state structure. The supremacy of Austria in Italy is reaffirmed. Lombardy and the Veneto become Austrian provinces. Tuscany is placed under Austrian rule, and Naples and Sicily are invaded. The papal states are reinstated.
- **1831:** Bellini's operas *La Sonnambula* and *Norma* are performed in Milan.
- **1831:** Following several popular revolts against the Austrians, Giuseppe Mazzini founds the secret movement for independence, "Young Italy." The national resentment of the Italians against the Austrians (the *Risorgimento*) grows.
- **1848:** A general insurrection against Austria under the leadership of the king of Sardinia is crushed by the Austrians.
- **1849–1850:** Victor Emmanuel II of the House of Savoy

becomes king of Sardinia. Cavour's government organizes the state of Piedmont.

- **1858**: Cavour and Napoléon III create an alliance at Plombières.
- **1859**: War is declared by Austria against France and Piedmont. Victor Emmanuel II places his army under the command of Garibaldi. Franco-Piedmont victories result in Piedmont obtaining Lombardy, and France obtaining Savoy and the county of Nice.
- **1860–1861**: Garibaldi frees the south from the Bourbons. The kingdom of Italy is proclaimed, with Turin as its capital. Victor Emmanuel II is crowned.
- **1866**: Italy declares war on Austria but is defeated. The Austrian admiral Tefgthoff sinks the entire Italian fleet. The Prussians join Italy and defeat the Austrians near Königgrätz, forcing them to retreat from Italy.
- **1870**: France withdraws its troops from the papal states and Rome becomes the capital of Italy. The Italian unification is complete. The pope retains sovereignty over Vatican City.
- **1882**: Italy makes peace with Austria. Under Umberto I, Italy forms the Triple Alliance with Germany and Austria-Hungary.

Italy in the 20th Century

- **1900**: King Umberto I is assassinated, and Victor Emmanuel III ascends to the throne.
- **1909**: Marconi receives the Nobel prize in physics.
- **1913–1934**: Works of Luigi Pirandello; receives the Nobel prize for literature (1934).
- **1915**: Although initially neutral, with territorial guarantees from Britain and France, Italy declares war on Germany and Austria, annexes Istria, Venezia-Giulia, and Trentino–Alto Adige.
- **1919**: With the peace treaty of St.-Germain-en-Laye, Italy receives South Tirol up to the Brenner Pass, Istria, and a number of Dalmatian Islands.
- **1922–1926**: After his march on Rome, Benito Mussolini is granted dictatorial powers by parliament and his Fascists take over the government.
- **1929**: The conflict between church and state is settled with the Lateran Pact. The Vatican is established.
- **1935–1936**: Italy invades and annexes Abyssinia in North Africa.

- **1936:** Germany and Italy enter into the "Rome-Berlin Axis." Italian troops fight for Franco in Spain.
- **1940:** Although at first remaining neutral, Italy eventually sides with Nazi Germany and declares war on France and Britain.
- **1941:** Italy loses Abyssinia.
- **1942:** Enrico Fermi splits the atom.
- **1943:** Allied troops land in southern Italy and conquer Sicily. Italian forces surrender; Mussolini is arrested and the Fascist government falls.
- **1945:** The German army surrenders. While fleeing, Mussolini is executed by partisans. The Christian Democratic Party forms a government led by de Gasperi.
- **1946:** King Victor Emmanuel III abdicates.
- **1947:** In the Treaty of Paris, Italy cedes Istria to Yugoslavia, and the Dodecanese to Greece. Italy renounces its colonies.
- **1953:** The Christian Democratic Party loses control; the frequent rise and fall of governments becomes the norm.
- **1954:** Trieste is divided between Yugoslavia and Italy.
- **1957:** The European Economic Community (EEC) is founded in Rome. The reconstruction of the country moves quickly.
- **1966:** Northern and central Italy are flooded; irreplaceable works of art in Florence and other cities are destroyed.
- **1970:** Following widespread strikes and unrest, the Statuto del Lavoratore (the Statute of the Worker) provides job security.
- **1976:** Earthquakes in Friuli and in the province of Udine cause severe damage.
- **1978:** Aldo Moro, chairman of the Christian Democratic Party, is kidnapped by the Red Brigade and found murdered 54 days later.
- **1980:** Severe earthquakes rock southern Italy.
- **1981:** Pope John Paul II is gravely injured in an attack.
- **1983:** Bettino Craxi is the first Social Democrat to become head of the Italian government.
- **1987:** Italy ranks fifth among Common Market countries as an economic power, nosing out Great Britain.

—Joanne Hahn

INDEX